Policy for Land

Policy for Land

Law and Ethics

Lynton Keith Caldwell
and
Kristin Shrader-Frechette

Rowman & Littlefield Publishers, Inc.

ROWMAN & LITTLEFIELD PUBLISHERS, INC.

Published in the United States of America
by Rowman & Littlefield Publishers, Inc.
4720 Boston Way, Lanham, Maryland 20706

British Cataloging in Publication Information Available

Library of Congress Cataloging-in-Publication Data

Caldwell, Lynton Keith, 1913–
Policy for land : law and ethics / Lynton Keith Caldwell and
Kristin Shrader-Frechette
p.   cm.
1. Land use—Government policy. 2. Right of property. 3. Land
use—Environmental aspects. I. Shrader-Frechette, K. S., 1944–.
III. Title: Work place ethics.
HD111.C3   1992   333.73—dc20   92-28586   CIP

ISBN 0-8476-7778-8   (cloth : alk. paper)
ISBN 0-8476-7779-6   (pbk. : alk. paper)

Printed in the United States of America

The paper used in this publication meets the minimum requirements of
American National Standard for Information Sciences—Permanence of
Paper for Printed Library Materials, ANSI Z39.48–1984.

Contents

Preface

We believe that the time is approaching when socially responsible Americans will seriously seek consensus on a new and sustainable land ethics capable of being translated into law and policy. Basic questions of policy for land remain unanswered in today's forum of politics. Incremental changes in popular ethics regarding land are evident in the news media and in citizen action. These changes have been influenced by increasing concern for the quality of life and the environment, by more sophisticated economic and technical analysis, by ecological insight, and by reaction against irresponsible land development, costs of which have been thrust upon an unwilling society. Disregard for ethical, aesthetic, ecological, and socioeconomic values in the treatment of land, however, remains widespread. Exploitation of land for short-term private, political, or economic advantage is common and still regarded by some Americans as a birthright. But this attitude has become increasingly unacceptable in many communities. Conflict over land use could be greatly diminished by wider agreement on the principles upon which land-related decisions are based. During the many decades when most Americans were trying to wrest a living from an often hard environment, there was little concern about the ultimate consequences of their actions on land, the resource base of society. Today, in a high-tech, relatively affluent, and better informed era, more people are able to concern themselves with environmental quality and sustainability for the future.

This book is offered as a contribution to the search for consensus. We are not providing detailed solutions to specific, present-day issues of land management, land law, or land evaluation. For these practical matters the reader is referred to publications and courses sponsored by the Lincoln Institute of Land Policy or to journals on land-use economics, law, and policy cited in the notes. Our purpose is to stimulate thought about the basic social and ethical values underlying land policy and their expression in the law. To achieve this goal, each of us has approached the topic of land policy from a slightly different, but complementary, standpoint.

Professor Caldwell provides the perspectives of a political and legal theorist. He synthesizes and explains a new, ecologically enlightened view of land policy. Professor Shrader-Frechette offers the account of a philosopher of science and ethicist; she defends the new land policy by analyzing and evaluating the arguments often brought against it. From our complementary stances, we come together to present our case for a new view of land. Our account is both biocentric and anthropocentric. It also draws on political and legal theory, as well as on analyses of both science and ethics. Because our subject is *policy*, our concern is inevitably focused on human attitudes and behaviors. Science and law both influence and implement human relationships to the land, but we believe that the fundamental element in these relationships is most accurately identified as philosophical. What people believe about their relationships with the Earth takes the form of ethical conclusions that are expressed in institutions defined by law. Although we approach our subject by two different routes, our perspectives are complementary and our objective is the same.

The General Thesis

As the chapters in this volume illustrate, many of the controversies over policy for land concern private rights versus public needs, or public rights versus private needs. Very often conflicts also arise among private needs: for example, among private persons pursuing incompatible interests or purposes, such as historic preservationists and land owners seeking a maximum return from their property. Controversy likewise takes place over private benefits from using a public "good," like grazing lands or scenic landscapes. Use of these public goods threatens a tragedy of the commons (mutual ruin when all persons seek to maximize their advantage over a limited resource). Conflicts also concern several kinds of costs, privately incurred but thrust upon the people as a public "bad," like soil erosion or a toxic-waste dump. Such a public "bad" threatens an inverse tragedy of the commons (all affected private owners are forced to share in a common disadvantage). Both of these tragedies are capable of being averted, provided that we develop appropriate ethics, political consensus, and laws regarding land use. There is little to be said about land-use policy that has not been said before, but until a more rational and sustainable consensus develops, there is justification for keeping the issues before the public and its political representatives. The purpose of this volume is therefore to present the case for more rational and sustainable ethics, politics, and economics for land.

Writing in 1989, David E. Dowall of the Institute of Regional Development at the University of California, Berkeley, stated what nearly all studies of land policy have discovered: "the USA lacks a coherent and explicit policy toward land use and development."[1] If an exception to this stance can be found, it would be that the American policy toward land per se is to have no policy in principle. That there has been a myriad of federal, state, and local policies affecting specific land uses is readily apparent. Even the dominant policy of the federal government throughout the nineteenth century—to privatize land ownership as rapidly as possible—had exceptions and these have become more numerous with the passing decades.[2] The absence of a coherent federal policy for land use, however, has increased the probability that policies for land use will emerge on the political agenda. Accumulating public concerns with environmental quality, health, economic rationality, financial investment, transportation, and energy will likely persuade persons that erstwhile unpopular choices are acceptable. Nevertheless, transformation of land-related assumptions, values, and interests—and their implementation in new policies—is certain to be contentious. Conflicts over ethical and legal principles will be reactivated as various groups advocate new land-use positions and introduce legislation based on them. We think conflict over land is more likely to accelerate than to continue as it is.

One unifying theme, implicit in our approach, is the search for a sustainable relationship between people and the land. During the early years of European settlement in America, limits to sustainable land use seemed inconceivable. Even when farms or pastures were "worn out," there was always new, "unused" land to be developed. Only the ending of the frontier and confrontation of the many costs of misused land opened the way to a reconsideration of America's cornucopian philosophy. Thus our theme does not give equal weight to all interests in land. We believe neither that market forces can provide rational solutions to all land-use conflicts, nor that they can be relied upon to provide sustainable futures for communities. Within limits, however, the market is an efficient way to allocate values and to make rational choices among particular alternatives. We also recognize the limitations of land-use planning as a political process. But we believe that we can discover ways to develop better policies and to plan for sustainability. We do not believe that the last word has been said on criteria for land decisions or on the methods and substance of public planning. We prefer a learning mode to confrontation and compromise in policy development, and we believe that there is room for reconciling most interests in the uses of land *if* consensus on basic principles can be achieved. Definition and acceptance of these principles are, of course, critical to the attainment of a popular consensus.

Overview of the Volume

Divided into three sections, the book begins with reflections on this lack of consensus. Several initial chapters survey the legal, political, and philosophical aspects of problems created by land policies that are contrary to the general interest. The second section of the volume, chapters 4 through 8, uncovers the philosophical assumptions and value commitments that underlie ecologically and ethically questionable policies and practices as well as the socioeconomic consequences that follow from them. The last section, chapters 9 through 12, offers a number of solutions, suggestions, and strategies that together comprise a new land-use policy.

Although this book examines some of the ethical, legal, and political foundations for a new land policy, it is neither as inclusive nor as analytic as many studies within a single discipline. Because of their multidisciplinary character, these essays do not cover all the topics of land use that might be important either to an economist, a political scientist, a philosopher, an attorney, or an ecologist. Instead, they bring the tools and insights of a variety of disciplines, including philosophy and political science, to bear on an issue whose range and policy implications lie beyond any single area of scholarship. Given the breadth of our focus, our aim is not systematic, specialized, disciplinary analysis. Rather, it consists, as Wittgenstein put it, of "assembling reminders for a particular purpose."[3] Our purpose is to call attention to the need for a new conserving, restoring, and sustainable policy for land.

In chapter 2, "The Ecology and Political Economy of Land," we begin the discussion by seeing where and why we have failed to develop an effective land policy. We explain that the game of land-use politics is played with a deck of cards stacked by history, a deck with political, economic, philosophical, and ideological cards. The most important of these cards, however, is political. Because land-use problems are people problems, chapter 2 outlines some of the general political strategies needed for land-use planning, identifies some of the persons who might implement them, and surveys some of the actions they might undertake. The goal of discussing general strategies is to explore how to correct the ways in which the political and historical cards have been stacked against the ecological, ethical, and sociocultural values that land-use planning seeks to protect. Toward this end, land-use strategies must take account of (1) how to estimate

the probabilities and consequences associated with various land actions, (2) how to expand the scope of opportunities for wide and sustainable land use, and (3) how to analyze and evaluate the assumptions underlying alternative land-use decisions.

Given the *political* and *legal* overview presented in chapter 2,
chapter 3 ("Four Land Ethics") offers a survey of land-related *ethical*
problems. Rather than only one "land ethics," this chapter argues that
there are at least four, each developed in response to a different set
of land-related problems. From an international perspective, land-
reform ethics has arisen in response to the political, economic, and
legal problems caused by faulty land distribution. Only a handful of
persons hold most of the land in many countries. The second ethics,
land-use ethics, has developed as a result of the economic, ethical,
and ecological difficulties caused by spillovers (e.g., of air, water,
sound, or pollutants) from one person's (or nation's) land to another's.
Land-community ethics calls for recognizing land as a member of
our moral community to which we owe duties of preservation. This
ethics has arisen in response to widespread environmental degradation,
especially destruction of land, which carries with it many other forms
of loss. The fourth land ethics, land-rights ethics, is a call to accord
land legal standing in court. It has developed as a response to the
failure to win protection for land in court. This failure has led to a
conflict between ecocentric and anthropocentric ethical positions and
to a reexamination of relationships between human beings and
nonhuman and inanimate nature. After sketching the land-related
circumstances and events that have generated these four land ethics,
chapter 3 outlines the assets and liabilities of each.

There is little chance of any of these four new land ethics being
put into practice, however, so long as the political deck of cards in
the game of land-use decision making is "stacked" to favor short-
term economic advantage over all other considerations. If we are to
adopt a new land ethics and policy, therefore, we must unpack and
"unstack" the historical and ethical traditions that have been interpreted, erroneously, to allow owners to do almost anything they wished
with their land. One of the most important of these traditions arises
from the alleged Lockean view that we have a natural right to property in land, and that landholders have virtually free rein to do as
they wish with their acreage. Neither capitalist nor socialist in intent
or argument, chapter 4 ("Locke and Limits on Land Ownership")
provides a revisionist account of John Locke's writings on ownership
of land. Arguing that Locke's claims ought to be reinterpreted, this
chapter shows how his texts provide a strong basis (because of the

"Law of Nature") for land-use planning and for community control of many rights to private property.

Chapter 5, "Concepts of Ownership and Rights of Use," continues the task of chapter 4, unpacking the historical, philosophical, and legal assumptions that are obstacles to effective land-use policy. The basic thesis of this chapter is that, because the legal legacy of conventional land "ownership," from seventeenth- and eighteenth-century England, is confusing and inconsistent, Americans need a new conceptual basis for land-use law and policy. As the chapter puts it: "Land law rooted in the conventions of Tudor England cannot be expected to serve the needs of the post-industrial society now emerging." Although the right to hold land was never absolute in English law, the shortcomings and ambiguities of English legal convention, together with American folklore that envisioned absolute rights of possession, enabled landowners in the United States to treat their land as something to which they had a "right," rather than a socially derived privilege. Chapter 5 offers three propositions as a new conceptual basis for land law and policy. The first proposition is to redefine rights of ownership so that they apply not to land itself but to rights to occupy or to use land. The second proposition is to redefine legal rights of occupancy so as to classify land according to its economic and ecological capabilities, reserving to the public the values added through societal "improvements." The third proposition is to tax land on the basis of the economic value of the rights actually possessed and exercised, not on the basis of the land itself or its anticipated value and potential rights.

Misinterpreted Lockean political philosophy (chapter 4) and ambiguous legal conventions of ownership (chapter 5), however, are not the only culprits in our failure to develop a desirable land policy. Part of the problem lies with our fundamental concepts of justice. Chapter 6, "Agriculture, Coal, and Procedural Justice," argues that justice requires restricting or prohibiting certain traditional property rights in land. Because we have been insensitive to the ways in which land ownership confers political and economic power, we in the United States have not recognized the ways in which the exercise of land-ownership rights may violate our accepted norms regarding procedural justice. Using the case studies of Appalachian coal land and California agricultural land, the chapter argues that violations of the conditions necessary for procedural justice in these two regions and elsewhere require a radical change in the definition of property rights. The needed change would subject them to societal control by a rationally defined public interest.

Besides our concepts of procedural justice, our ethical assumptions about rights to land use also influence our land policies. Chapter 7, "Limits to Policy: Problems of Consensus," shows how philosophical assumptions linked to individualism, short-term thinking, and discounting the future have helped Americans to avoid a reasonable land policy. Moreover, these assumptions and values are so strong that even declarations of national policy and law (like the proposed 1970 National Land Use Policy Act) can do little to achieve a stewardship ethics regarding land. Rather, the chapter claims, the new ethics and policy will only come about as a result of an evolution or revolution of values in the minds of the thinking community.

One of the values that must be reinterpreted and rationalized if effective land-use planning is to become a reality is national sovereignty. Chapter 8, "Land-Use Policy as an International Issue," argues that people must stop thinking of national sovereignty over their territories as absolute and exclusive. Sovereignty cannot protect a country from damage to its land and resources originating in other countries. Acid rain, radioactive fallout, and effects of global warming are transboundary phenomena. Just as individual land owners ought not use their property in ways that violate the rights of others, so also nations must come to recognize that they should not use their land in ways that jeopardize the interests of other countries. To alleviate the overemphasis on the value of national sovereignty, chapter 8 proposes several examples of international agenda-setting for national land-use policies. There is growing evidence that sovereignty is receding as a barrier to international cooperation and that more global issues relating to world trade, population dynamics, and threats of climate change may be more significant elements in future policies for land. But just as countries often have single-purpose goals in land policy (e.g., protecting their national sovereignty and promoting national growth), so also individual values may be distorted by single-purpose thinking. In our society single-purpose thinking tends to the maximization of economic values or political opportunities, and resulting policies are almost invariably short-range and discount the future. Chapter 9, "The Ecosystem as a Criterion for Land Policy," begins the third and final ("solutions") stage of the volume. It argues that our land policies must be founded on comprehensive, scientific, survival-oriented, long-term, holistic values, rather than on laissez-faire political philosophies. Our criterion for land-use decisions, it argues, must be the extent to which a particular land use enables natural systems to renew themselves and remain self-sustaining.

Replacing laissez-faire political values with ecological values, however, is not an easy task. Chapter 10, "Problems with Ecosystemic Criteria for Land Policy," discusses some of the science-based remedies for our land-policy problems and argues that general ecological theory, at present, cannot do the job that many moral philosophers, political scientists, and environmental policy makers ask of it. Because it alone cannot provide a predictable, unambiguous foundation for land ethics and policy, we need to infuse our land policy with more natural history and with practical, action-oriented ecology. We believe that although general ecological theory may have limited ability to contribute to resolution of particular land-use controversies, applied ecological analysis often can be successful in providing both practical insights and a basic framework for land ethics, policy, and planning. Chapter 10 closes with several suggestions for how to use ecology as a general guide in formulating land policy.

Continuing the discussion of solutions to our problems of land policy, chapter 11, "Practical Steps and Ethical Justifications," surveys the moral, political, legal, environmental, and economic arguments in favor of restrictions on property rights in land. With these arguments as a foundation, the chapter examines eight general solutions (such as taxation and controlling development rights) to our difficulties with land use, land ethics, and land policy. The chapter closes by answering some of the objections to these proposed solutions.

The final chapter of the volume, "A National Policy for Land," provides more detail as to possible ways to curtail our misuse of the land. It summarizes the objectives of a proposed national land-use policy act and then addresses specific political mechanisms for achieving the goals of a federal land-use policy. With this new policy, as chapter 12 reminds us, we will have put away our coonskin caps, our flintlocks, and our myths about private property in land. We will have developed a land policy that is consonant with the sophisticated, technological society that we have created.

Throughout these chapters the coauthors have emphasized different aspects of policy for land. This should not lead to an inference that their views are incompatible. There is no matter of principle on which they find themselves in disagreement. Focus on particular points of law or equity in individual chapters does not mean that there are no other issues to be considered. It demonstrates merely that not everything about a particular issue can be said simultaneously. The coauthors consider ecological, economic, holistic, and scientific concepts differently in differing contexts, even though their fundamental understanding of the concepts is complementary. Moreover, because this volume is addressed to a general audience, the author's use of terms is intended to convey meanings understandable by the general public. Consequently, they have chosen more common and general usage over more specialized definitions preferred by attorneys, scientists, or philosophers. Terms such as "ecology," "ecosystem," "biotic community," "biosphere," and "exosphere" should be understood within the context in which the expressions are used. The purpose of this book is to emphasize relevance over a precision that would exclude many members of a broad audience.

Finally, contrary to skepticism found at the extremes of so-called "right" and "left" contemporary ideologies, we believe that there is a reality presupposed by the concept of the "public interest." We recognize the abuse of the expression and the difficulty of discovering where the public interest lies. Yet we also believe that attempting to discover the public interest will make for a more just and sustainable society. We know that our use of the term "public interest" will raise more questions than we answer in this book. But without the reality of the public interest, even if imperfectly understood, this book would have little practical meaning.[4]

Acknowledgments

Pursuit of this project has placed us in the debt of many persons. Among them are the publishers of our previous books and articles, small portions of which appear here in significantly modified form.

For constructive criticisms of earlier versions of this book, we are grateful to many persons, including reviewers for Rowman and Littlefield, scholars at the Lincoln Land Institute, and our editor, Jonathan Sisk. Whatever errors remain are our responsibility. Dan Wigley and Jeannine DeBolt have done superb work as research and word-processing assistants, and we owe them great thanks. Our greatest debt, however, is to our spouses and children. They make everything worthwhile.

Part One

New Perspectives on Policy for Land

This first section presents the case for a reassessment and revaluation of the way people in general and Americans in particular conceptualize their relationships with the land. It explores the reasons why a new way of seeing the land is necessary to the welfare of humans and members of all other species. These first three chapters also identify some difficult ethical problems associated with human relationships with the land. Major legal and philosophical problems arise when one attempts to reconcile the concept of land as private property with the concept of land as a fundamental element in the biosphere upon which much of life depends. Ultimately, the law will follow ethical consensus. Today, no clear consensus regarding land policy can be found in most societies, and the value conflicts translate into political differences. An objective of this book is to assist a rational resolution of such differences. In this process, however, we argue that some assumptions and values will need to be displaced by others that are more conducive to ethically and ecologically enlightened stewardship.

1

Reconsidering Land Policy:
An Introduction

Lynton Keith Caldwell and
Kristin Shrader-Frechette

Among the ways of relating to the land and its uses, two concepts predominate in modern society. At the cost of over-simplification we may identify them as *economic* and *ecological*. Between the polarities of each position there are many intermediate or mixed attitudes. Within each grouping there are controversies over public versus private interests, over conflicting private interests, and over ethical judgments that complicate and deter the development of public policy for land. Because land is literally the base upon which all human societies are built, public decisions about how land is possessed and used have powerful implications for the character of a society and for the respective rights of individuals in that society.

How people relate to the land influences how they relate to one another. Deeply held values link us to things beneath, upon, and above the land, and we seldom perceive the earth solely as a biogeochemical phenomenon. Attitudes toward the land and its uses express economic, ethical, and aesthetic values, often held with deep emotion. Given these circumstances one can readily understand the reluctance of American public officials to move a graveyard, for example, or to condemn private, family-owned land for a national park. Land use is a contentious field of policy. As a consequence, many politicians would like to avoid any consideration of policy for land, regarding it as a "no-win" issue.

Economics and Ecology

Although it is not feasible to attempt precise descriptions of the two dominant concepts of land use, several characteristics seem representative of the differences in these two attitudes. The first and most widely accepted land attitude in the developed, industrialized world is economistic—an attitude based on exaggerated and unsustainable economic priorities. For those who share the economistic view, land

3

is primarily a financial resource—a commodity bought, owned, sold, and used for some form of financial return. Land is perceived as little more than legally described, discrete pieces of negotiable property. In their stated objection to the U.S. Land Use Policy and Planning Assistance Act of 1973 (S.268), Senators Fannin, Hansen, and Bartlett declared that "Historically, the marketplace has dictated the highest and best use of land."[1] This statement is supportable, however, only if one accepts the results of market transactions in land as its "highest" and "best" use—whatever "highest" and "best" are understood to mean within laissez-faire economic theology. Many persons have challenged this economic theology, and the terms "economistic" and "economism" are associated in particular with the critique of modern society by the ethicist and theologian Nicholas Berdyaev.[2] "Economism" in his view (analogous to scientism) was an inordinate and excessive attribution of importance to economics, narrowly defined, as against all other values. The criticism was not of economic values per se, but their exaggeration in relation to other values. (Some uses of the term "environmentalism" suggest a similar exaggeration of one set of values over others. It was this use of "environmentalism" that formerly gave the term bad repute among geographers.[3]) Berdyaev saw economistic attitudes dominating the modern world— equally under capitalism and socialism.

Economics, however, is neither an exact nor a unified science. There have been many and different economic theories—some in opposition to one another. Hence, when someone argues that "it isn't economical" or asserts that "economists believe," the response should be "what economists?" Economists of Marxist or laissez-faire market-forces persuasion are more like advocates than unbiased social scientists. Given the variety of economic philosophies, there is a fundamental sense in which economics and ecology are different, compatible ways of approaching an understanding of the real world. There are economic principles evident in nature, and economic behavior is both facilitated and limited by ecological processes.[4]

Where commercial considerations are foremost, approaches to decisions regarding land rights and responsibilities tend to be incremental, legalistic, and strongly influenced by prevailing economic dogmas—such as the right to and necessity for growth, and the use of monetary return as the measuring stick for the highest and best value of land. Public decisions for land use also tend to be case-specific and tactical in that, within the general parameters declared by law, they focus on respective rights among parties in conflict. This approach may be described as "fractionated." Its focus is upon individual increments of property in land (large or small), and neither upon responsibility for care of land as an ecological and economic resource, nor upon land as a basic element in a comprehensive natural system.

The second or ecological attitude toward relationships with land emphasizes organic, human uses of the land within a complex, interactive web of life for which the earth itself is the frame and indispensable support. This organic concept of the earth is characteristic of many so-called "primitive" or traditional societies. Drawing support from advancing science, this view is also held by growing numbers of broadly informed, environmentally concerned persons. Unlike the economistic orientation, it tends toward strategic rather than tactical approaches to land policy. That is, the ecological attitude toward land takes a comprehensive, long-range, systemic view. It views land, earth, humanity, and the entire biosphere in a mode that is, or seeks to be, integrated rather than incremental. Although the scientific application of this integrated ecological view has not been fully developed, it nevertheless represents an ethical and political ideal, a vision of real-life conditions and interdependencies. If specific land-use issues were seen in their larger ecological context, then the orientation of policy would tend to be integrative rather than fractional. Today this breadth of view is exceptional. If our society were guided by a concept of human interdependence with the land, a broad set of prevailing assumptions, behaviors, ethics, and legal principles would have to change. In the United States, where rights of individual land ownership have been deeply entrenched, ecology has encouraged modifications of and exceptions to conventional modern law and policy. These developments have arisen as a result of a growing understanding both of the linkages between causes and effects (e.g., leaching of toxins in landfills and resultant groundwater pollution) and of environmental science (including biogeochemical cycles, maintenance of biotic diversity, and the ultimate necessity for sustainability in human uses of the earth). For the modern mind of the twentieth century an ecological view of the earth has had to be acquired through learning. Ecological literacy has not always been a characteristic of modern authors. It will be an unavoidable feature of postmodern society.[5]

Whereas some changes in land policy and law have addressed practical problems of health, safety, and economics—restrictive use of flood plains, for example—ethical considerations are increasingly becoming factors in land-use legislation. The changes emerging in land ethics, however, are not wholly new. In some respects they are a return to preindustrial attitudes that presuppose—as economic methods characterizing the industrial era generally did not—an interdependence between humanity and the earth, and a human responsibility to use the land in ways that will be sustainable throughout future generations. But emergence of this ecologically based land ethics has aroused counterethics based on exaggerated individual rights to possession and use and defended as the American way of life. Powerful though they still may be, these ethics appear to be a "rear guard" defense of an attitude receding into history. To understand better how our society appears to be moving to a new land ethics, it may be useful to review briefly the route by which we arrived at the present juncture.

Attitudes Toward Land: A Retrospective

Were it not so often ignored in practice, it would be redundant to observe that air, water, land, and the biosphere are the basic physical elements upon which human life, indeed all life, depends. The properties and configurations of land present opportunities and limitations for human activities. Land is the ultimate habitat for the human animal and it is the essential base for ventures upon and under the sea and into the air and outer space. Land is thus the ultimate natural resource, but always in association with air, water, and plant life.[6]

The history of human culture and civilization is also a history of human relationships to land. These relationships have passed from successive stages of food gathering, hunting, and fishing through pastoralism and agriculture to urbanism, resource exploitation (e.g., mining and timbering) and recreation. Each of these stages has brought with it distinctive forms of social organization for cooperation, coordination, competition, or control. With the growth of complexity in the allocation of natural resources and social responsibilities have come institutional arrangements for establishing authority and providing governance over land. Custom regarding land evolved into law, and law was elaborated as populations increased. Environmental interrelationships became more numerous and complex. As land became a basis for economic, social, and political power, relationships with land were codified through statutes that were based on prevailing assumptions regarding equity, justice, ethics, and the perceived interests of dominant classes.

Rights to territory characterized early traditional societies.[7] But with the development of agriculture and urbanization, control of land became concentrated, organized hierarchically, legitimized by positive law, and even sanctified by religion. Historian Karl Wittfogel attributed the rise of despotic regimes in the ancient Middle East to the necessity for authoritative management of irrigated agriculture.[8]

Comparable concentrations of political power over agricultural land and its produce occurred in India, China, and Peru. But the most explicit linkage of land tenure and political power, prior to the Russian revolution of 1917, was effected under feudalism, notably as it emerged in medieval Europe. This linkage occurred at two levels that are still distinguished in Western law: the public domain and the royal domain. At the highest political level, policy for land pertained to the royal or national domain. Indeed, the medieval realm was defined by boundaries on the land. The monarch was chief tenant of the realm, which was subdivided among the nobility, the church, free cities, and corporations. Only gradually did these landholdings become private property in the modern sense, and even then the provision of eminent domain affirmed the prerogative of the state to assert prior rights over those of the immediate landholders. Under the old regimes, distinction was drawn between state lands that were regarded as "public," and those that comprised the royal domain (e.g., the personal estates of the monarch). A related distinction exists in the United States today between the public domain (e.g., unappropriated publicly owned land), and public land under the control of various governmental agencies (e.g., the Department of Defense, the National Park Service, and the Postal Service). The unappropriated domain is administered under the "protective" custody of the Bureau of Land Management.[9]

Whatever the political and legal arrangements for the custody and use of land, people have usually supported these arrangements by means of philosophical rationales that reflected particular ethical commitments. The open and uncontrolled character of American society, for example, permitted the privatization of land holding, assisted by public policies, to be carried to great lengths. Taken with very little economic cost from aboriginal inhabitants, the pioneers tended to regard their land tenure as absolute ownership. Their attitudes stand in contrast to the philosophic views of Thomas Jefferson on land tenure. Jefferson's ideas in this area do not appear to have been shared by many of his contemporaries. He believed that each generation had rights only to the usufruct (i.e., tenancy) of the earth, and that each was ethically obliged to pass this right on to succeeding generations "free and unencumbered."[10] The philosophical principle that a land owner was only the temporary holder of specified and conditional rights over the land also has not been congenial to many Americans. They have tended to see their land as *their land* and not merely as a bundle of rights to use.

It is paradoxical that people often assert a strong sentimental attachment to the land, yet they show little concern for its conservation, enhancement, or misuse. Americans, perhaps because of their historical and religious heritage, have generally taken a distinctly anthropomorphic and possessive view of the land. Their widely shared tacit assumptions have often been revealed in small, ordinary ways. For example, the folk singer Woody Guthrie's song, "This Land is Your Land," became very popular during the environmental movement of the 1960s, but its implications were seldom closely examined. The following lines are hardly consistent with ecological-geological reality or with the concept of humans sharing an interdependency with the land and the rest of living nature:

> This land is your land, This land is my land
> This land was made for you and me . . .[11]

Other lines make evident that *the land* is viewed primarily as a natural endowment that is possessed, rather than as a geopolitical entity. North America was certainly not *made* for humans, nor for the people who call themselves "Americans." The dispossessed aboriginal Americans generally saw themselves as separate neither from the earth nor from the rest of nature. Guthrie's lyrics suggest respect for the land, but they also incorporate a sense of possessiveness. Indeed, the choral lines suggest collective ownership, and this could lead either toward stewardship or toward Hardin's "Tragedy of the Commons" discussed elsewhere in the volume. Our point here is that Guthrie's lyrics are consistent with both the traditional dichotomy between humans and nature and with the prevailing notion that land can be possessed.

American attitudes toward land acquisition and territorial possession have historically been reinforced, in part, by certain Biblical interpretations. Just as God "gave" the Land of Canaan to the ancient Hebrews, European colonizers believed America was given to them. Canaanites and native Americans were not seen as having real rights to the land. The concept of "God-given rights" permeates American attitudes toward land and, at least in part, explains the moral indignation of land owners whose possession is threatened by a government takeover for a public purpose. They often claim that compulsory taking of land, whatever the purpose, "just ain't right."

Today, one of the most difficult environmental issues is how to reconcile traditional assumptions regarding *private rights* to land with important *public needs* that would abrogate alleged privileges of private owners. There is moreover a reverse side to this issue—how to reconcile *public rights* to land with *private needs*—with the health, safety, and preferences of private citizens, both those who hold land and those who do not. Examples of the former are the taking of land for public purposes from unwilling sellers or the prohibition of certain private uses through zoning or development restrictions. Public purposes include the siting of highways, power lines, nuclear reactors, hazardous-waste facilities, airports, or military installations. Failure to enforce public—measures intended to safeguard the welfare of individual citizens—is often a consequence of political favoritism for one private interest over another.

In his *Discourses on the First Ten Books of Titus Livius*, Niccolo Machiavelli observed "that whoever wishes to foresee the future must consult the past; for human events ever resemble those of preceding times." He reasoned that human events "are produced by men who have been, and ever will be, animated by the same passions, and thus they must necessarily have the same results."[12] Machiavelli's observations accorded with his view of history in which the circumstances of human life had not changed greatly in more than a thousand years. Machiavelli lived at the threshold of modern times. Science, technology, and the dynamics of human population had not yet combined to transform the circumstances of human existence. Robinson Jeffers likewise believed that in 10,000 years human nature had not changed more than had the beaks of eagles.[13] Machiavelli and Jeffers may be right, but both the material environment in which human nature is expressed and the human understanding of that environment have changed dramatically.

Although the passions of humans may not have changed—for example, feelings of altruism, anger, fear, envy, ambition, love, and hatred—the situation of humans in relation to their environments has altered the ways in which emotions translate into action. Over time, human feelings about interpersonal interactions may not have changed, but human reactions to those feelings has changed, as notions of socially acceptable conduct have changed. Thus, what we may learn through retrospection is the ultimate malleability of human behavior and therefore the malleability of social and legal assumptions and institutions. To study the past reveals the ways that humans have perceived and organized their relationships to the land and the environment. Such study shows that our present assumptions about land occupancy, ownership, and rights are products of the relatively recent past and are neither inevitable, inalienable, nor fixed for all time. Past experience, understood in relation to the circumstances under which it occurred, could help us devise more beneficial, acceptable, and sustainable land policies for the future.

The Route to Reconsideration

It seldom happens that attitude changes as fundamental as human relationships to land occur rapidly. When unforeseen change does occur suddenly, it has invariably been in the making for some time. As subsequent chapters will relate in more detail, changes in the beliefs of people regarding their relationships to the land often occur as the result of changes in a more fundamental societal paradigm (a set of assumptions regarding the way the world works). Changed circumstances and perceptions continue to call the validity of the paradigm into question, as they have in the past (e.g., in the dismantling of feudalism or of the democratic centralism of communism). One aspect of social relationships (e.g., between the sexes or between employers and employees) may change, however, while another (e.g., legal rights of land owners) may not. Moreover, the breakup of an old paradigm may not be followed immediately by a new and inclusive one. An intervening period may occur in which the times are out of joint. Rear-guard actions of those resistant to change are likely to occur where large financial interests or political hegemony are in jeopardy.

The period of postmodernism and the change in assumptions and values near the end of the twentieth century has weakened the moral and ethical support for conventional policies of land use and ownership, but the legal and political position of these policies is still relatively strong. The legal structure of land policy is undergirded by political commitments (e.g., a reluctance to interfere with the "rights" of inholders surrounded by public lands). To change land policy it is necessary to change the laws—or at least their interpretation. But before these changes can occur, we must have changes in political orientation and commitment. And for political change to happen, a critical mass of the population must demand a new order of land policy. In the absence of such a critical mass, policy makers are likely to stay with the status quo until forced by considerations of political survival to change.

The foregoing considerations set the problem of reconsidering public policy toward land. Contemporary efforts to obtain more ecologically and economically rational and sustainable land policies have enjoyed no more than local and incremental success. If the goal of a new land policy is to be attained, a strategy for conceptual change is needed. Such strategy must necessarily address the factors that inhibit and obstruct changes in attitudes and evaluation. An extensive and well-reasoned literature on the need for conserving and sustainable land policies has been available for many years. But to make it an effective agent of change we must first answer the question: "Why has it not yet been sufficiently persuasive to move the policy makers?"

Although subsequent chapters of this book deal with particular aspects of land policy, law, and ethics, they should be read against the background of a more general thesis. This thesis is that, to effect change in an element of social convention so deeply embedded as prevailing beliefs regarding land, a new way of seeing and understanding humankind's relationship to the earth must emerge. At first thought, this may seem like a very large order of dubious prospect. Yet it is hardly more "revolutionary" than many societal and conceptual changes that have occurred during the past half-century. A variety of so-called "blueprints" for a more generally rewarding and sustainable future have been proposed.[14] Not all are of equal feasibility, but out of a critical integration of their respective approaches, perhaps a sound and persuasive argument for a new perspective might be developed. Our point of departure is to identify the factors that obstruct a broader view of land-use ethics, policy, and law. If, as we believe, land policies are embedded in more general social conventions and values, then the question to be answered is why reform in land use tends to lag behind other aspects of environmental policy. The answer may be that change doesn't occur because a sufficient number of people are not ready for it. Why have they not been ready? There appear to be several reasons, and they apply to other environmental issues in addition to land policy.

First, familiar circumstances under "normal" conditions are rarely seen as "problematic"; most people seldom question them. Concerned with their own affairs, most people feel no apprehension regarding things going on around them that they have always regarded as "natural." They often accept current policies and practices as "normal" because they are part of the conventional way of thinking that assumes the inevitability of growth and development. This inevitability is expressed in the cliché—"you can't stop progress." If people more generally understood the ultimate costs of ever-expanding and speculative land development, however, then they might reconsider their assumptions. But like the dog that didn't bark because the intruder was familiar, people are not inclined to protest against that to which they have become accustomed.

Second, although the general public may be apathetic, people whose economic interests are served by freedom from interference with their uses of land will "bark" if a threat of restrictions and controls appears. In commenting on the defeat of the federal land-use planning bill in July 1975 by the House of Representatives Committee on Interior and Insular Affairs, Congressman R. Taylor of North Carolina said that lobbying pressure greater than any he had seen in the last fifteen years caused him to vote against the bill.[15] The bill was widely denounced as "legislating against growth" and as a "federal power grab." Its opponents were chiefly real-estate and land-development interests, agricultural land owners, local chambers of commerce, and intransigent libertarians. Even so, the bill—which had been endorsed by President Richard Nixon—passed in the Senate but was several times blocked by the Rules Committee from consideration by the whole House of Representatives. The moral here is that an intensely self-interested and committed minority can prevail over a less committed majority.

A third psychological element obstructing popular support of land-policy reform is a widespread belief (not without particular exceptions) that "government restrictions" are prejudicial to personal freedom and unfairly obstructive of the natural impetus for economic growth. The vestige of belief that "freedom" requires an uninhibited right to exploit nature—a belief exemplified in James Fenimore Cooper's novel *The Pioneers*—remains in the ethos of many Americans. This belief provided a pseudo-ethical justification for the Sagebrush Movement of the 1970s and early 1980s in which self-serving ranchers and natural-resource developers urged that unallocated federal lands in the American West (the public domain) be transferred to state control or, better yet, sold off to private individuals.[16] State ownership was generally seen as a "halfway house" toward privatization. But to some Sagebrushers the thought gradually dawned that a generally permissive and accommodating federal landlord might be replaced by a less sympathetic Japanese, Canadian, and corporate owner who could outbid the local interests in any open market not only for land but for water as well. They realized that preferential treatment of private owners who had leased the public lands that they hoped to acquire could easily be described as a special-interest land steal, and that it could hardly obtain congressional approval. Perhaps the most significant thing about the Sagebrush Rebellion was its failure—even when it was endorsed rhetorically by a popular president of the United States, Ronald Reagan. A movement for the privatizing of the public lands continues but seems unlikely to achieve its objectives. In any case, those objectives are difficult to separate from the perception of "land grabs" by politically favored private interests.

In August 1991, division between economic and environmental interests again broke out over a proposal of President George Bush. He wanted to revise the federal wetlands-protection policy to satisfy the objections of land developers; oil, gas, and mining interests; and farm owners. Environmental organizations were outraged by Bush's reversal of a 1988 campaign pledge of "no net loss" of wetlands. As of mid-1992, it remained to be seen whether environmental interests had gained sufficient political strength to prevent a repetition of the 1975 defeat of land-use reform. The wetlands issue has been in many ways a talisman of political commitment to environmental and land-use protection in the public interest. Restrictions on the draining or filling of wetlands by farmers and developers has been seen by opponents as a "taking" issue for which compensation must be paid. Legislation adopted by the U.S. Senate in July 1991 would sharply restrict the "taking" of private property for public purposes—a measure strongly endorsed by the National Association of Realtors. Such legislation continues to be controversial, because many Americans remain torn by simultaneous commitments to economic growth and jobs on the one hand, and to environmental quality and preservation on the other.

The unthinking commitment to growth is a common psychological disincentive for land-use reform. Most Americans are neither large land owners nor in the land-development business, and yet they have been persuaded that almost everyone benefits from growth—the more growth the more benefit. They have not understood that beyond a point, not always easily identified in advance, continuing growth is not helpful to most individuals or communities. It eventually leads to costs, inconvenience, insecurities, and diminished quality of life. Americans have viewed growth as desirable, however, in part because of "the American dream."[17] Examination of a large volume of writing, rhetorical invocation, and analysis of this "dream" leads to the conclusion that it has no clear or universally accepted definition. A widely held interpretation is the "dream" of freedom and opportunity to rise on the social ladder and, better yet, to gain wealth and celebrity. It is a "dream" of individual personal attainment in which social institutions are evaluated in relation to their making personal dreams come true. Responsible stewardship for land and natural resources does not appear in the American dream. Nevertheless, the dream includes justice in interpersonal relationships, primarily in order to permit everyone to share in its realization. The dream condones government controls and public laws that ensure the right of everyone to participate in the perceived benefits of an open and growing society, but it offers no agenda for an ecologically more just and sustainable life. The so-called "American way" is to make sure that everyone has a chance at a role in the play. It assumes, without critical inquiry, a happy ending to the action.

A fourth factor retarding land-use reform has been negative, ineffectual, or—at worst and all too common—dissembling leadership. Because land-use regulation often appears to be a no-win issue for elective politicians, there is an understandable temptation for them to evade commitment and to appease opposing camps. Unfortunately for the compromisers, many land-use controversies cannot be reconciled. The politician seeking "balance" is likely to satisfy nobody. Leaders in land-use reform find their support chiefly among people with no economic interest in the issue, but they are likely to be opposed by well-funded economic interests that will benefit financially from the defeat of land-planning measures. Such opposition is often easily able to neutralize leaders who call for land-use reform. After all, leadership requires followers, and if people will not follow, then no one can lead.[18] To be effectual as a reformer in so sensitive a policy area as land ownership and use, it is necessary to know how to rally visible and vocal support and to placate intransigent opposition. To accomplish this task, it is necessary to understand the causes of indifference or opposition to reform and to devise appropriate counteractive strategies. Strategic thinking has generally characterized neither the environmental movement nor the those wishing to reformulate land policy. Proponents of land reform have more often adopted the one-sided rhetoric of a moral crusade, and they have assumed that science and land ethics would carry the day. Experience shows that their assumptions have not always worked.

Aldo Leopold, whom many regard as the most eloquent and influential advocate of land ethics, believed that it must be achieved through social evolution, a consequence of enlarged public understanding.[19]   He believed that in respecting and protecting the land, one also protected the welfare and future of humanity. Views such as Leopold's must be kept in the forefront of reform efforts—but strategies for change are also needed. To be effective in developing land ethics, we must use science, logic, and moral conviction to overcome time-honored inhibitions. To accomplish this objective, we must study the opposition and anticipate the arguments that will be marshaled to defeat any proposed restriction on prevailing rights of land ownership and use. In addition, alternative approaches to the economics of land use must be discovered, evaluated, and disseminated. The intellectual goal must be a synthesis of personal, private, and public interest that is fair to the living world generally and to future generations. In order to achieve this goal, we must first gain the attention of the public. Even if land-use reform has enough support to win a legislative victory, it may suffer defeat by being eclipsed by an intervening and distracting event. Scandals like Watergate, Iran-Contra, or almost any international war will divert the attention of politicians, the news media, and the general public from issues of greater long-run significance. These events, especially foreign wars, enable politicians to divert attention from domestic issues that they find inconvenient to address. Before people can be persuaded to support land-use planning, it is necessary to gain their attention.

All of the foregoing factors must be taken into account in developing a strategy to modify or replace the prevailing economistic perceptual bias. It is not fundamental economics that is the conceptual enemy of reformed land policy. On the contrary, sound economic analysis is supportive of conserving and sustainable land policies. Economism is to economics what scientism is to science—in both cases there is a specious perversion of rational concepts into exaggerated and unsustainable dogmas. It is easy to build a case for more rational, equitable, and sustainable land policy, but difficult to surmount the ideological barriers that block its general public acceptance. It may be possible to identify the elements of a strategy that could penetrate the defenses of the prevailing land paradigm and open the way to new ethical and political perspectives. This book, however, does not attempt to do more than to point the direction that successful action must take. The task itself requires the concerted efforts of many and diverse publics and an informed and dedicated political leadership.

Institutionalizing a New Land Ethics

Assuming that a new, widely accepted land ethics can be developed, how can it be made operative? Behavior does not always follow consistently from professed belief. Ethical declarations and personal goals of people are not always compatible. Immediate personal concerns with economic implications are sometimes more likely to influence behavior than philosophic beliefs, especially when those beliefs concern the welfare of generations yet unborn. Moreover, it is difficult to be ethical by one's self alone. Without the aid of social institutions, few persons know how to be moral. "Liberty under law" suggests a society that protects and enlarges freedoms that could never exist under rugged individualism or anarchy. All Americans who espouse extreme individualism, who fear that their rights and freedoms are threatened by responsible, democratic, public planning should ask themselves these questions: What are the real constraints upon my personal freedom to obtain secure, predictable employment; to live unmolested in a neighborhood unthreatened by social disorder, physical deterioration, invasion by incompatible activities, or exorbitant tax increases; to travel to work, school, worship, or recreation over safe, uncongested streets; to have access to open skies, beaches, woods, fields, and uncluttered roadsides? Millions of Americans are today denied these freedoms by the unintended, inadvertent consequences of our planless patterns of land use, patterns often pursued in the name of individual liberty. How free can we truly claim to be when we permit our past investments to be depreciated, our present life experience to be impaired, and our future opportunities to be jeopardized by failure to create institutions and procedures that could help to safeguard these values?[20]

It is far easier to recognize the *need* for institutional arrangements that will assist people in making land-use choices that are socially and ecologically appropriate than to agree upon *what institutions* would be feasible and effective. There may be no one best way to respond to this institutional need and, indeed, not everyone agrees that a need exists. There has been in the American ethos since colonial times a deeply entrenched animus against any restriction of individual freedom and against governmental controls. This hostility is often expressed under circumstances of high emotion and low comprehension of the full dimensions of public issues. Conversely, there has always been popular enthusiasm for government as the great dispenser—the extender of benefits, the remover of obstacles to growth and progress. Laws governing land use have thus tended to be ad hoc, opportunistic, and issue specific. As a legacy from their status as self-governing colonies, the states retained their so-called "police powers" over the public interest in the use of land. Much of this power, however, remained unused until recently. Much of it was transferred to local units of government (e.g., towns, counties, and cities) or to special-purpose authorities (e.g., public utilities). During the late twentieth century, however, federal action has been invoked to extend, supplement, reinforce, or (in some cases) to prevent state action with respect to land policy. Because of its extemporized and local nature, unguided by any positive philosophy of conservation, land law in the United States is highly fractionated in substance, structure, and procedure. Thus, addressing it in a coherent, holistic manner is extremely difficult and unlikely (for the time being) to attain success. In the short run, specific land issues must be addressed as they arise. But addressing only specific cases is like fighting brush fires when a comprehensive plan for fire prevention is needed. Development of an alternative to the prevailing social-economic paradigm for land should move forward. At a time when environmental awareness is spreading throughout American society, when economic and demographic pressures are great and growing, and when it is understood that almost every environmental issue has land-use implications, questions of land policy cannot be put off or misrepresented as inherently threatening to the rights and liberties of a free people.

Described briefly in the preface, the chapters that follow deal with major aspects of land law and ethics. Strategies to reconcile law and ethics with fairness to future generations and to other living creatures will be considered largely in the concluding chapter. The authors do not propose here detailed solutions to land-use problems—many of which are site specific and often complex. Although they do not prescribe a blueprint for reform, the coauthors do propose principles and approaches that they believe will enable the American people to address land issues more effectively and constructively than they are usually addressed today. It should also be emphasized that the authors are not hostile to market mechanisms in land transactions. An efficient and expeditious method for facilitating land-use decisions, the market is a valuable operational tool for allocating property and resources. It ought not be, however, a political philosophy. Faith that market forces, if left unfettered, will solve most social and environmental problems is just that—a faith, an ideology.

Our purpose in this book is not to convert the reader to an informed ecological perspective on land policy. We hope that the reader will be prompted to think about the issues, to consider the evidence, and to appreciate the probable consequences of policy alternatives. The uses of the land have an unavoidable effect on the environment and on the quality of life. Policy for land, if consistent with any thoughtful concept of the public interest, must treat land as much more than a mere commodity. Land is literally the foundation upon which social orders and civilized societies are built.

2

The Ecology and Political Economy of Land

Lynton Keith Caldwell

As a consequence of historical experience, land in America has been viewed primarily as a commodity. Relatively narrow, short-term economic values have been protected by law, whereas more inclusive environmental values have been slow to win acceptance. But concomitant with increasing pressures of an expanding political economy upon basic and finite resource, science has been increasingly able to project probable consequences of decisions regarding land use. This information is effective, however, only to the extent of its acceptance by the owners and users of land, by governmental law makers, and by the general public. Statutory law is needed to make land policy legitimate and predictable, but public involvement and acquiescence is needed in the formulation of land use policies.

If population pressure is excluded as common and basic to most problems of the human environment, land use is our largest and most fundamental set of environmental problems.[1] Land use presents environmental problems for four reasons. The first is because improvident human uses may degrade the quality of the land, diminishing its ability to sustain life and causing it to degrade the quality of air and water. The second is because human uses often conflict and require public action to resolve differences. The third reason is that the political economy of land in our society is influenced largely by a relatively small number of large proprietors or users whose preferences may be inconsistent with the preservation of the land or the welfare of society and over whose decisions society has very limited influence. And fourth, partly for the foregoing reason, government policy and administration of land does not necessarily serve the long-term public interest. Government agencies have themselves too often been guilty of abuse of the land and its resources. Because of the large extent of government control over land in the U.S. public management or mismanagement may lead to serious land-use problems.

Yet contrary to some skeptical opinions, land use in principle must

19

be placed on the agenda of national policy; it has, in practice, always existed at the local level of government. This is not only because its various aspects require public decisions, but also because it is linked to almost every other major social and ecological problem: for example, to energy, climate, transportation, housing, urbanization, agriculture, health, recreation, and the protection of plant and animal life.

Nationally, relative to its importance, we have had relatively little success in developing effective land-use policy. Have we attacked land use as a policy problem from the wrong perspective? Are there alternatives to market or regulatory solutions? Have we misinterpreted the problem? Have our methods of solution been inadequate or inappropriate? If the answer to these questions is "yes," then what responses are required? What aspects of land use planning, necessary to the continuing social and ecological well-being of our society, ought to be raised?

A Problem for Policy

Many of our programs and proposals relating to land use appear to contain the cause of their frustration. We seem to have built negating components into many of our land-use plans. This has seldom been a calculated risk. It may best be described as inadvertent—caused because we have been looking at the problem from the wrong end. But misconception of a problem defeats its solution, and action based on mistaken premises cannot realistically be expected to prove effective. How can we develop land-use policy that is not self-defeating? Perhaps the way is not to attempt to legislate comprehensively enough to meet the full range of policy objectives, but rather to focus upon specific actions and behaviors that affect or involve the misuse of land. Our purpose here is to consider why this may (or may not) be an effective approach to policy problems of land use in the United States, avoiding the trap of self-defeating legislation. But by avoiding omnibus proposals that mobilize diverse opponents, there is risk of missing the larger ethical and ecological values basic to true reform.

Perhaps we can better understand how to develop a new and more effective approach if we understand how we arrived at our present formulation of land law and policy. To find out how to succeed, it may be helpful to assess the successes and failures of the past. We will return to this theme throughout this volume, for unless circumstances have changed, strategies to achieve successful reformation of policy will not be well served by past strategies that have not met with success.

Law expresses culturally derived principles and relationships and in the main is necessarily conservative, for its purpose has been to stabilize and regularize relationships and rights so as to make them predictable and reliable guides to behavior and to the resolution of disputes. Law is intended to expressly confirm patterns of accepted behavior and to provide means for resolving conflicts among asserted rights as variously interpreted.

For historical reasons, relationships among humans and the land are numerous, complex, and often inconsistent—representing in subtle and often unapparent ways the accretion of centuries of custom. The present law thus contains many (1) specific residual principles, doctrines, and assumptions pertaining directly to rights of land use and ownership and (2) more general principles of property ownership applicable to the use and possession of land. This historicity helps to explain why the conservative field of land law embodies tacit popular beliefs and accommodates behaviors derived from a long past.

Land law in the United States evolved from western European—largely English—precedent, in which land-tenure relationships had for hundreds of years been the basis of political power, social structure, and economic rights.[2] In medieval culture, land ownership or tenure was requisite to a larger degree of freedom.[3] Lack of personal rights in land use tended to correlate with lack of control over one's personal life. Land and personal freedom became especially associated in the minds of settlers in America. A free-market approach to land as a commodity became a basic element in the concept of economic freedom, in contradistinction to feudal and communal servitude and the encumbrances characteristic of medieval law.

The emotional hostility with which many people react to almost any land-use-control measure cannot generally be explained wholly by reference to economic self-interest. Very old ethical assumptions regarding human relationships to land reinforce perceived self-interests. Motives for land holding are numerous and diverse. They need not be explicit to pose formidable barriers to a rational consideration of land-use policy. Land owners, especially small owners, have often reacted violently to changes in law and policy that in broader perspective would seem to have been in their economic interest. The jurist Blackstone declared that "Regard of the law for private property is so great—that it will not authorize the least violation of it, not even for the general good of the whole community."[4]

A Stacked Deck

The game of land-use politics is played with a deck of cards stacked by a selective "history." Tradition invoked "selectively" may be taken out of its original context and present a biased view of actual experience. The properties of the several suits in the deck, which we may term (1) behavior, (2) economics, and (3) ideology, are more often the cumulative result of historical practice than a deliberate rigging of the game by interested players. Of course the interests of particular social classes and economic groups have been incorporated into law and practice. It is hardly exceptional for people to seek to institutionalize and so to protect their interests as they perceive them. And when, for whatever reasons, the larger society acquiesces in policies that favor some of its members more than others, the resulting arrangements may be taken as if they were consensual.

This consensus need not be truly intentional; people may accept as "given" arrangements that they see no prospect of changing, especially if the arrangements are of long standing, reinforced by habitual behavior, social status, and political power. One need no more than observe that the composition of the American deck in the land-use policy game is culture-specific to American experience. In other cultures the values of the cards may be different. For example, social consensus may not favor individual preemption or even control of land. In societies as contrasting as those representing nomadic pastoralism, communal agriculture, or Marxist socialism, the cards may be stacked against individual ownership or possession of land or against certain ways of using land. In the United States the cards, with few exceptions, favor the individual or corporate proprietor.

A major suit in land-use policy is behavior, and the shuffle in America has provided few means for guidance consistent with the public interest or control. "Behavior" should here be read as *the generally accepted practice of people* without regard to rationale or approval. For example, it is a time-honored practice in much of rural America to dump old automobile bodies, defunct refrigerators, bedsprings, and miscellaneous refuse in woodland ravines and along the banks of streams. Not all rural Americans accept the practice as desirable, but few would attempt to interfere, nor would many favor public prohibition provided that the owner of the trash dumped it on his own land. Only if and when a nuisance, generated by the dumping, can be shown to harm neighbors or the community in certain specified ways can the particular behavior affecting land be effectively questioned. Even then, it is seldom the land-use practice that is challenged; the effort is rather to force abatement of the nuisance.[5] The gully-washing of one farmer's misused land may give no cause for complaint to his neighbors until their drainage ditches are blocked by sediment from his eroding acres. Other behaviors often immune to policy interference include (1) destruction of wildlife habitat, (2) value impairment of an aesthetic nature, (3) speculation—land treated solely as a commodity. Behind these behaviors lie ideological explanations or justifications, but these rationales are rarely invoked, as the behaviors, per se, are seldom challenged. Legal action is more often directed toward after-the-fact correction of their allegedly harmful effects. And too often "after the fact" means ecologically too late![6]

The conceptualization of land as a commodity leads to less than its fully economic significance. Here again the cards of political economy are stacked against comprehensive policy. Economics may be aptly described as a "rational" science, but sometimes its rationality is of a limited kind, and not all economic behaviors are fully "rational" in all senses of the term. What seems rational for an individual human with a restricted life span may not be rational as defined by long-term community needs and values. And it is easier for the individual landowner to analyze and evaluate available options for the uses of his proprietary rights in land than for society to discover and agree upon long-term needs and values in relation to his land.

Reconciliation of short-term, long-term, and individual social rationalities has been attempted by public agencies, notably by the courts, in adjudication of public "taking" of private property (e.g., land), for public purposes.[7] Where national parks or monuments have been established in populated areas, a phaseout period is now normally provided, assuring present occupants of lifetime possession but consummating the transfer to public control whenever a "turnover" in possession occurs. Favorable as this type of arrangement may be for the occupants, it is nevertheless often rejected, sometimes for reasons of sentiment (for example, leaving a family heritage to heirs) but as often perhaps because of economic loss, demonstrable or conjectured.[8]

For example, there may be a great economic advantage in possession of an "inholding" surrounded by a state or national park or forest. The inholding owner or occupant may obtain, as a consequence of public investment, extraordinary protection from economic competition from other land holders and from damage occasioned by misuses of their lands—economic, aesthetic, or ecological. But, of course, the government may not always be a "good" proprietary neighbor.[9]

There are some "wild" cards in the economic suit. These include unforeseen or unforeseeable changes in land values resulting from, for example, oil or gas finds, an unannounced industrial or commercial relocation, or radical changes in community life-styles, such as an increase of second homes or forms of outdoor recreation requiring green space. These shifts in the values of otherwise unchanged parcels of land cause the windfalls and wipeouts addressed by Donald Hagman and others.[10] They create interlinking problems of law and economics and often arise because the right hand of public policy concerned, for example, with highway construction or low-cost housing, is oblivious or indifferent to what the left hand may be doing with respect to taxation, resource conservation, or environmental quality. Land is thus a medium through which the consequences of certain value changes may be projected upon individual land users and owners and indirectly upon society at large.

Were economics like physics, a conceptually unified science, a generally reliable calculus might be developed to measure and allocate the costs of changes in the valuation and uses of land. Yet physics, if a more integrated and exact science than economics, is more probabilistic and less dogmatic than some schools of economistic theory. Economics consists of not one, but many, schools of theory and analysis. And although there are principles of economic behavior upon which nearly all economists agree, debates over economic policy soon arrive at the juncture at which an answer must be given to the question "whose economics should prevail?" And the answer accepted may bear heavily upon the subsequent direction of policy development.

The task of sorting out and trying to reconcile differing values in land and its uses is, or should be, one of the principal miseries of land-use planners. Like the searchers for miracle drugs in medicine, planners have sought for practical, acceptable legal devices to accommodate and adjust value conflicts over land and to clear the way for rational planning. For a short time, the concept of transferable development rights was seen by some land planners as a "magic bullet" that would obviate much of the conflict resulting from the imposition of legal restraints upon hitherto acceptable economic uses of land.[11] Transfer of development rights has proved to be a selectively helpful tool of land-use planning and control, but it does not answer all needs and circumstances, nor was it intended to do so.

An obvious difficulty in finding equitable solutions to conflicts in value preferences is that the values are not always, or even often, commensurable. The constraints that some people wish to impose upon conventional economically motivated uses of land may be aesthetic, ecological, ethical, or even a contrary order of economic considerations. Even if one were to accept the hypotheses that everyone has his price, and that even the most deeply and intensely held ethical value can be reduced to monetary terms, the proposition would not help the policy planner if enough people perversely rejected its validity. Problems of land-use policy choice cannot be solved through economic reductionism unless some means are found to persuade almost everyone to accept a translation of all values into econometric terms. The prospect for this conversion in an age of apparently increasing ecological and aesthetic awareness would appear to be poor.

A third suit in the political deck whose cards may reinforce, weaken, or cancel the value of behavioral and economic cards is the ideological. Here one finds ethical beliefs and aesthetic values that may or may not be translatable into conventional economic terms, but may also either censor or legitimize particular economic behaviors. Most behavior in any society, including economic behavior, is in some sense legitimized by some prevailing ideology. Thus it is logical in our culture to "own" or to "buy" land in a way that is in effect quite different from acquiring access to common properties in air, water, or sunlight. What is usually acquired from common properties are "rights" to transitory and specified uses of these hard-to-hold resources. One buys a "view" on a hillside subdivision, but may lose it if it is obstructed by high-rise buildings or defaced by chimney stacks or electric power lines. One buys measurable quantities of water only to lose them in use.

Some technical legal principles of long-standing application to property rights pertaining to land have adversely affected groups and individuals deficient in power or knowledge. Historic legal doctrines grew out of a social ideology that, among other things, did not question capital punishment for offenses now regarded as misdemeanors and denied to women most economic and many personal rights. Although no legal principle or doctrine can continue indefinitely to be regarded as politically more valid or persuasive than the social ideology that sustains it, a legal principle that has become questionable theoretically may continue to be sustainable until supplanted by a feasible alternative. Several interrelated reasons explain this with particular reference to land law in the United States.

One reason is that ideological change in American society has largely been issue specific, not comprehensive. Although there have been radical or utopian exceptions, reform movements characteristically have been directed to specific discovered abuses, not toward the social system as a whole. For another, the law, being conservative in tendency, is not likely to change in the absence of pressure upon some specific principle or provision. A third reason is the complex set of interrelationships involving land, law, and economics manifest in the traditional emotional aura surrounding the concept of ownership. Land is widely regarded as our most important commodity, and transactions affecting its disposition and use are almost invariably locked into the real-estate triangle of land owner, money lender, and lawyer (at bar and on the bench).[12] The law governing land ownership and uses is thus strongly reinforced by linked and convergent interests. In many communities, the real-estate triangle is the most potent single fact of politics.

It should not be surprising, therefore, that broadly based land-use politics that are not consistent with generally accepted and mutually advantageous relationships among landlords, lenders, and lawyers are likely to encounter resistance. Many of the concerns motivating policy changes in land laws fall outside the real-estate triangle and do not serve the interests that it symbolically represents. The objectives of land-use reform today are characteristically sociological or ecological; their economic rationales tend to be those of communities rather than of individuals, but their impacts may be felt by land-owning interests. Even when the proposed reforms could benefit individual proprietors, the advantages are not always specified or clarified in a manner adequate to overcome a generalized fear of loss of control.

Present-day attacks upon the traditional structure of land use law are, moreover, far from consistent with one another. Some are mutually antagonistic. The sociological objectives of some reformers, for example, to promote racial and economic diversification within communities, to break down various form of de facto segregation, have sometimes run counter to ecological objectives such as the preservation of open space and the control of population densities.[13] The aesthetic values of harmony in cultural and natural landscapes that reformers, often including land owners, attempt to protect through changes in traditional law may conflict with other changes sought by advocates of massive public technologies (e.g., highways, airports, landfills) who object to legal provisions that slow progress or increase costs by protecting "rights" of individual land owners or occupants.[14]

In sum, land-use problems are people problems. The critical issues and disputes have often more to do with the implications and consequences of particular uses than with the uses themselves. It is accordingly difficult to draft statutory declarations of land-use policy at less than a very high level of generality. High-level generalities, unless expressive of strong emotional bias, are notoriously poor catalysts of popular enthusiasm and support. On the land-use issue in America, the emotion is largely weighted against long-term comprehensiveness, supporting individual rights against social infringement, real or fancied. If comprehensive land-use policy is sought, a problem of strategy must be faced.

Needed—A Strategy

A strategy may be described as a plan of action designed to achieve a generalized goal by increasing proponents and diminishing opponents. In our society a public strategy will be most effective if overt and honest, not covert or disassembling. To win friends by straightforward efforts to help people reconcile their short-term interests with the longer-term needs and interests of society cannot fairly be described as subversive, and that is what an effective strategy for land-use policy must achieve.

In the United States, most statutory proposals for comprehensive land-use planning have attracted too few allies to offset hard-core opposition. It is plausible that, if fairly understood, legislation such as the National Land Use Policy Act (S. 3345, 1970, and its successors) would be favored by a majority of the national electorate.[15] At the state level, comprehensive planning has been enacted for limited and specific purposes—for example, by initiative in California (Proposition 20: The California Coast: environmental preservation and public access)[16] and by legislative action in Vermont.[17] But this state legislation has been largely confined to areas of conspicuous vulnerability—the coastal zone and land adjacent to lakes and streams. Legislation requiring restoration of strip-mined land has been enacted in many states, but its uneven effectiveness prompted demands for federal regulation.[18] More inclusive land-use measures might win approval if they could be debated and could come to a vote. But the commonly successful strategy of the opposition has been to prevent land-use planning measures from reaching the legislature as a whole by "bottling them up" in committee. Thus, consideration of general federal land-use legislation has been blocked by the Rules Committee of the House of Representatives. Frank J. Popper, in his book *The Politics of Land Use Reform* (1981), has described this complicated and often contradictory effort toward formulating land policy in greater detail than is attempted here.[19]

The hard-core opposition to comprehensive land-use planning may not be as formidable numerically as it is strategically. Its principal cohorts are the real-estate lobby, the building trades, mortgage and land investment companies, and development interests generally. Their stakes in land-use policy are their preferred economic futures. Their legal responsibilities as land developers seldom include protection against adverse economic, let alone social or ecological, consequences of their actions. There are few practicable ways to hold land developers accountable for their actions other than bonding for specific performance.[20] For many land abuses, the only remedy is prevention.

Prevention, however, requires constraints upon land owners, users, and developers, obviously diminishing their economic freedom in relation to the uses of the land.

Free-enterprise development interests tend to respond aggressively to planning that places desirable tracts of land out-of-bounds for subdivision. Opponents of land-use restrictions and advocates of market mediated laissez-faire land policy have sometimes alleged that land-use planning discriminates against the poor. This allegation is generally specious. Local ordinances for land use or controlled growth are vulnerable to judicial review if, by intent or affect, discrimination against any sector of the population is inferred. However, the 11th Circuit Court has held that to demonstrate that a zoning action violates equal protection rights there must be proof of both a disproportionate impact on a particular class and that the government acted with discriminatory intent or purpose.[21] There is a certain irony in efforts by developers of luxury housing and shopping malls for the affluent to coopt the civil rights movement in opposition to public land-use planning and control. Demagoguery is not an attribute cultivated exclusively by candidates for political office.

The allegation that land-use regulation has a tendency to deprive the poor may be reversed, as plausibly, to the opposite conclusion. For example, under Senate Bill 268 (1973), which would have become the Land Use Policy and Planning Assistance Act, the Secretary of Housing and Urban Development was required to review and comment on grants requested by the state, notably with respect to a state's participation in programs pursuant to Section 701 of the Housing Act of 1954. The poor have little influence on the market for land—they are seldom in a position to speculate on land futures—and the surest protection of their interest in land is through planning and through administrative and judicial review of private as well as public land-use plans. Exclusionary zoning has usually been sought by private interests not always disposed to favor land-use planning.

Owners are not necessarily disadvantaged, even economically, by land-use controls and may indeed be advantaged. For example, owners wishing to retain lands in farms, forests, or for residential use can be protected against pressure to develop accompanied by increased tax assessments.[22] But land owners can be frightened by the prospect of unspecified and unforeseeable consequences of changes in their legal rights that comprehensive land-use planning might entail. The hard core of unconvertible opposition to public control over land use has effectively exploited this uneasiness. Its success may be the most significant single reason for the general failure of the comprehensive approach thus far.

If comprehensiveness in land-use policy is necessary to its effectiveness, but not attainable by statute, a different approach must be sought. The pragmatic approach that many jurisdictions have begun to follow has been to focus efforts on specific aspects of land use and environmental objectives, for example, through implementation of Section 208 of the 1972 amendments to the Federal Water Pollution Control Act.[23] Yet the unhappy consequences of ad hoc approaches to land-use policies and controls have provided some of the most convincing arguments for comprehensive perspectives in planning. It can hardly be too strongly emphasized, however, that the *goal* of comprehensiveness does not imply an attempt to deal with all aspects of land use. Planning may be technically centralized or broadly participatory, but it is more likely to be truly comprehensive if an appropriate allocation of responsibility prevails so that account may be taken of all aspects of planning that are relevant to achieving its objectives. One objective is to avoid mutually conflicting developments.[24]

A major rationale for a federal land-use planning assistance act was illustrated by a series of transparent overlay maps prepared for a hearing before the Senate Committee on Interior and Insular Affairs on March 24, 1970, pursuant to S. 3354.[25] These overlays depicted existing and some projected land uses by the federal agencies. Points of competition, contradiction, and conflict were made explicit. The maps indicated localities in which tax dollars were being spent by federal agencies, in effect, to negate one another's efforts. Lack of coordination in land-use planning was obviously costly in both dollars and program effectiveness.

Prudent public investment in land public works requires a degree of comprehensiveness in planning and control sufficient to reconcile and coordinate existing and proposed usages. It is poor logic for Congress to grant public-works funds to the states for airports, highways, land and water conservation, and similar land-related purposes when most states have made no effort to see that the land-use intentions of these projects have not been contradicted by other land-use commitments. But this logic alone was insufficient to enact federal legislation in 1970 or 1973 that would have assisted statewide land-use planning.

Separate attack by statute or ordinance upon particular land-use problems does not afford a practical alternative to a comprehensively conceived planning unless two conditions are present. The first is that particular action be taken within a broad perspective and evaluation of land-use interrelationships and priorities. The second is that there be some operational institution or agency to make this overview and to obtain, by whatever means appropriate, an approach consistent with

long-range ecological values and public welfare. These two conditions are essential components of a strategy to obtain by a skillful
combination of existing means the policy coordination heretofore
unobtainable through categorical statutory authorizations (e.g., separate legislation for various types of land use unrelated to other land-
use issues).

This approach to policy may modify but need not negate the general body of legal principles governing land use and tenure. It need
not be prejudicial to the proprietary rights of an individual or a corporate body in land, with an important exception. Exercise of these
rights ought not be permitted to impair or destroy the integrity or
self-renewing capabilities of natural ecosystems or human communities without the strongest social justification and review by those who
must in various ways bear the cost of resulting damage. This is a
large exception, but one consistent with the concept of an inherent
power in government to protect the public health, safety, general
welfare, transgenerational equity, and by implication, the environment.

There are, of course, commentators and professional skeptics who
contend that land-use planning will never work as intended—produc-
ing unforeseen adverse consequences or merely failing to achieve its
purpose (at an unjustifiable cost).[26] There are indeed formidable obstacles to the implementation of land-use plans. Most formidable
among these is excessive population growth, and it will continue to
be a hazard in this as in other respects as long as high levels of growth
continue and a large sector of the public and its government are ob-
sessed with the notion that more and bigger are necessarily better.
There are numerous examples of both successful and failed planning.
It is not necessary to argue an inherent weakness in planning to explain the reasons for the failure of some land policies and land-use
planning methods.

An effective strategy for comprehensive land-use planning must
enlist the support of a critical mass among persons who have traditionally opposed the planning concept. These include, principally,
persons holding proprietary interests in land for these, as Donald
Denman has reminded us, are the primary land-use planners.[27] It has
been a failure-inducing paradox of many land-use planning proposals
that no clear or appropriate role was provided for these primary planners. A strategy is needed that will avoid uniting land owners against
planning and will bring as many of them that respect ecological and
cultural values and sustainable economic rationality into an influential and constructive role in the planning process.

An effective strategy of implementation does, however, imply a
well-conceived and concerted set of objectives—in effect, a plan that

is comprehensive in the scope of its consideration and intended results, but flexible and opportunity-seeking with respect to practical means. In theory, although rarely in practice, political-party platforms afford a rough analogy. They set forth a set of (sometimes) interrelated goals indicating an intended direction of policy, but are usually noncommittal as to means. It is, of course, commonplace for candidates for the offices of state governor or president to declare in favor of policy objectives without specifying a particular course of action. To fit together pieces of authorized action to form a coherent and consistent policy may be regarded as effective administration; it may be called policy making by implementation.

Implementing a Strategy

Any effective strategy for comprehensive land-use planning must provide answers to three questions. *What* is the strategy? *Who* is to implement it? and *How* is the strategy to be implemented? Our definition of strategy has a consensus-building plan of action, directed in this instance *toward* ecologically and economically sustainable patterns of land use, yielding optimal levels of human satisfaction. Obviously this is not a self-explanatory definition. The expressions "sustainable patterns" and "optimal levels of satisfaction" do not represent broadly understood criteria in our society. Although their meanings may incorporate significant and even objectively demonstrable findings of fact, and to this extent may be called "scientific," they may also contain subjective, preferential aspects that are not demonstrably right or wrong in an ethical or a scientific sense. Optimal satisfactions may most easily be isolated through discovering those circumstances that almost no one would regard as optimal. For example, exhausted soil fertility or water supply would hardly be regarded under any circumstances as optimal. Optimality might be posited as a goal and some of its major parameters identified through objective analysis. But its ultimate meaning as a goal of policy would have to be discovered through the implementation of an optimum-seeking strategy, for there appears no other way that in societies holding multiple values, consensual definitions of optimality can be achieved.[28] The attempted balancing of values by the courts may be regarded as a practical effort to approximate optimality. But equitable balancing may be compromised by limited information in a case under review. Judicial review is restricted to the evidence at hand and may be unable consider related but noncontested issues. Posterity may not have standing in court, and the implications of the controversy may extend to social and ecological considerations beyond those reviewable in the court.

Practices that are ecologically sustainable, meaning protective of the self-renewing capabilities of ecological communities, including those serving the ecological needs of people, are less difficult to define and confirm than are propositions regarding economic optimality. In neither case is prediction wholly dependable. But ecological probabilities may more reliably be conjectured by evidence of cause-effect relationships, regardless of human preference or value. Strategy therefore also calls for making explicit and widely understood the interrelationships among natural systems, including the systems that humans contrive through the manipulation of natural forces. This strategy assumes that people can be persuaded to act more often in their own interest in a manner consistent with that of others and of posterity to the extent that probable consequences are understood. A strategy is, after all, an effort to advance human purpose; in our context it is a corrective, not a panacea, for the limitations of human altruism and foresight.[29]

The incidence and origins of land-use problems indicate who should be involved in their solution. The traditional base for land-use decisions has been the real-estate triangle of landlord, lender, and lawyer, with the speculator and developer playing roles intermediate among the three principals. And because decisions within the triangle have historically been made largely exclusive of general public interests or external costs, public authority has been sought to afford at least minimal protection to the community. Land-use controls, notably zoning, have been the generally accepted forms of public involvement in land-use policy.[30] But conventional methods have been widely criticized as ineffective and clearly have not prevented many of our worst land abuses, including many perpetrated by governmental agencies.[31]

Among the more obvious weaknesses of conventional public controls are these: first, the owners and users of land are seldom involved in representative or constructive ways that are open and protective of the public interest; second, the policy machinery is easily captured by economically focused development interests that may preempt representation of proprietary interests in land; and third, no systematic way is provided for scientific or cultural considerations to influence the decision process. In many communities these circumstances have been conducive to skulduggery, conspiracy, favoritism, and a bad name for land-use planning. Zoning and planning boards are often dominated by persons whose interest in land is almost wholly in short-term economic profit. The interests of small landed proprietors are often overridden in favor of big developers, builders, speculators, and government public works agencies. Development interests may numerically represent a small minority in a community, the proprietors a much larger number. But the development interests invoke the magic symbols of jobs, economic growth, and especially of increased taxable assessments, whereas the individual land owners are likely to be seeking protection for preferred private uses of their property. Stability rather than growth may often be their objective.

Land-use control, therefore, risks becoming a manipulative and adversarial process, with insufficient regard for its long-range effect upon the community, state, or nation. When the big public and industrial eminent-domain decision makers enter the process to obtain rights-of-way, power plant sites, airports, or housing tracts, they have characteristically done so with advanced plans, narrowly focused on their economic missions, without significant public input, and ably defended by lawyers and economists. Invariably the public interest is invoked in addition to theoretical economic justification for overriding the preferences of adversely affected communities and property owners. "Economic growth" has been the magic word invoked to ward off threats to development.

Bureaucratic and industrial enterprisers define the public interest in terms consistent with their missions and assume with good logic that the courts will entertain a presumption in their favor. Under the present structure of land-use decision making, it may be regarded as logical to assume that duly constituted representatives of the public such as the Department of Defense, Tennessee Valley Authority, and the Federal Highway Administration are more broadly representative of the public interest than any probable combination of individual land owners or users. It is similarly logical to assume that a legislative grant of eminent domain to energy and mining corporations confirms their interpretations of public convenience and necessity as more valid than any combination of citizens, short of an electoral majority. However, courts may not always agree that this assumption holds in particular land-use or environmental disputes.[32] Legislation such as the National Environmental Policy Act of 1969 injected a new set of ecological considerations into the land-use policy process.[33] Nevertheless, the political and legal cards continue to be stacked against the ecological and sociocultural values that this legislation was designed to protect. Protection of the environment and the land—unlike civil rights and property—have no standing in the U.S. Constitution.

The matter of *who* is involved in the decision process significantly influences its outcome. If land-use policy is to serve comprehensive long-range and ecologically defensible values, the structuring of par-

ticipation in the decision process must be consistent with this purpose. The excessive influence of the real-estate triangle and of the
narrowly focused eminent-domain decision makers needs to be leav-
ened by participation from the full range of interests in land use. These
include land owners and many users (especially residents), representatives of the affected and concerned public that does not own land,
and scientists, engineers, and environmental planners with special
knowledge and operational skills pertaining to the utilization and
conservation of land and its associated resources.

In simple language, a workable strategy for comprehensive land-
use planning calls for a greatly broadened base of real and not superficial or symbolic participation. Institutional arrangements are required
that will go as far as formalities can toward ensuring this broad participation. To serve its purpose, however, the participation must be
informed, and this implies a learning experience for the participants.
Finally, it must result in demonstrable accomplishment, in action and
not mere rhetoric.

Only to the extent that participation makes a difference in the
outcomes of land-use decisions will it be possible to sustain a broad
spectrum of disinterested involvement. The interests within the real-
estate triangle ensure *their* participation. The outstanding loans and
bank balances of developers and builders ensure their readiness to sit
past midnight in sessions of planning boards—this public business is
their business, and its outcomes determine their economic futures.

Paradoxically, individuals and relatively small landed proprietors
are often the most vocal opponents of public land-use planning. A
free-enterprise bias may persuade them that the representatives of the
real-estate interests are their allies and protectors. This dubious proposition has been cultivated by real-estate lobbyists, reinforced by the
often heavy-handed and uncomprehended behavior of governmental
planning and development agencies, and sharpened by a sense of
powerlessness among individual land owners. Powerlessness breeds
fear that broadly inclusive statutory controls over land will be used
to the land owners' disadvantage. The historical record of government land policy, at all jurisdictional levels, tends to confuse the
prospects rather than to refute the fear. The private development sector may threaten the values of many individual land owners, but it
often obtains acquiescence through the persuasive power of money
plus propaganda. Government tends to resort to administrative regulations or judgments-at-law, but it might serve the public interest more
effectively through efforts to educate and inform public opinion regarding the issues and the reasons for government action.

Who implements a land-use planning strategy depends greatly on how the decision processes of society are organized and evolve. We have argued that comprehensiveness in the scope of land policy requires the participation of large numbers of people involved in or affected by land-use decisions. How to obtain this participation in an appropriate, constructive, and responsible manner is a major aspect of the land-use policy problem. The *how* of implementation therefore includes the building of an institutionalized public coalition to accomplish the purpose of comprehensive land-use planning that, within prevailing limits of ecological facts and social values, is broadly consensual. To achieve an operative consensus that is democratically constituted and scientifically informed, it is necessary that the substance of the consensus, however minimal, be explicit and that a critical mass of civic leadership is committed to it. The consensus would be agreement regarding the preferred future quality of the environment with particular reference to the effects of land-use decisions. Consensus need not imply universal agreement; some measure of conflict is safely predictable. Consensus is more widely and surely achieved through the interchange of information and experience by persons representing the broadest range of concern with land. Brought together on boards or commissions, these persons may find a level of consensus through coping with land-use problems against a background of generally accepted preferences. To plan toward preferred outcomes implies some structuring of the decision process so that a connection is established between what is decided in particular cases and the preferred outcomes. A major purpose here is to avoid the tyranny of small decisions that, taken incrementally, foreclose future options. Gradually emerging from this collaborative decision process should appear the elements of democratic and realistic land-use planning, evolved through a broadly representative and responsible effort to approximate land-use wisdom.

To serve its purpose effectively, this process must be characterized by order, system, and directness. The weaknesses of conventional land-use controls have been their superficial neutrality and ad hoc modification. Zoning and subdivision controls, for example, have sometimes proved to be unreliable instruments of protection against powerful socioeconomic pressure.[34] These controls have at times paradoxically been both vulnerable and obstructive, for they often represent a barricade or status quo psychology but possess no power to alleviate or redirect the pressures that they were intended to resist. Nevertheless, when they work as intended they may protect stability in neighborhoods and prevent disruptive uses of land. They should not be abandoned without more effective substitutes and may be combined with other forms of policy implementation, for example, siting and architectural standards, historic preservation, and ecological conservation.

The *how* aspect of developing land-use policy has three interactive components: citizen representation; professional, scientific and technical advice; and administrative implementation. First and basic is the structure of representation. Local, regional, and state commissions, broadly representative of the legitimate interests in land (not "packed" by developers and real-estate enterprisers) could provide this component. California and Vermont have provided examples of citizen commissions for the review of land-use decisions in the vulnerable areas of the coastal zone and the shores of lakes and rivers.[35] These commissions function pursuant to statutory authority, but governors and local executives might appoint advisory and fact-finding bodies whose actions could be influential without the force of law. A statutory basis for such bodies would be desirable, however, expressly to define their roles and representative character and to provide, as far as possible, against their misuse. The need for informed judgment on many land-use issues also calls for professional, scientific, or technical opinion. Here advisory panels could be useful; some could be continuing, others ad hoc. The study group of the National Research Council on the extension of airport runways into Jamaica Bay, New York, illustrates the role of this component in the decision not to extend, and its findings may have decisively influenced the outcome.[36] The administrative component is divided between the secretariat function essential to effective citizen committee work and the executive responsibilities of public officials for the decisions that make or implement land-use policy. These officials include not only general executives such as governors, mayors, and city/county managers, but they also, and often more importantly, include the administrators of airport, highway, park, and sanitation programs, among others.

To implement a land-use strategy, these three components must constitute an effective network of communication. American civic behavior is long experienced at combining official and unofficial action to serve public needs. Let us accept as plausible that irresponsibility in land-use decisions results more from an inadequate system of information and consensus building than from inadequacies in the law. If so, then to focus corrective efforts on statutory reform to the neglect of building a structure of popular understanding and consent is to attack the policy problem from the wrong end. Statutes are often necessary but per se are insufficient to achieve the purposes of law. Our statutory codes are replete with unenforced or indifferently enforced provisions. Law most effectively administered is usually law that has substantial public support. The *how* of formulating land use policy includes consideration of what it is about land use that requires attention. Because prevention of misuse is usually more effective than its cure, policy needs to be anticipatory as well as reactive. Both citizen and official bodies need to look at the uses of land, present and prospective, in relation to (1) probabilities, (2) potentialities, and (3) values.

Probabilities

The policy-formulating process should search for best estimates of the consequences of socioeconomic or ecological trends affecting land and its uses. To arrive at rational decisions regarding land use, the decision makers, unofficial as well as official, need to know what will probably happen if they do nothing and the prevailing forces of humanity, economics, and nature work toward their most likely consequences. To obtain this information, the assistance of science is needed. Trends and impacts, and the results toward which they appear to lead, must be compared with those that the society generally prefers.

As of today, building a consensus on preference is a major challenge to strategy. This task implies a broad educational effort of multimedia dimensions and with multiple sponsorships. In developing this strategy those policies and practices, public and private, impairing the terrestrial environment should be identified. It should be possible to locate the pressure points and more pervasive forces threatening the quality of the environment. Impact analysis is becoming a widely used instrument for this purpose.

This estimate of probable impacts could become an important instrument of consensus building. To arrive at estimates meaningful for policy, analyses of true costs and benefits of impending actions are needed. Cost-benefit analysis is a tricky tool of policy. But in principle, and when all true costs are considered and value preferences made explicit, it affords a means for discovering who gains what and who loses what in specific land-use decisions and policies. In particular, it may help individuals to discover their personal stake in land-use decisions and what they have to gain or to lose in particular circumstances. It is plausible that if most land owners and members of the non-land-owning public had a more realistic understanding of the impact of land-use decisions upon themselves, they would be more favorably disposed to broadened perspectives in planning. They might seek a more effective voice in governmental decisions and be less easily coopted by the emotion-charged propaganda of liberty lobbies and predatory development interests. Emotional appeals are also made by environmental-protection and preservation groups. In any case, a rational assessment of the claims would depend upon access to the full and accurate facts of the respective allegations.

Few allies are won by recitations of abstract social or ecological costs, but individuals may be aroused by the threat of impositions upon themselves personally. It can be demonstrated that the absence of socioecologically rational land-use planning is not in the interests of most land owners and the general public. But in our society, the burden of proof that planning may be advantageous is on its advocates. Conventional wisdom points to an opposing conclusion.

Potentialities

A second aspect of the planning process relates to potentialities or opportunities for optimal land use. It is a point of faith, but not of demonstrable fact, that free-market decisions always result in optimal land use. Individual land owners and decision makers characteristically act upon imperfect knowledge regarding the consequences of their actions. The probable consequences of opportunities overlooked or foreclosed may be ascertained from future projected cost-benefit analyses and estimates of opportunity costs. No less important is analysis of what might be done to enhance environmental quality and self-renewing productivity through alternative, rational, land-use initiatives.

Conventional definitions of the scope and substance of the land market may be unduly restrictive. In some respects the land itself, beyond proprietary rights pertaining to it, is a common-property resource comparable to air and water.[37] As common property in the sense of societies' terrestrial life-support base, all society is affected by land-market transactions as well as by planning, regardless of the distribution of legal rights over land. In various ways all members of society receive the impacts of "goods" and "bads" in land regardless of their awareness of participation in the land-use decision process. Yet there are few ways in our society for most of the involuntarily involved public to obtain a voice in what they, in effect, "buy" and what they "sell." Nevertheless, for many purposes a "free" market for rights of use in land within appropriate parameters is an efficient way of implementing land-use decisions.

Doctrinaire socialization of land ownership and land-use decision making is fraudulent in that it offers no reliable promise of ecologically or economically rational, unique solutions to most substantive problems of land-use policy. It substitutes one form of ownership status for another but cannot guarantee that responsible concern or foresight or wisdom will thereby be enhanced. It is one thing to recognize that there are widespread but differentiated public interests inherent in land-use decisions that have certain characteristics of a market, and quite another to regard the land as a "commons" in which privileges and responsibilities are equally distributed. No sustainable socialist or communal scheme of land control could for long risk a "tragedy of the commons" in which each user seeks to maximize his advantage, thus destroying the commons for all.

To replace the relatively unstructured system of land-use accountability afforded by a socially perfected system of private ownership, a socialized system would need to find an alternative form of motivation. The historical substitutes for personal interests have usually been coercive. In self-styled socialist states, costs and risks of initiative traditionally borne by the owners of land have been assumed by public bureaucracies wholly paid for by the people and ostensibly accountable to them. Individual users of the land, however, are no longer independent agents; they are part of a hierarchical structure of authority. Shortsighted or destructive land-use decisions by official bureaucracies are difficult to challenge and reverse, even where independent judicial review is available as in the United States. But the argument that private owners are always more reliable caretakers of their land than public custodians does not stand up under real-life scrutiny. There is no substitute for a system and consensus in law and ethics that inculcates and requires responsible land use and management regardless of ownership.

Students of land policy could benefit from the findings of cultural anthropologists regarding the various patterns of ownership and rights of use among traditional societies.[38] The dichotomy of government or private ownership and control is not the only alternative in human experience—nor is it necessarily the most rational and responsible choice. There is opportunity and need for more creative thinking about the management of land-use decisions.

Values

A third aspect of systematic policy development linking prospects with opportunities is the consideration of values.[39] American politics and public administration have not been distinguished by sophistication in value analysis. Values are often asserted in dogmatic and simplistic language. Unexamined assertiveness regarding land ownership and land use makes more often for antagonism than for cooperation. Value analysis is necessary to successful coalition building. Conflicts over land use often occur because alternative means are never explored for the reconciliation of apparently conflicting values. It is not always the values that conflict, as often it is the proposed means to their realization. Discovery of what values can be reconciled and what cannot would obviously serve land-use planning strategies. Meritorious land-use propositions have miscarried because they failed to accommodate legitimate and compatible values, thus making enemies out of persons who could have been friends. But if fundamental values and assumptions are incompatible, not all interests can be accommodated; hence the importance of building a broad consensual societal base in environmental values and ethics.

The Essence of Policy

The argument of this chapter has been that the goals of broadly beneficial land-use planning are more surely achieved through a progressive and broadly participatory development of policy than through premature legislative or judicial assertion, although official action will ultimately be necessary. The task of strategy is essentially the building of a coalition or critical mass of popular understanding and acceptance. The strategic means include the responsible involvement of all the major interests in society concerned with the consequences of land-use decisions. A suitable institutional arrangement to accomplish this purpose would need to be invented, but we are not without models or precedents. Many types of federated citizen-action groups, soil and water conservation districts, and neighborhood associations are examples of a multiplicity of institutional arrangements that might afford guidance to the architects of a novel but feasible structure for broadly participatory, but scientifically informed, systems for the implementary development of acceptable land-use policies. An outcome of this strategy would be a generally agreed upon hierarchy of priorities, reflective of a broad range of values and guided by considerations of (1) immediacy of threats to the environment, (2) nature and extent of costs of remedial measures, (3) alternative means to the realization of values sought in land, and (4) constructive opportunities for optimizing the values attainable through people-land relationships. Procedures toward this end include consensus building through citizen involvement and by making explicit the sociological, ecological, economic, and political consequences of specific policies and actions affecting the land. Unlike most conventional land-use controls, this approach is more positive than negative. It would be characterized by citizen-based public initiatives in which land owners, both public and private, would play major roles within a social content broader than the traditional real-estate triangle.

Obviously, not all owners and users of land would benefit from this approach. It is not calculated to serve the interests of speculation or of action having destructive consequences. Yet it preserves and, in principle, helps to define the place of market mechanisms in land-use decisions. To put this consensual strategy into effect would be a major task of political innovation. To build the minimum required base of understanding and consent would require time, reliable and adequate information, and a high order of dedicated persuasiveness. Both the extension and the restriction of freedoms over land usage might be facilitated by the prudent use of incentives and compensatory provisions. Abuses of land-use policy are not fairly attributable solely to landlords and land users as some reformers allege. Efforts to achieve social goals may have inadvertent consequences that are ecologically and economically destructive. For example, so-called agrarian reform, whatever its justification, has seldom been motivated by regard for the ecological renewability of the land or for enlarging the values served through uses of the land. More often, the objective has been the reduction of a social class dependent for its economic status and political power upon control of the land, and elevation of landless peasantry to a higher economic status. In our times, redistribution of land to the landless has often been followed by collectivization, once the holders of centralized political power have eliminated independent sources of opposition.

Economic power derived from landownership has traditionally been an instrument of political power. But in the independence of the individual land owner it has also been a brake against the abuse of centralized political power. A broadly distributed pattern of ownership with the size of holdings appropriate to usage and terrain have characterized most societies in which personal freedoms and widespread responsible participation in public decisions have flourished. What implications does this thesis hold for law? Most importantly it suggests that the conservatism of law should reflect the need to conserve land as a basic resource for life support and a broad range of human values. The growth of scientific knowledge pertinent to land-use policy has not yet been adequately accommodated in the law. Policies to protect aquifers, ground water, soil quality, and deposits of essential materials such as sand, gravel, and building stone often run against the grain of the law of property rights. Policies to protect the public from hazardous uses of land, as, for example, on flood plains and unstable subsurface terrain, have been handicapped by legal provisions and presumptions that in effect favor the immediate economic interests of the real-estate triangle over the long-range interests of the community.[40] To bring the law more nearly in line with current needs implies more legal research into its present state of inadequacy. Much work has of course been done on various aspects of land law, but there is still need for a systematic taxonomy of problems and related legal provisions that case books do not adequately provide. The need relates to what the law does not provide by way of guides for policy as to what may be done under the law as it now stands.

This discourse on the law-land relationship began with the proposition that focus on specific land abuses might offer a more meaningful and acceptable approach to land-use planning than general statutory authorization, which has historically attracted more opposition than support. Knowledge of specific problems and available remedies is obviously essential to this approach. More than legal research is needed, because the range of land-use related problems is very broad. Many of these problems are well known to the people who have experienced them, but the remedies in law or in policy are not always obvious nor are the relative merits of alternatives generally perceived. This survey of the problems and the law of land usage should therefore be designed as much for average citizens and public officials as for lawyers. The primary purpose of this chapter has been to address the practical need for broadened participation in land-use decisions; that implies that more people not professionally trained in the law participate in its interpretation and administration. This development would not be unique to land-use policy; citizen participation in public administration and planning has been growing across the spectrum of public affairs.

Complexity and specialization in modern life have increasingly separated the citizen from personal involvement with the law as an instrument of self-government. Alienation of people from their legal system can hardly be healthy for the practice of self-government or for an individual sense of civic responsibility. And although citizen participation in government is now on the increase, signs of popular alienation from government and public affairs have also been increasing, and at a time when precisely the reverse of this trend is needed. If we are to cope effectively with the environmental problems of our times, ways must be found to establish a relationship between people and the law that will be widely regarded as meaningful. Land use is an area of public affairs in which rapproachment between the citizen and the legal system is an essential condition of developing and achieving sound and acceptable policy goals. The linkage between law and land is the commitment of the public, which now and in the future is unavoidably affected by whatever happens to the land.

3

Four Land Ethics: An Overview

Kristin Shrader-Frechette

Lynton Caldwell has noted that land use comprises our largest and most fundamental set of environmental problems.[1] For centuries, land has been the focal point for numerous ethical and environmental difficulties. In chapters one and two, we surveyed a number of these difficulties—such as reconciling alleged private rights in land with public needs, overcoming the prevalent economistic paradigm for land, and determining long-range effects of particular land-use controls. Most of these ethical and environmental problems arise as a result of at least four distinct land crises.

Introduction

Policy makers throughout the world have been trying to deal with the first type of land crisis ever since at least 1798 when Malthus wrote his influential *Essay on the Principle of Population*. Malthus described a land crisis of *distribution*; it arises from the fact that land supply (unlike labor and capital) is constant, while the demand for it is increasing. A second sort of land crisis arises because of *spillovers*. Spillovers arise because land sites are immobile and because the value of specific tracts of land derives not only from their own characteristics but also from the use made of neighboring sites. Nuisances (like air pollution from a factory) that spill over onto neighboring sites reduce their value, whereas amenities (like expensive and well-landscaped housing) spill over and increase the value of nearby land parcels.[2] A third type of land crisis arises, not because of the political and economic problems associated with land distribution or spillovers, but because of the environmental difficulties that develop as a result of treating land as a mere object or economic commodity, rather than as a part of the biosphere. Such economistic attitudes (see chapter one) have resulted in a crisis of land *degradation*. A fourth land crisis involves *legal standing*. Because the land does not have standing

43

in court, as do (for example) persons, corporations, and trusts, legal actions cannot be instituted at its behest. Courts cannot take into account injury to land, but only injury to *owners* of land caused by damage to the land. One of the most famous attacks on the failure to accord land legal standing is Christopher Stone's classic work, *Should Trees Have Standing?*"[3]

In this chapter, we attempt to investigate these four land crises and the major ethical and political solutions offered to alleviate them. First, we outline the problems associated with each of the four land crises. Next we summarize the four main "land ethics" proposals for resolving these crises. Finally, we sketch the assets and liabilities of each of the four land ethics.

Four Land Ethics

The classic response to the land crises of distribution, spillover, degradation, and legal standing has been to argue both for new ethics regarding land and for new constraints on the ownership and the use of land. Acceptance of these new constraints, however, appears (to some persons) to require acceptance of several revolutionary new land ethics. These ethics appear, at least at the outset, to challenge the validity of our deepest Lockean and Jeffersonian traditions and to strike at the heart of our pursuit of economic growth, individualism, and the notion of inalienable property rights. At least in the United States, many of us were raised to believe Locke and Jefferson, who argued that land ownership gives citizens independence from the state and strengthens democracy. Locke, in particular, claimed that property is the most basic of the natural rights. Moreover, the history in many of our textbooks told us that economic growth came about only because the institution of private property replaced more communal feudalism, thus providing capital and the means to increase productivity. For a variety of historical and cultural reasons, anyone who proposes new land ethics runs the risk of being viewed not primarily as an environmental messiah, but as an anti-Christ threatening the two religions of capitalism and democracy. (In chapter 4, we argue that at least one of these four new land ethics is consistent with our authentic legal, philosophical, and political traditions—through John Locke—and may be required by our traditions.)

Let's look more closely at the four main land ethics, all of which propose solutions to the land crises just mentioned. We call them "land-reform ethics," "land-use ethics," "land-community ethics," and "land-rights ethics." Although a brief chapter does not provide the space for a full discussion of all four of these new frameworks, let us sketch them briefly and then outline the assets and liabilities of each of them.

Land-Reform Ethics

The first land ethics, land-reform ethics, focuses on a set of moral imperatives designed to correct allegedly inequitable distributions of land. Typically, we think of land-reform ethics as being needed primarily in second- and third-world countries, where a minority of the population usually controls the vast majority of the land acres. In appealing for social justice and equal opportunity, however, proponents of land reform point out that, even in the United States, the bulk of land and assets are owned by only a few people. Haar and Liebman document, for example, that the wealthiest 20 percent of the population own over 75 percent of all the private assets in the United States, and that the wealthiest 8 percent own 60 percent of all private assets. The wealthiest 1 percent own 26 percent of all private assets, and the poorest 25 percent have no net worth.[4] A more recent, federally funded study concluded that the top 5 percent of all U.S. land owners owned 75 percent of the land, but the bottom 78 percent owned only 3 percent.[5] Examples of the results of such statistics are graphically illustrated in regions of the United States like Appalachia and the San Joachin valley. Both of these areas have been called third-world "colonies" of monopolistic, absentee landlords. In many areas of Appalachia, typically 80 percent of the land, both surface and mineral rights, are owned by monopolistic, absentee corporations, while local families have access neither to land nor to nonmining jobs. A recent report of the Appalachian Regional Commission pointed out that virtually all of the economic problems of Appalachian people, especially small farmers, could be traced to the central problem of monopolistic, absentee control of land.[6]

One of the proposed solutions to problems such as these in Appalachia is land reform. Defined most generally, land reform is expropriation, compensation and, finally, "redistribution of property or rights in land for the benefit of small farmers and agricultural labourers."[7] Let's look briefly at some of the positive and negative aspects of our proposed land-reform ethics.

Probably the main philosophical motivation for new land-reform ethics is to abolish extreme social, political, and economic inequality; many philosophers have noted that avoiding great economic inequalities is often a necessary condition for helping to attain political equality among citizens. For example, persons who are so economically deprived that they cannot feed themselves are unlikely to be able to exercise their equal political rights (e.g., to vote).[8] But if this is true, then reducing extreme economic inequalities, through strategies like land reform, might be one way of helping to reduce extreme political inequalities. Another motivation for new land-reform ethics is not philosophical but economic. When Thomas Jefferson and other colonial leaders championed land reform in the United States, for example, they were motivated not only by new democratic politics but also by the desire to realize the older dream of the economically disenfranchised Saxon freeman to hold land.[9] Other economic arguments for land reform come from Adam Smith, who, in his *Wealth of Nations*, argued that land reform would stimulate production and investment. Part of his reasoning was that land owners would work more effectively on and with their own land than they would as sharecroppers or wage laborers on the land of others. More recent economists make the same point and note, for example, that a very clear inverse relationship exists between farm size and net farm income per unit of land.[10]

Although social justice, productivity, and economic incentives provide strong arguments for land-reform ethics, there are a number of arguments against land reform. First, many people claim that land reform is unethical; it interferes with property rights and free competition. One of the most eloquent proponents of this point of view is Harvard philosopher Robert Nozick. Nozick defends an entitlement theory of justice, according to which a person is entitled to all holdings obtained in accord with principles of justice (e.g., the holdings were not stolen or obtained through cheating). Because he claims that one is *entitled* to all holdings obtained justly, Nozick even goes so far as to say, for example, that taxation of earnings is on a par with forced labor. On the entitlement theory, any redistribution (whether of land or of other property) is unethical, for at least two alleged reasons. One reason is that such a redistribution would require "continuous interference" in people's lives (because even after a redistribution, Nozick claims that the more shrewd or hard-working citizens would soon gain control of the lion's share of assets, thus requiring further redistributions). Another reason why redistribution is unethical, on the entitlement theory, is that it allegedly involves "the violation of people's rights," especially property rights.[11]

Opponents of the entitlement theory maintain that both the "interference" argument and the property-rights argument are suspect, since they beg the question. Nozick's "interference" argument, it can be claimed, is questionable because it presupposes (but does not substantiate) an important thesis. This thesis is that government interference in land holdings, via redistribution, is a worse evil than political inequality (which is in part generated by extreme economic inequalities, such as extreme inequalities in land holdings). The property-rights argument against redistribution can likewise be said to be suspect because it presupposes, rather than defends, an equally important thesis. This thesis is that property rights are absolute and can never be modified. This argument also presupposes that it is more important, ethically speaking, to maximize property rights rather than to minimize extreme economic inequalities that might threaten political equality. Both presuppositions deserve careful analysis, since many theorists have conceded that property rights belong to the class of "weak rights" and hence can be amended in order to serve the common good.[12]

A second argument against land reform, in addition to those based on the entitlement theory, is practical. This argument is that, even if land reform could be justified ethically, there are economic grounds for believing that it wouldn't work—either to improve political equality or to enhance land productivity. This is because powerful land holders would use their influence to encourage government to set up stumbling blocks designed to thwart any attempts to carry out land reform. Some of these stumbling blocks include legalistic land-transfer procedures, inadequate farmland financing, faulty transportation systems for farm products, inadequate technical help for new land owners, lack of irrigation and planning, and inequitable expropriation of land. As one prominent author put it: "revolutionary governments can carry through reforms which genuinely abolish the old structure without being able to replace it with anything more productive, even though that is their intention."[13] Hence, land reforms don't necessarily cause things to be better in the long run, because there can be a reaction against them. Their success also depends on economics and on government help and planning, both of which can be thwarted. Denmark, for example, is a success story in land reform, primarily because the populace supported it and because a number of cultural, governmental, and economic factors contributed to the feasibility of land reform. Because these or similar factors are absent in other countries, it would be naive to assume that the Denmark case can be applied to other parts of the world. The failure of land reform in Italy, to cite another example, shows that one cannot just redistribute poor land and then expect reform to work.[14] Numerous other conditions besides redistribution are necessary for successful land reform, and an unwilling citizenry can block implementation of these conditions.

A third argument against land reform is that, even if it does work to reduce inequity or to increase agricultural productivity, it could have undesirable economic consequences. Land reform could reduce savings, for example, since poorer, smaller tenants have a lower propensity to save and a higher propensity to consume.[15] Another alleged negative consequence of land reform is typically a permanent, or at least a temporary, setback in agricultural production, as occurred in Cuba.[16]

All these reasons suggest that, even if land reform is in theory ethically defensible, it is not clear that land reform is in practice workable. A basic moral dictum is that "ought implies can"; one is ethically obliged only to perform those actions that are in practice possible. It is impossible to be morally obliged to perform the impossible. This means that, at best, land-reform ethics is only morally obligatory to the degree that it is possible. And only to the degree that it is possible to achieve, does land-reform ethics provide a viable solution to the problem of poor land distribution.

Land-Use Ethics

A second class of new land ethics, land-use ethics, constitutes a moral response to the crises caused by environmental spillovers such as air and water pollution. To correct or at least control these abuses, many philosophers, planners, economists, and political scientists have argued that we have a moral imperative to control land use and property rights so that they serve the public, as well as private, interest. The best way to serve the common good and the public interest, so the argument goes, is to restrict some of the many rights included in the bundle known as "property rights."

Included in the set of rights known as "property rights" are eleven subrights typically known as "incidents of ownership." These are the right to possess; the right to use; the right to manage; the right to income; the right to the capital; the rights to security; the incident of transmissibility (the right to pass on property to one's successors); the incident of absence of term (the right to hold on to property forever, if one lived forever); the prohibition of harmful use; the liability to execution (property may be taken to cover debts); and residuary rights (full rights to property after other limited interests in it cease). When one speaks of limiting property rights, one typically means limiting at least one of these eleven incidents.[17] Land-use ethics typically is implemented by restrictions on the right to use property. These restrictions are accomplished through mechanisms such as zoning, taxation, land-use planning, easements, and deed restrictions.

Those who argue that there is a great need for new land-use ethics point out that there are numerous spillovers, or negative externalities, arising from poor land use and threatening the common good. Each year, for example, we concrete more and more land in urban areas, making it difficult or impossible for the aquifers to recharge.

We lose valuable farm land to erosion and development. We degrade soil through improper agricultural, mining, and industrial activity. We allow persons to make substantial unearned profits through speculation in land.[18] Heavy taxing of those who cultivate erosive soils or leave mined soils unreclaimed, withholding subsidies from them, or simply prohibiting certain uses of erosive land are all examples of land-use control mechanisms that could address the joint problems of soil loss and water pollution. Whether such spillovers are addressed through land-use controls, however, is in part a function of whether a solid case can be made for new land-use ethics, ethics that justify further restrictions on property rights. As subsequent chapters of this volume will explain, notably chapter 11, society has enacted few limitations on property rights in land and has made little attempt to control land use.

Foot-dragging in enacting national, state, and local land-use legislation is perhaps more surprising than the failure to adopt one of the other systems of land ethics (e.g., land reform). For one thing, since land-use legislation is an attempt to be responsive to undesirable spillovers and to community, rather than merely private, interests, it is consistent with existing, widespread government intervention in many other property uses, from securities to FCC licensing. Land-use controls have their analogues in other areas of property legislation. Land-use ethics also appear *prima facie* more acceptable than other land ethics, because their primary focus is redressing harm to *human interests*, rather than merely to the *environment*.

Because of its emphasis on human interests, one of the normative foundations of new land-use ethics is the concept of equity. As we shall argue in chapter 11, minimal fairness dictates that a situation is inequitable if it allows some persons to use their property in such a way (e.g., poor mining practices) that it harms the interests of others (e.g., in clean water). To correct this inequity, we argue in chapter 11 for a system of amenity rights that require strict land-use controls.

In response to arguments about the need for greater land-use controls to promote wise use of land, prevent environmental degradation, and restrain spillovers, opponents of the new land-use ethics respond that they would limit competition, unfairly restrict property rights, and give government, rather than the free market, the power to control land use. Rather than deal now both with all the arguments, objections, and responses concerning land-use controls and with all the factual particulars associated with them, we shall examine them later. Chapters 11 and 12 in this volume will be devoted entirely to analysis and criticism of the many arguments for new land-use ethics, as well as to a consideration of what land-use controls these ethics might dictate.

Anthropocentric and Ecocentric Land Ethics

Although both land-use ethics and the earlier land-reform ethics call for a new land philosophy and a new land practice, they are primarily *anthropocentric*. They demand a change in our behavior so as to prevent harm to humans, whether the harm comes from political and economic inequities caused by monopolistic land holdings, or whether the harm comes from spillovers and degradation of the environment in which we must live and work. Because the first two land ethics are anthropocentric, they are more in keeping with classical ethical traditions in the West. In all of these traditions, moral right and wrong are defined in terms of what is good and bad for humans.

The two remaining land ethics, land-community ethics and land-rights ethics, however, are primarily nonanthropocentric or ecocentric. They issue moral imperatives, not for the sake of human well-being alone, but also for the good of the land (the entire biosphere) as a whole, apart from human interests. Although humans are included in the biosphere, presumably somewhat different actions might be mandated by an ecocentric or biocentric ethics that attempts to maximize the good of the whole biosphere, as opposed to an anthropocentric ethics that attempts to maximize the good of one subset of inhabitants (humans) of the biosphere. To use Holmes Rolston's language, ecocentric ethics (land-community ethics and land-rights ethics) are environmental ethics in a *primary* sense, because they give environmental interests primacy over merely human interests. Anthropocentric ethics (land-reform ethics and land-use ethics), however, are environmental ethics in a *secondary* sense, because they make environmental interests secondary to human interests.[19] (Admittedly human and environmental interests are one and the same in many cases. What hurts the land almost always eventually hurts people and vice versa. In other cases, such as short-term economic interests of humans versus long-term environmental interests, human and environmental interests are not the same.)

Since land-community ethics and land-rights ethics are biocentric or ecocentric, and because they are environmental ethics in the primary sense, they represent a more radical departure from classical ethical traditions. For this reason, they are probably less likely to be adopted than the anthropocentric land-use ethics, despite the fact that biocentric or ecocentric ethics appear to be important to conservation. Let's examine these two new ethics and discover why they have caused so much controversy in traditional philosophical circles.

Land-Community Ethics

Much of land-community ethics owes its inspiration to Aldo Leopold. Recall that, for Leopold, "land" encompassed not only soil but all the living things associated with the earth. Leopold maintained that everything is interconnected, and hence that ethics ought not be merely among individuals and society, but rather ought to be extended to a third sphere: our relation to the land and other living things. The chief tenet of land-community ethics is thus that land ought to be treated as a member of our moral community, and consequently that we ought to be said to have duties to land, just as we have duties to other humans. In *A Sand County Almanac*, Leopold bemoaned the fact that land, like Odysseus's slave girls, is still property, and that the land relation is still economic.[20] Instead, says Leopold, it is "an evolutionary possibility and an ecological necessity" to recognize new land ethics that enlarge "the boundaries of the [moral] community to include soils, waters, plants, and animals, or collectively, the land."[21] For Leopold, the land community provides a new touchstone for ethics; an action is right if it preserves the integrity, stability, and beauty of the biotic community.[22] Preserving the integrity, stability, and beauty of the biotic community was all important for Leopold both because protecting the land is necessary for protecting humans and because he viewed the earth as "a living being," an organism with organs, coordinated functions, and metabolism or growth.[23]

Because Leopoldian land-community ethics dictates enlarging the moral community to include soil, water, plants, and animals, one consequence of his land ethics is that land is not a commodity to be bought and sold, any more than humans are commodities to be bought and sold. And if we can't have property rights in humans, then we can't have property rights in land; we and the land are both living beings, for Leopold, and we are members of the same moral community. Some of these same Leopoldian sentiments are found in other writings. In more recent years, a number of ecologists have popularized the idea that the planet earth is one great organism, GAIA, just as Leopold believed. They have argued that this great organism regulates itself, circulates energy, and responds to human treatment or mistreatment.[24]

Despite the obvious truth that everything in the biosphere is connected to everything else, and that ethics cannot ignore this connectedness without courting environmental disaster, most classical moral theorists have rejected Leopoldian land-community ethics. And most practicing ecologists have rejected the GAIA hypothesis as unproved speculation. They admit the ecological fact of interconnectedness, and they recognize the importance of safeguarding those connections; nevertheless, either they reject land-community ethics as incoherent or unworkable, or they remain agnostic about the GAIA hypothesis, alleging that it is unproved. (See chapters 9 and 10 for a discussion of the relationship between GAIA, ecology, and land-use control.) For example, the distinguished Australian philosopher John Passmore quickly dismissed Leopold's views.[25] English philosopher Robin Atfield wrote that "Leopold the philosopher is something of a disaster."[26] Atfield and the Canadian philosopher L. W. Sumner called Leopold's work "dangerous nonsense."[27]

One of the greatest moral philosophers of this century, William Frankena, recognizes the fact that humans have duties to preserve the environment, so far as preservation is necessary to human health and interests. Frankena admits that there are pragmatic reasons for protecting the land, *for the sake of humans*, because the well-being of both land and humans is bound up together. Nevertheless, he disputes Leopold's land-community ethics. He denies that there are *moral* reasons for protecting the land, *for the sake of the land alone*. He claims that it makes no sense to say that a nonsentient being has interests or that there could be a moral community that includes nonsentient beings, like land and soils. Frankena writes:

> I see no reason, from the moral point of view, why we should respect something that is alive but has no conscious sentiency and so can experience no pleasure or pain, joy or suffering, unless perhaps it is potentially a consciously sentient being, as in the case of a fetus. Why, if leaves and trees have no capacity to feel pleasure or to suffer, should I tear no leaf from a tree: Why should I respect its location any more than that of a stone in my driveway, if no benefit or harm comes to any person or sentient being by my moving it? . . . I also cannot see at all directly that we ought to consider the Whole as such, at least not if the Whole is not itself a conscious sentient being.[28]

Admittedly, Frankena would probably recognize the distinction in scale between tearing a leaf from a tree and destroying an entire tropical rainforest. He would likely maintain that the latter act is wrong for pragmatic reasons, because it would adversely affect human interests. His point, however, is that there appear to be neither pragmatic nor moral grounds for calling other acts (e.g., tearing a leaf from a tree) wrong, if they do not adversely affect human interests or the interests of some sentient being. Frankena appears to accept the view that Rodman labels "sentientism," that it is only possible to benefit or harm a conscious, sentient being or one that is potentially so.[29] The famous utilitarian moral philosopher, Peter Singer, makes a similar point; the capacity for suffering or enjoyment is a prerequisite for having "interests." Singer maintains that beings without interests cannot be members of our moral community, because moral obligations to beings are based on recognizing their interests.[30]

Although Frankena, Passmore, Singer, and others probably represent the opinion of the philosophical "establishment," a few thinkers have disagreed with them and have claimed that rocks and land can have interests.[31] In response, Singer has noted that claiming that beings such as rocks and trees have interests involves using a very loose, nonphilosophical sense of the term "interest." We might as well say, writes Singer, that automobiles have an interest in being lubricated, and therefore that we have a moral obligation to lubricate them.[32] Of course, keeping a car lubricated makes sense if we humans want it to work, and if not changing the oil "harms" the car. Nevertheless, because autos are not sentient, they do not have interests. Singer's point is that, if we argue that land is a member of our moral community and that it has interests that we are obliged to protect, then virtually anything could likewise be said to have interests. We would have no criterion for "having an interest." Singer believes that if we say that land has interests that we ought to protect we have claimed too much; if we accept Leopold and consistently apply his beliefs, then we shall have to fulfill a great many bizarre moral obligations (e.g., to lubricate cars) and alleged "interests" which are patently absurd. Moreover, it would be impossible to protect the interests of all beings.

Also, according to proponents of sentientism, how can the earth (which is allegedly a whole, but not sentient) have a "good"? If it can have a good, how can we, as individual moral agents, know what that good is, if it cannot tell us? Even if we can know what the good of the whole is, claim Rodman and others, why should we care, apart from how its good affects human welfare? In response to such questions, proponents of new, ecocentric ethics have provided criteria for when to recognize human rights and when to recognize the priority of environmental interests over purely human concerns. For example, they have argued that we have a prima facie duty to respect all living beings, human and nonhuman, and that this duty can be overridden only to protect basic human rights to bodily security.[33]

Critics of ecocentric ethics, like Rodman, however, are often unaware of the compelling arguments in favor of ascribing inherent worth or inherent value to all living beings. Instead they focus on early views like those of Leopold, or they point to the failure of ecology to provide clear directives for environmental policy. Many ecologists and policy makers, in fact, have admitted that ecology has not been able to deliver the theories, understanding, and predictions needed for environmental reform. Because of this fact, Leopold's critics are asking how it is possible to provide ecological criteria for the "integrity, stability, and beauty of the biotic community." They maintain that, since ecosystems and the biosphere naturally change over time, there is no clear notion of stability available to guide environmental policy. Moreover, they claim, the evolutionary foundations of ecology seem to suggest that whatever happens is stable, integral and beautiful. They allege that there is no moral reason, short of human welfare, to prefer one temporal arrangement or stability over another. In other words, they charge that the evolutionary foundations of ecology undercut Leopold's land ethics. (See chapters 9 and 10 for a further discussion of this point.[34]) In response, defenders of ecocentric ethics argue that, despite the problems with the scientific foundations of ecology, it is possible to build a new, ecocentric ethics not merely on science, but also on notions of inherent worth, moral considerability, and so on— notions like Schweitzer's "ethic of life."[35]

Critics have also leveled at least two other philosophical charges against Leopold's land-community ethics. First, they say, since Leopold's ethics defines "right" in terms of community, not individual, welfare, his system provides for no individual, inalienable natural rights (for example, to life and to equal protection). In his scheme, both humans and everything else on earth are subordinate to the integrity, stability, and beauty of the biotic community. But if so, then from the point of view of Leopold's ethics, massive human deaths might be good, indeed even morally required, in order to check the population problem and therefore protect the integrity, stability, and beauty of the biotic community. This is why moral philosopher Tom Regan calls Leopold's ethics a clear case of "environmental fascism."[36] Regan charges that, within the alleged fascism of the supremacy of the biotic community, Leopold leaves no room for the individual, inalienable rights that are the foundation of this country. Such rights also provide the justification for the Nuremburg War Trials and the rationale for protests against apartheid. In a century wracked by murder of Jews, discrimination against women and blacks, and totalitarian regimes, many moral philosophers are reluctant to relinquish our hard-won, inalienable, *individual* rights in favor of the holistic welfare of the biotic community. And if so, then Leopold's views stand little chance of being adopted.

Continuing the attack on land-community ethics, Peter Fritzell (1987) notes that there is a fundamental dilemma at the heart of

Leopoldian ethics. Either we humans are on a par with other creatures on the planet or we are not. If we are on a par, as equal members serving the biotic community, then it is no more wrong for humans to kill and eat other humans than it is for wolves and alligators
to do so, says Fritzell. If we are on a par, then humans have no special rights and consequently no special responsibilities. We are just
members of the biotic community. On the other hand, claims Fritzell,
if we are not on a par with other members of the biotic community,
owing to our special moral responsibility and our alleged free will,
then we share moral community only with other beings who also have
moral responsibility and free will. But in this case, land cannot have
moral responsibility and free will, and so is not a member of our
moral community. And if not, then we have no obligations to land per
se but only to humans whose interests are served by protecting the
land. This means we are faced with a dilemma, says Fritzell: (1) Either we humans are equal to other members of the biotic community
and therefore have no special moral responsibilities to other humans,
contrary to what all the ethical traditions have claimed, or (2) we are
not equal to other members of the biotic community and therefore,
because of our moral primacy, have no moral responsibility to anyone
or anything except other humans, since we are superior to all beings
except humans. The upshot, says Fritzell, is that if Leopold's ethics is
correct then, on pain of inconsistency, it must either allow humans to
perform heinous actions, like murder, so long as the whole biotic
community does not suffer, or it must admit that there is no responsibility to beings that have no sense of moral responsibility or free
will. He concludes that Leopold's ethics is either heinous or incorrect.[37]

In response to criticisms of persons like Fritzell, defenders of
biocentric ethics maintain that they need not fall victim to the problems that beset Leopold's version of environmental or land ethics.
Rather, they claim to have criteria for when to recognize human rights
and when to protect the environment. Hence, they avoid both fascism
and moral dilemmas. (See note 33.)

A third charge leveled against Leopoldian land-community ethics
is that, if land ceases to be a commodity and private property, and
instead becomes a commons, then it could succumb to the tragedy of
the commons. As Garrett Hardin so eloquently maintained, if everyone is responsible for land but no one owns land or treats it like an
economic commodity, then the land is likely to be abused. Abuse is
likely, says Hardin, because regulation is not a successful way of
avoiding the tragedy of the commons. The implementation and en-
forcement costs of regulation would be high and, for Hardin, it would

not be in a person's short-term self interest to preserve the commons.[38]

As the preceding account reveals, critics of Leopold's land-community ethics have at least three main worries: (1) It is not reasonable to claim that land can be "hurt," since sentiency is a criterion for having interests that one is morally bound to respect. (2) Ecology provides no clear, precise criteria for how to judge what promotes the integrity, stability, and beauty of the land. (3) Since the Leopoldian ethics accords primacy to ecosystemic or community well-being, it renders individual rights subservient to this well-being.

Are there ways of defending land-community ethics against these charges? Although there is no space here to address these charges in full, we can provide a sketch of what such a defense might be like (see note 33). Regarding claim (1) and sentiency, it can easily be argued that sentiency is not necessarily the primary basis for having interests that others are bound to respect. If the capacity for sentiency (experiencing pleasure and pain) were the basis of moral obligation, then we would have no moral obligations to persons who are completely anesthetized, hypnotized, deeply comatose, or who are victims of a well-documented condition known as "congenital universal indifference to pain."[39] Yet we do believe that we have moral obligations to such persons; hence it is not clear that sentiency is always a criterion for having interests which one is morally bound to recognize. Indeed, if philosophers such as Paul Taylor are correct, then being alive could be a sufficient condition for having interests,[40] and one could base a biocentric or ecocentric ethics on the duty to recognize, and avoid interfering with, the good—life—of all beings that are alive.

Regarding charge (2) and the limitations of ecology, it is important to point out that ecology can give us some precise directives about exactly what is harmful or helpful to particular environments. Ecology has no grand theories that uncontroversially tell us when an ecosystem is in dynamic equilibrium or when some "balance of nature" has been reached. Because ecology can deliver no general theories, however, does not mean that it can deliver no directives at all. It can often solve particular problems (e.g., how to control the vampire bat and how to eliminate California red scale). And it can often tell us what *not* to do. Ecologists can often tell us, for example, what interventions in ecosystems are likely to reduce species diversity. *If* we define natural beauty in terms of species diversity, *then* indeed ecologists can give us some help with Leopold's directives. Ecologists cannot provide us with a general definition of an *end* or *goal* of ecosystemic activity but, if we humans can agree upon some of those goals (e.g., promoting species diversity), then ecologists can often provide details about the *means* for attaining those ends. Community ecology is particularly helpful in providing a foundation for environmental policy through specific case studies and through natural-history information.[41] (See chapter 10 for further discussion of these issues.)

There is no quick way to counter charge (3) of "environmental fascism" and Leopold's according primacy to the biotic community, over and above the individual. One can claim, as has Rolston, that one must *interpret* Leopold's directives in the light of ordinary ethical theories that recognize inalienable human rights. (See note 33.) If Leopold did not intend such an interpretation, then land-community ethics is seriously incomplete, and it is at odds with liberal political theory. If Leopold did intend an interpretation such as Rolston's and Shrader-Frechette's, then the remaining task, for philosophers attempting to make sense of land-community ethics, is to continue to spell out the rational criteria for deciding when human interests ought to override the interests of the biotic community and vice versa.[42] In other words, the remaining task is to clarify, defend, and evaluate biocentric ethics so that it does not fall victim to some of the charges just discussed.

Land-Rights Ethics

The problematic issue of human interests versus the interests of the biotic community also arises in connection with the fourth land ethics, land-rights ethics. Like Leopold's land-community ethics, land-rights ethics are primarily biocentric or ecocentric and nonanthropocentric. Proponents of these ethics accept at least one of the two following propositions. (1) Land ought to be accorded *civil rights*, as attorney Christopher Stone argues.[43] Or (2) land ought to be accorded *natural rights*, as Abbey, Leopold, Muir, Nash, and Watkins claim.[44] Regarding (2), Leopold, for example, maintains that communities of plants and animals, both included in what he calls "land," have a "right to continued existence and, at least in spots, their continued existence in a natural state." Watkins makes a similar claim: "nature has a right to exist." Edward Abbey puts it even more bluntly when, in *Desert Solitaire*, he states he would sooner shoot a man than a snake. Still other people, notably John Tallmadge and John Bennett, view nature as worthy of existence on its own terms (as a person is), as possessing intrinsic value, and, perhaps, as possessing natural rights.[45]

The obvious advantage of both variants (1) and (2) of land-rights ethics is that they would provide great protection to the land. This is because they would put the "burden of proof" on the person attempting to violate these alleged rights. As Ronald Dworkin pointed out, "rights arguments" trump all other claims.[46]

Let's look more carefully at land-rights ethics. Consider first version (1), that land has legal rights, as Stone argued. Stone's main reasons for proposing that land be treated as a jural person and be accorded legal rights are that, historically, women, the insane, blacks, etc., were treated as objects, and the notion of legal rights was expanded to include them. He also argues that the concept of "legal right" is a product of historical, pragmatic, and mental baggage, rather than the result of clear analysis, and that there are presently other inanimate rights holders (e.g., corporations, trusts, municipalities, and ships). Stone likewise maintains that the legal machinery for extending legal rights to land already exists, and that land meets all the criteria necessary for making something count jurally: the thing can institute legal actions at its behest; the court would be able to take into account injury to the thing; and relief would run to the benefit of the thing.[47] Moreover, says Stone, court-appointed guardians could initiate legal actions on behalf of land. An obvious measure of damages to land would be the cost of making it whole again, and trust funds could be established to administer the benefits awarded.[48]

Viewed as a proposal to change legal convention and to treat land as a jural person, Stone's proposal (1), for according civil rights to land, has much to recommend it. Perhaps its greatest benefit is that it could soon change the way we think about land, and such changes in our thinking could result in more desirable environmental behavior. The main shortcoming in Stone's position, however, is that even if one agrees that it is correct, and land ought to be said to have legal rights, we still have no foundation for asserting that land ought to be accorded natural rights. Saying (1) that land ought to have *legal rights* does not entail (2) that land ought to have *natural rights*. Affirming (1) merely amounts to the claim that human conventions and institutions ought to change, and we ought to treat land in a certain legal way. If proposed changes in our legal conventions are to have a philosophical foundation and therefore the most powerful rational defense possible, then those who claim legal rights for land also need to be able to claim either *natural* rights for land or a strong pragmatic justification for legal rights. To make the strongest case, they need to be able to argue either that land possesses natural rights, *independent* of human institutions and conventions, or that pragmatism requires such legal rights. They need to show that land rights are more than a mere legal convention, that instead they are either "in the nature of things" or absolutely necessary, on practical grounds, to insure desirable consequences.

This point is obvious if one considers that perhaps the most effective way of arguing that a particular country ought to accord certain *legal* rights (e.g., to blacks) is either that blacks have *natural* rights that ought to be recognized by society or that, without recognition of their legal rights, disastrous civil discord will follow. Hence, goes the argument, one ought to recognize their legal rights. Analogous reasoning supports our theories about civil disobedience. Presumably what justifies civil disobedience, in certain cases, is that existing *legal* rights do not accurately represent authentic *natural* rights (see chapter 4, especially the discussion of Locke and natural rights), or that extension of legal rights is necessary to avert catastrophe. In other words, our legal and moral traditions appear to support the view that legal rights ought to be based either on authentic natural rights, or on very strong consequentialist arguments, if they are to command our recognition.

Although a case can be made for legal rights of land, even if there are no natural rights, it may be more difficult and tenuous to do so. If one argued for legal rights on grounds other than natural rights, then presumably the justification would need to be purely pragmatic (rather than based on "the nature" of things). But if a purely pragmatic defense of (legal) land rights were used, then it might be more likely that short-term, economic interests could outweigh it. Because Stone gives us merely a practical, legal way of protecting the land, his arguments might be subverted by short-term, anthropocentric, or purely economic interests. He gives us no *philosophical* justification for land ethics. He gives us no reason that we should recognize certain legal rights rather than others. He never argues that land has a "sake" for which we ought to act. Rather, his arguments for legal rights are formulated in pragmatic terms.[49]

Defenses of thesis (2), that land has *natural* rights, are also problematic, but for different reasons than Stone's arguments. For one thing, the standard view among moral philosophers is that only subjects of experience can be injured or benefited, and only what can be injured or benefited can have rights. Therefore, according to the standard view, only subjects of experience can have rights; since land, soil, rocks, and plants obviously are not subjects of experience, therefore they cannot have rights.[50] A second problem with maintaining that land, soil, plants, etc., have natural rights is that it appears somehow "discordant" with nature. Natural, individual rights presumably are asserted in order to protect a particular being from harm; yet nature "red in tooth and claw" does not protect particular beings from harm. It seems peculiar to claim that nature has accorded rights to beings when nature herself produces enormous suffering through the mechanisms of natural selection. Even more peculiar is the fact that persons such as Muir glorified the "waste and death" in the natural kingdom, even as they claimed that rocks and plants experienced happiness, were capable of being injured, and therefore had some sort of "rights."[51]

The root of the apparent difficulty with according natural rights to nature, when nature does not accord natural rights to nature herself, is the asymmetry between rights and duties. Moral philosophers have traditionally believed that, for every ascription of *rights* to a particular being, there is a corresponding ascription of a *duty* to other beings to recognize those rights. Yet if both land and humans are said to have natural rights, then an asymmetry occurs: humans allegedly have duties to recognize the rights of other humans and of land, but the land has no duties to recognize the rights of humans and of other beings also collectively referred to as "land." The solution to this philosophical difficulty, if there is one, probably lies with (i) agreeing to use "rights language" in asymmetrical ways; or (ii) agreeing not to ascribe rights to beings that are not also capable of exercising corresponding duties. Consideration of arguments for and against (i) and (ii), however, is beyond the scope of this chapter, since they strike at the foundation of many, many years of complex moral theorizing.

A third problem with maintaining that land has natural rights is how to adjudicate conflicts of rights between, for example, humans and plants. Does the plant's right to exist take priority over the human's desire to eat it? Why or why not? On the one hand, it will not do to say that humans are superior and therefore take priority, since the whole point of according *natural rights* to rocks or land or plants is to guarantee both that they are not harmed by humans and that the land's interests receive consideration equal to that of humans. If, on the other hand, one settles rights conflicts by appealing to the good of the biotic community, then this move is likewise problematic. Making individual *natural rights* subordinate to the welfare of the biotic community merely collapses land-rights ethics into land-community ethics, the position already discussed. It "solves" the problem, but at the price of doing away with the fourth land ethics, land-rights ethics. Moreover, as was already pointed out, such a move could conceivably result in the discrimination and totalitarianism earlier described as "environmental fascism."

There is at least one possible way to ameliorate the third problem with land-rights ethics, viz., the difficulty of adjudicating rights conflicts among humans and nonhumans. This is to specify criteria for rights claims, including the conditions under which human interests take priority, given a case of conflict, and conditions under which nonhuman interests take priority, as we suggested earlier (see note 33). Moreover, it is important to recognize that although there is no easy answer to such conflicts, they can be resolved. After all, even after 3,000 years of theorizing about ethical conflicts, there are still great conflicts regarding which rights (e.g., equal protection) take precedence over which other rights (e.g., property).[52] There are also heated controversies over whether community interest can ever override individual rights.[53] Such controversies are unlikely to end soon, and for at least two reasons. One reason is that the two most basic ways of dividing classical ethical theories, into utilitarian and deontological views, is based in large part on two different accounts of the place of rights in ethics; utilitarians typically give more weight to community well being, and deontologists typically give more weight to individual rights. A second reason that rights conflicts are unlikely to "go away" is that no alleged right is absolute, even the right to life. And no right is absolute, because each person's right ends where another person's right begins. This being so, rational analysis of rights conflicts is an unending task. Recognizing such facts does not resolve the problem of conflicts in land-rights ethics, but it does place these conflicts in perspective. The real issue is not whether land-rights ethics can adjudicate rights conflicts, but whether its doing so is, in principle, more difficult than adjudicating such conflicts within classical ethical theory (see note 33). If it is not more difficult, then land-rights ethics faces no insurmountable obstacles. If it is more difficult, then land-rights ethics may be hard to implement.

Conclusion

Where does this brief survey of four land ethics leave us? Although an in-depth analysis of the many particulars of each of the land ethics remains to be accomplished, a few preliminary conclusions are in order. Land-reform ethics appears to have strong rational and ethical justifications, but there are pragmatic grounds for doubting the extent to which it is achievable in a variety of cultures. Since "ought implies can," the moral imperative to implement land-reform ethics is contingent on the possibility of actually being able to do so. The viability of land-reform ethics, therefore, is likely a function of a factual question. Is it possible for government to provide sufficient incentives for land owners to give up their holdings and to "make" land reform work?

Land-community ethics, on the other hand, faces quite different obstacles. If it is to be implemented, then either we must abandon certain individualistic tenets of liberal political theory, or we must be able to show that the consequences of land-community ethics are consistent with liberal political theory and the primacy given to the individual, rather than to community, well being. This we can do if we continue to develop criteria for when to give primacy, in a situation of conflict, to human over nonhuman interests and vice versa.

Land-rights ethics is confronted, not primarily with opposition from liberal political theory but from classical philosophical traditions in the West. Its success may be determined by our willingness to change our traditional moral philosophy about natural rights. Because of the skepticism of most philosophical theorists regarding attributing *natural* rights to land, it appears unlikely, as we argued earlier, that the natural-rights version of land-rights ethics will come to be accepted. Nevertheless, there are no insurmountable difficulties with attributing *legal* rights to land, as Stone proposes. Hence the legal-rights version of land-rights ethics may come to be accepted. Land-use ethics, however, appears to require neither a change of heart of land owners (as land-reform ethics might), nor new developments in liberal political traditions (as land-community ethics might), nor a change in classical philosophical traditions (as one version of land-rights ethics might). As the next chapter in the volume will argue, land-use ethics, despite the sweeping reforms it dictates, appears consistent with some of the best Anglo-American philosophical, political, and legal traditions—through John Locke—provided that those traditions are correctly understood.

Part Two

Philosphical Assumptions and Policy Implications

In this section we explore the dichotomies between land as property and land as a critical element in the planetary life-support system. Given an historical perspective, we recognize that many of the ethical and practical problems of land ownership and use are not new. Numerous historical concepts and practices related to private property rights in land are invoked today. They do not uniformly support the same conclusions, however, as they did in the past. Some practices are no longer defensible in the world of the twentieth century, considering what we now know regarding the interactions of soil, plant and animal life, atmosphere, and water. Few actions regarding land are now seen as "private." In addition, the proliferation of populations of humans and domestic animals, the increased mobility of persons and natural resources, and the economic and social consequences of these developments have made land use an international as well as a national public issue. Our new ecological understanding has altered our interpretations of many philosophic assumptions regarding policy for land. Consequently, it also has influenced our political and legal thinking regarding the rationality, feasibility, and equity of various policies for land.

4

Locke and Limits on Land Ownership

Kristin Shrader-Frechette

Revisionist history often upsets our ordinary ideas of right and wrong. We once believed, for example, that the Europeans who discovered and settled the new world were courageous in bringing civilization and its benefits to a new continent. It is now more common to recognize that some, perhaps many, of these explorers and settlers were tyrants who stole land from native Americans and often violently destroyed indigenous cultures.

Just as scholars have provided a revisionist account of the history of settling America, in this essay we provide a revisionist analysis of Locke's theory of property rights. After providing a brief overview of his theory, we explain that Locke has traditionally been hailed as the defender of unlimited capitalistic appropriation of property, including land. Arguing that both the traditional capitalist-bourgeois and the Marxist-socialist interpretations of Locke have serious shortcomings,[1] we opt for a middle ground between these two extremes. We suggest that, although Locke ought not be interpreted in any doctrinaire, ideological way, his account may be ambiguous enough to support restriction of certain property rights in natural resources like land. And if so, then Locke's writings may provide a philosophical basis, in traditional political theory, for a welfare-state capitalism that includes land-use planning.

Our arguments for the plausibility of this revisionist account of Locke attempt to avoid (what Quine called) "nothing but" explanations. Such simplistic explanations focus only on one aspect of complex views, and they may be responsible for whatever bias is exhibited in both the capitalist and the socialist views of Locke. Appropriating neither of these interpretations, we believe that Locke's own words provide a basis for limiting or denying property rights in land and other natural resources. Our belief rests on at least four theses, for each of which we provide arguments: (1) Locke makes property subject to the requirements of the original community and

65

to natural law. (2) The first proviso, that land may be appropriated, provided that as much and as good remains for others, holds for all time. (3) Because the value of land is not derived completely from labor, some control over property rights to it rests with the community, not merely with those who labor over it. (4) All property, including land, is subject to the productivity criterion and hence to the control of the community regarding its use. Moreover, although Locke does not always present his moral beliefs as philosophical arguments (some are based on religion, for example), we show that at least one of these beliefs tends to support the four arguments already given. This is Locke's view that desiring more than we need is the root of all evil. For all five reasons, we claim that it is possible to find Lockean grounds for asserting that the community has at least a partial right to control certain property rights, especially in land. We maintain that, although the *historical* Locke may not have meant to do so, his writings provide a basis for such control.

Locke's Justification of Property Rights

Locke's basic justification for the acquisition of private property is the labor theory. According to this theory, people are entitled to hold, as property, whatever they produce by their labor, intelligence, and effort. The labor-theory justification has such a foothold, in the minds of scholars and the common person, that Becker calls it "virtually unchallengeable." As he puts it: "One might ignore it [the labor theory] (as Hume did), but would not deny it, even if one were attacking the whole notion of 'primitive acquisition'."[2]

Locke's general argument is as follows: Because one owns one's body, one owns the product of the labor accomplished by one's body. For Locke, one can appropriate (from the commons) anything with which one's labor has been "mixed," provided that there is enough and as good left for others (the first proviso), and the property does not spoil but is used (the second proviso). Thus, for example, the settlers in the early days of the West could fence off land for farming and grazing, and their labor established a moral claim to it as their property. As Locke puts it:

> every man has a *Property* in his own *Person*. This no Body has any Right to but himself. The *Labour* of his Body and the *Work* of his Hands, we may say, are properly his. Whatsoever then he removes out of the State that Nature hath provided, and left it in, he hath mixed his *Labour* with, and joined to it something that is his own, and thereby makes it his *Property*. It being by him removed from the common state Nature placed it in, it hath by this *labour* something annexed to it, that excludes the common right of other Men. For this *Labour* being the unquestionable

Property of the Labourer, no Man but he can have a right to what that is once joined to, at least where there is enough, and as good left in common for others. . . . Thus this Law of reason makes the Deer, that *Indian's* who hath killed it; 'tis allowed to be his goods who hath bestowed his labour upon it, though before, it was the common right of every one. . . . The same Law of Nature, that does by this means give us Property, does also *bound* that *Property* too. . . . But how far has he given it us? *To enjoy.* As much as any one can make use of to any advantage of life before it spoils; so much he may by his labour fix a Property in. Whatever is beyond this, is more than his share, and belongs to others. Nothing was made by God for Man to spoil or destroy.[3]

Moreover, the argument continues, because the invention of money made it possible to exchange every commodity for pieces of metal, we no longer need to worry about owning only as much as does not spoil. Through implicit consent to the use of money, we "have agreed to disproportionate and unequal Possession of the Earth."[4]

In Locke's words:

This *measure* [the laborer being able to appropriate as much as he could without its spoiling] did confine every Man's *Possession*, to a very moderate Proportion, and such as he might appropriate to himself, without Injury to any Body. . . . That same *Rule of Propriety*, (*viz.*) that every Man should have as much as he could make use of, would hold still in the World, without straitening any body . . . had not the *Invention of Money*, and the tacit Agreement of Men to put a value on it, introduced (by Consent) larger Possessions, and a Right to them. . . . This partage of things, in an inequality of private possessions, men have made practicable out of the bounds of Societie, and without compact, only by putting a value on gold and silver and tacitly agreeing to the use of Money. For in Governments the Laws regulate the rights of property, and the possession of land is determined by positive constitutions.[5]

One of the difficulties with Locke's argument, of course, as commentators from Hume to Nozick have pointed out, is why one should think that mixing one's labor with a thing is a way of making it one's own, rather than a way of losing one's labor.[6] If one dumped a can of tomato juice into the sea, for example, wouldn't one lose the juice rather than own the sea? Locke's rationale for believing that mixing one's labor with a thing gives it value—and gives one property rights to it or to its product—is fourfold. The rationale is based on need, efficiency, desert, and on a labor theory of value.[7] First, Locke claims that there is a *need* for appropriation based on labor; if such appropriation were not permissible, then people would perish while waiting for consensual agreements about property to be set up. He says that

Man's *Property* in the Creatures, was founded upon the right he had, to make use of those things, that were necessary or useful to his Being. . . . Was it a Robbery thus to assume to himself what belonged to all in Common: If such a consent as that was necessary, Man had starved, notwithstanding the Plenty God had given Him.[8]

Second, Locke maintains that it is *efficient* for appropriation to be based on labor. He claims that

he who appropriates land to himself by his labour, does not lessen but increase the common stock of mankind. . . . he, that encloses Land and has a greater plenty of the conveniencies of life from ten acres, than he could have from an hundred left to Nature, may truly be said, to give ninety acres to Mankind.[9]

Likewise, Locke notes, for example, that nations in the Americas

have the materials of Plenty, i.e., a fruitful Soil; . . . yet for want of improving it by labour, have not one hundredth part of the Conveniencies we enjoy: And a King of a large and fruitful Territory there feeds, lodges, and is clad worse than a day Laborer in *England*.[10]

Third, Locke attests that those who labor are industrious and rational persons who, because of their initiative, *merit* the results of their labor. He says, for example:

He that in Obedience to this Command of God, subdued, tilled and sowed any part of it, thereby annexed to it something that was his *property*, which another had no Title to, nor could without injury take from him. . . . He that had as good left for his Improvement, as was already taken up, needed not complain, ought not to meddle with what was already improved by another's Labour: If he did, 'tis plain he desired the benefit of another's Pains, which he had no right to.[11]

Fourth, Locke claims that, because labor is often responsible for so much of the value in a thing, the laborer is entitled to the resource in much the same way that the creator is entitled to his creation. He says that

if we will rightly estimate things as they come to our use, and cast up the several Expenses about them, what in them is purely owing to *Nature*, and what to *labour*, we shall find, that in most of them 99/100 are wholly to be put on the account of *labour*. . . . *labour makes the far greatest part of the value* of things, we enjoy in this World: And the ground which produces the materials, is scarce to be reckon'd in, as any, or at most, but a very small, part of it; So little, that even amongst us, Land that is left wholly to Nature, that hath no improvement of Pasturage, Tillage, or Planting, is called, as indeed it is, waste; and we shall find the benefit of it amount to little more than nothing.[12]

Various commentators have argued that Locke offers a labor theory of value to justify acquisitions of property rights.[13] Some authors, however, have claimed that Locke's property rights are based both on labor and on merit or desert.[14] Other scholars have argued that Locke's theory also is tied to utility or efficiency,[15] while a few persons have argued that Locke's justification is based on all four rationales (need, efficiency, merit, and labor).[16]

We shall not discuss the extent to which Locke relied on claims of labor rather than on efficiency, merit, or need, in part because there appears to be some textual basis in Locke to support all four claims (see the discussion in previous paragraphs), and in part because there are numerous interpretational controversies among Locke scholars, including allegations of inconsistencies in his texts.[17] Rather than address particular details of such questions, to which we do not have the time to do justice, our approach will be to sidestep highly specialized controversies like those over whether merit or need is more important for Locke. Instead, we shall focus on what logical consequences follow from Locke's four claims, if one is interested in the question of ownership of natural resources. In other words, we prefer to examine what might follow from Locke's views, important as they are, rather than to take part in the highly stylized squabbles about the historical Locke or about how to interpret particular Lockean tenets. The two activities are connected, of course, but emphasizing the latter types of analyses would take us too far afield from our main concern: justification in the Lockean texts themselves for controls on property in land.

We also shall address neither the question of whether Locke himself would have argued for controls on the property of wealthy owners such as his patron, the Earl of Shaftesbury, nor the question of whether or not Locke's views are defensible.[18] Instead, our aim is to determine whether the consequences of Locke's own words, correct or not, support restrictions on property rights in land. Our rationale is that, because much U.S. property law is grounded in Jeffersonian and Lockean notions,[19] as well as in common law, if one can show that Locke's texts might be used to support such limitations, then this is a powerful argument that at least some U.S. traditions and institutions might support land-use restrictions.[20]

Traditional Interpretations of Locke's Theory

Scholars such as C.B. Macpherson and Leo Strauss have typically thought of John Locke as the classical defender of capitalism and the right to private property, especially property in land.[21] One of the many reasons that scholars have interpreted Locke as a defender of unlimited capitalistic appropriation is his claim that consent to the use of money has provided for "disproportionate and unequal possession of the earth."[22] In other words, one argument is that because Locke notes that money can be exchanged for land and other properties, therefore there is no upper limit on a person's owning only what can be used before it spoils. Avoiding the constraints of the second proviso, they reason that one can pay others to work the land for him.[23] (In subsequent paragraphs, we shall argue, on the contrary, that there are a number of continuing Lockean constraints that provide an upper limit on what and how a person may own.)

Other scholars who interpret Locke as a proponent of unlimited appropriation claim that his first proviso, about as much and as good being left for others, is a fact about acquisition in the early days, not a normative restriction on all appropriation. Hence they argue that this proviso does not stand in the way of unlimited accumulation.[24] As one capitalistic interpreter of Locke put it: "a developed market economy with a system of money exchange removes any practical limit on the quantity of nature that can be made one's own by means of labor."[25] Both Strauss and MacPherson have argued that Locke's account of property provides an ideology of the bourgeoisie and a moral basis for laissez-faire capitalism.[26] (We shall argue, on the contrary, that both the law of nature and the first proviso—in addition to Locke's religious views—prevent his account from being interpreted in the ways that Strauss and Macpherson prefer.)

There is also a traditional, but less influential, Marxist interpretation of Locke. In this view, the Marxist notion that value derives from labor is based, in part, on the fundamental Lockean ideas that labor creates just ownership, and that anyone who appropriates others' unpaid labor (as capitalists are said to do) violates the Lockean strictures on appropriation of property. Although the Marxist view of Locke is important, there are several reasons why we shall not pursue it here. For one thing, it is not the dominant interpretation of Locke, and our concerns lie elsewhere. Because our goal is to show that the logical consequences of some of Locke's views support severe restrictions on property rights in land, our main theoretical target is the traditional capitalist interpretation. Finally, although we shall not take the time to argue the point, we believe that the Marxist interpretation errs largely because it fails to take adequate account of Locke's theory of value and natural rights and his law of nature. Engels, for example, made it clear that (for him) Locke's theory of value and natural rights does not express basic principles of justice, but rather an historical formulation of political demands arising out of particular economic institutions.[27] As later paragraphs of this chapter will make clear, such a Marxist view fails to account for the moral demands of Locke's "Law of Nature" and its eternal, rather than historical, character.

Even Tully's brilliant anticapitalist analysis fails to do justice to important aspects of Locke's views. It is arguable that it errs: in interpreting all Lockean property rights as use rights; in affirming that, in civil society, all Lockean property is owned by the community; in claiming that Locke believed it was "logically impossible for an agent to alienate his labor"; and in denying that, in civil society, there is a natural right to property. We shall not take the time to argue against Tully's claims, both because they are not part of the traditional interpretation of Locke (our target), and because others have already done so.[28]

Labor and the Limits on Property in Land

Although traditional theorists are surely correct in saying that Locke justifies individual appropriation of property beyond what is necessary for individual use, there are grounds in Locke for believing that there are limits on this appropriation, especially in the case of land. We shall argue that the basis of such limits arises not only from our duties to make the land productive and to practice Christian charity, but also that such limits include the degree to which there is an "original community" that establishes a natural-law framework for just distributions of goods in society. (Admittedly, if Locke is a natural-law theorist, he is certainly not one in the traditional sense, because he claims that rights to private property are completely natural, not conventional or based on solely on consent.)[29] Other reasons for Lockean restrictions on property rights to land are that the first proviso holds for all time; that land value is not derived solely from labor; that ownership of property is subject to the productivity criterion; and that desire for more than we need is for Locke the root of all evil.

Property, the Original Community, and Natural Law

Beginning his discussion of property, Locke points out that God gave the earth to Mankind in common. . . . all the Fruits it naturally produces, and Beasts it feeds, belong to Mankind in common, as they are produced by the spontaneous hand of Nature; and no body has originally a private Dominion, exclusive of the rest of Mankind, in any of them, as they are thus in their natural State.[30]

As Locke's own words reveal, it is important to clarify that his explicit starting point is that the earth is common property given by God. Indeed, Locke speaks of the "common right" of other persons which is excluded by the labor of one person when he makes property his own.[31] This means that Locke has to explain the conditions under which common property, to which we all have common rights, can give way to private property. Many philosophical, political, and environmental commentators, however, have missed this starting point and, like Nozick,[32] have claimed that Locke is explaining how what is *unowned* can become private property. Schwartzenbach speaks of "this lack of prior assignation"; Stone claims that Locke believed in a "'natural right' to unowned goods"; and Mautner talks of things that are "nobody's" property.[33] Griffin claims that Locke tells how "one may appropriate *unowned* land."[34]

When Nozick and others simplify Locke and speak of "unowned" property like land, their words eliminate more than a redundant theological framework.[35] They also, incorrectly, fail to recognize Locke's original state of liberty and equality in which the world belonged equally to all persons. They eliminate what Locke called "the common state" or the "State of Nature" in which there was an "Original" community.[36] In this "Original" community,[37] although Locke did not define it clearly, humans enjoyed common ownership of the goods of the earth, "a State of perfect Freedom . . . and. . . . Equality. . . . by Nature."[38] In this state, Locke says that "the Law of Nature . . . willeth the Peace and *Preservation of all Mankind*, the *Execution* of the Law of Nature,"[39] "the law of *reason* and common Equity."[40]

The law of "reason and common Equity," the law of nature, "still takes place," says Locke.[41] It governs, for example, the distribution of common properties, like the "Fish any one catches in the Ocean,"[42] or "the Possessions of a Private Man [that] revert to the Community," if he has no heirs.[43] Moreover, for Locke, whenever anyone becomes a member of a commonwealth, he thereby subjects his property to the government of that commonwealth. Locke writes:

Every Man, when he, at first, incorporates himself into any Commonwealth, he by his uniting himself thereunto, annexed also, and submits to the Community those Possessions, which he has, or shall acquire, that do not already belong to any other Government. For it would be a direct Contradiction, for any one, to enter into Society with others for the securing and regulating of Property: And yet to suppose his Land, whose Property is to be regulated by the Laws of Society, should be exempt from the Jurisdiction of that Government, to which he himself the Proprietor of the Land, is a Subject. By the same Act therefore, whereby any one unites his Person, which was before free, to any Commonwealth; by the same he unites his Possessions, which were before free, to it also; and they become, both of them, Person and Possession, subject to the Government and Dominion of that Commonwealth, as long as it hath a being. *Whoever* therefore, from thenceforth, by Inheritance, Purchase, Permission, or otherwise *enjoys any part of the Land,* so annext to, and under the Government *of that Commonwealth, must take it with the Condition* it is under; that is, *of submitting to the Government of the Commonwealth,* under whose Jurisdiction it is, as far forth, as any Subject of it.[44]

The law of nature induces humans to join together in societies and to leave the state of nature so as "to supply those Defects and Imperfections which are in us." "[L]iving singly and solely by our selves, we are naturally induced to seek Communion and Fellowship with others . . . in Politick Societies. . . . all Men are naturally in that State [of Nature], and remain so, till by their own Consents they make themselves Members of some Politick Society."[45] Humans consent to join some society because they are unable to enforce the law of nature and to protect their property, either because of the ignorance of others or their own lack of power. That is,

> though the law of Nature be plain and intelligible to all rational Creatures; yet Men being biassed by their Interest, as well as ignorant for want of study of it, are not apt to allow of it as a Law binding to them in the application of it to their particular Cases.[46]

Because humans consent to the law of society, so as to insure that the law of nature is understood and enforced, it is clear that the law of nature continues to govern human communities, even after the end of the state of nature. Indeed, Locke says that the law of nature continues to limit the actions of society:

> Their Power in the utmost Bounds of it, is *limited to the public good of the Society.* It is a Power that hath no other end of preservation, and therefore can never have a right to destroy, enslave, or designedly to impoverish the Subjects. The Obligations of the Law of Nature, cease not in Society, but only in many Cases are drawn closer, and have by Humane Laws known Penalties annexed to them, to enforce their observation. Thus the Law of Nature stands as an Eternal Rule to all Men, *Legislators* as well as others.[47]

By virtue of the law of nature, moreover, Locke asserts that humans have a fundamental obligation not only to preserve themselves and all other humans, but also to avoid harming "another in his Life, Health, Liberty, or Possessions."[48] Because of this obligation, "no Man could ever have a just Power over the Life of another, by Right of property in Land or Possessions; since 'twould always be a Sin in any man of Estate, to let his Brother perish for want of affording him Relief out of his Plenty."[49] In the *Second Treatise*, Locke stresses that one has obligations to others in need, and that the state of liberty is not a state of license, in part because all persons and possessions are the property of their maker, God.[50] This is consistent with Locke's claims in the first *Treatise*, where he makes rights to property subservient to rights of persons to what they need to live.[51] "The same Law of Nature that does by this means give us Property does also bound that Property."[52]

Why have a number of commentators apparently missed the Lockean point that in the state of nature, land and resources were common property? Or Locke's claim that the law of nature and hence the foundation for property rights are eternal? Part of the reason may be that they have overemphasized Locke's distinction between the state of nature and civil society, between natural property rights that hold in a state of nature and those that arise later with the introduction of money and the creation of government. Or, commentators may have overemphasized the role of consent after the creation of society. Thomas Scanlon, for example, claims that once money is introduced and society is created, "the original moral foundation for property rights is no longer valid, and a new foundation is required. Locke takes consent to be this foundation."[53]

If one refers to the passage just cited (see note 48), however, Locke does not seem to posit a "new" foundation of property rights. Rather he appears to say that the foundation, "the fundamental law of nature," remains in part the same. In both the state of nature and civil society, the law of nature is (for Locke) a necessary condition for the justification of property rights. After the introduction of money and the creation of society, however, consent also becomes a necessary condition for the exercise of property rights. Scanlon and others, in presenting Locke's view of consent, seem to suggest either that consent is a sufficient condition for the exercise of property rights in civil society or that, with the transition from the state of nature to civil society, the necessary condition for property rights changes from the law of nature to consent. One of Locke's biographers, Maurice Cranston, for example, makes exactly this point. He wrote that, for Locke "the consent of the people was the sole basis of a government's authority." Cranston also claimed that protection of property was "the chief end" of political society for Locke, and that Locke was an early champion of the minimal state.[54] Cranston and others, however, seem wrong to overemphasize consent, because they ignore the continuing role of the law of nature. They appear not to notice that consent to the laws of society, for Locke, is predicated in part on their conformity with the eternal law of nature.

Even if one denies, contrary to Locke (see note 48), that the law of nature is eternal, and instead says (as Scanlon and others appear to do) that the laws of society, justified by consent alone, govern rights to property, then one is not able to claim that property rights are unlimited and exclusive. One is not able to make this claim because, to the degree that one separates the "Law of Nature" from the laws of society (after the introduction of money), then to that extent does one lose the *natural* foundation for property rights. If there were no law of nature after the introduction of money, then property rights would be conventional, and there would be no sacrosanct (nonconventional) protections against violations of property. Hence there are additional conceptual reasons for believing that the law of nature continues to circumscribe property rights, and that Locke's own words provide a basis for arguing that government ought to regulate property in accord with the principles of natural law.[55]

Yet another reason for believing that natural law or the law of nature could provide a basis for government regulation of property is that this belief is consistent with Locke's attempt to limit the power of the sovereign over the property of subjects. Locke was eager to establish the natural rights of laborers to property. He was eager to assert that "the king has no right to take what the subject has acquired by the sweat of his brow," and that government has no right arbitrarily to take the earned property of citizens.[56] If Locke believed that the king and government ought to be subject to the dictates of natural law and natural right, so as to protect citizens' welfare, it is reasonable to claim that others—those who appropriate great amounts of property—likewise ought to be subject to the dictum that they not injure the life, health, liberty, or possessions of others (see note 49). In other words, just as Locke employed natural law to counter the power of the sovereign, so also it is reasonable to believe that his words provide a rationale for employing natural law to counter the economic and political power of persons who injure others through their accumulation of vast properties. Admittedly, although the Lockean text can be interpreted as providing such a rationale, the historical Locke may not have intended such a rationale, given his career and the revolutionary epoch in which he participated.

If our arguments and suggestions are correct, then Locke's text provides arguments for adherence to a law of nature that exists both before and after the state of nature. His words also support a notion of community, both in the state of nature and to which humans are drawn in civil society. The law of nature and the bounds of community that it includes (e.g., human freedom, equality, and a right to preservation) function as limits on the accumulation of property, including land. This means that to argue that Locke sanctions unlimited accumulation, without concern for the needs of other persons, denies what is *explicit* in Locke. He claims, for example, that "the end of government is the preservation of all,"[57] and that "the Law of Nature stands as an Eternal Rule." (See note 48.) To argue that Locke sanctions unlimited accumulation is also to deny what is *implicit* (the original community) within his general theoretical framework.

Macpherson, for example, seems to ignore both these explicit and implicit points when he says that Locke developed a "conception of the individual as essentially the proprietor of his own person or capacities, owing nothing to society for them."[58] Indeed, although there is no time to defend the point here, both Macpherson and Strauss appear able to interpret Locke as supporting unlimited accumulation precisely because they underemphasize Locke's discussion of the law of nature and his "Original" community.

The First Proviso Holds for All Time

If the law of nature "stands as an eternal rule to all men," not a temporary norm for the state of nature, prior to the introduction of money,[59] then certain consequences follow, particularly with respect to the way that we interpret the first (as-much-and-as-good) proviso. One important consequence is that, while Locke's two provisos must be *reinterpreted*, as a result of the tacit consent to money, they are not completely removed, as many Locke scholars appear to have argued.[60] Other authors claim that, because of the introduction of money, the first (as-much-and-as-good) and second (spoilage) provisos still exist for Locke but are rendered inapplicable.[61]

On the contrary, we believe that Locke neither denied, nor rendered inapplicable, the first proviso. We suspect that he merely wished this proviso to be reinterpreted, as a consequence of civil society and its laws. After all, Locke never denied the right to preservation or subsistence, as a consequence of the consent to money. He believed that the introduction of money justified an "inequality of Private possessions,"[62] but he did not revoke his claim that such possessions ought *never* injure the life, health, or liberty of others (see note 49). In fact, in the first treatise, he writes:

> Man can no more justly make use of another's necessity, to force him to become his Vassal, by with-holding that Relief, God requires him to afford to the wants of his Brother, than he that has more strength can seize upon a weaker, master him to his Obedience, and with a Dagger at his Throat offer him Death or Slavery.[63]

Moreover, he specifically affirmed the right of government and law (via natural law) to "regulate the right of property."[64]

Even Macpherson, to some degree, appears to have recognized this reinterpretation of the first proviso. He writes that, after all land has been appropriated and after humans have consented to the use of money, Locke assumes "that the increase in the whole product will be distributed to the benefit, or at least not to the loss, of those left without enough land. Locke makes this assumption."[65] Hence, even Macpherson appears to believe that Locke assumes that persons will not be made worse off as a result of the scarcity of land. If Locke makes this assumption, however, then it is likely part of a larger Lockean argument that, if accumulation of land/property is ethically acceptable, then no one will be made worse off; but if someone is made worse off as a result of another's accumulation, then the accumulation is ethically unacceptable.

To the degree that Macpherson is correct in attributing this assumption (that persons will not be made worse off as a result of scarce land) to Locke, and to the degree that the assumption is part of a larger Lockean argument like that just formulated, then to the same extent it is arguable that the (first) proviso holds for all time, even after the introduction of money. It is arguable that it holds, at least in the sense that "having as much and as good" means "not being made worse off." In other words, Locke's text supports the claim that the eternal law of nature, directed at human preservation, places at least some limits on property rights.[66] Because of the restrictions on property rights set by the law of nature, the first proviso (about as much and as good being left for others) must hold for all time. If the law of nature holds for all time, and if the law of nature requires the first proviso, as we have just argued, then the first proviso also holds forever. As a consequence, the first proviso ought not merely be applied at the moment of acquisition, as Nozick and others do, but for all time.[67]

If the first proviso holds forever, then it specifies a negative version of Rawls's principle that inequalities of wealth, power, and so on, are justified only if they work to the advantage of all members of society.[68] But if Locke's eternal law of nature entails the eternity of his first proviso, and this proviso, in turn, entails a negative version of one of Rawls's principles, then Locke's own words support a patterned conception of justice. This patterned principle (a principle calling for a particular distribution of property, like land), of course, is contrary to the position that Nozick and others attribute to Locke.[69]

Further evidence that the first proviso is a patterned principle is that it specifies not that acts are unjust but only that resulting situations (patterns) are unjust; it is relativized to material conditions. Moreover, because the proviso must invoke limits in transfers—limits based on distribution of resources—it has no significant procedural content, but mainly a pattern content. It also mandates inspection and monitoring activities, both of which are characteristics of pattern principles.[70] Hence, there is a basis for arguing that, once one accepts the logical consequences of Locke's claims, one is bound to support restricting property rights by means of a patterned (distributive) principle of justice. For the historical Locke, of course, such restrictions are generated in part by the duty of the property owner to achieve heightened productivity and to practice Christian charity. Hence, even though the historical Locke might disagree with us regarding the precise nature of contemporary restrictions on property rights, nevertheless there is a precedent, in Locke's text, for the community decisions required by land-use planning and for societal limits on the exercise of property rights.

Land Value Is Not Derived Only from Labor

Another reason that there is no Lockean support for full property rights in land and other natural resources is that no humans have labored to create them. Locke himself claims that "'tis *Labour* indeed that *puts the difference of value* on every thing."[71] Hence if labor puts the value on everything, and if human labor did not create land, then human labor is able to put value only on the product of the land, not the land itself. Admittedly, Locke erroneously believed that land on which humans had not labored was of little value. Nevertheless, he also admits that there is some portion of land value not created by human labor:

> of the *Products* of the Earth useful to the Life of Man 9/10 are the *effects of labour*; nay, if we will rightly estimate things as they come to our use, and cast up the several Expenses about them, what in them is purely owing to *Nature*, and what to *labor*, we shall find, that in most of them 99/100 are wholly to be put on the account of labour.[72]

Locke's words suggest that, if there is some fraction of land value not created by human labor, then perhaps there is some fraction of property rights in land that cannot be appropriated from the commons. And if it cannot be appropriated, then it must remain in the commons. And if all land, in some respects, remains in the commons, then all land, in some respects, is subject to land-use planning on behalf of the common good.

Indeed, Mill and others recognized that full rights of ownership in land could not be created by reference to the deserts or labor of a person who cultivates it. Proudhon, for example, points out that

> property is the daughter of labour! . . . we want to know by what right man has appropriated wealth which he did not create, and which Nature gave to him gratuitously. . . . the creator of the land does not sell it; he gives it; and, in giving it, he is no respector or persons. Why, then, are some of his children regarded as legitimate, while others are treated as bastards?[73]

Henry George reasons similarly:

> If production give to the producer the right to exclusive possession and enjoyment, there can rightfully be no exclusive possession and enjoyment of anything not the production of labor, and the recognition of private property in land is a wrong.[74]

As a number of thinkers have recognized, the person who labors on land would, at most, deserve the rights of use and the right to the product. Hence, on this view, Locke's labor theory of value undermines an exclusively proprietary theory of ownership, full acquisition, with respect to land. Moreover, to the extent that most working on the fruits of nature is cooperative, and most economies are complex, to that degree is full acquisition of any private property rights (independent of other persons) in natural resources impossible.[75]

Yet another reason, a practical reason, that no humans have exclusive and unlimited ownership of land, of property taken from the commons, is that most property rights are derivatively acquired, and almost no record of property rights is a clean one, without fraud and conquest by force. In California, for example, land titles go back to the Mexican government, which took them from the Spanish king, who took them from the pope when he divided yet-to-be-discovered lands between the Portuguese and the Spanish. Everywhere, as Henry George put it, the title to land goes back "not to a right which obliges, but to a force which compels."[76] But if much contemporary private property in land has been illegitimately acquired, and if "force and

fraud have reigned supreme in the history of mankind,"[77] as one com-
mentator put it, then it is questionable whether any alleged current
owners of land have full claim to it. This is both because no human
labor created the land, and because most land probably has not been
transferred according to (what Locke would call) principles of the
law of nature. And if not, then it is arguable that land, in at least
some respects, might be part of the commons, and hence that the state
or the people as a whole ought to have some voice in how such property is used.

Property as Subject to the Productivity Criterion

If the first argument (about Locke's positing an "Original" community and a "Law of Nature" that serves the value of preservation
of life) is correct, then as a consequence property rights, even after
the introduction of money, are circumscribed by the requirements of
this community, the law of nature, and human preservation. But if
there is a Lockean obligation to help preserve humankind, then consequently there must also be an obligation to use property in such a
way that preservation is served. Using property in this way, in turn,
requires that it be productive, that resources be used "to the best
advantage of life and convenience."[78] Locke states again and again
that the purpose of property is that persons should not only use resources, but make the best possible use of them. His argument, in a
nutshell, is that extensive accumulation is justified because the practice works to the benefit of others. From this it follows logically that,
if the practice does not benefit others, then extensive accumulation
cannot be justified.[79]

One problem with Macpherson's interpretation is that he fails to
take account of Locke's claim that extensive accumulation ought to
benefit others. Macpherson, in other words, takes inadequate account
of Locke's utilitarian justification for appropriation beyond need, that
is, the benefit of accumulation to society as a whole.[80] Locke assumes
that it is acceptable to appropriate more land than one can use, provided that this appropriation works to the benefit of all, provided that
it serves the duty "of Preserving all Mankind," provided that it dis-
tributes the productive benefits of land and hence fulfills the natural
law. It follows that, to the degree that the appropriation does not work
to the benefit of all, then the excessive appropriation is not clearly
justified.[81]

If owning property is tied to making the best possible use of resources, then we need to avoid waste,[82] even when there is no danger
of violating the spoilage proviso, and we need to use property in the

most advantageous way possible. Indeed, Locke believes that individual property ought to maximize production: "he who appropriates land to himself does not lessen but increase the common stock of mankind."[83] This is because the opportunities to preserve life ought to be much greater when one has improved land. And if so, then the person with property rights in land has a duty to use them to improve the stock of humanity or at least to insure that persons are made no worse off. "Property rights are rights to use nature productively (improve it), not just to use it," as O'Neill puts it.[84] And if so, then although Locke argues for private property in land, clearly his text does not support full property rights, including the right to destroy or to idle productive resources, or to use them in less than productive ways. Instead, Locke makes property rights subject to the productivity/improvement criterion.

Productivity and improvement are required, for Locke, to satisfy the natural-law demand to preserve all humankind.[85] On this view, although the historical Locke may not have done so, one could imagine a contemporary Locke arguing for extensive restrictions on property rights in land (e.g., prohibiting filling in wetlands) and for agricultural zoning or preservation, for example, to prevent fertile land from being developed or paved. In other words, one could imagine a contemporary Locke concerned about land productivity, applying the consequences of his views in the light of current land-use problems, and arguing for various land-use controls.

Moral Grounds for Believing That Locke's Text Supports Limited Property Rights

In addition to the previous *ethical* reasons for believing that Locke's own words provide a basis for limiting the appropriation of property, even after the introduction of and consent to money, there is at least one *moral* reason for believing that even the historical Locke might not have been wholly opposed to such restrictions. In his *Essay, Some Thoughts Concerning Education*, Locke spoke of the importance of curbing children's acquisitive tendencies. He wrote:

> They would have property and possession; pleasing themselves with the power which that seems to give, and the right they thereby have to dispose of them as they please . . . he who thinks that these two roots of almost all the injustice and contention that so disturb human life are not early to be weeded out, and contrary habits introduced, neglects the proper season to lay the foundations of a good and worthy man.[86]

Locke also argued that children love dominion more than anything else, and that "this is the first original of most vicious habits, that are ordinary and natural."[87] Moreover, although Locke obviously does not believe that owning property is evil, he is convinced that possessing more than one needs is wrong because of "covetousness" and because "the desire of having in our possession, and under our dominion, more than we have need of, being the root of all evil." As a consequence, he recommends that children be taught very early to give away some of what they have "easily and freely to their friends."[88]

To claim that Locke's moral beliefs—about educating children not to want more than they need—provide support for the interpretation of property rights discussed in this chapter, of course, is questionable on at least two grounds. First, it is not obvious that Locke's *Thoughts Concerning Education* are as reliable a source of his views as some of his other works. Second, this account of Locke's moral beliefs is contrary to what some major commentators claim about his position. Macpherson says, "Not only is the desire for accumulation rational, according to Locke but accumulation is the essence of rational conduct."[89] If Locke's words on education, the law of nature, and the duty to preservation are correct, however, then it is questionable whether his text provides an unequivocal defense of capitalism and unlimited appropriation as "the essence of rational conduct."

Conclusions

Admittedly Locke's educational remarks about limiting possessions and covetousness do not constitute arguments for restricting property rights in land.[90] They do at least suggest, however, that some of his *moral and educational injunctions* (about the dangers of power given by excessive possessions) might be consistent with the revisionist account we have given of the *ethical and political views* about property in the Lockean text. This consistency lends some credence to the revisionist arguments that we have sketched. If our four arguments for limitations on property (based on religious duties to those in need, on the "Original" community, and on "the law of nature"; on the continuity of the first proviso; on land value not derived from labor; and on productivity) are correct, then contrary to traditional views, Locke's text does not provide clear support for bourgeois capitalism. The existence of these and other limitations on property rights might support, at best, a welfare-state capitalism in which property rights, especially in land, are restricted in ways necessary to serve the common good.

The revisionist interpretation of the Lockean text that is offered in this chapter may be more plausible to the extent that we are willing to distinguish the "historical" Locke from the "conceptual" Locke, the Locke that must take account of the logical consequences of certain claims in his text. This revisionist interpretation also may be more plausible to the degree that Macpherson is correct in his assertion that Locke's theories about property and the state of nature are unclear.[91] Other commentators claim that the relationship between Locke's natural law and property rights has a "central structural ambiguity."[92] Locke also offered little guidance regarding how civil society might regulate property.[93] If indeed such notions are ambiguous or inadequately treated in Locke, then earlier commentators may have been too quick to read Locke as a Nozickian capitalist. However, if notions like natural law ("Law of Nature") are not ambiguous and are treated adequately in Locke, then perhaps they deserve more of our attention, in part to see what guidance they might offer in areas like adjudicating claims to property rights in land.

5

Concepts of Ownership
and Rights of Use

Lynton Keith Caldwell

The conventional concept of "ownership" of land in America has been obstructive to rational land use and related environmental policies. It is deceptive to those persons who would trust it for protection. A new consensual basis for land-use law and policy is required to reconcile the legitimate rights of the users of land with the welfare of the larger society in a high-quality environment. This chapter is intended to promote discussion of ways to reconcile these objectives.[1] A rational substitute for ownership of land per se would be the purchase by owners of rights to use the land in specified ways and under specified conditions. In fact, this is the right that ownership of land technically confers. The equity issue is who should pay for what, so that land would be used with benefit to the user and without harm to the public welfare. One may question whether the public must pay to prevent uses of land that are found to be contrary to the public interest. The "taking" clause of the U.S. Constitution has often been interpreted in ways protective to private rights in property without regard to the responsibilities of government in protection and enhancement of the public environment. The Constitution explicitly protects private rights in property, but only by inference does it afford protection of the environment.[2]

A letter from the U.S. Department of Justice to Senator Paul Fannin relating to the proposed Land Use Policy and Planning Assistance Act of 1973 stated that:

> it has long been established that state regulation based upon the police power may substantially diminish the economic value of private property without giving rise to an obligation to compensate the owner. . . . [T]here is a very hazy boundary between takings (compensation required) and "police power" regulation (compensation not required). The Supreme Court itself has acknowledged "that there is no set formula to determine where regulation ends and taking begins. [*Goldblatt* v. *Hempstead*, 369 U.S. 590, 594, 1962][3]

The extent of the police power—to protect the public health, safety, and morale—is ambiguous and changes with public beliefs and scientific findings. Relationships among health, safety, and environment have been amplified during recent years by scientific evidence, but more perhaps by popular beliefs. Environmental considerations alone still have little judicial protection. Absent a constitutional amendment for environmental protection, the conservative Supreme Court of the Reagan-Bush administrations has continued to place a high value on property rights as against other values. But in this, as in many other issues of policy and law, its decisions are very likely to be overturned at a future date.

If the strictly legal concepts of land ownership prevailing in the United States did not now exist, it is highly improbable that a similar body of doctrine would be adopted. Law more appropriate to present-day realities would be more likely. The existing aggregation of laws and practices pertaining to the ownership and use of land have been beneficial primarily to persons interested in exploitation or litigation. They provide deceptive protection to the land owner who lacks continuous economic and legal counsel and who is unable personally to influence lawful decisions by other land owners that may be prejudicial to his interests. Moreover, land laws as generally interpreted are even less helpful to communities or to the general public in preserving or restoring the quality of their environments.

Persistence of "pioneer" concepts of ownership rights is possibly the principal obstacle to effective land use planning. A redefinition of the meaning of ownership in land is thus a needed concomitant to both land use planning and environmental management. Land law rooted in the conventions of Tudor England or pioneer America cannot be expected to serve the interests of post-industrial society in the twenty-first century. Archaic concepts and perceptions may persist for a long time if, as in the American judiciary, they may enjoy political protection. As of the early 1990s, one finds a highly discordant and inconsistent mix of "conservatism" and "liberalism" in judicial opinion. But this is what might be expected in a society undergoing a massive and multidirectional cultural transition.

At least one theory of political economy has been based upon the proposition that land is the primary source of all wealth and that its use should be consistent with the laws of nature. This was "physiocracy," a theoretical system of economics largely confined to France in the eighteenth century.[4] The physiocrats, Quesnay, Mirabeau, du Pont de Nemours, and Holbach, relied for the production of wealth upon the operation of natural systems undistorted by the manipulations of government and other "artificial" institutions. A single tax on land (*impot unique*) was believed to be the most logical and least harmful form of taxation. In effect, laissez-faire economics was a concomitant of this theory; it might be regarded as antecedent to present-day libertarianism. It was an expression of the natural law–natural rights assumptions of the eighteenth-century "Enlightenment." Physiocracy per se had little direct influence in America, although Thomas Jefferson was doubtless familiar with its tenets, which corresponded closely to his views regarding the primacy of agriculture and of natural rights of land ownership. Henry George resurrected its principles in his proposal for "a single tax."[5]

The Confusing Legacy of Conventional Land "Ownership"

In his essay on "Control of the Use of Land in English Law," W.O. Hart, then Clerk of the London County Council, observed that: "The English Law of real property never developed a true theory of ownership: title was, and still is in essence, possessory and, moreover, relative rather than absolute".[6] The prevailing principles, terminologies, and deficiencies of English land law were transplanted to colonial America, and although changed circumstances led to changed interpretations and practices, the basic elements of law as applied in seventeenth- and eighteenth-century England continued to influence land law and policy.[7] The absence of an adequate theory of the obligations of land ownership, and the unappropriated status of land in America at the time of the English colonization, have at least in part permitted the growth of the tough resistance in the American political-legal system to regulatory public control over the uses of land. Nevertheless a substantial body of law governing land use has gradually evolved.

Throughout the history of law in Western society, property in land has been distinguished from other forms of property, and rights of ownership have been distinguished from right of use. Rights pertaining to land have never been absolute *in fact*, and not consistent in theory. As R.G. Crocombe observes, "The word ownership is misleading. A person does not really own land: he owns rights to land."[8] Authority over the uses and disposition of land has always been residual in society as represented by the community, the monarch, or the state, and has survived today in the concept of "eminent domain."

Except as allocated to specific persons for designated uses, land in Anglo-Saxon England was "folcland" (e.g., belonging to the folk).[9] Under feudalism distinctions between the rights of ownership and of use continued, but the English economy outgrew the provisions of the common law, and disputes over the uses of land began to be taken to the Court of Chancery where adjudication was not bound by precedent and tradition. In the twenty-seventh year of Henry VIII (A.D. 1535), Parliament enacted the Statute of Uses to clarify and reconcile the complexities that had accumulated regarding rights in the conveyance, utilization, and alienation of land. But economic forces and legal conservatism combined to diminish public benefit from this legislation. The legacy of English land law that was transmitted to the American colonies was highly technical, complex, and unsystematic. Subsequently belonging to the jurisdiction of the states, not the nation, the unsystematic complexity of this body of law has increased over the years; its social and ecological deficiencies remain unremedied.

The status of people-land relationships during the period of European colonization in America was transitional from vestiges of feudal land tenure to the treatment of land as a market commodity. The transition proceeded over several centuries and was influenced by economic forces and opportunities rather than by theory. In America the great opportunity was on the frontier, where land was free from the traditional encumbrances of communal, seignorial, or royal authority. Of larger long-run significance, possession of land carried no responsibility for the possessor, who could do whatever he liked with his property short of failure to pay assessed taxes. The possession of land conferred security, economic freedom, and social status—and the settler in America developed a deep hunger for ownership of land such as he could never hope to satisfy in the Old World. As an owner of land he owed few obligations to neighbors, none to posterity, and very little to the state. He came closer to holding his land in "fee simple absolute" in a literal sense than anyone ever has under Anglo-American law.

Freed of the vestigial constraints of feudalism, the landholder in America developed a tenacious attitude toward unfettered rights of private land ownership. Most important of these rights was the right to treat land as a commodity—to buy, to sell, to speculate, and under the right of ownership to take from the land whatever might be of value. This strong sense of private ownership, along with the abundance of unpreempted land, and the disinclination of government to interfere with land use, combined to establish a tradition of private property in land that has proved highly resistant to the imposition of public land-use controls or to any general sense of owner responsibility beyond legal liability. With few exceptions (pertaining chiefly to public nuisances) the rights of ownership fully covered the rights to use or to dispose. No other society appears to have gone so far in leaving the fate of the land to the discretion of the private owner and the largely unguided operations of a market economy.

This historically exceptional state of affairs in America lasted long enough to implant deeply the idea of unrestricted private property rights into law and politics. But attrition of this extreme form of economic individualism began as population growth and pressure on available land caused public needs to impinge upon the exercise of unfettered private ownership. Increasing growth in the American economy also occasioned third-party claims against the owners and users of land; in brief, the laws of liability expanded. Thus the development of public land-use policy in the United States began inauspiciously with a people deeply committed to a myth of near-absolute rights in ownership. This widely held assumption limited consideration of rational use of land in the public interest, and often failed to protect the real interests of the private land owner. Public opinion nevertheless continued to adhere to the belief in largely unrestricted individual ownership of the land itself as a natural right and a moral principle.

Anomalies of the Ownership Concept

The history of American land law and its English antecedents make evident that, in fact, the right to hold, enjoy, develop, and protect land, as well as to profit from its use, was never absolute. American folklore vaguely envisioned a natural moral right in lawful possession that stood against all claims except those of the state to taxes and those of creditors to whom land was mortgaged. But there was also the residual doctrine of eminent domain that gave the state an ultimate right of possession that, where applicable, overrode private ownership.

Some forms of nuisance or threats to public safety traditionally have limited the uses to which an owner may lawfully put his land. As an obvious example, no right of possession permits a land owner to start an untended and unauthorized open fire on his land during a weather condition of extreme fire hazard. But this prohibition pertains to use and not to ownership. The point at which legal and political conflict over the rights of use characteristically arise is where these rights are claimed to follow from the rights of ownership. And the highly valued advantage of ownership has been in relatively unrestricted freedom to use and especially to sell or otherwise convey for a consideration—in brief, to treat land as an ordinary commodity.

Legal fact and popular concept are seldom entirely consistent in any field of law. With respect to land, the emotional fixation on pri-

vate property has tended to obscure the reality that peaceful possession rests upon the public affirmation and protection of whatever right
to use in fact exists. A priority of public interest may be asserted not
only with respect to taxes, but also for generally accepted public uses
such as highways, military installations, airports, parks, or waste disposal sites; these uses may be obtained by a public taking of private
land upon payment of what the courts determine to be just compensation. The rights of ownership being, in fact, conditional, the practical question of the meaning of ownership consequently relates to
the conditions under which alleged rights of owners may be enforceable, primarily against exactions by government. As often, however,
conflicts over rights are between private owners.

Anomalous (at least in logic) are the laws of states that confer upon
privately owned public utilities the power of eminent domain over
privately owned real property. If the exercise of this public power is
essential to the siting of power plants and to the routing of transmission lines, it would seem dubious that the generation and distribution
of electrical energy is an appropriate activity for private enterprise.
It would be more consistent with popular concepts of private property rights in land were eminent domain to be invoked only by agents
of the public. Under this logic, the sites and routes of power lines,
pipelines, and generating plants would be publicly owned and, if privately managed, would be leased or franchised from the government.
An obvious difference between the use of eminent domain by the
government and by a privately owned public utility is that the public
does not elect the board of directors or chief executive officer of the
utility—they are not answerable to the public for the exercise of this
power.

In addition to these practical exceptions to theories of absolute
ownership, the right of land ownership has been clouded by differences in the philosophic justification for ownership rights. Although
Anglo-American law per se did not develop a theoretical foundation
of continuing relevance for the rights of ownership and use of land,
an approximation to such theory was provided by the doctrine of
natural law.

Theories of land use and ownership in colonial America were influenced by the political philosophy of John Locke. But as Kristin
Shrader-Frechette has demonstrated in the preceding chapter, Locke's
theories were drawn upon selectively to emphasize the rights of ownership to neglect of attendant obligations. Like others of his time,
Locke's interpretation of natural law was based upon an anthropocentric view of human relationships with the earth, a viewpoint some see
as consistent with Old Testament Biblical theology.[10] Locke's *popu-*

lar influence thus tended to be weighted on the side of the rights of ownership, overlooking the reservations set out in his writings. Locke's opinions may have gained more currency through hearsay than through examination of what he actually said.[11]

One of the more influential American expositors of natural-law doctrine in relation to land was Thomas Jefferson, but his views were qualified by his commitment to civil law.[12] His opinions tended to be broadly philosophic and political rather than more narrowly jurisprudential and they frequently embraced contradictory propositions for which he offered no resolution. In a prerevolutionary political treatise prepared for a general convention of the Commonwealth of Virginia meeting in Williamsburg in 1774, Jefferson argued that the system of land inherited from Norman England could not be applied to colonial America without the consent of its inhabitants. He compared the European settlers of America to the Saxon invaders of Britain declaring that

> Their own blood was spilt in acquiring lands for their settlements, their own fortunes expended in making their settlement effectual; for themselves they fought, for themselves they conquered, and for themselves alone they have a right to hold.[13]

Jefferson thus alleged that the British crown had no claim to title over unoccupied lands in the colonies (i.e., lands unoccupied by British colonists) and that their use and disposition by the Americans was justified by conquest and occupancy. This taking of possession of "unoccupied" land appeared to be a natural right, but Jefferson believed that certain natural rights could be abridged or modified with the consent of the people or their deputies. Upon this reasoning he concluded that the personal ownership of property must be deemed a civil rather than natural right. And although he believed that society should guarantee to everyone "a free exercise of his industry, and the fruits acquired by it," he held that the rights of an individual, natural or civil, never extended to harming the equal rights of others.

Moreover, Jefferson did not believe that the civil law of one generation could bind succeeding generations. "Each generation," he wrote, "has the usufruct of the earth during the period of its continuance. When it ceases to exist, the usufruct passes on to the succeeding generation, free and unincumbered, and so on successively, from one generation to another forever."[14] This philosophic proposition was hardly applicable in the practical world beyond the obvious consideration that every generation to some extent reinterprets existing policies and laws. But it was clearly not supportive of conventional practices regarding land ownership that honored Jefferson's individual and natural rights philosophy but disregarded his reservations. In any case, land degraded and impoverished by one generation could not meaningfully be transmitted "free and unincumbered" to succeeding generations.

And so the man who more than any other may be described as the father of American democratic ideals left a confusing legacy of thought regarding the rights of the individual and the rights of society in the ownership and use of land. No other public figure in the formative years of the nation had greater concern for land policy and for the rights of the individual farmer and homesteader. His belief in the linkage between rights of possession in land and protection of personal freedom was a reinforcing although not unique contribution to American political ethos. But his insistence upon the need for the adaptability of law and institutions to the changing circumstances of society is the most principled and pertinent contribution of his thought to the present debate over land-use policy and law.

Is There a Natural Right to Ownership?

Differences in opinion regarding the source and interpretation of human rights have been fundamental to policy differences over land ownership and use. John Locke assumed a natural right to property; Jefferson preferred the anomalous concept of "pursuit of happiness" as a more inclusive and less binding proposition. But the era of American constitution making after 1776 tacitly accepted existence of natural law and natural rights, allegedly inferred by enlightened human reason. The natural-rights assumption is the principal philosophic substrate of the doctrine of an unalienable right to ownership of land as property. But this assumption is most persuasive when least examined. It is a proposition to be believed, not to be questioned. Yet if the reality of such rights is asserted or assumed, there must be persuasive answers to the following questions. If such rights are real, from whence are they derived; who and where is their arbiter? In the Judeo-Christian tradition, we may assume the giver and judge is God, but where do we find the judgment of God on the legal rights of land ownership? If from Nature, then where is the evidence that such rights exist independent of human intuition or convention? How do we know what rights Nature confers upon mankind—and does humanity have enforceable rights against Nature? Does natural law confer upon humanity immunity from consequences of its own behaviors? Are natural rights subordinate to natural law that, in effect, ordains penalties inherent in violation of natural systems (e.g., soil erosion, contamination of groundwater, depletion of the ozone layer)? The Amazonian rain forest, the Great Lakes, or grizzly bears may have no rights that humans need respect, but does humanity have a dispensation from the consequence of their loss or degradation? And dispensation from whom? The processes of nature make natural rights in the uses of land conditional upon behavior consistent with the "laws of nature."

Have I a right to continued good health if the physiological consequences of my behavior diminish my pursuit of life and happiness? A draft version of the National Environmental Policy Act of 1969 declared that Americans had a right to a healthful environment. But who could guarantee such right against natural conditions inherently unsafe for human health (e.g., conditions of extreme heat or cold or endemic disease, such as malaria, fungal infections, or schistosomiasis)? In brief, if Nature has no rights that persons need respect, may we also conclude that persons have no rights that Nature "need" respect? This interpolation of a commentary on the implications of belief in natural rights to property is not a deviation from our main thesis regarding the social or utilitarian justification for natural and legal rights. Nearly all of our environmental issues are significantly affected by how humans behave in relation to the land, and those behaviors are significantly influenced by the tacit assumptions and beliefs prevailing in human societies.

Nothing in our knowledge of the natural world, including the nature of being human, supports the concept of inalienable legal rights, nor does our knowledge of history or anthropology confirm natural rights to property as inherent in human rationality. Legal rights as understood in the social and behavioral sciences, are cultural artifacts, socially derived and justified through philosophical analysis. A sense of such rights is no less valid for having evolved out of human experience and knowledge of cause and effect in human behavior. There is an important distinction in human society between legal rights and rights believed to inhere in nature—essentially moral rights apprehended through experience, and through reflection upon the consequences of human behavior. For if persons alone are responsible for defining their rights, they bear responsibility for exercising those rights and for the obligations that nature (in effect) imposes on behavior. This principle would be basic in a new socioecologically rational land ethic.

The definition of rights to land use (legal or natural) ultimately depends upon an interpretation of humanity's relationship to the natural world. This relationship is inherently transgenerational and evolutionary, for human life is successional and the earth abides. The dynamics of natural systems and the limited lifetime of humans preclude ownership in relation to land as no more than socially confirmed rights to its temporary custody. Thus the society that recognizes such rights also has a responsibility to determine what those rights should be and how they should be used in relation to the generations to follow. On this point, the authors emphasize somewhat different aspects of the rights issue. If "rights" imply natural ethical or moral principles, then one may logically hold that they do not depend upon societal fiat. If, however, "rights" are also viewed as legal authorization or social consent without regard to ethical or moral implications, then one may argue that such "rights" are socially conferred. Legal rights socially conferred may be socially withdrawn. Human slavery was legal in the United States when the Constitution was adopted, and the right to sell alcoholic beverages was withdrawn and later restored conditionally.

These interpretations of "rights" may conflict on certain land-use issues. They may in some cases lead to differing assessments of justice, as when one declares that "it isn't right, but it's the law." So it seems that not all legal rights are moral rights, and some people would say that there are moral rights that are not legal. The beneficiaries of socially conferred legal rights may seek their justification on moral grounds; "vox populi vox Dei." But Moses did not need the intermediary voice of the people in asserting a rightful claim to the land of Canaan. Today, the prevailing view of rights in property has been based on an abstract and anthropocentric concept of the relationship of the individual to the world of which he is a part. As summarized by one observer of the interpretation of property rights, "there is wide agreement that the cause, not only of the environmental crisis, but of many of our other economic, social and political problems as well can be traced to Western man's denial of his interdependence with his fellow man and with his environment."[15] The dichotomizing of people and nature in modern Western society (i.e., mankind *outside* of nature) is not demonstrably more just or moral than interpretations of human societies and individuals as within and belonging to the natural order.

The biological unity of life is scientifically demonstrable. People cannot exist apart from the biosphere and thus at least minimal respect for nature and protection of natural ecosystems is necessary for the continuing survival of the human species. This is the basis of efforts toward holistic interpretations of person-environment relationships, and it places nature neither completely above humans nor vice versa in the scale of values. For example, Robinson Jeffers expressed the ethical essence of ecological holism in poetry.[16]

If we interpret our own rights, and if the consequences of their exercise are significant, should we not take care what rights we declare? If we consider the consequences of exercising our rights, are we not then logically moved to consider what obligations, if any, those rights entail? Obligations characterize every human culture and grow with growth in societal complexity and enlarged understanding of risks and consequences of behaviors. Posterity is unable to assert any claims against us, nor can the natural environment in which we live and of which we are a part. Nature asserts no rights against abuse by humanity, but it may levy penalties against transgressions of its processes and parameters. In recognition of this reality does not our understanding of cause-consequence relationships and the ethical maturing of our culture oblige us to cultivate foresight and to express in our conduct an attitude of fairness and of respect for the living world that makes our survival possible? We develop this expression as both an ecologically imposed and a self-imposed obligation, and by these obligations we place limits on our self-declared rights, many of which are exercised on and in relation to the land. By acting within those limitations that are inexorable in nature, we lose no freedoms that may be made enduring.

Deficiencies in the Ownership Concept

The case for traditional ownership of land cannot therefore be made solely by reference to history, philosophic theory, or theology. The strongest defense of all alleged rights to ownership of land is the empirical fact of widespread social acceptance of their legitimacy. The concept of moral right to absolute possession is not supported by interpretations of natural law, which would leave the owner in possession only so long as he could physically defend his tenure. Nevertheless, ownership of property as a civil right does carry certain social advantages that account for its persistence and that will presently be explored.

The authors are hostile neither to the concept of private property nor to the protection of property rights. Private property is a mainstay of personal freedom. Our criticisms are directed only to its overextension or abuse. We do not expect the principle of private property in land to wither away. Not all advantages associated with private ownership of land, however, are derived from the mere legal fact of ownership, and there are a number of contingencies for which ownership alone unsupported by other legal rights offers only limited protection. Examples are numerous: land ownership per se may not protect against air pollution, offensive noise or odors, obstruction of sunlight by high-rise buildings, or deterioration of adjacent property. If privacy is an objective, then ownership of land may protect but does not assure. The privacy of an owner may be invaded by public authorities for many reasons, among the more obvious of which are tax assessment, public works, and criminal investigation. Nor is mere ownership a barrier to the intrusion of such unwanted externalities as those cited above. Ownership supports a right to sue (and be sued) for damages or to seek injunctive relief. In most communities defense against casual trespass is a responsibility of the owner, whose ability to enforce his rights is limited by law and often by circumstance. Today, neither ownership nor privacy are defenses against alleged violations of someone's civil rights.

If security (both personal and economic) is an objective, then conventional ownership alone cannot guarantee it. Persons have been robbed and murdered on their own land. The market value of land may fall as well as rise, and the burdens of ownership may be increased through taxation, by special assessments, by acts of nature, and by the personal ability of owners to bear the responsibilities of ownership. The relative permanence of land makes it acceptable as collateral for loans, and this economic advantage along with the relative stability of land values offers the most reliable benefit from ownership as presently defined. But *these* benefits are obtainable only to the extent that land is treated as a commodity, enjoyed primarily by the owner and sometimes at the expense of his neighbors and society-at-large.

The best-advertised abuses of the land tend to be associated with its treatment in the marketplace. There are of course abuses, notably soil erosion, resulting from carelessness and neglect. Among those "legal persons" who deal in land as a commodity, the more significant are corporations whose activities in land development or speculation are not even necessarily advantageous to all of their stockholders. Some holders of stock in enterprises that profit from transactions in land might be adversely affected by the consequences of corporate policies. For example, a stockholder who admired an "unspoiled" valley in the Rocky Mountains might be dismayed to discover that "his" company was subdividing the valley into five-acre ranchettes.

A direct consequential economic loss by a stockholder would doubtless be exceptional but not inconceivable. Such a case could arise if corporate land development in which an individual owned shares impaired the value of other land or property possessed by that individual. But if persons experience a loss of environmental amenities, even in an area removed from their immediate environment, the negative effects of land development entailing future social costs should also logically be weighed against the monetary benefits received from land transactions. Future costs are borne by future generations so that an ethical question arises regarding exercise of rights allegedly derived from ownership to the disregard of consequences in the future.

It should be noted, however, that land development by corporations is not always destructive. The worst practices are often perpetrated by companies solely engaged in promoting land sales and speculation. Some corporations have engaged in land development for purposes of economic diversification and, not being wholly dependent upon turnover in real estate, have tried to administer ecologically responsible policies. Some have given substantial tracts of land to environmental protection organizations, such as the Nature Conservancy.

Although it is demonstrable that the principal beneficiaries of present land ownership laws are not necessarily individual land or home owners (and certainly not a majority of the American people), belief in a moral right to the inviolability of private property from public action is pervasive. Psychologically, many Americans have been committed to land ownership policies that are not necessarily in their individual or collective interest. Here again, moral rights and legal rights tend to be confused. An extreme example was a militant conservative movement organized as the Committee to Restore the Constitution, Inc., which argued that federal legislation as mild as the proposed National Land Use Policy and Planning Assistance Act of 1973 threatened: "The right of private property, guaranteed to the people under the provisions of the Fifth Amendment, and respected as fundamental to individual freedom since December 15, 1791."[17] Such allegedly "conservative" positions are not in fact conservative, being advanced characteristically by speculators and developers who seek to retain freedom to alter the land for their private benefit with little regard to consequences for the public or for other private land owners. Moreover, it is not the right to private ownership per se that the planning process would affect. It is rather a process to ensure that proposed uses, public or private, do not entail undesirable long-range economic and environmental costs for everyone.

The ill-fated National Land Use Policy and Planning Assistance Act of the 1970s established no policy and conferred no new powers upon government. Its principal institutional effect would have been to encourage the states to assume the rights over land that have always been theirs but had largely been unasserted or had been delegated to the roughly 10,000 units of local government. As among uses, the Act was essentially neutral, but injection of land-use policy into the public forum in each state might arouse latent issues and dissatisfactions. For this reason, and because they viewed any suggestion of federal regulatory activity in relation to privately owned land as dangerous, representatives of the land development and building interests opposed statutory action at the federal level. Federal involvement with the rights of private ownership of land, historically a state concern, has occurred chiefly in interpretations of the "taking" clause in the Fifth Amendment to the U.S. Constitution and in the exercise of eminent domain.[18] Such interpretations have been subject to re-interpretation by the Supreme Court. A case can be made that an amendment to the U.S. Constitution would be necessary to stabilize a principled policy for public "takings" and to allow environmental and transgenerational considerations appropriate weight in adjudications.[19]

The possible limits on federal power to take privately owned land for a public purpose are, as previously noted, conjectural. Determination of just compensation for a "taking" and of the requirements of due process of law are subject to the changing opinions of the courts. It would be naive to assume that no future changes will occur in the judicial interpretation of these provisions. Throughout the history of the American judiciary new rights (e.g., the "right to travel") have been discovered and long-standing rights (e.g., prayer in public schools) have been declared invalid. There is need for the adaptation of law to changing circumstances, but there is also need for predictable interpretations grounded in principles that transcend contemporaneous political controversies or ideological predispositions in the Supreme Court.

That there are diverse possibilities in the law was illustrated by a legislative taking under Public Law 90-545 for the purpose of establishing a Redwood National Park in California. Section 3 (b) (1) declared that "Effective on the date of enactment of this Act, there is hereby vested in the United States all right, title, and interest in and the right to immediate possession of all real property within the park boundaries." The Act provided for just compensation to former owners and for the termination of all private operations on the property acquired by the United States. Unlike the usual federal condemnation proceedings, claims against the government were to be heard in the Court of Claims rather than by a jury in a federal district court.[20] This summary method has obvious advantages in the protection of land threatened by immediate damage, but it also demonstrates that under certain circumstances private ownership of particular land can be terminated by legislative action and with a stroke of a presidential pen.

The composite picture of land ownership rights in the United States is, therefore, anything but consistent. A basic deficiency in the traditional American law of land ownership lies, as we have noted, in the ultimate insupportability of its philosophic foundations. It is difficult to build a logical case for or against a body of law that has grown, virtually ad hoc, in response to pressures and events and justified by tacit assumptions. As K.E. Digby observed with respect to the evolution of the English law of real property: "the nature and attributes of the various classes of rights are to be accounted for by reference rather to their history than to any principles of jurisprudence."[21]

Writing more than a century ago, Digby concluded that the confusing provisions of the Statute of Uses [27 Henry VIII, c 10.], "and the marvelous interpretations to which its interpretations have been subjected—renders any real simplification of the law of real property impossible, without a more thorough rebuilding of the whole structure from its foundations and the substitution of a systematic or scientific for a historical classification." Since this time significant rationalization (if not simplification) has occurred in English law, notably through the Town and County Planning Acts. In the United States, however, there are as many different systems of land law as there are states (and their 10,000+ local subdivisions), with additional legislation pertaining to federal lands and territories. The mere fact of legal variation does not in itself imply deficiency, but it does reflect the absence in American society of a guiding philosophy of relationships between people and the land.

The conventional belief that land may be "owned" as of "right" rather that as a socially derived privilege is undercut by a number of considerations, several of which have shaped land use arrangements in other societies. A consideration common among primitive and pastoral peoples is that because no man made the land, no man may possess it as his "own." This argument has been adopted in some sectors of the ecology/environmental quality movement. It is unrelated to Marxist theory of collective ownership, being derived from a belief about environmental relationships rather than from socioeconomic philosophy. In exceptional instances land may be "made," in the sense of being made available to human use through human effort. But an individual is rarely equal to this task. For example, manmade land, as in the polders of the Netherlands, has been socially engineered.

The conditional use of land (usually for specified purposes) has been the custom among many people, as it was among the Anglo-Saxon settlers in Britain. Law in some societies, as in the United States, distinguishes so-called "improvements" to the land from the land itself—and the rights and obligations of ownership reflect this consideration. The definition of "improvement" is, however, a matter of convention and political determination. Not everyone would consider the filling of marshes or the replacement of open fields by shopping centers to be improvements. Nevertheless American legislators, judges, and tax assessors have generally assumed that improvements to land result in increases in its monetary value. Taxable value may fall if the "improvement" is removed, thus the wrecking of solid, usable, but unused buildings to reduce assessed valuations.

A tacit consideration that has persisted throughout the evolution of the law of property is the transiency of human individuals and artifacts as opposed to the relative permanence of the land. This circumstance has underlain the distinction between real and personal property. Real property cannot be separated from its environment, and although its qualities may be depreciated, successive generations of mankind will depend upon it for sustenance. And so integrity of the land and its ecosystems may make the arbitrary personal use of any part of it subject to social intervention if the acts of an owner obviously threaten the continuing welfare of the community. For example, topsoil may be regarded as landed property and, if allowed to erode, the value of the land itself will be diminished.

From this consideration follows the principles of stewardship under which ownership or possession of land is interpreted to be a trust, with attendant obligations to future generations as well as to the present.[22] The ownership concept as it developed in America emphasized the rights of personal possession and did not lead to an attitude of responsibility to the public or to posterity. However, an ethical concept of stewardship, beyond the law, has been latent in a minority sector of opinion. Aldo Leopold's "land ethic" has become analogous to religious scripture for many environmentally concerned people.[23] This attitude may, in fact, assume a semireligious or mystical character, as illustrated by Liberty Hyde Bailey's *The Holy Earth*, and in many of the more poetic expressions of the ecology movement of recent decades, exemplified in the lines by Robinson Jeffers quoted earlier in this chapter.[24] Its roots are ancient and multicultural, but its assumption regarding humans as a part of the totality of nature is more consistent with reality as revealed by science than are the legal technicalities of ownership rights.

There is an additional consideration with respect to ownership, which has no historical tradition but reflects historical fact or, more precisely, the changing social environment in which land is owned and used. The ownership concept developed historically under relatively constant social relationships with no massive rapid changes in land value or in concepts of its appropriate usage. In America the relative abundance of cheap land and the minimal demand of society upon land owners continued from the time of the European settlements until nearly the end of the nineteenth century. By mid-twentieth century radical changes in environmental relationships were effected by a great increase in population and per capita wealth. The impact of technology upon land use was dramatic—the automobile and the airplane making every part of the nation readily accessible to popular use and exploitation. Air conditioning and cheap energy enlarged human opportunities for settlement and development and altered land use patterns over large areas of the nation.

Following World War II, the escalating market value of land was equaled only by the concurrent degrading of the American landscape and the economically and ecologically costly dispersion of housing and commercial activities over the countryside. To sustain this dispersion an inexhaustible supply of cheap energy is necessary. No such permanent supply is presently accessible to industrial society, and the costs of the "spread city" in time, space, and energy are great. If permanent supplies of cheap energy are developed, the spread city may be the settlement pattern of the future. If removable sources of cheap, environmentally acceptable energy are not developed, the "spread city" may be a short-lived urban phenomenon with drastic alterations in the relative monetary value of land depending upon location.

The cumulative effect of present and prospective changes has been to bring into question the social and economic implications of the rights of land ownership as presently construed. The case for ownership rights to land would be stronger were the personal freedom and independence of most Americans actually dependent upon it. In fact, the present legal status of land ownership (*not the principle of private possession*) is beneficial especially to developers, to speculators, and to the exploiters of values attached to the land. To the individual home owner, mere ownership offers little more than the illusion of security while the advantage accrues to the indifferent exploiter of land and landscape whose interest is neither with the future of the land nor the environment, but rather with the prospective economic returns from transactions in land and its resources.

Needed: A New Conceptual Basis

The right to use land in particular ways and for particular purposes, and to obtain reliable protection from invasion of legitimate rights that are consistent with the public interest, requires more appropriate mechanisms than conventional rights of ownership as we have them today. Systematic means are needed to balance the various appropriate uses of land in society. And the proposition guiding all alternatives is that, next to human society itself, land use in its various aspects is the fundamental element in the human environment and a major influence in shaping the character of a society.

The need for change in laws governing land arises as a concomitant of other major social changes. English land law experienced periods of major change at critical junctures in English history. The first change, from a communal to a feudal land system, followed the Norman Conquest in A.D. 1066. The second, from feudal to commercial, followed the birth of modern England and was exemplified by the Statute of Uses in 1535. The third phase occurred when England reached "saturation" in demands upon the land and when social and ecological considerations began to override market considerations. The series of Property Acts taking effect in 1926 and the subsequent Town and Country Planning Acts have restated and restricted the rights of the landowner for more inclusive benefits of the land user (i.e., the society in general). The changes have been incremental and reformist in a characteristically English manner, rather than expressive of a radical new ideology.

English land law was transplanted to America at a time when the entitlements of private land ownership had reached an all-time high. The conditions favoring their free exercise continued for roughly 300 years, becoming deeply ingrained in American ethics, attitudes, and expectations. The radical changes in the American economy and lifestyles in the mid-twentieth century found the nation poorly equipped by psychology or by law to cope with the rapidly mounting problems of land use. The persistence of traditional land ownership concepts represents a failure of perceptual and political adaptation to the changing circumstances of human relationships to the land.

Cheap energy along with a free market in land encouraged the disintegration of cities and the sprawl of economic activities and settlements across the country, entailing heavy fixed costs in public services, in the transportation of people and materials, and in attendant losses of environmental amenities. The energy crisis of 1973–1974 demonstrated (briefly) how the decentralizing effect of land policies had defeated the efficient use of mass transit in suburban areas. Following the passing of the energy crisis (actually an access-to-energy crisis) of the early 1970s, the object lesson of the vulnerability of a highly decentralized settlement pattern without public transportation was rapidly forgotten. It remains to be relearned at a future date. By the early 1970s the cumulative effect of a quarter-century of private land-use decisions had created a costly and generally inconvenient disintegration of the physical infrastructure of American society. These decisions had been influenced by public policies relating to enhanced revenues and assessed valuations, banking and credit, highway construction, low-cost housing, and civil rights. An interlocking set of policies and conditions converged to destroy both urban and rural environments and to overwhelm the burgeoning suburbs with expenses and problems. Land-use planning and the control of urban growth appeared to be emerging as major subjects of political concern. But in a milieu of public distrust of government, of apathy and misinformation, growth and development advocates successfully smothered federal action before significant legal reforms could be undertaken. Cities were compelled, by judicial solicitude for private economic rights and protection for alleged civil discrimination, to pursue a cautious course in land use policy. Some innovations were achieved, but it was primarily at the level of state government that the more general public concern was reflected in new land-conserving policies and legislation.

In the absence of a fundamental change in the rights of land ownership, serious efforts to implement land-use planning legislation are likely to be ineffectual and frustrated in a long uphill struggle toward ecologically sound and socially economical uses of land. But fundamental change in legally sanctioned rights was not what public opinion has seemed to favor. In many communities there has been visible public dissatisfaction with the politics of land-use decisions. This may at least be partially directed toward inept governmental planning and decisionmaking. It has often been the planners rather than planning per se that were at fault. Reform without pain has been the preferred objective. Protests tend to be directed toward symptoms. The basic causes of ills attributable to improper land use are poorly understood, if understood at all, by the public at large. Arguments against planning and regulation are often presented as the opinion of "economists" whereas many differing views are held by economists, some of which are as critical of market-driven practices as others are of planning.

Some Elements of Rational Policy

In the search for alternative principles of land policy one should distinguish between the temporary economic advantage (or disadvantage) to particular individuals, and definable long-range benefits that satisfy social and ecological criteria. Both require consideration. It is also necessary to distinguish between theory and actual effect. Failure to so distinguish would almost certainly increase the probability of opposition from persons owning land even though many of the traditional rights of ownership would be replaced by rights of use. If those rights of ownership that are presumed to safeguard the privacy and security of the individual land owner could be provided for more effectively in some other way, there might be a general advantage in abandoning the conventional concept of outright ownership of land. Assured protection of socially and ecologically harmless rights that are now allegedly protected by ownership would certainly be a prerequisite to the willing acceptance of land owners of any new set of legal principles under which land itself was not "owned."

A second prerequisite would be provision against the "Tragedy of the Commons" effect.[25] Land, as such, would be no more "ownable" than air or water, but the *uses* of land would be the object of law and of rights as is currently the case of water and is becoming the case with the atmosphere. Rights to uses of our air and water are already, under some circumstances, treated as commodities. But the sale or trade of specific rights by public authority or under government supervision is different from establishing property rights in air or water (or in wildlife). The objective of land-use control would not be to substitute bureaucratic for commercial decision making, but rather to provide an open and informed review of the decision process, as well as assuring more adequate protection both to the legitimate property interests of individuals and to the present and long-term needs of society. Basic to this assurance is that land is more than a commodity and market forces alone should not determine its use.

Following are some propositions that might answer these purposes. None of these propositions is intrinsically new. Their novelty would lie in their combination to form a new conceptual basis for land law and policy—to help construct a foundation in jurisprudence for policies that must be devised to safeguard our future in a finite environment. For clarity and convenience the following propositions are presented in semioutline form.

A.   Rights of ownership would be redefined to apply not to land itself, but to specific rights to occupy and/or to use particular parcels of land in accordance with publicly established criteria. Rights to use might be bought and sold, and could confer possession—the land itself ceasing to be property. Property would inhere in the ownership of specified rights, not in the land per se. The ultimate repository of these property rights would be in society. Their administration would be through government, but could involve extensive citizen participation in policy making in which all available information relevant to a decision was made public and subject to testing for validity.

B.   Rights of occupancy and use would be defined by law (as they are today), through classification of land according to its economic and ecologic capabilities, with provisions governing (a) obligations of occupancy (stewardship), (b) acquisition of additional rights, (c) transfer of rights, and (d) abrogation of rights.

1. "Rights" would specify those activities in relation to the land in which the occupant or user might freely engage, and it would also define those aspects of privacy and of security from external damage or annoyance that society through government would undertake to defend and protect.

2. Obligations concomitant with custody of land would be specified and, in addition to traditional restrictions against public nuisance, would reinforce measures to protect the quality of soil, air, and water, the integrity of ecosystems, protection of nonhuman species, and the character of the landscape—both manmade and natural.

3. Allocation of particular rights to particular areas of land would take place through public planning involving citizen participation and expert assessment. For any piece of land only those rights allocated to it could be exercised, though not all available rights might need to exercised. Some provision should be made to prevent or undo speculation in rights whereby owners might decline to employ their "rights" to meet an urgent public need in order to raise the price of rights for particular uses. A purchaser might buy some, but not all, of the rights pertaining to a given piece of land (e.g., the right to farm but not the rights to mine or to develop). This is the present situation, but provisions may be needed to reconcile the exercise of different rights by different individuals on the same land, (e.g., rights to subsurface minerals, to timber, to water, or to road construction).

4. Rights and obligations may be defined for communities and public authorities as well as for individuals and corporations. These provisions would especially apply to land for public works (e.g., for power plants, energy transmission lines, airports, highways, military and administrative purposes, scientific research, recreation, historic preservation, and natural resources development).

C. Taxation would apply to the economic value of rights actually possessed and exercised—not to the land itself, nor in anticipation of rights that *might* be obtained for a particular piece of land. The tax rate could be adjusted to compensate the public for any burden that a particular use of land might place upon a community.

1. This arrangement would put an end to the practice of as-

sessing land at its presumed market value regardless of its use. For example, the owner of the right to farm a tract of land could be taxed only in relation to that right, even though the farm were surrounded by land for which highly taxed development rights had been granted.

2. Capital gains in land per se would not be obtainable. The owner of the right to farm a piece of land would gain no advantage in the present practice of holding the land itself off the market in anticipation of an increase in value. He could not develop the land or sell development rights to others unless he possessed those rights. Any increase in the uses of land not covered in rights possessed by the users would require purchase of additional rights from the public authority concerned. For example, to convert farm land to an industrial site would require the purchase of a right or franchise to develop for this purpose. The assessment of these rights could reflect the prospective profitability of the development and the costs and benefits to the community.

3. The right to remove minerals, soil, timber, and aggregate from land would require conditional permits drafted to protect the ecologic and amenity values, and to ensure the efficient handling of the materials. This arrangement could replace existing severance taxation.

A major objective of these changes in land law would be to assure that publicly created values in land would accrue to the public. For example, increases in the value of land at newly constructed interchanges on interstate highways would afford no opportunity for excess profit to the adjacent land owners. Whether development rights or franchises would be granted would depend upon considerations of physical planning and public necessity and convenience. A development franchise could not be granted without an environmental impact study and, if granted, could stipulate parameters of architectural style and construction, siting, landscaping, and provision for traffic flow and public utilities, including waste management.

Surrender of development rights, and avoidance of accrued financial liabilities, would require restoration of land to a condition equivalent, in most cases, to its predevelopment status. Derelict billboards, abandoned buildings, mines, quarries, and other residuals of discontinued development would continue to be taxed at rates sufficient to compel their owners to undertake remedial or restorative measures. The intent of these provisions would be to make development more responsible and more carefully considered. It would also make it less spontaneous and less profitable to would-be speculators in land values. Special provision should be made, however, to prevent the destruction of potentially useful structures or of buildings of artistic or historic value. Certificates of exemption might be issued to relieve the owners of these nonproductive "improvements" from being taxed at development rates.

A secondary purpose would be to prevent socially and ecologically harmful speculation in development. A grant of development rights would confer limited authority to change the uses of land in certain ways, but for major environmental changes involving public services and transportation, (e.g., a shopping center), an impact assessment and an additional franchise would be required. If, as has been suggested, development taxes must be paid so long as a right to develop exists, developers could not escape errors of judgment or miscarriage of projects merely by walking away from them. Until the development rights were sold or surrendered they would continue as accruing liabilities to the holder of the rights. Some form of public receivership would doubtless be necessary to take custody of abandoned property and to restore the land with funds obtained from forfeited equities or from penalties for failure to restore the land.

A virtue of the foregoing approach to land-use policy is that decisions affecting the public could in effect become public decisions—a circumstance that occurs very imperfectly and often not at all under the laws currently prevailing in most of the United States. The decision process could be made more open and explicit than it usually is under the system of private land ownership. The "rights to use" approach could direct public action away from litigation and toward planning and administration. Some critics will find these proposals utopian—pointing out that land-use decisions that we regard as "bad" are made in collusion between public officials and developers. We do not regard our proposals as ideal or immune to abuse; we do believe them to be more responsible and less subject to connivance than most present practices.

Among the probable effects of removing land per se from the market or as an object of speculation would be the following:

(a) Values in land would be unstable until their redefinition in terms of use could be completed. During this interim the price of land might be depressed. If, however, the assessed or estimated market value were redefined to be the value of its present use, a traumatic effect on the real-estate economy might be avoided.

(b) The immediate effect upon expansive economic growth would be negative, but the long-range effect would be to stabilize economic activity and reduce the incidence of failure in land development projects.

(c)   Taxation of land would be replaced by taxation of rights to use. Careful attention however should be given to the treatment of vacant land. Pro forma or actual premature development ought not be encouraged. In so far as speculative values relate to rights and not to the land per se, low tax rates could encourage keeping land in green space. Structures built on the land could, as at present, be taxed separately. The incidence of these taxes would require careful study as there would be no inevitable direction toward which the tax burden could be shifted.

(d)   Some forms of economic growth would be hurt, at least temporarily, but these would chiefly be instances of growth bearing long-term social and economic liabilities. A relatively stabilized population is both a conditional factor and a likely consequence of a more stable and predictable pattern of land use. Land use policy and controls alone will not meet all of their objectives. Additional socioeconomic factors must be considered.

Feasibility of These Propositions

The principal effect of the foregoing propositions would be to take from private persons—individual, corporate—and even from public authorities the power to alter significantly the environment without generally accepted standards of quality and sustainability. It does not necessarily follow that the power of environmental planning and management would be transferred to public bureaucracy or that universal acquiescence in a decision would be required. Use of citizen boards of review, of open planning, of provisions in the decision process for inputs from science and the design arts—all these methods could result in more socially and ecologically responsible land-use decisions than might be expected under the existing technicalities of land law. The objectives of these propositions are conservative in a very fundamental sense. They are intended to preserve and to conserve, to encourage and to enforce responsibility toward society and posterity, and to reduce the likelihood of rash and destructive uses of land and resources. And they are intended to do these things without loss to the real freedoms currently enjoyed under land ownership except where their exercise would be determined to be prejudicial to the community or to the broader environmental life-support system (i.e., ecosystem or biosphere).

It should be apparent that the proposal to replace rights of outright land ownership with rights of use implies the possibility of major changes in the power structure of society and in the processes of decision making with respect to land use. It should also be apparent that the direction of the policy changes suggested here would be opposed with vigor by many politically influential interests and institutions. We would not expect, nor attempt to persuade, representatives of banks, real-estate boards, developers, and speculators in land futures to accept the reasoning advanced in this book. But among them some might, upon reflection, find merit in our suggestions. In certain respects our propositions may bear some similarity in principle to those advanced more than a century ago by Henry George in his first book, *Our Land and Land Policy* (1871), and subsequently in his better-known *Progress and Poverty* (1879). The philosophic foundation for these works is in ethics and ecology: assuming that in a logical and meaningful sense land, as such, can no more be owned than air or water. But the purpose of the propositions advanced here is more limited than George's and the alternatives are more numerous, more complex, and less definite. No general reformist device such as the single tax is proposed, nor would the tax on uses suggested in this chapter necessarily force land into economic uses or cause it to be withheld from the market. It is the economic value of the actual use that would be taxed, not the prospective value of the land. Payments for rights of use correspond to Henry George's rent, but no claim is made that this form of taxation would invariably be more equitable in all cases than those presently practiced in the United States, although we believe that it might be made so. The effects of taxation might be made clearer and criteria for equitability might more adequately be defined.

Whatever its deficiencies, the existing system of land ownership and its variations and modifications has produced relationships and results that are generally if imperfectly understood. Remedies exist for most abuses, although their practical availability is often expensive and belated. Substitutions of another set of legal principles will not be easily accomplished. This chapter has advanced the proposition that the changes that have been occurring in present-day society have made the present land ownership system increasingly dysfunctional to rational basic economic and ecologic objectives. But recourse to a different system should be preceded by careful study of its probable consequences. The importance of research on the relationships between land use and laws governing proprietary land units was stressed by D.R. Denman, Professor of Land Economy at the University of Cambridge.[26] There is a large body of published work on law and practice of land use and we are unable to digest it all here.[27] The Lincoln Institute of Land has undertaken and sponsored numerous studies of practical importance. Comparative studies of land law and policy as practiced in other countries could be useful to Americans. An example would be a study of the proprietary unit (ownership) and the enterprise unit (use) undertaken by the National Institute of Agrarian Research in France.[28] The problem of finding an optimal relationship between rights of ownership and rights of use is not unique to the United States. In his inaugural, professorial lecture D.R. Denman declared that "Property rights in land or rights analogous to them are, in the last analysis, the only power by which men can execute positive plans for the use of land and natural resources." [29] Denman argues persuasively that much of the frustration and failure in present-day land-use planning has resulted from the failure of planners to recognize adequately "the positive influence of property rights in land" and that "the planning process has not superseded the property sanction."

The argument that the ownership of property in land should be in specified rights of use rather than ownership of the land per se does not attack the concept or legitimacy of private rights in property. It argues for redefining those rights, making them more like property in patents or copyrights rather than the ownership of personal property consisting of tangible assets such as houses, furniture, or jewelry. The institution of property is indispensable to social stability and responsibility, and its demise is neither likely nor desirable.[30] The redefinition of property in land to comprise uses rather than the physical land also is not a panacea. Rights, however defined, could be abused or misused. Conversion from present practices in land ownership to the concepts proposed here would be difficult and would require changes in assumptions, expectations, and ethics, changes advocated throughout this book. Temporal compromises would probably be necessary in certain instances to avoid gross injustice to individuals. Nevertheless, the ultimate goal should remain. The tentative nature of human lives makes all changes possible over extended time.[31] To attain a sustainable economic and environmental future of high quality, we need to find an appropriate institutional means for reconciling the rights of the individual to own with the need of society to plan. Rights of ownership in land as they have been conventionally interpreted in the United States have not met this need. The wise course would therefore seem to be to identify those alternative rights that, even if retaining the terminology of property rights in land, would redefine those rights to better serve the public interest.

6

Agriculture, Coal, and Procedural Justice: Case Studies for Land-Use Planning

Kristin Shrader-Frechette

If the arguments of the two preceding chapters are correct, then the history of property rights in England and America reveals that land has often been interpreted in terms of private rather than public interests. Part of the reason for this individualistic emphasis may be that we have been insensitive to the ways in which land ownership confers political and economic power inimical to the common good. Such insensitivity is not unique to the property issue, however.

More than 400 years before the birth of Christ, Thucydides bemoaned the fact that many Athenians were dedicated to their own private interest, rather than to the public interest. Like an early Walter Lippmann, he wrote that his fellow citizens

> devote a very small fraction of the time to the consideration of any public object, most of it to the prosecution of their own objects. Meanwhile each fancies that no harm will come of his neglect, that it is the business of somebody else to look after this or that for him; and so, by the same notion being entertained by all separately, the common cause imperceptibly decays. [*The History of the Peloponnesian War*, bk. I, sec. 141]

Like the Athenians of Thucydides' time, many of us are more concerned with our private, rather than public interests. Even among public goods, like clean air and water and land, we are often busy carving out our private interests. One of the most common ways in which we reduce public goods to private ones is in our ownership of finite natural resources, like land. And one of the ways that the contemporary Thucydides among us attempt to remedy our graspingness is to argue for land-use planning.

Perhaps the most basic assumption underlying all land-use planning is that land, as a natural resource, ought to serve public, rather than merely private, interests. For example, if farmland needs to be preserved in order to safeguard the U.S. agricultural base, then zon-

111

ing laws, taxation, and other forms of land-use controls ought to secure this societal goal. If citizens need to be protected from the dangerous spillovers of agriculture or industry, then planning and other forms of land-use controls ought to secure this public good. Every public good, however, is bought at a price. And part of the price of land-use controls is greater restrictions on property rights. Of course, property rights have already been restricted somewhat, as in cases of eminent domain. At least in the U.S., however, they still are often held more sacrosanct than civil rights. This means that the more extensive the land-use controls we propose, for example, the more powerful must be the philosophical arguments attempting to justify them.

The argument in this chapter is twofold. (1) Procedural justice (see note 23) requires, *in particular* cases, that we restrict property rights in natural resources (e.g., California agricultural land or Appalachian coal land). (2) Conditions imposed by Locke's political theory and by expanding population require, *in general*, that we restrict property rights in finite or nonrenewable natural resources such as land. If these arguments are correct, then we have a moral imperative to use land-use controls (such as taxation, planning, zoning, allocation of water rights, and acreage limitations) to restructure land ownership and land use in a far more radical way than has ever been undertaken in the past. Moreover, we need to be sensitive to the ways in which our philosophical assumptions about procedural justice (see note 23) contribute to our misuse of land and other resources.

Background for the First Argument: The California Farmer

Consider first the more particular argument, (1) that there are ethical grounds (the public interest), in specific cases, for restricting property rights in natural resources, especially among large land owners. As background for this argument, consider the role of the small farmer, first in California, then in Appalachia.

California agricultural land presents an important case study for land-use controls because owning even a small piece of it may confer a great deal of economic and political power. California is the largest producer of many specialized crops, and ownership of several hundred acres with rare soil and a specific climate can give one a great amount of power: for instance, in setting the price of broccoli, asparagus, or artichokes. For example, 88 percent of California macadamia nuts are grown in only one county (San Diego), 56 percent of California avocados are grown in only one county (San Diego), 54 percent of California asparagus is grown in only one county (San Joaquin), 50 percent of California brussels sprouts are grown in only one county (Santa Cruz), and so on.[1]

One of the most interesting things about California land is its concentration in the hands of a few; the top 25 private owners hold at least 58 percent of all land in the state.[2] A 1987 government study revealed that 67 percent of California farmland is held in farms that are larger than 2,000 acres each. Another report on land ownership in California revealed, moreover, that 45 corporate farms, representing less than one-tenth of 1 percent of the commercial farms in the state, control approximately 61 percent of all farmland in California.[3] Also, approximately 81 percent of all acres benefited by government-subsidized irrigation for California farmland are for farms larger than 200 acres, while approximately 19 percent of the acres irrigated are for farms of less than 200 acres.[4] Of course, it is true that homesteading and sales reduced California's land empires of the eighteenth and nineteenth centuries. Since at least 1958, however, land concentration has begun to enter another upswing. Increasingly, diversified and absentee landlords own most of California and most of the agricultural lands. According to a recent survey done by the U.S. Department of Agriculture and the Agricultural Extension Service of the University of California, the larger the number of acres held by owners, the more likely they are to be nonresidents of California.[5]

The same study reveals that this highly concentrated, absentee ownership of land has resulted in more concentrated and effective political and economic power and greater ability to oppose contrary interests than does widely diffused ownership. Large land owners, said the authors of the study, direct far more of their earnings toward political ends than do smaller owners, resulting in a situation in which the large holders' land-use decisions have a greater public impact and give them greater bargaining power with officials. Only a few large land owners are sufficient to unite to advocate particular legislation (e.g., subsidized water). As the authors of the study put it: "The few, who own more and more of California's land, control their own political and economic destinies; the many are more subject both in economics and politics to the automatic regulation of competition."[6] Such a situation suggests, therefore, that large and small land owners do not have equal opportunity in the marketplace, because of the distorting political and economic effects of large real-estate holdings. And if they do not have equal opportunity, then it is questionable whether the demands of procedural justice are met in situations where large, absentee landlords and small, resident farmers compete in and for the same agricultural and economic markets.[7]

Some of the practical reasons why small farmers cannot compete with the large absentee-controlled conglomerate farmers have to do with inflated land values in California. Such land values benefit the large holders (i.e., big growers, big speculators, and big investors) who drive up the land prices even further. Inflated land values, in turn, hurt the small farmers who attempt to do all or most of their own work.[8] If they are to compete with the larger holders, then they must continually purchase or rent more land. But inflated land values make purchase or rental even more difficult, and the pressure for expansion inflates real-estate values further. Moreover, because of higher land costs, the farmers receive proportionately smaller returns for their labor. Even government farm-income maintenance programs have not helped this problem but only aggravated it, since they have made the relatively richer farmers wealthier, at considerable expense to the public.[9]

Why do state and federal policies put the small farmer at a disadvantage relative to the large, absentee, conglomerate owners? Substantial capital gains, favorable depreciation rates on equipment and machinery, and tax losses written off against nonfarm income are major benefits that return sizeable tax savings to absentee investors and large corporations that engage in farm and nonfarm enterprise. The tax benefits permit the large, absentee owners of farmland to operate with a cost structure entirely different from that of the small owner-operator. The independent owner-operator of a small farm who earns his living entirely from farming may, of course, make some use of depreciation and capital-gains provisions but, unlike large corporate farmers, he is not likely to have taxable nonfarm income against which to offset farming losses. For this reason, a recent U.S. Secretary of the Treasury told the House Ways and Means Committee that current tax policies "create unfair competition for farmers who may be competitors and who do not pay costs and expenses of tax dollars, but who must make an economic profit in order to carry on their farming activities."[10]

Recent statistics on the difficulty that the small farmer has in competing with the large, absentee corporate farms bear out the preceding observation on the effects of current tax policies. Between 1954 and 1973, small farms (under ten acres) declined by 53 percent, whereas farms between 500 and 999 acres decreased by only 9 percent, and farms larger than 999 acres decreased by only 8 percent.[11] 1989 census data reveals equally grim statistics: Since 1982, the number of California farms under 180 acres increased by *less than* 1 percent, whereas the number of California farms larger than 180 acres grew by 4.8 percent.[12] Moreover, since 1982, family farms in California decreased by 0.8 percent, while the number of corporate farms increased by 10.7 percent.[13] Likewise, since 1982, the number of farms operated by blacks in California has decreased by 13 percent, and the number operated by native Americans has decreased by 4 percent.[14] Smaller farms and farms owned by members of minority groups thus have fared significantly worse than large farms and/or farms owned by whites. Part of the problem is that, because the profit margins in farming are so narrow, smaller farmers have a credit squeeze. They lose their credit base because they are losing their land and, therefore, their ability to secure a loan. Large, conglomerate, absentee-owned farms and small family farms operate in completely different capital situations. The local bank is usually the only source of funds for the small farmer, while the corporate farms enjoy a broader source of capital that includes issuing securities and bonds as well as obtaining loans.[15] Hence the small farmer is clearly no match for the huge corporate conglomerate. Because of both intentional and unintentional discrimination, he is unable to accumulate the resources of land and credit that would give him opportunities equal to those of the corporate farmer.

The California data suggest that land-use controls such as acreage limitations and increased taxation of larger corporate farms (to offset their existing tax advantage relative to the small farmer) might help to solve a number of problems. They might, for example, help to decrease the amount of prime farmland lost to other uses, since equalizing the tax advantage might enable small farmers to purchase more land. Land-use controls also might help equalize competition between the small farmer and larger corporate land owners. Other controls, aimed at reducing the likelihood of absentee landlords funneling all their profits out of the region, might insure that local residents received a portion of the value derived from the land in their area.[16] Which land-use controls are most appropriate for a given region, however, is not the subject of this chapter. Our concern here is more theoretical: first, how to determine when particular land-use controls are in the public interest, and second, how to justify philosophically any such controls and the restriction on property rights that they entail. Before examining a philosophical justification for more extensive land-use controls, let's examine another case study, this one concerning the Appalachian farmer.

Background for the First Argument: The Appalachian Farmer

Even though California is geographically, demographically, culturally, and economically quite different from Appalachia, the conditions affecting the small farmer in both regions are quite similar. California land has increased in value primarily because of the desirable climate, fertile soil, and federal subsidies (for example, for water). Appalachian land has increased in value primarily because of its vast coal reserves. The two areas are quite similar in that natural resources (agricultural land in California, coal land in Appalachia) have invited speculation and caused much of the heightened real-estate value. In both areas, most of the land is concentrated in the hands of a few absentee, corporate holders. In both places, this situation has resulted in unequal political and economic opportunity for everyone (except those involved with large, corporate agriculture) and in the subsequent decline of small farms.[17]

A major study of land ownership patterns and their impacts on the small farmer and on life in Appalachian communities was sponsored by the Appalachian Regional Commission and completed in 1981. It is one of the most comprehensive land-ownership studies ever completed in the United States. Presenting profiles of eighty counties in Alabama, Kentucky, North Carolina, Tennessee, Virginia, and West Virginia, the researchers (sponsored by the Appalachian Alliance, Appalachian State University, and Highlander Research Center) traveled 75,000 miles and gathered information on more than 20,000 acres. The conclusions of the study were that most of the region's woes—that is, the decline of the small farmer,[18] the housing shortage, and environmental degradation—were caused by concentrated, absentee ownership of most of the land. The researchers discovered that almost all owners of mineral rights pay less than a dollar an acre in property taxes, and three-fourths pay less than twenty-five cents. The researchers also determined that 53 percent of the total land surface in the eighty counties is controlled by only 1 percent of the total population—by absentee individuals and by corporations. Furthermore, they showed that about three-fourths of the surface acres surveyed are absentee-owned, and four-fifths of the mineral acres are owned by out-of-state or out-of-county owners. Of the top fifty private owners, fourty-six are corporations.[19]

Using more than one-hundred socioeconomic indicators, the land-use researchers drew some startling conclusions: (1) that the greater the concentration of land and mineral resources in the hands of a few, and the greater the absentee ownership, the less of the money generated by coal production remains in the counties giving up their resource wealth; (2) that little land is owned by, or accessible to, local people; and (3) that because of (1) and (2), many ills plague Appalachia: inadequate local tax revenues and services; the absence of economic development and diversified job opportunities; losses of agricultural lands; insufficient housing; a lack of locally controlled capital, and a rate of outmigration from Appalachia that is proportional both to corporate ownership and to concentration of land and mineral wealth in the hands of a few.[20] Fifty-eight percent of Kentucky farms, for example, are under 99 acres, and 62 percent of Tennessee farms are smaller than this size.[21] The sixty researchers (who worked for two years on the Appalachian study) argued that the concentrated absentee ownership of mineral-rich land was the cause of virtually all of the social and economic ills besetting Appalachia. Both in California and in Appalachia, researchers concluded that land reform or land-use controls were a necessary, although not a sufficient, condition for correcting socioeconomic ills and providing equal opportunity to the small farmer.[22]

Procedural Justice and End-State Principles

The researchers who drew these conclusions about the cause of the dispossession and subjection of both Californians and Appalachians admittedly based their causal inferences on mere correlations. Nevertheless, even though social scientists could spend years arguing about the methodology of precisely these causal inferences, they raise an interesting philosophical question: If one assumes that the researchers are *factually* correct (both about the causes of unequal opportunity for small farmers, whether in California or in Appalachia, and if one assumes that they are correct about at least one necessary remedy, land-use controls), then are there important *ethical* grounds for limiting the property rights of California's and Appalachia's corporate, absentee landlords? One might attempt to establish such grounds by some sort of argument based on principles of *equal distribution* aimed at land reform. One might build a case for the claim that, because most Appalachian land and most California land is concentrated in the hands of so few persons, the property rights of these large owners should be limited, so that the land could be distributed equally. Such an argument, however, has the shortcoming that it appeals to a socialistic, rather than capitalistic or libertarian, political philosophy. Apart from whether such an underlying philosophy can be justified in this case, land proposals based on socialistic presuppositions are unlikely to be accepted, much less adopted. This means that the potentially most successful sort of philosophical argument, whether for land reform or for land-use controls, is likely to be based on philosophical considerations equally acceptable to persons of a variety of political persuasions. The most compelling sort of argument would be one that begged no questions about the validity of a particular political philosophy.

The constant struggle among socialists, libertarians, and moderates indicates that people notoriously disagree on "end-state" principles about how to distribute societal goods. (See note 23.) Socialists typically prefer end-state principles based on equality, for example, and libertarians admit of no end-state distribution principles, but argue that everyone ought to be allowed to keep, free from redistribution, what he has legitimately acquired. In other words, libertarians and many moderates recognize no principles of "end-state" or distributive justice; the only principles they recognize are those based on *procedural justice*, on the legitimacy of the procedures by which lands and goods are acquired; procedural justice hence prohibits cheating or stealing so as to obtain goods, but it does not prohibit unequal distribution of any goods.[23] Since an argument based on procedural justice would likely be less controversial than one premised on end-state principles, we are left with a key question. Is there an argument for land-use controls based purely on the procedural justice of the land transactions by which the alleged property rights were acquired?

A Procedurally Based Argument for Extensive Land-Use Controls

Using the conclusions of the recent California and Appalachian land ownership studies, one could develop a procedurally based argument. A rough formulation of one such line of reasoning is as follows:

1. Concentrated, absentee ownership of Appalachian coal land and California agricultural land leads to concentrated political, legal, and economic power in the hands of the owners.[24]
2. Such concentrations of political, legal, and economic power limit the *voluntariness* of land transactions (as well as other transactions) between the large owners (holders of power) and others, especially small farmers.[25]
3. Apart from legitimate reparation or punishment, whatever social institutions limit the voluntariness of transactions (between large property owners and others) limit the "background/conditions" necessary for procedural justice and hence limit procedural justice.[26]
4. Whatever limits procedural justice should be avoided. (See note 23.)
5. Concentrated, absentee ownership of land ought to be avoided.

Of course the main stumbling blocks in this argument are premises 1 and 2. They are factual (and therefore contingent) propositions whose truth depends on the soundness of a number of related arguments, all made in the land-ownership studies. These premises appear plausible, not only because they are conclusions drawn by the authors of the recent California and Appalachian land-ownership research, but also because they rest on the intuitive soundness of several insights.

Why Land Transactions May Not Be Voluntary

One such insight is that monopolies tend to reduce the freedom of market transactions. The other insight is that property generates inequality, and inequality menaces liberty. Land economists, in particular, have explicitly noted how concentrations of rural land in the hands of a few owners leads to monopsony (owners' control of wages), the absence of developable land, the lack of a diversified economy, and the absence of local capital.[27] These factors (lack of a diversified economy, etc.) in turn limit the voluntariness of transactions between large land owners and others.[28] Because they limit voluntariness, they thereby limit certain "background conditions" (e.g., the existence of a *free*, competitive market) necessary for procedural justice. When transactions are not voluntary, then presumably they are made under duress, extorted consent, and the like—conditions that limit procedural justice because they limit fairness. For Nozick, Rawls, and virtually all moral thinkers, procedural justice requires fairness, and fairness requires background conditions such as the existence of voluntary transactions. Rights and obligations incurred in justice arise only if the transactions generating them are voluntary.[29]

Perhaps the main reason for claiming that transactions between large land owners and others in Appalachia might not be voluntary is that the small farmers and land owners often cannot do otherwise than to sell their land to the large absentee landlords and coal companies. A number of philosophers, including Aquinas, Hume, Bradley, Campbell, Melden, Ryle, Moore, Gustafson, and others maintain that a person's action cannot be called free or voluntary unless the person could have done otherwise.[30] If land concentration, monopsony, and the absence of local capital and developable land mean that small landowners are forced to sell their land, then obviously their selling is not voluntary in the sense that they could have done otherwise than they did. And if the selling is not voluntary, then its ethical defensibility is highly questionable, for the reasons sketched in the previous paragraph.

But what does it mean to say that the small land owners "could" not have done otherwise than they did? In order to understand the sense in which their actions were voluntary or not voluntary, we must analyze the concept "could." Such an analysis would be difficult to accomplish, however, because of the great ambiguity in the word "could" and because of its many uses.[31] This ambiguity is so great that, when Nowell-Smith, Austin, and others fought over the meaning of "could" and "voluntary," they decided that it was better not to try to unravel the "notoriously difficult" concepts.[32] Instead, they joined Ryle, Hart, and Honore in claiming that they could merely attempt to specify when an action was *not* voluntary, (that is, when it was accomplished under external coercion or when it was done by mistake, by accident, in the absence of muscular control, under duress, under pressure of legal and moral obligation, or even under the pressure of making a choice as the lesser of two evils).[33] In other words, Hart, Nowell-Smith, Austin, and others (following Aristotle) have claimed that words like "could have," "freedom," and "voluntary" are not positive but negative terms. Austin claimed that the negative use of words—such as "freedom"—predominates, and that to say that one behaved freely or voluntarily is primarily to say that one behaved in a way that was not nonvoluntary. Hart, for example, argued that although voluntary actions are a subset of intentional actions, there is not anything positive common to all voluntary actions and that is missing from all actions that are not voluntary. Instead, he and others claimed that words like "free," "unfree," "voluntary," and "involuntary" are defeasible concepts, concepts not definable in terms of necessary and sufficient conditions or by means of any criteria, but understandable only in terms of the various particular ways in which an action may be unfree or not voluntary (e.g., by accident or duress). And admittedly, the ways in which an act may be rendered not voluntary or unfree are numerous; hence there is no general criterion for when an action is voluntary or not voluntary, other than to say that when persons act voluntarily, they could have done otherwise.[34]

Note, however, that when we claim that persons did not act voluntarily, meaning that they "could not have done otherwise," we really mean that persons "could not be *expected* to have done otherwise." This is because even persons ordered to perform an action under threat (by someone holding a gun on them, for example) "could have done otherwise" than what the gunman ordered. The persons could have chosen death rather than to perform the action. Hence "could not have done otherwise" must mean "could not be expected to have done otherwise."[35] Also, when we ask whether persons "could not be expected to have done otherwise," we do not typically mean, in a sense of exclusive disjunction, whether they could or could not be expected to have done otherwise. Rather, we typically mean to inquire into the degree to which the persons could have done otherwise. The issue is not simply either/or. The issue is, *ceteris paribus*, the more duress or external coercion imposed on persons to perform an action, the less the persons could be expected not to perform it, and hence the less voluntary the action.[36]

Using the case of the small California or Appalachian farmer, the argument has been that they could not be expected to do otherwise than to sell their land, that factors such as monopsony and the absence of local capital have coerced the small farmers to such a degree that their land transactions likely are voluntary only in some minimal sense. As was already explained, what makes such an argument problematic is that there are no necessary and sufficient conditions rendering an act voluntary or involuntary. Hence one can only point to factors such as the lack of a diversified economy in order to show how they render small farmers incapable of not selling their land.

In arguing that the decisions of many small farmers to sell their lands are not voluntary, we are relying in part on moral philosopher Alan Gewirth's analysis of voluntary action. Gewirth argues that voluntary action is uncoerced and unforced, and that nonvoluntary or coerced action has at least three characteristics; it is compulsory, undesirable, and the result of threat. As Gewirth points out, a choice is compulsory if it is between undesirable alternatives, none of which persons would choose if they were totally free. The choices of many Appalachian land owners are surely compulsory in the sense that they likely do not wish to choose either of the main options open to them: either to lose their small farms or to live on the brink of starvation. Likewise the main options open to them are undesirable. What decisions they make, because of the power of monopsony, the lack of local capital, and the absence of developable land, appear to be made in order to avoid a threat of serious harm. Hence Gewirth would probably say that such Appalachians' choices probably were "irreducibly involuntary," like choices between taking a pay cut or being fired, when jobs are scarce.[37] Moreover, as Gewirth notes, just because "the normal or natural or expected course of events" is that many people face just such choices (e.g., between taking a pay cut or being fired), does not mean that their choices are voluntary, just because their incidence is so great. "Surely the forcedness of choice is not removed when these features [of compulsion, undesirability, and threat] are a regular part of someone's life or of the institutional structure of a society. . . . [For example,] when industrial workers function as cogs in vast machines and as dominated by huge impersonal corporations, their choices to work under such conditions might be held to be forced by the threat of unemployment and the unavailability of alternative conditions."[38] Likewise, we have argued that some Appalachians' choices are forced. Of course, the obvious objection to the claim that a great many choices made in contemporary industrial-agricultural society are forced or not voluntary is that such a claim makes the conditions of morality (e.g., voluntariness, irrelevant and unrealistic), since virtually all choices may be alleged to be nonvoluntary in the sense discussed. This objection will not hold, however, and for two reasons.

First, a number of choices in contemporary society are not made in the context of serious threats to well-being, at least in the sense that a number of persons are well off and financially secure. Obviously they do not face as many undesirable threats as persons who are less financially secure and hence more likely to be coerced in their decision making by external factors. Second, many of the alternatives persons face in their choices are not all undesirable. To say that all choices were undesirable for all persons, as in the case of the Appalachian deciding whether to sell his land, would be to presuppose a great exaggeration of human desire. Such exaggerated desires are probably more characteristic of Plato's insatiable tyrant and of Freud's id than they are of many human beings. Normal human beings have more modest desires and hence often have choices among several desirable alternatives, provided that they (the persons choosing) are not severely constrained by factors such as illness and poverty.[39] But if so, then it is plausible to claim that the land transactions of many small Appalachian farmers, and others like them, are likely not voluntary.

It is not difficult to show that Appalachia, for example, provides a clear instance of how concentrated property holdings limit the voluntariness and hence the fairness and procedural justice of many land and other transactions. Concentrated property holdings cause the choices of those "less propertied" to be made under compulsion, among undesirable alternatives, and under threat. To see this, consider how background conditions very likely affected historical land ownership patterns. In the early days of this country, in New England, land was divided fairly evenly among the many; in the South, mostly because of large royal grants, it was concentrated in the hand of the few. As a consequence, New England politics revolved around such institutions as the town meeting, while all aspects of Southern society and politics were dominated by the landed gentry. This means that, in Appalachia, where most of the land was and is held by only a few individuals, their speculation had the effect of driving up land prices and impeding settlement by poor Americans.[40] As a consequence, because there is little industry in Appalachia and because the population is rural-agricultural, the small farmer has rarely been able to compete fairly with the large landowner, who very likely owns the community bank and the general store and "noncoercively" controls the whole community. Now suppose a mining company, owned by a multinational corporation, makes a contract with a small farmer to purchase title to this land. Granted, the farmer may not be coerced or defrauded; he may "voluntarily" sell his property. Yet, consider the following factors: he has been chronically impoverished, perhaps poorly educated, and (in part because of tax laws) faces the impossibility of competing with the large farmer. He has no capital investment for keeping his land and farming or mining it himself, and there are no other (i.e., nonagricultural, nonmining) jobs available. Surely, he is not in an equal bargaining position with the large absentee landlord, and surely he is not wholly *voluntarily* selling his land.[41]

Although his contract with the landlord may be legal, nevertheless it may not be completely ethically justifiable. This is because (perhaps through no fault of the landlord) necessary background conditions (e.g., the possibility of voluntary transactions between the small farmer and the large land owner, or the existence of a free, open market) for the exercise of procedural justice have not been met. Justice cannot be met if allegedly voluntary decisions or transactions are coerced or forced. Just transactions presuppose just background conditions. But if the necessary conditions for procedural justice are unlikely to be met, especially in cases such as those described in California and in Appalachia, then there may well be ethical grounds for additional limitations on the property rights of large, absentee landlords (like those in California and Appalachia). If their property rights were limited, then perhaps they would be less likely to hold coercive power over typical market transactions. And if so, then decision making and land sales might take place in a situation providing more background conditions for the exercise of procedural justice.

Suggestions for Limiting Property Rights

But if there are ethical grounds for additional limitations on the property rights of large, absentee landlords, then the obvious issue is what sorts of limitations ought to be pursued. One reasonable position would be to argue for the least restrictions necessary in order to meet minimum requirements regarding background conditions for procedural justice. If certain minor restrictions were successful in meeting these minimum requirements, then greater limitations need not be considered. If they were not successful, then greater restrictions might need to be discussed. We shall not take the time to argue here for which limitations are likely to meet these minimum conditions. However, we believe that it is not difficult to show that certain controls on the *right to use* one's property and specific limitations on the *right to income* from it would counteract most ill effects of concentrated ownership.[42] One might limit the right to use agricultural land or coal property, for example, by requiring that for every 1,000 acres held by a large farmer, he would have to help create "x" number of jobs in nonagricultural or nonmining industries in that county. Such a land-use control might lead to a number of benefits affecting background conditions. It might help to diversify either the agricultural or coal economy (rendering it less susceptible to booms or busts), create more job alternatives, and provide residents with greater freedom not to sell their lands. Likewise, one might limit the right to income from one's property, for example, by requiring that concentrated land holdings be heavily taxed or that "x" percent of a large corporation's income from mining or agriculture in a given county be reinvested in that county. Such a limit on property rights would clearly help economic diversification and job opportunities. As a consequence, it would enhance the voluntariness with which small farmers and large landlords made transactions.

Another relatively minor version of land-use controls, certain to have desirable effects in terms of procedural justice, would be to place acreage limitations on landholders. Just as the U.S. Preemption Act of 1841 and the U.S. Homestead Act of 1862 limited ownership by a single person to 160 acres, so also there could be similar restrictions on California agricultural land or Appalachian coal land. Minnesota, North Dakota, South Dakota, and Kansas already have acreage limitations on the amount of farmland that can be held by corporations.[43] Such acreage limitations, as well as taxation or restriction of the right to income, constitute powerful vehicles for avoiding land concentrations.[44] Admittedly, however, these alone are not necessarily *sufficient* to address all the land-related problems associated with maintaining the public interest.[45]

Basically, the argument to limit property rights (through acreage limitations, restricted right to income, or restricted right to use, requires us to accept the premise that we ought to avoid certain societal institutions to the extent that they preclude the existence of important "background conditions" (such as a free, competitive market) necessary for procedural justice. The key insight on which this argument rests is fundamentally Rawlsian: "Only against the background of a just basic structure. . . . . and a just arrangement of economic and social institutions, can one say that the requisite just procedure exists."[46] If one accepts this argument for limiting property rights, then one has admitted that, *in some instances*, the actual operation of the market runs afoul of the Lockean proviso that the condition of others not be worsened by our appropriation and use of property. Nevertheless, in theory at least, all market proponents desire just background conditions, such as a free and competitive market, because they are essential to the smooth and continuing function of the market. Hence, our argument is not against the market but against improper operation of it. (Note also that this argument has only attempted to establish that in some instances, like Appalachia, property rights in land produce poverty and social instability. Hence the argument is that, in these particular cases, property rights ought to be limited. It would be far more difficult to make the argument that, *in all cases*, property rights in natural resources limit democracy, produce poverty and social instability, etc. This chapter has not attempted to argue for the larger claim.) But if the operation of the market, at least in Appalachia and in California, runs afoul of the Lockean proviso then, on their own terms, even libertarians would be required to accept limitations of the property rights whose exercise is responsible for violation of the Lockean proviso. (See chapter 4 for discussion of Locke.[47]) Given this argument, the burden of proof is on the proponent of unrestricted property rights (e.g., a libertarian, such as Harvard philosopher Robert Nozick). Given this argument, the consistent Nozickian must either accept the limitation of property rights demanded by the argument, or show where both the argument and the two land studies went wrong.

Objections to the Argument

In response to this procedurally based argument for land-use controls (or even land reform), a number of objections can be made. One of the most likely criticisms comes from the camp of libertarian philosophers like Nozick. They might claim that the argument rests on end-state principles (see note 15) that are socialistic, since its net *effect* would be the same as an end-state argument (that is, redistributing some advantages currently held by absentee landlords with large holdings).[48] Such a counter does not work, however, and for several reasons. For one thing, it erroneously assumes that two principles are the same if following them leads to the same actions or events. However, principles are obviously specified by criteria other than actions to which following them might lead.[49] Otherwise, it would make no sense to speak of doing the right thing for the wrong reasons.

Further evidence that this argument for land-use controls does not rely on socialistic justification or on end-state principles is that it specifies no *particular* distribution of land as desirable. As Scanlon would probably agree, it does not specify that end-state principles, such as equality or need, be followed, but only that land not be so concentrated in the hands of a few owners that this concentration itself limits the voluntariness of transactions.[50] Moreover, on Nozick's criteria,[51] this argument does not rely on any end-state principles. This is because "it focuses on a particular way that appropriative actions affect others, and not on the structure of the situation that results."[52] Admittedly, in not having some specific end-state principles to guide the limitations on property rights for which we have argued, we have no clear criterion for when social processes are truly voluntary and for when the background conditions for procedural justice have been met. We can show, however, that this flaw is neither devastating nor unique to this proposal. In fact, a similar problem faces someone who argues for reparation for blacks who have been victimized by illegal discrimination. Just as there is no clear criterion for when social processes are truly nonracist, likewise there is no criterion for when social processes are voluntary or when background conditions for procedural justice are met. In both cases, however, it is possible to make a reasonable judgment that certain social transactions are, for example, blatantly racist or blatantly unfree, and that they require, respectively, reparation or limits on property rights.

Another likely objection to these arguments for extensive land-use controls is that, as Nozick puts it, "no one has a right to something (e.g., background conditions for procedural justice) whose realization requires certain uses of things (property) and activities that other people have rights and entitlements over."[53] This objection, however, begs the relevant question, namely, whether people do *continue* to have rights over things when their exercise of them limits the autonomy or equal opportunity of someone else. Still another objection to this argument for land-use controls might be along the lines of a Nozickian claim that, so long as the absentee landlords had a *right* to act as they did, in obtaining concentrations of property, then their actions cannot be said to have made either Californians' or Appalachians' actions nonvoluntary. The problem with this objection, however, is that it appeals to Nozick's definition of property rights, which he interprets as near absolute, without showing precisely why rights ought not to be limited in order to provide background conditions for justice. This question cannot be met simply by reasserting the very property rights in question.[54]

A Second Argument for Limiting Property Rights in Resources

Obviously, a great many other objections could be made to the first, particular argument for land-use controls in Appalachia and in California. Likewise, a great many other questions could be raised concerning various theories of property rights and procedural justice. Rather than deal with them here, let us turn now to a second, and more general, argument for limiting property rights, especially property rights in natural resources. Recall that the first argument (above) presupposed that it was possible to have property rights in natural resources. The second argument calls into question this very presupposition.

There are at least two general, and different, grounds for doubting the claim that one can hold property rights in natural resources that are as extensive as other property rights. First, it is not clear that one can have full property rights in anything that was not created by his labor, and natural resources are not created primarily by human labor. As numerous Lockean commentators have pointed out, it is not clear that mixing one's labor with something gives one full property rights over it, rather than merely property rights over that part or aspect of the thing created by his labor. This is because one could conceivably be said to have property rights only to the *value added* to the property, since one did not generate, by his labor, the initial value in the property. This point is illustrated aptly by Robert Nozick who points out that, if I pour my can of tomato juice (labor) in the ocean and mix it around, then I don't thereby gain property rights to the ocean. Rather, I simply lose my tomato juice (labor). Proudhon makes a related point: if society didn't ask a person to labor on land, then why should society repay the person with property rights in the land?[55] But if one only has rights to the value added to property by his labor, then it is highly questionable whether any alleged owners of natural resources have full property rights to the resources. Second, it is not clear that property rights to land and other natural resources could be justified if their implementation involves (or renders highly probable) the exhaustion of a significant resource (e.g., coal, by a subset of the total population). To see why this is so, recall that Locke's theory is generally acknowledged to be the foundation of property rights. Recall also that Locke stipulates that one may own or appropriate property only so long as "as much and as good" is left for others. In other words, one may not take or retain property, so long as one's doing so is a loss to others. (See the discussion of Locke in chapter 4 for further details.)[56]

But consider the situations in which one's taking or keeping property is a loss to others. As applied to land and finite resources, Locke's proviso (as much and as good be left for others) seems to require that one's appropriation of property not put others at a competitive disadvantage. Whenever acquisition of property takes away another's competitive parity, or causes another's competitive situation to deteriorate, then one has indeed taken away a "good" from his neighbor. This "taking," it could be argued, would likely constitute (a) a loss to those left out; (b) interference with their liberty, or (c) production of a net disutility.[57] Hence the extent to which one has full property rights to finite natural resources, especially in a competitive situation and especially as population and demand for such resources increases, appears to be quite limited.

Objections to the Second Argument

The second (general) argument claims that property rights in finite natural resources like land ought to be limited, because one's labor does not create their value and because appropriating them puts others at a competitive disadvantage. As such, this argument is open to several objections. Among the more important of these objections are that (1) even though one's labor does not create the value in natural resources, there are utilitarian grounds for property rights in natural resources; and (2) there is no reason why the industrious should not gain competitive advantages over the nonindustrious. Let's consider each of these objections. Robert Nozick formulates one of the best versions of objection (1). Nozick admits that there are grounds for denying property rights in natural objects, but then argues that "social considerations" favor private property in resources. Some of these social considerations (which he alleges outweigh the failure to rationally justify property rights in natural objects) include the claim that private property increases the social product by putting the means of production in the hands of those who can use them most efficiently (profitably). Proponents of this view argue that allowing property rights in natural resources encourages experimentation, since only one person (property owner) has to decide to try out a new idea. They say that private property enables people to choose the risks they wish to bear, and that private property protects future persons by leading some to hold back resources from current consumption for future markets.[58] The main thrust of Nozick's objection is that although one cannot rationally justify property rights in natural resources, one can do so on utilitarian grounds. This means that if property rights do not contribute to the alleged benefits he claims, then he has no justification for them. Therefore, a crucial question besetting his objection is whether his factual assumption about the benefits (derived from property in natural resources) is correct. There are several reasons to believe that it is not.

First, it is not obvious that private property in resources encourages experimentation with them. If people are eager to use resources profitably and efficiently, as he claims, then this desire seems to run at odds with any tendency to experiment. People are unlikely to experiment with valuable resources if their doing so risks the loss of such resources. Second, it is not obvious, factually, that private property protects future generations by leading some persons to hold back resources from current consumption for future markets. For one thing, as numerous studies have documented, the pervasive tendency is to use resources at an exponential rate; the current market provides little evidence that people are "holding back" resources for the future.[59] For example, both the 1974 MIT study, *The Limits to Growth*, as well as its 1992 successor, *Beyond the Limits*, conclude that the world usage rate of every natural resource, including land, is growing exponentially, in part because technologies and markets "overshoot."[60] Moreover, even if resources are occasionally "held back" (in order to gain a higher profit), it would be difficult to show that such a "holding back" actually benefited future generations, as Nozick claims. Owners of resources would appear to hold them back within their lifetime or that of their children. It seems unlikely that a person would hold back resources so that their future owner, many generations later, could realize a profit. Such a situation would contradict economists' notions of the supremacy of the net present value. It would also presuppose an altruism not much in evidence in a profit-oriented market focused on short-term gains.

Apart from whether Nozick's arguments for benefits derived from private property in natural resources are factually correct, there are reasons for suspecting that they are ethically and logically misguided. One alleged reason for property rights in natural resources, says Nozick, is that resources are put in the hands of those who can use them most efficiently. This reason is ethically suspect because it assumes that natural (therefore common) resources can be employed for private gain, even though private labor did not create them. It assumes that resources ought to be placed in the hands of economically efficient users rather than in the hands of all persons, including future generations. It assumes that economic efficiency outweighs con-

siderations of equality and rights of future generations. Most importantly, all these ethical assumptions lead Nozick to beg the very question at issue: that there ought to be property rights in natural resources.
Only if one makes this assumption (that there ought to be property
rights in natural resources) do his other claims about maximizing
economic efficiency make any sense. It makes no sense to say that a
private individual ought to be allowed to maximize the economic
efficiency of something unless he antecedently has property rights
over the "something." Nozick's arguments for property rights in natural resources are also suspect on ethical grounds because he assumes
that risk taking and experimentation with natural resources, at the
decision of only one person, the owner, is desirable. If land is indeed
a common resource, then it is questionable why any single person
could be said to have the right to risk it and experiment with it. Again,
Nozick's alleged arguments beg the very question (that there ought to
be private property in natural resources like land) he addresses. Only
if one presupposes, ahead of time, that there are property rights in
natural resources does it make any sense to claim that an owner could
experiment or take risks with those resources.

What of the second objection to the claim that one cannot have
full property rights to finite natural resources, since "as much and as
good" would not be left for others? This objection is that there is no
reason why the industrious should not gain competitive advantages
over the nonindustrious. After all, Locke himself remarks that God
gave the earth "to the use of the industrious and rational."[61] The main
flaw in this objection is that it assumes that according property rights
in resources gives advantages to the industrious over the
nonindustrious. This is false in many cases. If an industrious person
obtains property in natural resources because of his hard work, intelligence, and ambition, it is not clear that he has won something "away
from" the lazy, unintelligent, and unambitious. In large part, he has
won something away from future generations, most of whom have not
even been born yet. And many of them are likely to be hard working,
intelligent, and ambitious. Moreover, even if one concedes (erroneously) that allowing property rights in natural resources allows the
industrious to be rewarded over and above the nonindustrious, there
remains a major ethical problem. Why should the aggressive inherit
the earth (as they have)? Why should the natural advantage of intelligence, whether its origin is genetic or environmental, allow one to
receive greater benefits than those who, through no fault of their own,
did not also receive such natural endowments? Moreover, as Becker
points out, the Social Darwinist rationale for the rights of the strong
to the advantages conferred by property reduces to an absurdity. To

the extent that property rights protect possession and inheritance, the strong do not need them. Such rights protect the weak against the strong.[62] But if so, then there are no clear grounds for arguing that certain persons have full rights to property in natural resources.

Conclusion

If the preceding analysis, despite its admitted incompleteness, is largely correct, then there are strong grounds for further consideration of two conclusions, one particular and one general. *In particular*, in areas such as Appalachia and California that are prone to monopolistic control of land, procedural justice suggests that property rights to finite natural resources ought to be limited. *In general*, because one's labor does not create most of the value in natural resources and because appropriating them puts others at a competitive disadvantage, there are ethical grounds for severe limitations on property rights in finite natural resources.

But if there are rational grounds for limiting property rights in finite, natural resources such as land, what land-use controls might be appropriate? As was already mentioned in connection with the particular argument concerning areas such as Appalachia and California, such controls might include acreage limitations, restrictions on the right to use land when certain uses obstruct operation of a free and competitive market, and heavy taxation of owners with large holdings, so as to offset the tax breaks they have relative to persons such as small farmers. In response to the general argument, ownership of vital, finite, natural resources such as land may have to be restricted to the rights of income, transfer, and limited transmissibility. Rights to management, use, and actual possession might have to remain under full public control.[63] In the last two chapters of this volume, we shall outline some of the ways to implement our conclusions regarding the desirability of land-use controls. Before doing so, however, we need to examine some of the political and scientific constraints on such controls. Apart from being philosophically justified (see chapters 4 through 6), land-use controls must also be politically realizable. The next chapter analyses the extent to which controls are politically feasible, as well as the obstacles to their realization.

7

Limits to Policy: Problems of Consensus

Lynton Keith Caldwell

This chapter employs two different approaches to the relationship between land and the law and the limits to policy for land use in the United States. The first approach considers ways to prevent the harmful exercise of alleged rights in land and looks at the basis of these "rights" in traditional American social attitudes and assumptions—now made questionable by scientific knowledge and changing concepts of public interest. The second concerns the feasibility of general laws to reflect changing perceptions of rights over land through declarations of national policy implemented through specific procedural requirements. Each approach reveals difficulties for any effort to achieve a legally defined set of principles that would reinforce a basic stewardship ethic for the land without unduly burdening the benefits of ownership. Rather than omit relevant aspects of the problems of consensus, this chapter will refer back or reintroduce issues discussed in previous chapters of this book.

The United States presents a strongly marked, although not unique, example of the persistence of claims for rights of land owners as against (1) rights asserted on behalf of the society generally, (2) rights attributed to nature, or (3) rights reserved for future generations. Attempts to enact comprehensive national land use legislation in the United States have not succeeded. Even with presidential and substantial congressional support, at least three successive tries were unable to obtain adoption of the proposed National Land Use Policy Act of 1970 and its subsequent 1973 modifications.

At the state government level, however, land-use legislation with varying degrees of coverage has been enacted. Except where prohibited by some specific constitutional provision, the states have residual (i.e., police) powers to regulate uses of the land.[1] State policy toward land has varied greatly and without any well-defined pattern. Yet some states have experimented with various devices for land-use control, establishing new legal norms where the United States government has been unable to move. These states are much in the minority, but may be vanguards of changes yet to come. Particular aspects of land use are directly or indirectly controlled in more states, as, for example, restrictive protection of the coastal zone, conservation of groundwater, or maintenance of forest preserves.

Why, when government today intervenes extensively in a wide range of property uses (for example, in relation to intangible negotiable securities), does the prospect of government controls over land arouse an inordinate degree of opposition—often expressed with fervent emotion? For 300 years land ownership in the United States has been strongly linked in the popular culture with individual personal freedom—especially freedom from the exactions of government. Land was historically a way to wealth, and speculation in land became a part of the American way of life from its very beginning. There has probably been no other aspect of property ownership in which "what's mine and what's yours" has been more jealously guarded, and in which tradition-sanctioned beliefs have had a more restrictive bearing upon public policy. While there are more highly sensitive areas of beliefs and values in which governmental intrusion is resisted, there are none in which ingrained popular attitudes have more persistently influenced and limited public law and policy.

Even today, when most Americans are no longer land owners, there is a widely shared bias against governmental guidance of basic land use decisions. We do not see mass rallies or street demonstrations demanding general land use standards: As John Ise explained, as a result of their historical conditioning:

> Americans are land value animals. For three hundred years they have been moving westward seeking titles to land they hoped would rise in value; for three hundred years they have been following the lure of unearned increment, the beacon light of "something for nothing," boasting, bragging, puffing, whoopin' 'er up for the home town and the home state, hoping to sell real estate at an advance.[2]

Even in urban America large numbers of people who own no land still psychologically wear the coonskin caps of land-hungry pioneers and the rose-tinted glasses of speculators. Hardly a mindset receptive to ecologically rational land-use policy.

This strong commitment of rights to private ownership in land and especially the right to profit from that ownership may explain why land-use policy has lagged behind the other areas of environmental reform which have won wider acceptance. But unlike air, water, and most wildlife, land can be owned and may be used as a source of security or profit. Even in an industrial economy, ownership of land still confers economic and political power. Although a large number of the great fortunes in the United States were won in oil, steel, timber, or railways, they were and many still are sustained and enlarged through control over real estate.

Land law has been structured primarily to protect the established economic rights of private owners. Today, changes in popular values—and advances in scientific information regarding the properties of soils and the interrelations of land with the rest of the ecological environment—have raised a set of policy considerations against assumptions that have been dominant since the eighteenth century. The old values continue to prevail, but are challenged by new values, asserted in the public interest and seeking to modify or reinterpret the rights of ownership that presently limit the scope of land-use policy.

Defining Rights to the Land

Land law, like all other legislation, is culturally derived and is reflective of politically dominant social attitudes and conventions. When social attitudes change to form an altered critical mass of activated public opinion, the law will follow even though belatedly. Once adopted, law often affects attitudes—more often behaviors. Enacted legislation rarely represents a unanimity of public opinion, but if it persists it often attains general acquiescence and becomes the norm. If one believes that social attitudes and information regarding land use today are changing more rapidly than the law, there is justification for considering what the law should be, although practicing lawyers are appropriately concerned with the present state of the law in relation to established rights and equities.

The key to deciphering the intended meaning of the law may be found in the assumptions underlying its substance and application. These assumptions are more often tacit than explicit. Rights are more freely asserted than are defended by recourse to their presumed basis in history and philosophy. Concepts of natural rights to possess and use land as property are widely accepted as "given," without knowledge or curiosity regarding the historical origins of the alleged rights. As related in Chapter 5 it is the ownership of these privately held rights rather than of the land itself that the law really protects, except where a specific public consideration is judged to be superior.

But rights of use, abstractly defined in absence of knowledge or regard for the consequences of particular uses, may lead to environmentally and socially destructive results. Where, as in the United States, rights to land have been defined essentially as rights to property, the legal responsibilities of owners and users have to a large extent conformed to rights as defined in relation to property generally. These rights concern possession, occupancy, transfer of title, obligations to public authorities and to other land owners on specific issues such as taxation, trespass, fencing, drainage, hunting, liabilities, subdividing, and rights of government to take land for public purposes. These and other rights and obligations are defined by custom, statute, and adjudication, consistent with historical cultural norms, and these norms have imposed no general obligation to safeguard the quality of the land or its renewability.

The law characteristically lags behind changing social norms, except in those circumstances where the judicial interpreters of the law assume the role of legislators and reformers. But courts rarely rule in anticipation of changing social norms without at least an influential nucleus of supporting public opinion (as in civil rights cases). Under circumstances of divided or apparently transitional public sentiment, the way in which controversial issues are defined, and the philosophic references of the judges affect judicial behavior.[3] Many scientific and particularly ecological concepts gaining acceptance in modern society are judicially novel and involve modes of analysis and reasoning unfamiliar to many judges and lawyers. Law is thus conservative; yet ultimately it may be subject to change through judicial interpretation if public opinion changes, especially that opinion to which judges listen. In brief, laws regarding land use assume a set of rights that embody past circumstances and inherited values. Stewardship, or socially and ecologically responsible custody of the land, has been handicapped because of the way in which rights to use the land have been defined. If the law is to reinforce the concept and practice of stewardship, prevailing popular and judicial assumptions regarding rights to land use will require modification.

Relationship of Ownership to Stewardship

A basic problem for land-use policy, as noted in Chapter 5, is determination of the rights of the land owner versus the "rights" (i.e., long-term interests) of society. These rights need not conflict but often do. To an individual, the benefits of ownership—especially economic benefits—are limited, except through a legacy to posterity, to the owner's lifetime. The interests of society, however, are logically extensible into an indefinite future. As more is known about the long-term relationships between the environmental and economic importance of the land in the life-support base for society, public interest in land use increases quite apart from who owns it. Legitimacy of rights asserted by owners is increasingly tested by the effect of those rights on present and continuing social interests.

State and national legislation to prevent or to correct misuse of land has been present for many years, but with only modest success. There are often divided opinions over what, in a particular instance, is misuse. Political obstruction of direct land use controls has inspired alternative, often indirect, strategies —often to save the land through saving something on or associated with it (e.g., an endangered species, an historic site, etc.). Such alternatives to land-use policy are less often perceived as subversive of owners' rights because those strategies attempt to avoid direct challenge of those rights and are not described as land-use control measures.

Success in legal protection for land as a resource has been attained primarily under either of two circumstances, neither of which challenges directly the in-principle right to private ownership. In the first circumstance, land-use controls as a means to limit, to plan, or to direct growth have been sought in various communities, but with mixed success and failure. Control of land use through planning is exceptional among the states—Vermont being an early example.[4] Only in a few states, and in some relatively small homogenous communities, have the costs and burdens of laissez-faire land use prompted governing bodies to adopt unconventional land use policies by law. And where there has been near consensus to limit growth, as in communities such as Petaluma, California, Boca Raton, Florida, or Ramapo, New York, external interests (e.g., developers, building contractors, and civil rights groups) have challenged land-use controls that limit growth or movement of people as unconstitutional and have won some victories in the courts.[5]

Attempts to control land use through zoning encounter a predisposition of the courts to declare against any measure that suggests exclusionary intent.[6] State courts, for example in Pennsylvania, have held that local governments may not obstruct the natural flow of population or diminish the residential opportunities of low-income groups.[7] Limitations or restrictions on growth because communities have been unwilling or unable to extend sewer or water systems, as in Ramapo, New York, are defensible in the courts if it can be shown that no covert attempt to limit growth is intended.[8] The position taken by courts on limitations to growth and the right of communities to shape their futures is essentially ideological and broadly equalitarian. These positions restricting the rights of communities on behalf of rights of individuals and "minorities" reflect a late twentieth-century political liberalism rather than jurisprudential reasoning. For so long as "growth" is the holy grail of the American civic religion, one may expect the courts to find implied principles for the defense of growth in an "explication de texte" interpretation of the Constitution.

In the second instance, land and its resources are controlled through purchase or gift for preservation in a natural or unaltered state. Rights to certain uses of land may be limited through purchase of scenic or conservation easements or through purchase or trade of development rights. In all of these cases the principle of private ownership is respected. The methods of acquisition may not differ from land transactions for commercial or governmental purposes. But the land thereafter is no longer treated merely as a commodity. It becomes, in designated respects, a public asset or trust for cultural, scientific, economic, or historical purposes, and its tenants are bound by judicially enforceable deed restrictions in its custody and management. Ownership thus implies stewardship, utilizing but not challenging conventional legalities.

Land-use control through purchase has been undertaken in the United States by a diversity of organizations for the preservation of natural and historic sites, monuments and buildings, and in special cases to protect agricultural land. A notable example through purchase (or gift) is provided by The Nature Conservancy, which has acquired more than two million acres for scientific, natural history, and educational purposes.[9] The Nature Conservancy (TNC) in the United States, unlike the Nature Conservancy in the United Kingdom, is a nongovernmental membership organization that resembles charitable trusts for conservation, historic preservation, and nature protection.[10] Land law in most of the United States was based on British precedent, and it is thus not exceptional that control of land use through purchase should have followed the pattern established in Britain in 1907 by the National Trust.

The purchase of special development rights, as noted, is another way of controlling land use through conventional noncoercive means that do not transgress conventional values.[11] This device is particularly useful for preserving large areas of open space—farmland—for example. It will only work, however, if assessed valuation of the land for taxation is reduced to reflect diminished market value. Deed restrictions on use may also be attached to particular parcels of land, but the ability of these legal devices to provide continuing control over uses can be determined only on a case-by-case basis. American lawyers can be very artful in finding ways to break deed restrictions. In matters of land use, conventional mores, reinforced by political influence, tend ultimately to prevail over legal proscriptions.

For a great part of privately owned land, few of the aforementioned options, even when technically available, may be feasible ways to implement general land use policy. They work only with willing sellers; owners intent upon exploitive uses or garnering the unearned increment of rising land values are unlikely to sell their commercial advantages for prevailing prices. There are, moreover, many ways of challenging land-use restrictions, and if restrictions are not firm there is no guarantee that changes in owners or judicial interpretation may not open the way to altered uses. The Nature Conservancy requires reverter clauses in deeds to land that it sells or transfers in cases where protection of scientific or ecologic value is sought. Failure of a new owner to honor the deed restrictions may open the way to legal action for reversion of the property to its former owner. But the former owner may no longer be present or may be unwilling to take legal action, especially if the new owner is government.

Public ownership does not guarantee protective custody. The exercise of stewardship may be frustrated, as in lands owned by the federal government for which Congress neglects to provide funds for protection. Misuse is often difficult to challenge where government is legally responsible (e.g., as with grazing permits on public land), and even more so when private owners take the position that "my land is mine to use as I please as long as I do not create a public nuisance." But "nuisances" are judicially definable and a "nuisance" to one owner may be a "right" to another. For example, the activities of a very unconventional religious colony just outside the north boundary of the Yellowstone National Park has been widely viewed as harmful to the park and to the values it has been intended to protect. Nevertheless the U.S. government is reluctant to intervene or to buy out the colony. Similarly, Congress has been generally unwilling to regulate or buyout inholders in the national parks and forests regardless of the problems that they create.

Inholders in national parks, forests, and nature preserves pose chronic problems for land managers. Land owners in or adjacent to national parks, for example, have often used their strategic locations to demand services from the government and to try to use the adjoining public land for private business purposes. These inholders are well organized in a national association and their vigorous opposition to any lessening of their privileges or to forced sale to the government has caused Congress and the state legislators to be reluctant to buy them out.

Ambiguity pervades the law of land use and few generalizations will stand without qualification. For example, to attempt to control or direct the land use practices of private property owners is to risk an encounter with the "taking" clause of the U.S. Constitution, previously considered in chapter 5. Here the issue is not one of ownership but of consensus. Unless a compelling public necessity can be shown, restrictions on uses of land that work a demonstrable economic disadvantage on the owner may be found by courts to constitute a "taking." But what constitutes a public necessity, and how compelling must it be? Opinions differ. There is probably no matter of land policy in the United States on which there is less consensus than on the justification and compensation for "takings." Restrictions on uses of land that work a demonstrable economic disadvantage on the owner may be found by courts to constitute a "taking" regardless of ecological or social justification. Downzoning of land that reduces its market value has commonly been viewed as a "taking"; however, the judiciary of the Commonwealth of Virginia upheld downzoning in a 1974 opinion.[12] But judicial opinions differed in the case of *Lucas v. Carolina Coastal Commission* (404 SE 2d. 895) wherein a property owner was denied the right to build beyond a setback line on the beachfront, under a statute enacted subsequent to his purchase of the land.[13] There appears to be no general consensus in the United States over criteria to determine priorities between public and private rights over land. In the Lucas case the issue was one of public amenities and environmental prudence versus private economic interest and expectation.

Where government purchase is precluded for various reasons, public efforts to prevent misuse of private lands or to guide their use in ecologically and socially sustainable ways is to that extent limited. Legal provision for transferable development rights and trading of public for private parcels of land may provide a means to obtain better uses of particular lands but does not guarantee stewardship. The state police power, as presently understood, does not extend to a taking of privately owned land merely to prevent its abuse. However, practical considerations of government responsibility for allocation of clearly limited resources (such as groundwater in arid regions) may entail a consequential limitation on land use. Arizona has restricted the right of land owners under certain circumstances to extend irrigation systems, in effect depriving them of the economic value that water would bring. The constitutionality of this apparent "taking" was upheld in the Supreme Court of Arizona.[14]

Some innovative purchasing of land has been occurring at the state level and may involve cooperation with nongovernmental organizations concerned with environmental quality. Florida, for example, has adopted a tax on official documents required for transactions in real estate and is using the proceeds to purchase and thereby protect ecologically sensitive areas.[15] The Nature Conservancy, a private organization, can often purchase land from willing sellers more expeditiously than can slower moving government. It may also persuade land owners to recognize ecological values when land is up for sale, whereas government representatives may encounter the old residual resistance to government ownership or control. In the state of Indiana, the legislature has limited the right of the U.S. Forest Service to purchase land for addition to the national forest, even from willing sellers.[16] The Forest Service pays local governments an "in lieu of" equivalent to tax moneys foregone because of government acquisition, and so the real force behind the restriction is an emotional urge to limit further federal landownership in the state.

Control of use through voluntary sale and purchase might appear neither to challenge nor expand public policy, yet it is not wholly acceptable to those adherents to public choice or libertarian doctrine who oppose government ownership, or government action on behalf of purposes not universally shared. There are, however, ways of evading this objection. For example, the Florida program to purchase threatened areas is only indirectly a land-use measure. It is, in fact, a tax on a conventional source of revenue. That it has land use results does not invalidate exercise of the power to tax. Such legislation might be difficult to challenge as an unwarranted extension of government control over land, as its validity rests upon the power of the state to tax and spend. Objection might be made to the ultimate objective of the expenditure—but hardly to its legality. In several states land trusts have been established by private groups to acquire or otherwise protect specific values on the land for which government protection is unavailable. This method of getting around the limitations of governmental action appears to be gaining popularity and does not challenge traditional ownership principles.

The federal government is the nation's biggest land owner, and the land-use policies of the federal agencies, determined by statutory law and administrative action, are also conventional exercises of ownership rights.[17] But the role of government as a land owner is often opposed by persons (as in Indiana) whose unit of human value and legitimate action is the hypothetical individual. In their view all property ownership, including land, should be vested in identifiable individuals. Joint and corporate land ownership may sometimes be acceptable, provided that individuals as shareholders have an identifiable interest in and responsibility for land-use decisions. But the identification of actual "owners," what they in fact "own," and how equities are apportioned among multiple owners are matters that may be exceedingly complex, and these too may create problems for policy that may be limiting.

In a discussion of the facts of ownership, Gene Wunderlich has observed that

> The ownership of land can be ambiguous in at least two aspects: (1) specification of the owner, that is, the principal holder of rights, and (2) identification of others holding separated interests in land other than those of the owner. To these conceptual ambiguities can be added (3) the problem of valuation, for it is through price or some other expression of value that ownership is given weight and substance.[18]

Criteria for valuation grow with diversification of the values that people attribute to land and that are regarded throughout society and by the courts as legitimate. Conventional valuation recognized by law has been almost wholly commercial. Money has been the denominator common to valuation. However, economic criteria have not been exclusively, uniformly, or universally accepted. The use of a monetary measure to evaluate noncommercial rights and sites appears to some people to be arbitrary and subjective; some see market mechanics as no less arbitrary than bureaucratic decision making. For aspects of the land having unique, irreplaceable characteristics, no socially acceptable market may exist and there may be no practical way to establish a monetary value. How, for example, could a socially acceptable monetary value be placed on the Grand Canyon, the Everglades, or the Big Trees of Sequoia National Park? In theory a monetary value can be assigned to anything—in actuality, cultural values and unique characteristics limit this form of economism. But cultural values realized through economic means (e.g., prolonging jobs in lumber camps by cutting virgin forests) may also be invoked to limit protection for ecologic or scientific reasons. Controversy over cutting the ancient Douglas Fir forests in the Pacific Northwest is a case in point.[19]

Where the value of land cannot adequately be quantified or limited to the interests of ownership, a problem of nonowner interests is encountered, and land appraisers and courts face a problem that conventional law is not well-equipped to resolve. Class-action lawsuits have provided a means whereby a group of nonowners may seek to restrain uses of land alleged to do cumulative harm to a community of interest, but the harm (usually material) may be difficult to establish for any particular individual.

In the absence of general ingrained ethics of stewardship, ambiguity of ownership has been a major deterrent to obtaining responsible land management. To the extent that land ownership is diffuse, fractionated, and indirect, fixing responsibility for its custody and care becomes difficult. Successive ownership has also handicapped efforts to establish a stewardship obligation, for example, under circumstances in which a land owner has inherited a contaminating toxic dump site from previous owners no longer accessible to legal action to recover costs of remediation. In principle a present owner inherits the liabilities together with the rights of his purchase. Here a widely accepted, ecologically conserving consensus on the responsibilities of land ownership could provide an unwritten policy for land. As Aldo Leopold suggested several decades ago, stewardship—responsible custody of land—would more readily follow from a strongly held universally accepted land ethic than from a comprehensive system of government regulations.[20]

Ecologically based land ethics have been growing but as yet are far from dominant in American public life. Legal and economic circumstances place the power to decide land-use policies in persons who have the greatest incentive to regard land as a commodity and a resource for economic growth and to discount noneconomic and long-range considerations. Even a clear and active majority of people committed to ethics of stewardship and ecological sustainability cannot impose its convictions upon a politically influential minority whose right to make land use decisions is confirmed by law and is based upon very different ethics, which regard economic development and monetary return as the highest and best uses of land.

There may be conceptual ambiguities in the relationship between ownership and stewardship. Garrett Hardin, in "The Tragedy of the Commons," described the fate of land (and other resources) held in common and subject to no restraint beyond the individual conscience.[21] Under such circumstances the aggressive exploiter benefitted in the short run. Restraint was in no one's economic self-interest. The land suffered first, and subsequent generations suffered later. This "tragedy" has doubtless occurred but is more likely the exception than the rule. Many peoples holding land in common have had agreed-upon rules—sometimes detailed—regarding its usage. Particularly in so-called primitive or traditional societies reverence for ancestors, for ancient custom, and regard for the omnipresent spirits of nature endow an individual conscience more powerfully restrained than any modern statute or title of ownership is likely to effect. The parable of the commons, however, has been taken by opponents of government ownership to demonstrate the economic and ecologic merits of private over public ownership.[22] Yet government responsibility and administration are not the same as ownership in common. The argument has been that government is incapable of taking care of the land because it will be unable to prevent special interests from using political influence to exploit the public domain; and public bureaucrats—having no personal interest in the fate of the land—will not exert themselves on behalf of its protection at risk of political reprisal.

In this perspective, public land is viewed as if it were a commons, although, in fact, government agencies may be bound by such statutes as the Federal Land Policy and Management Act (FLPMA, 1976), the National Forest Management Act (NFMA, 1976), the National Environmental Policy Act (NEPA, 1969), and by specific provisions of clean air and water legislation to observe specified precepts and procedures in land-management decisions and practices.[23] There is no necessity that government ownership of land results in a commons. The U.S. government has maintained restrictions on many uses of the public lands. Public opinion has increasingly provided support for such provisions. Yet the historical record shows that government custody of public lands in the United States has been characterized by political corruption. The U.S. Department of the Interior has been distrusted by environmental protection groups because of its partnership in lawful corruption and its indifference toward exploitive uses of the land.

Experience does not demonstrate an inherent superiority of either government or of private ownership in the custody and care of land. Why would one expect otherwise if the assumptions and values relating to economic behavior and the land are basic to the culture of the greater number of Americans? But the behavior of government agencies in management of the public land is theoretically more open to public control than is land as the property of private owners. If administration of public lands were viewed as a public trust, stewardship should be the controlling ethic in public lands policy. Instead, the popular ethics of "come and get it," not government ownership per se, historically has made the public lands a common pool for plunder.

Working through congressional committees and the federal agencies (especially at the regional level) both economic and environmental interest groups have sought to influence public policy and administrative action. Historically the big resource-using interests in timber, grazing, mining, and mass recreation have often been able to skew land-use decisions to serve their particular purposes without regard to larger and longer-term considerations. The fact that contending interests—economic and environmental—use similar methods to influence policy does not mean that their objectives equally serve the collective and future interests of society.

Efforts Toward Stewardship Through Law

There now appears to be a slow and uneven development of public opinion that may in time cause stewardship to become a requirement of landownership. Evidence of this change has been found by students of opinion on environmental values. Although land use has seldom been the direct focus of these inquiries, it is implicit in the attitudes that they reveal toward the environment. There is reason to infer that a growing sector of the public in the United States is prepared to go further than legislators and judges in the direction of public action on behalf of stewardship in uses of the land.[24] The National Environmental Policy Act of 1969, a reflection of changing public attitudes toward land and its uses, directed all agencies of the federal government to: "Identify and develop methods and procedures . . . which will insure that presently unquantified environmental amenities and values may be given appropriate consideration in decision making along with economic and technical considerations."[25] Action on this and other provisions of the act have been forced through the well known, but not so well understood, environmental impact statement requirement.[26] A large number of federal actions affect land and rights attached to land and its resources, both public and private, direct and indirect. Regulations on agency-administered land and the public domain, and a long list of provisions regarding clean air and water, agriculture, antiquities, historical preservation, endangered species, and native American religious sites have been authorized or required by statute, and constitute a body of federal land-use law. Additional provisions governing specific uses of land have been provided by state and municipal legislation. Laws governing public health and maintenance of nuisances have added new dimensions and land-use significance as science-based evidence accumulates regarding contamination of air, land, and water. Legislation at all political levels extends qualifications over rights to use land and to evaluate uses solely by economic criteria.[27]

The multiple involvements of the federal and state governments in many private land-use decisions and the effects of private land-use decisions upon public interests indicate that any general public policy for land use in the United States must be applicable in principle to all land, regardless of the legal status of owners. In an ecological or sustainable environmental perspective there is seldom good reason for differentiating among parcels of land merely because of ownership. From legal or economic viewpoints, rights and equities must be considered, but these considerations are subject to changing values and perceptions. The economic equities of individual persons are more ephemeral than are the continuities of nature and society, involving problems of legal philosophy to be worked out with regard to changing knowledge and concepts of responsibility for the uses of land. Knowledge of the probable consequences of decisions and actions may carry ethical implications relevant for both public and private land use policies.

Law that declares the sense of a community regarding rights and obligations confirms prevailing ethics, but law may also be anticipatory of future standards of conduct. In a social environment of diversity and paradox, where ambiguities and anomalies confuse the adoption of common land-use ethics, an anticipatory declaration of principles and standards may be the most practicable way of moving toward an accommodation of changing social preferences in relation to land use. The operational question is: "At what point in social evolution can new assumptions regarding the uses of land be translated into legal precepts?" The answer seems to be empirical; the point of legislative feasibility can be determined only by testing legislative proposals.

Allowing for obstacles to the adoption of substantive goals, the cause of responsible land use might be advanced by a national set of standards and criteria to protect the nation's basic assets in land. In 1970 a National Land Use Policy Act in its successive versions was proposed to prod the states into action which was protective of environmentally sensitive lands.[28] Introduced by Senator Henry Jackson, Senate bill S.3354 would have required the states to address the issue of land-use planning for the more vulnerable and critical areas. The states, not the federal government, were to do the planning.

This proposed statute, presently to be considered, was a logical sequel to the National Environmental Policy Act, but responsibility for its implementation was laid upon the states with federal grants to induce action and fiscal sanctions for noncompliance. In effect, it was an effort to persuade the states to assume a role of stewardship for environmentally sensitive areas. This legislation was endorsed initially by President Richard Nixon and, under several iterations over the succeeding three years, passed in the Senate, only to be sidetracked in the House of Representatives through maneuvers on behalf of land speculators, developers, and self-styled libertarians.

The National Environmental Policy Act became law because of an undeniable groundswell of public demand in the late 1960s for government "to do something about the environment." No such public pressure demanded land use legislation. A Coastal Zone Management Act was passed and, like the more general proposal, it also required state implementation. Its effect on coastal development has been mostly modest in those states that have adopted it.[29] It appears that the public wants action in general on environmental issues but, with the exception of toxic contamination, is uncertain about action in particular, especially where customary folkways may be threatened or certain opportunities for jobs or income may be diminished.

An Emergent National Issue

That land use could become a public and national issue became evident in 1970 with the introduction of a land-use planning bill into the U.S. Congress, and a call for land-use legislation by the president of the United States. Following enactment of air and water pollution legislation, and the declaration of a national policy for the environment, land-use legislation was a logical next step. The way in which land is used is basic to all environmental policy. Public support for land-use planning had grown during the 1960s, not so much from acceptance of a land ethic as in response to the frustration growing out of conflicting land-use demands. As often happens with large public issues, different groups supported land-use action for differing reasons. For example, the National Forest Products Association advocated a national land-use policy to stabilize the resource base of forest industries. A major objective of the industry was to stop the withdrawal of forest lands from commercial use into national parks, wilderness, and recreation areas. But the enlargement and strengthened protection of these and other reserved areas was a major reason for the support of land-use planning legislation by many conservation groups, notably the Wilderness Society, the National Parks and Conservation Association, the Sierra Club, and by planning groups such as the American Institute of Architects, the American Institute of Planners, and the American Society of Landscape Architects. Thus an unlikely convergence of organizations supported land-use planning, in principle, but each in its own interest.

Even a cursory survey of American newspapers during the 1960s would show that people were more than ever getting in one another's way. Public demands for environmental amenities were rising at a time when their attrition by commercial and industrial activity was rapidly increasing. Suburbanites and second-home owners in scenic areas were not universally welcoming drive-in theaters, overhead power lines, electric generating plants, and airports. Large environment-shaping government agencies, long immune to effective public criticism, found their former popularity giving way before the demands of an environment-conscious public. These demands were for greater respect for nature and for neighborhoods, and for counterbalancing traditional economic and engineering criteria for public works by ecological and esthetic considerations. By 1970, the agencies were confronting events that had hitherto been hardly imaginable. Citizens were actually obstructing completion of interstate highways; opposing construction of dams, canals, and pipelines; and preventing the expansion of airports. Obviously, some people wanted these so-called "improvements," but many did not or not in the way they were being engineered, and they were now sometimes able to persuade courts that their objections should be considered.

The complex diversity of environmental issues affecting land use was illustrated by the White House Conference on Natural Beauty (May 24–25, 1965).[30] The concerns of the nearly one thousand participants in the conference went well beyond environmental esthetics. Land use as such was not on the agenda, but nearly every issue considered at the conference involved uses of land, and few conference recommendations could have been carried out without modifications of existing land-use practices (for example, with respect to surface mining, real-estate subdivision, highway construction, and outdoor advertising). The failure of the conference to achieve more than minimal practical results should not obscure its greater long-range significance. It publicized the environmental issue and heightened public expectations for greater governmental responsiveness to environmental-quality considerations. The Johnson Administration, enmeshed in foreign war and ethnic discontent, disappointed these expectations. But the environmental issue had gained a visibility and political legitimacy that found legislative expression in the 90th and 91st Congresses.

Concern for national land-use policy was also stimulated by the work of the Public Land Law Review Commission. The report of the Commission, *One Third of The Nation's Land*,[31] issued in June 1970, dealt with lands administered by federal agencies, but its recommendations held implications for privately owned land as well. Note for example the following excerpts from chapter 3 of the report, "Planning Future Public Land Use":

1. Goals should be established by statute for a continuing, dynamic program of land use planning.
2. Public land agencies should be required to plan land uses to obtain the greatest net public benefit. Congress should specify the factors to be considered by the agencies in making these determinations, and an analytic system should be developed for their application.
5. All public land agencies should be required to formulate long range, comprehensive land use plans for each state or region, relating such plans not only to internal agency programs but also to land use plans and attendant management program of other

agencies. Specific findings should be provided in their plans, indicating how various factors were taken into account.

12. Land use planning among federal agencies should be systemically coordinated.

14. Congress should provide additional financial assistance to public land states to facilitate better and more comprehensive land use planning.

15. Comprehensive land use planning should be encouraged through regional commissions along lines of the river basin commissions created under the Water Resources Planning Act of 1965. Such commissions should come into existence only with the consent of the states involved, with regional coordinating being initiated when possible within the context of state and local political boundaries.

The phrase "comprehensive planning" has been regarded by commentators as unrealistic and unworkable.[32] Its opposite, "disjunctive incrementalism," has been cited by some critics of planning as descriptive of how the real world works. The difference of opinion here seem to be differences in how the word "comprehensive" is understood. Planning may be comprehensive if all major relevant factors are taken into account. It need not, and cannot, consider every aspect of a proposal that might have numerous and future impacts—many of relatively minor significance. But antiplanners may attack the concept of comprehensive planning using the "straw man" analogy, by attributing to "comprehensive" an all-inclusive meaning that few if any of its advocates have proposed. Incremental planning or ad hoc decision making that fails to consider the broader implications of an issue risks "the tyranny of small decisions." Ad hoc decisions today may forestall beneficial options in the future.

Premise 4 of the Public Land Law Review Commission Report stated that "in planning the use of public lands, the uses of non-public lands must be given consideration." Clearly effective management of public lands, particularly in those states with large land holdings, requires a use of nonpublic lands consistent with public land management practices. Public land policies ought also have regard to their effect on nongovernmental land uses, consistent with the larger, long-range general interest. The recommendations of the Public Land Law Review Commission were merely recommendations, not policies, but they added to the growing weight of argument for a comprehensive national policy for land use regardless of ownership. They did not, however, indicate what criteria should govern land-use planning and decision making. They could be weighted toward economic values and could limit policies that would restrict economic development (such as wilderness areas or wildlife refuges).

Passage of the National Environmental Policy Act (NEPA, PL 91-190) in December 1969, and its signing by President Richard Nixon on January 1, 1970, as his first official act of the new year, marked an official commitment of the United States to environmental quality as a national policy. An explicit rationale for land-use planning was now provided. Although the act did not directly address land use, actions of federal agencies having significant environmental impact upon land were subject to review under Section 102 of the act (the environmental impact statement). It was hardly surprising therefore that Senator Henry M. Jackson, principal sponsor of the National Environmental Policy Act, followed up this initiative by introduction on January 29, 1970, of a Bill (S.3354) to provide for a national land use policy. The 91st Congress, however, adjourned before the bill could be acted upon. Substantially the same bill was again introduced into the 92nd Congress as S.632. The Nixon administration now introduced its own bill (S.992). The bills were similar in most respects but the administration measure tended to be the more conservative and to rely more on voluntary action at the state level. That land issues were at the time matters of public concern is indicated by the large number of land-related bills (200) before thirteen committees in the 82nd Congress. But these bills were not all to the same purpose. Diverse sponsors had diverse objectives. Some, in effect, could be used as defenses of particular land uses against ecologically motivated land-use planning restrictions.

A brief account of the inability of Congress in the early 1970s to enact national land-use legislation illustrates the problem of politically addressing a recognized need in the absence of consensus regarding how it should be met. The Nixon administration was persuaded of a need for national legislation but was not prepared to leave the initiative on land-use policy to the Congress. In its first annual report (August 1970), the Council on Environmental Quality recommended adoption of a national land-use policy, and this position was endorsed by the president in his message transmitting the Report to the Congress. The president declared that

> We have treated our land as if it were a limitless resource. Traditionally Americans have felt that what they do with their own land is their own business. This attitude has been a natural outgrowth of the pioneer spirit. Today, we are coming to realize that our land is finite, while our population is growing. The uses to which our generation puts the land can either expand or severely limit the choices our children will have. The time has come when we must accept the idea that none of us has a right

to abuse the land, and that on the contrary society as a whole has a legitimate interest in proper land use. There is a national interest in effective land use planning all across the nation.

I believe we must work toward the development of a National Land Use Policy to be carried out by an effective partnership of federal, states and local governments together, and, where appropriate, with new regional institutional arrangements.[33]

The administration might have supported the Jackson bill, which had already received public hearings before the Senate Committee on Interior and Insular Affairs. It elected instead to propose its own bill (S.992), which was introduced into the Congress on February 17, 1971. Although sponsors of the Jackson bill were prepared to make various modifications in their proposals to meet administration objections, it became evident that the Nixon administration wanted its own bill and no other. The consequence was mutual checkmate. Meanwhile, efforts were renewed to enact a coastal land-management bill to provide protection for those lands most acutely threatened by development activities. This legislation was, at least initially, opposed by the administration on the argument that coastal zones and estuaries were explicitly covered by the administration bill. Nevertheless, a bill, S.582 (the Coastal Zone Management Act), was favorably reported out of the Senate Commerce Committee on December 1, 1971.

Among the differences between the original Jackson bill and the administration bill, the following were significant. The administration bill, S.992, would have encouraged the states, through federal monetary grants, to classify and to assert state control over "areas of critical environment impact." In his testimony before the Senate Interior Committee on May 25, 1971, Russell E. Train, chair of the Council on Environmental Quality, explained that, whereas the Jackson bill involved classification of all lands outside the largest urban areas into six land uses, the administration bill was "designed to be selective by inviting state involvement only over matters of state concern or priority, while leaving the remainder of land use problems of purely local significance subject to local control.[34] The Jackson bill, by contrast, in effect required the states to undertake comprehensive land-use planning, with a threat of progressive loss of federal grants by states that failed to comply.

A superficial and unsophisticated reading of the bills might lead to the erroneous conclusion that the administration bill favored local self-determination, and that the Jackson bill provided a more centralized and coercive procedure. In actual practice, the opposite could have been true. The administration bill would have authorized the Secretary of the Interior to approve planning grants to the states and, subsequently, to administer program management grants where states met certain specified criteria. The Jackson bill placed federal control in a Land and Water Resources Planning Council with a considerably more detailed specification of responsibilities. Of the two measures, the Jackson bill with its action-forcing provisions was the more forthright. The administration bill, in the words of Russell E. Train, would leave "land use problems of purely local significance subject to local control." But what these purely local matters would be was difficult to predict with certainty.

The administration bill provided a means of interfering intimately and directly in local land-use decisions through Paragraph (4) of Section 104 of the bill, which authorized the Secretary of the Interior to make state grants only if in his judgment the state has "a method of assuring that local regulations do not restrict or exclude development and land use of regional benefit." But "the Secretary shall not approve a grant pursuant to Section 104 until he has ascertained that the Secretary of Housing and Urban Development is satisfied that those aspects of the state's land use program . . . meet the requirements of section 104 for funding a program management grant." The purpose of this provision appears to have been to enable the federal government to strike down local land-use plans that, in effect, would result in restrictions against low-cost public housing. But almost any other state or federal intervention in local land-use decisions might be justified under this provision. "Regional benefit" is an exceedingly flexible term and all local regulations, however ostensibly local and innocuous, would exist on the sufferance of state and federal judges with better than average imaginations regarding the possibilities inherent in interpretations of "regional benefit." And what they lacked in imagination would no doubt be supplied by lawyers for airport promoters, public utilities, gravel pit operators, civil-rights groups, and all other interests whose objectives might be frustrated by local regulations.

To make our point we need not follow this legislation through its numerous revisions, resubmissions, and reversals from 1973 to its final *coup de grâce* on July 15, 1975, when by a 23–19 vote the measure was finally killed in the House Committee on Interior and Insular Affairs. Three members that had previously supported the measure switched their votes under lobbying pressure described by Congressman R. Taylor of North Carolina as greater than any that he had seen in the preceding fifteen years. The National Wildlife Federation reported that "massive lobbying by land use opponents had steadily eroded support for the bill in the 94th Congress.[35] The history of efforts to enact national land-use legislation reveals the major limitations to public policy making in the United States. The White House, discredited by scandal and fraud (e.g., Vietnam and Watergate), and staffed in many positions by antipublic allies of powerful moneyed interests in land development, supported only the semblance, not the substance, of land-use controls. The Congress was characteristically sensitive to the interests of those who provide the money needed to pay the ever-increasing costs of election to public office. The structuring of American politics is thus obstructive of policy in the long-term public interest. There is money to be made in the exploitation of land and natural resources, but no one profits financially from their conservation.

Under present conditions, it is uncertain whether communities can continue to protect themselves from what they perceive as undesirable development where economic growth or civil rights are at issue. Public confidence in the honesty and reliability of government generally appears to have declined to a degree that makes doubtful that there will be willing widespread acceptance of comprehensive national land-use planning in the near future. Nevertheless there may be grudging acquiescence in planning as a "lesser evil." Acceptance of planning, however unenthusiastically, is plausible primarily because among the environmental penalties for being without it may be further exposure to the damaging economic and social consequences of unrestricted growth and development. More people are beginning to understand that they will carry the costs of indiscriminate economic growth while speculators and developers gather in the profits.

State and Local Action

The inability of the federal government to deal effectively with most land-use problems has been partially offset by state action. But no more than one-fifth of the states have enacted comprehensive land-use legislation. Still, some states, acting under their residual constitutional powers, have undertaken legislative experiments that could provide models for the nation.[36] Whether, as a practical matter, state action alone could provide effective land-use control is doubtful. The tendency of the U.S. Supreme Court to strike down state restrictions under the constitutional due-process and takings clause suggests that many of the objectives of present-day land-use planning advocates would be frustrated by judicial interpretation. However, the Court has reaffirmed the power of the states to regulate land and natural resource usage to serve public needs. In what some persons regard as an extreme case, the Supreme Court unanimously upheld a 1967 Hawaii statute authorizing the taking of land from large estates for division among small property owners.[37]

But consistent with customary vagaries of American democracy, the states have not consistently exercised their inherent powers over land. Instead some have ceded authority to local jurisdictions or to favored private enterprises with a "public interest," such as public utilities.[38] There have been, however, efforts in a few states to initiate a larger degree of state control over land use. It may be significant that the states that have taken a lead have important outdoor-recreation industries whose future could be jeopardized by haphazard, discordant development. Hawaii, California, Wisconsin, Florida, Oregon, Maine, and Vermont are among those states. Hawaii was the first state to adopt comprehensive land-use legislation under direct state administration. The first Hawaiian statute was enacted in 1961 and has survived determined attacks by land owners and developers. The law provides for the classification of land into four categories (urban, agricultural, conservation, and rural) and is designed especially to protect the agricultural and scenic resources of the Islands from uncontrolled development. The act is administered by the State Land Use Commission, which alone has power to grant variances from the classification applied to particular parcels of land.[39] Strong development pressure, however, is a continuing threat to ecological considerations in the administration of Hawaiian legislation.

In 1970 the Colorado legislature, with much urging from the governor, passed a "watered-down" bill establishing a State Land Use Commission. Opposition to state action to implement the measure came particularly from ranchers, developers, and other large land owners who disliked the prospect of anyone restricting the ways in which they might choose to use their land. The prognosis for effective results from most state efforts has not been good. California, Florida, New Jersey, and New York have adopted land-use control measures with varied success. Basic legal concepts in the United States continue strongly to support private property rights as against public purposes. Even so, qualified progress toward effective land-use policy has been achieved in a few states in addition to Hawaii, but not without encountering difficulties.[40]

Wisconsin was one of the earliest states to undertake land-use studies. In 1927 the state initiated a land-use survey, and subsequently adopted county zoning, especially to control occupancy of the impoverished "cut-over" lands of northern Wisconsin.[41] In 1966 a Bureau of Water and Shoreline Management was established to develop criteria for shoreline and floodplain protection, and to supervise their administration through ordinances adopted by county governments and municipalities. A continuing interest in land-use problems and policies has been maintained at the University of Wisconsin.

Pressure of expansive growth of population and development impelled the Florida legislature to enact a variety of measures to control land subdivision and prevent or reduce environmental degradation. The Environmental Land and Water Management Act of 1972 marked a significant advance in policy at a time when land-use legislation was bottled up in the U.S. Congress.[42] Extraordinary pressures of moneyed interests for development have put a great stress on implementation of Florida's land-use legislation. Some limited success has been achieved in protecting Areas of Critical State Concern. This concern takes cognizance of the importance of tourist visitation as well as the desire of retirees for environmental amenities. Thus economic considerations work both for and against protective landuse policy in Florida.

Oregon adopted comprehensive land use legislation in 1973 in response to a sharp upturn in population and economic growth during the preceding decade.[43] Local governments had proved unable to deal with urban sprawl, misplaced commercial development, and loss of visual amenities and could not address important the nonurban problems of farmlands. The act has been repeatedly challenged through the courts and by referenda, but continues to find support among an apparent majority of the electorate. In the state of Washington a comprehensive land-use control proposal was defeated in a 1990 referendum. This action was consistent with the generally negative attitude toward expansion of government and tax increases evidenced across the country. Environmental quality measures including land protection were voted down in California and New York in 1990 elections. Lack of positive consensus toward land policy continues to be its biggest limitation.

For the greater number of states, federal action will be required to induce legislation. More states will adopt land-use policies, but the prospect of all states, on their own initiative, administering effective policies in coordination with one another and with federal agencies, seems too improbable to merit optimism. But state experience, even though limited, should be helpful in formulating whatever federal statutes are eventually enacted.

A "Response Analysis" survey of American's beliefs about the environment undertaken in 1991 found the general public unconvinced that a significant environmental problem really existed.[44] People become excited when their persons or property are exposed to an environmental hazard such as toxic wastes or polluted air. But this study found only a minority concerned about endangered species, loss of natural areas, water quality, or urban amenities. Apart from any judgment on the validity of this survey, it seems that polls indicating strong public support for environmental protection may be misleading. Public response seems to be site specific and issue specific, and indicates no massive conversion to a biocentric viewpoint. If true, this may explain the lack of general public support for land-use planning. Politicians may assess the environmental concerns of their constituents as essentially neutral to indifferent. Few candidates for elective office win or lose on the strength of the "environment vote." Hence they logically resort to rhetoric or calls for balance or compromise on environmental and land-use issues.

Possibilities and Prospects: Problems of Consensus

The immediate future of land-use planning in the United States is uncertain. The absence of a pervasive coherent national philosophy of land—a land ethics—handicaps all efforts toward formulating a general policy. Traditional, individualist, and opportunist attitudes are well-served by the arrangements that now exist. And the diverse and contradictory interests that make a land-use policy desirable also make it difficult to formulate and to enact. In our concluding chapter we suggest a number of steps that could be taken toward obtaining land policy that we regard as sustainable, rational, and in the public interest. But we think it improbable that general consensus on land policy will be attained. A plurality or majority of opinion is all that it is reasonable to expect. Interests hostile to land-use restrictions or environmental regulations found encouragement in the pro-private, antigovernment stance of the Reagan and Bush presidencies. Attacks have been mounted upon land-use regulations generally, and especially upon the Endangered Species Act and on beachfront and wetlands regulations.

A coalition of natural resource interests, conservative advocates, mechanized recreationists, and antigovernmental activists have been organized through the Multiple-Use Land Alliance, and more than half a dozen other groups are well funded and have been well connected at the White House. Under the rubric of "wise use" they would open up wilderness and national parks to mining, log the ancient forests of the Pacific Northwest, severely cut back the protection of the Endangered Species Act, and remove restrictions on the development of wetlands.[45] It seems plausible that present methods of financing campaigns for election to political office give these well-funded coalitions and their sponsors more influence in the Congress than either their numbers or arguments could justify. The American Land Institute and the American Bar Association have tried to develop model legislation that would lead toward equitable resolution of differences and clarify legal ambiguities.[46] But these efforts seem unlikely to remove strong interest or ideological fixations.

A decentralized and selective approach to land-use planning may be the only politically feasible alternative. But decentralization implies some degree of centralization. There is a need at the federal level for establishing those principles and standards that will assist ecologically and economically sustainable land-use policy in the public interest and help to develop a consensus for its implementation. The ecological logic of land use calls for comprehensiveness, but it also may require a greater degree of like-mindedness than is now found in the United States. As political scientist Norton E. Long observed in 1966: "There are powerful reasons limiting cooperation to piecemeal and ad hoc palliatives."[47] There are also unresolved problems of political ethics with which American society has not seriously attempted to cope. These questions in particular must eventually be answered if environmental quality is to be sustained.

1. How much freedom does or should a local community have to determine or to preserve the character desired by a majority of its citizens? What if a community choice would result in irreplaceable loss or in a burden for the rest of the nation?

2. Does an individual have a right to live where he chooses when his choice may condemn him (and his family) to poverty and indefinite dependence upon the public treasury or may intrude upon the preference of his would-be neighbors?

3. By what criteria should an individual be permitted freedom to use or dispose of land to which he holds title when his choice has implications for the future welfare of his community or the nation?

4. Should the criteria for tax assessment of land be more than economic, to prevent the incidence of taxation from discouraging conserving and amenity uses of land?

The tax assessor has by tradition been a notorious destroyer of environmental quality and a malign influence on the rational and conserving uses of land. Assessed valuations of land and buildings may have little relevance for their "highest and best use"—if that use is determined by more than economic criteria. Owners of the Seagram Building in New York City were, in effect, penalized by the tax assessor for adding nonprofitable amenities for the general public.[48] On the taxation of certain environmental amenities, however, the courts appear to be adopting a broader, public-benefit rationale in place of a narrow, bookkeeper's conservatism.

In a crowded, mobile, and swift-moving society possessing unprecedented economic and technological opportunities, the validity of past assumptions regarding land use and community development must be questioned. What the future character of American society will be is not clear—projections of present trends notwithstanding. Land-use planning to cope with the traditional ad hoc, opportunistic, incremental, and reactive course of land use will be difficult and contentious. It will inevitably involve compromises in which the quality of the public environment will be endangered by politically opportunistic expediencies. Increasing population will accentuate all land-use problems, and differing preferences among economic and ethnic groups will intrude into the decision process. There is also the less probable possibility that some significant part of the body politic might embrace a sociopolitical ideology with strong land-use implications. This has already happened in such groups as Greenpeace, Earth First, and Friends of the Earth among others. There is a movement toward "green politics" among, primarily, younger Americans. This movement has not yet achieved significant political influence and has aroused considerable conservative hostility. Nevertheless it appears to be gaining strength. Its success, however, would very likely produce more sharp divisions in politics, and would allow less latitude for accommodation or compromise.

Those parts of the country that can, and do, establish effective, ecologically informed land-use policies will be the more fortunate. And if we cannot be optimistic about the early enactment of an effective nationwide land-use planning act, it is encouraging to see the extent of popular commitment achieved thus far. There are grounds for hope in state action and in the generally favorable public response to national legislative proposals for environmental protection. The limits to land-use policy are basically deficiencies in public foresight and consensus. Where opinions are divided and environmental quality votes do not swing elections, the normal susceptibility of politicians to accommodate their sources of funding and publicity may be expected to prevail. These sources rarely include interests sympathetic to land-use planning, other than planning to promote development and growth and to restrict "preservationist" efforts. It is the unseeing, uncaring, and self-serving side of American society that rejects land-use planning in principle. If the American people grow in moral and civic stature and in the capacity for foresight, they will, in time, demand wiser policies than we now generally have for the care and custody of land.

Meanwhile, public apathy, lack of understanding, and vigorous opposition to land-use controls on the part of industrial, agricultural, and development interests continues to threaten existing land-use planning and protective measures. For example, in August 1991 the Bush administration proposed legislation to reopen millions of hitherto protected areas to builders.[49] Reinforcing this self-serving lobbying effort by economic development interests and the administration has been the uncompromising opposition to controls over land by extreme libertarians.[50] Here is a limit to policy for protection of environmental values in land that will be fought out in the political arena.

8

Land-Use Policy as an International Issue

Lynton Keith Caldwell

Few public issues appear to be more strictly national than land use, and the legal rationale and defense of national jurisdiction is the doctrine of national sovereignty.[1] In environment-related United Nations conferences, third world representatives in particular have asserted absolute national control over land and natural resources. Nevertheless, international concern over land use is growing. This concern is scientific, economic, political, and demographic. It is heightened by the recognition that use and misuse of land has international implications and repercussions. How land is used or misused effects transboundary qualities of air and water, genetic diversity, and migrations of people and wildlife. Economic refugees from "ecologically bankrupt" countries have become difficult social and political problems for more provident nations. Yet up to now, the sovereignty doctrine has obstructed any significant international effort to influence destructive land-use practices. In many countries government policy could be described as schizophrenic. On the one hand international assistance is welcomed, even solicited, for specific land-use problems, but on the other there is resistance to remedies that would diminish the options of big land owners or arouse tribal opposition.

Developing countries, facing disastrous consequences of unwise land use (e.g., soil erosion, desertification, waterlogging and salinization, laterization, and loss of agricultural land to urbanization), have appealed to international organizations for aid. The Food and Agriculture Organization, the U.N. Industrial and Development Organization, the U.N. Environment Program, the International Conference of Scientific Unions, the U.N. Economic Commissions, and the World Bank group have undertaken land-use-related research and assistance programs. But political sensitivities have precluded external involvement in national land-use policy except in dire circumstances as, for example, in the drought-stricken African Sahel. Land-use issues of international concern are increasing (e.g., tropical

161

rain forests, pollution of international waters and Antarctica), yet these issues are largely viewed incrementally and are defined more by their visible effects than by their basic causes.

A paradox is encountered in the consideration of land use as an international issue. Land, above all things, has been regarded as an object of national sovereignty. Human rights—relations between governments and the people they govern—are now subject to international declarations, resolutions, and international sanctions, even overt interventions. Nations have adopted coercive measures to force the government of South Africa to change its racial policies, but no government proposes to punish Indonesia or Brazil for destruction of the equatorial rainforest. Absolute and unconditional sovereign rights over land and resources have frequently been asserted by representatives of national governments. Yet representatives from those countries, on occasions such as the 1972 U. N. Conference on the Human Environment at Stockholm, have endorsed qualified resolutions calling for national adoption of land-use and resources policies and practices proposed by international agencies and experts, and have accepted national obligations to other countries in certain matters affecting land use. Third World countries have also sought relief and migration for refugees from areas impoverished by improvident, ecologically uninformed land-use practices of their inhabitants. El Salvador, Haiti, Ethiopia, and the sub-Saharan Sahel are cases in point. In sum, international relations regarding land use are inconsistent and contradictory.

Paradox of National Sovereignty

International organizations and some developing countries have urged programs of technical and financial assistance for land-related purposes (e.g., agriculture and forestry) that are at variance with prevailing patterns of use and ownership in particular countries. And national governments have objected when their natural resources and the quality of their environments have been impaired or diminished by land use policies of their neighbors (e.g., Canada vs. the United States, the Scandinavian countries vs. Great Britain, India vs. Nepal, and Syria vs. Israel). Today the issue of global climate change, in effect, makes all nations neighbors. Destruction of the equatorial rainforests with disastrous consequences projected for the earth's atmosphere and genetic diversity has placed land use on the continuing agenda of international relations. Were national sovereignty over land really absolute and supreme, expressions of international concern would intrude upon matters over which international action was inappropriate and which had no foundation in international law. But a widely accepted principle of international law brings the concept of exclusive national jurisdiction into question.

That a nation may not lawfully permit the use of its territory in ways that harm other nations was successfully argued in the Trail Smelter Arbitration between Canada and the United States. The principle was asserted by Australia and New Zealand in the Nuclear Test Cases before the World Court and is implicit in numerous international agreements relating to international waterways, air pollution, and migratory animals.[2] If territorial jurisdiction is modified by responsibility to other nations for the consequences of land use, then national sovereignty over land cannot be absolute. This qualification being conceded, no clear line in principle unequivocally separates (1) the right of a nation to control its land laws and practices from (2) its responsibility to other nations, or to what may be called the world community, for care and custody of the land. And because land, and resources in and on the land, are basic to the sustainability and future quality of life, the issue of fairness to future generations should be a national concern with international implications. But too often contemporary, powerful land owners and governments are ready to sacrifice future opportunities to contemporary objectives. What logic then explains the apparent contradiction of vigorous assertions of exclusive national control over land, but equally vigorous statements of national obligation to refrain from land use injurious to other generations and countries? In theory the logic is that nations assert sovereignty with respect to their land, qualified by an obligation to implement that sovereignty with respect to the rights of others. But the growth of international environmental policy during the past decades shows that once the camel's nose of obligation pushes under the tent of national sovereignty, the future of the sovereignty dogma cannot be taken for granted.

Sovereignty in theory is fixed and absolute, but obligation is conditional and expansible. In recent years science has been an expander of national obligation and a modifier of sovereignty. As an agent of change in many other aspects of life, science has inadvertently undermined long-standing legal conventions over land, and by implication has suggested new principles by which land use should be governed. During the past quarter-century there have been great advances in environment-related science. Heretofore unrecognized effects of land-use practices have been discovered, and prior theories regarding such matters as deforestation and watershed protection, overgrazing, salinization of irrigated land, uses of herbicides and inorganic fertilizers, value of wetlands, and effects of mining technologies have been refined, corrected, or confirmed. As the often multiple effects of land-use practices becomes better understood, and alternative land-use technologies become available, the responsibilities and options of nations regarding these uses are clarified. Previously unperceived or unexperienced transborder damage becomes identified through scientific investigation. As in the issue of acidic precipitation, science may enlarge national responsibility in ways uncongenial to some national governments and economic interests that are increasingly transnational in organization.

Nations may continue to assert their inalienable sovereignty in principle, but significant if subtle modifications in interpretation may occur over time. For example, the Belem Declaration on the Amazonian Cooperation Treaty of 1978 was a ringing assertion of exclusive national sovereignty over land and resources. But on May 6, 1989, in the Declaration of Manaus, the presidents of the eight Amazonian treaty states, without qualifying their unequivocal claim to sovereignty over their national resources, nevertheless stated their willingness to cooperate with other countries in environmental protection efforts in return for external technoeconomic assistance and an easing of their burden of foreign debt. Similarly, ministers of Latin American and Caribbean states issued on March 31, 1989, the Declaration of Brazilia, pledging cooperative attack upon environmental problems but calling on developed nations for technical assistance and reduction of foreign indebtedness.[3] It remains to be seen to what extent international considerations will modify the invocation of national sovereignty in defense of traditional land-use policies and practices. The emergence of nongovernmental environmental protection movements in many developing countries may complement external pressures for more ecologically rational and sustainable national land-use policies regardless of the sovereignty issue. Conservation of natural resources and preservation of the "national patrimony" is also a sovereign right declared in many national constitutions.[4] Need it be added that these formal declarations are almost invariably ignored in practice.

Spillovers of Land Uses

That the effects of certain land-use practices cannot be contained by national boundaries can be demonstrated by numerous examples; several will suffice here. Flooding and siltation of rivers in India and Bangladesh have contributed to massive deforestation and watershed erosion in the Himalayan mountains and foothills—especially in Nepal. Contamination of international waterways by residual products of irrigation agriculture has become an issue between Canada and the

United States, and Mexico and the United States. Canadian objections to certain features of the Garrison Diversion project in the Missouri River Valley stalled efforts of the U.S. government to replace dry-land farming with irrigation in North Dakota.[5] Proposals to open a coal mine on a tributary of the Flathead River in British Columbia have brought protests from the United States in protection of wilderness areas adjacent to Glacier National Park.[6]

Global circulation of air in the atmosphere also carries other transnational environmental problems. Intercontinental transport of soil dust from Asia and Africa has now been measured and monitored.[7] Some of this atmospheric dust may originate in undisturbed areas of the Sahara and Gobi deserts, but there are grounds for suspicion that some of it may be attributed to malpractice in agriculture and grazing, leading to desertification. The transnational atmospheric transport of toxic contaminants has also emerged as an international issue; as, for example, in North America where herbicides and pesticides used heavily in agriculture in Mexico and Central America may be carried northward by high atmospheric currents and deposited in Canada and the United States.[8] Land use thus becomes a factor in transboundary pollution prevention and control and has led to the international Convention on Long-Range Transboundary Air Pollution and Protocols. With the health, nutrition, and economic welfare of people being pushed onto the agenda of international relations, the linkage of these conditions to environmental and especially to land-use policies and practices gains pertinence. For example, agrarian reform has been a popular prescription to alleviate third-world poverty. But "reform" usually means redistribution of ownership and does not often address ecological problems of land use, which require solution if the condition of the rural poor is to be permanently improved. Indeed, the so-called reforms sometimes make bad situations worse, and collectivism uninformed by an ecology-based agricultural science may be no better.

Where land is in jeopardy people are in jeopardy—or will be when the productive and restorative capabilities of the soil give out. Rapidly increasing populations and expanding markets for natural products have intensified and extended agriculture through the world. In many of the tropical and subtropical countries, this explosive growth of agriculture has had disastrous effects: it has impoverished both soils and people and diminished biotic diversity. Massive deforestation for cattle raising and farming has generated effects felt at far distances. Increase in the carbon dioxide and methane balance in the atmosphere has been one consequence. Impairment and loss of genetic diversity among species and ecosystems is another. Improvements in ecologically sustainable agriculture and farming could contribute greatly to both environmental protection and the quality of life on a global scale.[9] Sociopolitical disorders have followed as populations increase faster than their economic support base, which is limited by the carrying capacity of the land and by their technological capabilities. Domestic and international conflict has been exacerbated by these circumstances. There is growing realization that unchecked population growth and concomitant misuse of land for survival are breeders of war and revolution affecting the entire community of nations.

The case of El Salvador illustrates how bad land use may contribute ultimately to international disorder. How Salvadoreans have used or misused their land may be regarded as no business of other countries only if no connection is perceived between the ecological disaster that Salvadoreans have brought upon themselves and their social war in which neighboring countries and the United States have been deeply involved. In 1961, long before the present political disorders had begun, Gary S. Hartshorn, Forest and Man Fellow of the Tropical Science Center in Costa Rica, in a letter to Peter Martin of the Institute of Current World Affairs, described the process of ecological impoverishment leading directly to poverty, social disorder, political upheaval, and mass migration to the United States.[10]

The case of Haiti is even worse. Reporting in the *New York Times* on June 12, 1991, Howard W. French wrote:

> In the dustbowl valleys and rocky hills of northwestern Haiti, generations of environmental destruction have turned a land once prized by the Conquistadors for its mahogany-rich forests into a cactus wasteland whose dry climate and desperate living conditions resemble the poorest of sub-Saharan Africa more than any Caribbean island.
>
> For northwest Haiti's growing pool of the disinherited, those without productive land or trees left to cut down, there is little choice but to flee. In addition to those joining the squalor of the already overcrowded capital, Port-au-Prince, thousands have set out from the northern coast in rickety boats, hoping to reach Florida.

The foregoing examples of the international effects of land abuse within nations show why national land-use policies are becoming international concerns. At present there are no conventions or other international agreements committing nations to a conserving and ecologically sustainable use of the land. Declarations of principle regarding land use (e.g., at U.N. conferences) have not received the follow-up accorded to treaties regarding trade in endangered species, protection of migratory animals, management of fisheries and marine animals, or transboundary air and water pollution (inadequate as this response often has been). Yet a number of international organizations, both governmental and nongovernmental, carry on activities relating directly to national land-use policies and practice. Is it possible that nations collectively are, so to speak, reluctantly backing into an international set of policies for land use? There is evidence to suggest that this may be happening.

In many developed countries the siting of polluting industries and waste disposal practices and facilities adjacent to international borders (e.g., the United States and Mexico) have forced consideration of appropriate land use.[11] Expanding economies in many places have encountered water problems above and below the surface. Restrictions on pumping groundwater, for example, are in effect restrictions on land use for agriculture which a national government may be reluctant to impose for the benefit of its neighbors. Where mining, farming, and forestry contribute to salinization, soil erosion, and sedimentation of rivers and reservoirs, governments must somehow intervene in the destructive use of the land in order to protect investments in their own public works in addition to obligations to downstream states.

International considerations influence national action in other ways. The case of Israel is instructive. The great initial success of Israel in intensive agriculture based on irrigation has led to depletion of surface and groundwater reserves. Reporting to the *New York Times* on April 12, 1991, Henry Kamm writes that "Israel's Farming Success Drains It of Water": "Israel, having made the desert bloom, a proud early achievement, is now counting the costs of its remarkable development of agriculture. It finds this symbol of national success withering." Conflict between Israel and her Arab neighbors over allocation of Jordan River waters has been of long standing. For example, as early as 1953 Syria appealed to the U.N. Security Council to stop Israel from diverting Jordan River water in demilitarized territory.[12] Nearly all water allocation issues are also land-use issues, and where available water is scarce and national claimants are several, international political problems are inevitable.

Rationalizing Sovereignty vs. International Responsibility

Historically a major obstacle to the rational development of an international responsibility for land use has been the concept of absolute national sovereignty. But, this concept, more accurately termed "political myth," however firmly believed, has more formal than factual significance. In actuality, sovereignty may be a shield protecting the perceived self-interests of powerful land owners to whom government officials feel beholden. A large part of the corpus of international law has developed in the course of resolving disputes among states where sovereignties collide. The fiction of sovereign control over land and resources is exposed by its most fervent advocates in the Third World in their demands for compensation if developed countries, for whatever reason, reduce purchases of Third World exports, which are nearly always products of the land (e.g., minerals, timber, and agricultural products). To the extent that a nation is dependent upon other nations for income from sale of the products of its lands, it does not actually have absolute control over the use of those lands. An exceptional but nonetheless significant case is the growth of coca and production of cocaine in rural areas of northwestern South America. Some years ago economic missions sought to help Colombia find a marketable crop alternative to coffee that could grow on forested and mountainous land. The missions were not notably successful, but Colombians subsequently discovered an "ideal" crop to make cultivation of the land worthwhile. The consequence was an international traffic in addictive drugs. An issue basic to this international problem is appropriate land use by the poor backcountry campesinos of Colombia, Ecuador, and Peru.

The concept of national sovereignty, like the concept of land "ownership," is becoming much more flexible in practice than in theory. As long as the concept itself is respected and acknowledged, there are various ways of getting through or around it. One of the more useful of these, for purposes of international cooperation on environmental issues, is the proposition that national sovereignties may be merged. Through treaties and other international agreements nations may collectively agree to action that they could not or would not take as separate and equal sovereignties. An atypical but well-known case that illustrates this principle is the treaty (1916) between the United States and Canada (officially with the United Kingdom) for the protection of migratory birds. Because the exercise of sovereignty over wildlife was believed to be allocated under the U.S. Constitution to the respective states, a treaty with another nation was necessary to permit the federal government to assume jurisdiction.[13] A land-use development was an outgrowth of this international treaty for it reinforced the legal foundation for the establishment of the National Wildlife Refuge System, which now involves the federal management of 452 refuges covering 89 million acres of public land.

Thus sovereignty may be extended or merged, and it may be self-denying—as in cases in which nations agree to limit or prohibit certain actions by themselves or their nationals. Sovereignty per se is no remedy for poverty and does nothing to improve the health, education, or economic opportunities of a people. It has been invoked very often to protect the interests of elites engaged in governing, resource exploitation, and military command. At the domestic level a defense against economic colonialism has been invoked to offset economic dependency from selling raw or only slightly processed raw materials. In the western United States assertions of "states rights" against Federal or "foreign" land ownership and control of exports is analogous to the sovereignty argument advanced by less-developed, resource-exporting countries. In both cases the sovereignty–states rights argument masks apprehension over loss of control of the resource base (e.g., land) upon which the local economy depends.[14] As social and economic pressures build within countries and governments encounter increasing difficulty in coping with events, the possibility of exchanging some intangible national sovereignty for tangible international economic aid becomes acceptable. We have noted the example of Latin American countries, which have been most vigorous in their assertions of sovereignty, to suggest that environmental cooperation with other governments might be possible if linked with financial and technological assistance. In the declarations of Brazilia and Manaus environmental cooperation—which largely involved land use—was offered provided that the burden of international financial indebtedness was eased.

Thus neither principles of international law nor of national sovereignty are impenetrable barriers to the development and extension of international policies regarding the uses of land. International policies may be incorporated in national legal doctrines that may be accommodated through skillful use of rhetoric, politics, and money. Developed with regard to national and geoecological circumstances, they may be made to serve positive transnational purposes, as in implementation by the United States and Canada of the 1916 North American migratory bird treaty. The more obdurate barriers to international environmental policies are ideological, but not excluding the economic factors that influence political behavior at the national level. With respect specifically to land use, economic factors have been paramount, although factors of health and sentiment may sway political decisions in particular instances.

Influence of Science on International Policy for Land

A broad range of environmental policy issues have been illuminated by scientific inquiries that frequently reveal the basic causes of environmental problems in the misuse of land. It is hardly an exaggeration to say that the numbers of people and the uses that they make of the land are at the root of most environmental problems. These basic factors underlie surface issues that people and governments generally regard as the real issues. Especially in their international context, issues such as exponential population growth are not perceived to be the ultimate cause of environmental disorders and hence are seldom seriously considered by public authorities.

In the developed countries people who appear to be in many ways intelligent seem unwilling, perhaps unable, to see the connections between population, environment, ignorance, poverty, and social disorder. The developed countries and especially the United States are self-appointed victims of fatuous policies that have abetted the migration of millions of destitute people from socioecologically bankrupt countries seeking better lives in the developed world. The refusal of the United States to contribute to the U.N. Fund for Population Activities has been regarded by critics as egregious short-sightedness contrary to the national interest. The self-imposed incomprehension of connections among population, resources (especially of land), poverty, and politics is at least in part a failure to understand their interactive character. A holistic or synthesizing view of environmental interrelationships might open the way to socioecological rationality. Land-related programs of the international agencies fall short of effectiveness as a consequence of their inability to deal holistically with land-use problems. Too often national and international efforts to alleviate poverty and famine caused by exhaustion or collapse of environmental life-support systems of land and water is to move people and livestock from degraded areas to undamaged lands where the process of wearing down the environment can begin again. However, an example of international scientific cooperation for addressing land use problems is the U.N. Plan of Action to Combat Desertification.[15] This program involves multiagency cooperation and is closely related to efforts to cope with the major international land-use problems presented by prolonged drought and misuse of grasslands in the African Sahel. A large number of international agencies and interagency organizations are involved in these efforts, including the Permanent Inter-State Committee on Drought Control in the Sahel, the U.N. Sudano-Sahelian Office, UNESCO's Man and the Biosphere Programme, and the FAO-UNEP program on Ecological Management of Arid and Semi-Arid Rangeland (EMASAR). Arid-lands research has been promoted by UNESCO, by ICSU through the former International Biological Programme, and by the International Geographical Union. Scientific survey and analysis of land use on a world scale was begun in 1949 by the International Geographical Union with financial assistance from UNESCO. Survey techniques had been developed in the United Kingdom in the early 1930s by L. Dudley Stamp, a pioneer in examining world land-use issues.[16]

Scientific knowledge of land-use capability could assist rationality in national and international land policy, but not necessarily in peaceful relationships among nations. For example, Hitlerite Germany was covetous of the agriculturally productive lands of Ukraine. Political ignorance of tropical forest-soils ecology has permitted misplaced settlement and land-clearance policies to flourish, with destructive consequences affecting the biological diversity of the Earth and the stability of its climate.

An important aspect of international scientific assessment of land-use capability is the identification and classification of the various types of soils. Land-use capability is in large measure dependent upon the properties of soils, and understanding their character and capability is basic to scientifically informed programs of international assistance in agriculture, forestry, and land use generally. The Food and Agriculture Organization of the United Nations has published a revised multivolume *Soil Map of the World* (1988).[17] Ironically, soil science and the mapping of world soils was pioneered by Russian academicians L.I. Passlov and N.N. Rosov.[18] The agricultural problems of Russia and the Soviet Union are not attributable to lack of diligence among their scientists. In the United States a response to the severe agricultural problems of the 1930s, illustrated by the notorious Dust Bowl, led to passage by the Congress of the Soil Conservation Act of 1935 and establishment of the Soil Conservation Service.[19] Under the vigorous leadership of its first director, Hugh Hammond Bennett, the SCS brought about a major turnaround in the historically wasteful attitudes of Americans toward land. Unfortunately, in the absence of a national policy for rational, conserving land use, economic temptations and the convoluted federal policies regarding agriculture eroded much of the good work of the early SCS. Even so, the agency has the institutional capability of playing a significant role in international cooperation in soil conservation.

Clearly soil science could make an important contribution to land policy, but there has been a strong tendency to focus soil research on food production. Indeed, some advances in the science and technology of soils and agriculture have contributed inadvertently to socioecological problems. Some critics of the Green Revolution in agriculture argue that the world food crisis is as much a problem of too many mouths as it is of too little food. Even so, scientific technology is contributing information regarding the effects of land uses that should assist the development of more rational land policies. For example, the ICSU Scientific Committee on Problems of the Environment (SCOPE) has undertaken a program of study of land transformation processes.[20] Case studies have been provided by fourteen countries and the number of case studies has been estimated as probably between forty and fifty. The committee enlisted the cooperation of the International Soil Science Society in this effort and joined with the ICSU Committee on Space Research (COSPAR) in a Symposium for the Study of Land Transformation Processes Using Observations from Space and the Ground.

Aerial photography and satellite remote sensing have provided technologies greatly facilitating the mapping and monitoring of land-use concerns of several types. For example, as many as fifty-five countries and five international organizations have undertaken various mapping or survey projects in cooperation with the U.S. Landsat System. But there is sensitivity in many countries about having their natural resources and land-use developments surveyed by "uninvited eyes."[21] Land-use changes of economic or military significance are of special concern to governments (in other countries as well as in their own). The unavoidable international impact of satellite surveillance led a committee of the U.S. National Research Council in 1977 to declare that remote sensing systems "constitute, in effect, an international public utility destined for international governance."[22] Here is a not unusual case of technique preceding policy. If the application of the technique (e.g., remote sensing) arouses political concerns, then technique may be said to drive policy. Visible evidence of what is happening to and on the land will almost certainly have policy implications. In any event the use of remote sensing technology now make possible the accurate, timely, and continuous monitoring of changes in land use—an essential concomitant of international land-use policy.

Concomitant with satellite surveillance is computer-aided mapping and the development of integrated geographic information systems.[23] These science-based technologies are now largely restricted to technologically advanced countries, but could be of great assistance to the implementation of land policies throughout the world. We include these technologies here because they could advance research around the globe in land-use trends, land-use capability, and monitoring of changes. The ultimate benefit of science applied to land-use problems could be its feedback effect upon popular attitudes, beliefs, and behaviors. Moreover, techniques such as impact analysis reveal blank spots or anomalies in our scientific understanding of the environment and thus stimulate efforts toward a more reliable science and more benign technologies.

The Economics of International Land-Use Issues

Adequately defined, with its many interrelating aspects taken into account, land-use economics and international relations afford persuasive arguments for consideration of international implications in national land-use planning and decision making. To the extent that national governments are persuaded that ecologically sound and sustainable value-conserving uses of their land are in their continuing economic interest, they may more readily accede to international policies and agreements designed to assist these uses. Knowledge of what to do, what not to do, what may be done, and probable consequences of decisions for international relations ideally should precede the formulation of policy. In the real world of politics this type of rationality seldom prevails. For example, the United States preempted the water of the Colorado River for agriculture and development with minimal regard to land-use consequences for Mexico. And plans of the U.S. Bureau of Reclamation to transform North Dakota agriculture from dry-land farming to irrigation were promoted without regard for effects upon the neighboring province of Manitoba.

Until basic facts about land use, its effects, and alternatives have been ascertained and translated into decisionable propositions, there is no adequate basis for sustainable land-use policy. As long as the uses of land are regarded as the exclusive business of land owners or national bureaucracies, and no facts are ascertained or data analyzed respecting land use and its effects, the ingredients of sustainable policy are likely to be missing. But even in some countries wherein the private ownership doctrines are most strongly held, governments collect large amounts of information regarding land use, (e.g., in the United States). The science of statistics had its origin in the inquisitiveness of national governments regarding the sources of national wealth and productivity, especially relating to land. The extent to which this information influences policy formation is customarily determined by politics.

The necessities of government may become opportunities for safeguarding the terrestrial resources of the biosphere through sustainable and ecologically sound economic policies developed through cooperative international action. Almost every major change in land use in developed countries today requires some form of governmental action (e.g., permits, licenses, loans, grants, variances, and inspections—among others). And in their insatiable quest for more revenues, and in efforts to improve living standards, governments have characteristically attempted to increase what comes off of and out of the land. As we have noted, the sources of reliable information for this purpose are to be found in the sciences and their related technologies. Governments have sought knowledge to advance economic objectives, but although acquired for purposes of economic development, knowledge may also illuminate environmental consequences and introduce further considerations into economic policy choice. Consider, for example, the environmental costs and consequences of surface mining of coal, the pulverization of rock in oil shale development, hydraulic mining of gold, and soil-erosive farming—consequences that may spill over across international borders.[24]

Knowledge uncovered is not easily held back indefinitely from the common domain. Moreover, knowledge tends to expand; the more that is learned about land use and its effects the more difficult it becomes to hold policy to customary prescientific principles. And as land owners and managers are initial beneficiaries of advancements in knowledge regarding land, they have been (e.g., in agriculture, forestry, and mining) among more active proponents of policy-relevant scientific experimentation and research. The resulting knowledge (for better or worse depending upon one's criteria) affects the way in which land is used. Histories of agriculture and forestry in the United States, and of the Green Revolution throughout the world, confirm the conclusion that science, narrowly applied, may not lead to generally beneficial results.[25]

Technoeconomic Influences

Clearly related to the influence of scientific knowledge and economic considerations are the effects of technology. Science tells the land owners what can be done; technology, economics, and finance provide the means to do it. Machinery and chemistry changed land-use patterns and practices over much of the world. Energy-intensive, capital-intensive, mechanized agriculture is characterized (perhaps deceptively) by low unit cost if total yields are sufficiently high. The conventional economics of this agriculture requires large-scale production and facilitates it. Mechanization and the Green Revolution are effective collectivizers. Smaller family-type farming is displaced by corporate-owned farming; small farms or fields are aggregated into large units; and the face of the land, the political economy, and the lives of many people are changed.

Patterns of land ownership and land use vary widely throughout the third world—small holdings in some countries—plantation monocrop production and latifundia in others. Trends in these economies, in land use more than many other aspects, are influenced by external aid programs and technology transfer. The U.N. development

programs and bilateral and multilateral technical and financial assistance in effect make international agencies and aid-giving governments participants in land-use decisions in many countries (e.g., the
Lomé Conventions of 1975 and 1981 between the European Community and African, Caribbean, and Pacific countries).[26] Within the U.N.
system, policies and programs for improving land use have been affected by a wide range of technologies influenced by the economic
policies of the development banks. Very often these activities are
jointly organized with one or more of the UN programs and specialized agencies especially UNDP, UNIDO, and FAO. This is especially
true with land-transforming projects involving agriculture, water resources development, land clearing, road construction, reforestation,
grassland restoration, and rural settlement. The past policies of the
World Bank and regional development banks often resulted in
unsustainable uses of the land and in social disruption in the interest
of relatively short-term financial (not truly economic) advantages. The
cumulative evidence of harm—economically, ecologically, and ethically—led in 1980 to the formation by the development banks and
associated lending institutions of the Committee of International
Development Institutions on the Environment (CIDIE).[27] During the
1980s this committee seemed to have gradually become more effective in considering the effects of international lending policies on land,
its natural resources, and ecological values.

These developments might be considered more economical than
technological, but in reality applied science, technology, economic
theories, and financial practices are bound together in a matrix of
international lending and assistance policy. No one of these factors
proceeds in international affairs without the others. All, for example,
were elements essential to the Green Revolution in which interna-
tionally promoted innovations in science-based agricultural technology brought about major economic and social changes in many third
world countries.

The Geopolitics of International Policy for Land

Throughout historic times and doubtless earlier, the possession and
use of land has been a major cause of conflict between peoples.[28]
Acquisition and control of land has probably been the principal objective of wars and invasions. Incursions out of Central Asia and the
European conquest of the Americas are conspicuous examples. As we
have noted, changes in land use and the condition of land internal to
a country may have ultimate, although sometimes indirect, effects upon
international relations. An example would be the land-enclosure move-

ment in nineteenth-century England, which, by driving people off the former common lands, in effect enlarged the pool of labor needed for the Industrial Revolution—which in turn had far-reaching effects upon international relations, commerce among states, and the mechanization of agriculture. Another development in land use with international repercussions was the plantation system and large-scale monocrop agriculture. The former led to the African slave trade; the latter widely replaced subsistence agriculture and nutritional self-sufficiency in many countries. Cash monocrop agriculture has had profound effects not only upon the land itself, but has also affected population distribution and urbanization, and has been a major factor in international trade and finance. The mercantilist practice of using less-developed countries as suppliers of raw materials to manufacturing nations, which in turn looked to these countries as markets for their products, has had profound environmental effects. Land conversion from forest to agriculture and grazing, deforestation, destructive mining practices, adverse effects of large dams, and excessive urban concentration by impoverished people driven off the land are some of the negative consequences of land-use practices beneficial in the short term to a relatively few people but with larger human national and international consequences noted earlier in this chapter.

Traditional attitudes and policies are slow to change especially if no militant group is pushing for new policies. So-called "agrarian reform," which characteristically has meant the breakup of large estates and the redistribution of land among landless peasants, has had mixed consequences. The process has led to social conflict within countries, which has often led to foreign involvement and intervention. Mexico, Cuba, and El Salvador are cases in point. Except through the international lending institutions, there are currently few ways in which timely international action can prevent or correct national policies for land that will almost certainly lead to adverse international repercussions.

The goal of sustainable development, which is now widely promoted by both intergovernmental and nongovernmental organizations, has the potential of inducing a new form of global geopolitics. We have noted that national sovereignty over land and resources is not an impervious barrier to international cooperation. Population policy, especially as it relates to growth of numbers and "colonization" of so-called undeveloped lands and migration to developed countries, is a more obdurate barrier. The ill-founded belief that economic market forces can more effectively adjust these matters than can national and international policies is especially obstructive at the present time. The economic and political interests of all people are delimited by their prospective lifespans. Some individuals and a few organizations do look beyond their lifetimes to the longer future. But it is difficult to persuade people to abstain from placing priority on their immediate foreseeable self-interest. In too many cases impoverished or financially overcommitted people are unable to do so. They are locked into practices that tomorrow will be self-destructive but will enable them to survive today. As we have observed in other chapters in this book, the social utility of the market in land-policy decisions is severely compromised by its inability to restrain policies and practices that currently benefit land owners and users but at opportunity costs, often irretrievable, to the larger social and economic good in the future. Thus the obvious difficulty in developing an ecologically rational policy for land at any institutional level lies in reconciling the factors influencing its use—demographic, ideological, economic, and ecologic. The process for attaining this reconciliation is unavoidably political. But for the political process to attain this objective, a "critical mass" of popular understanding and active support would be needed.

It is difficult to obtain or sustain rational and appropriate uses of land without ensuring the neutrality support or replacement of the currently dominant land-use decision makers. Unless the causes of misuse are overcome, mere legal prescription of remedial measures are unlikely to succeed. In some cases destruction of the environment occurs through default of policy. The point is illustrated by the repeated invasion of forest reserves and national parks in third world countries by poor landless peasants unimpeded by the responsible public authorities. There has always been a defining relationship between land tenure and forest policy exemplified in diverse culture, but overpopulation may overtake and overwhelm law and tradition.[29] Land-use policy implies policies governing population growth, settlement, and economic enterprise. It could hardly be otherwise, as land is a basic resource in any nation or economy. Still, the connections are widely overlooked.

At present, the international approach to land-use policy is necessarily largely incremental, addressing among other issues, specific land-use issues in cultivated agriculture, forestry, wetlands, natural-area preservation, and urbanization. The Food and Agriculture Organization (FAO) has had a major and continuing concern with land use. Its programs alone would be sufficient to put land use on the agenda of international relations. An elaborate structure of research, experimentation, advice, and planning has developed to bring experts and officials from national governments and international agencies into continuing interrelationships. For example, FAO, through its consultative group on international agriculture research, and the FAO

Panel of Experts on Forest Gene Resource and the International Board
of Plant and Genetic Resources assists the development of trees important to agriculture, especially food-bearing trees suitable for tropical agroforestry, and with obvious implications for tropical forest ecosystems. These efforts are intended to promote a more equitable,
sustainable, and harmonious international order, and so may be regarded as a constructive form of geopolitics.

There have been various U.N. efforts to stimulate and assist national and multilateral regional cooperation for natural resource conservation. An example of land use effecting action was the agreement
of nine African nations meeting in 1980 in Yaounde, Cameroon, to
negotiate a treaty on the improved management of tropical forest ecosystems and, with UNEP assistance, to establish a regional center for
scientific information and documentation in tropical ecology. The
ecological and environmental implications of agroforestry involve
concerns of UNEP and are studied by its Ecosystems Task Force. A
collaborator in these investigations is the International Council for
Research in Agroforestry (ICRAF), located in proximity to UNEP
headquarters in Nairobi.

Land-use policy with respect to wetlands has also become a focus
of international attention. For many reasons, but especially in the
interest of protecting migratory waterfowl, intergovernmental and
nongovernmental agencies have sought national action to prevent the
draining, filling, or contamination of wetlands of international importance. Leaders in this effort have been the International Council
for Bird Protection (ICBP) and the International Union for Conservation of Nature and Natural Resources (IUCN). UNESCO through its
Programme on Man and the Biosphere (MAB) and UNEP have also
been involved. An international Convention on Wetlands of International Importance especially as waterfowl habitat was adopted by an
international conference in Ramsar, Iran, in 1971. This treaty requires
each adhering government to conserve wetlands and designate particular wetlands of international importance for recording on a list
maintained by IUCN. Implementation involves either public acquisition of privately owned wetlands or restrictions on their use or both.
In many countries neither of these alternatives are likely to be elected.
As of 1989, fifty-four governments had signed the treaty, and a study
on the dynamics of continental wetlands was initiated under sponsor-
ship of the International Conference of Scientific Unions (ICSU).

To deal comprehensively with the subject matter of this chapter
would require book-length treatment. Many examples of international
aspects of land policies could be substituted for those described here.
Some topics of potential future significance, such as international

promotion of biotechnology, especially in agriculture and forestry, have not been discussed although sources of information have been indicated in the notes.[30]

As the twentieth century nears its close, there is little evidence that the political heads of state have understood the significance of land policy in relation to the broad spectrum of international issues. Political "leaders" appear to see the various aspects of mankind's environmental predicament, but seldom perceive their interrelationships forming a global problematic with implications for all nations everywhere. This chapter has documented major advances in international cooperation on behalf of land and resources. We have noted that scientific information and science-based technologies for surveillance and monitoring are far in advance of utilization in most countries. If information and technology can drive policy, and international cooperation permits, the land-use problems of the Earth could be far more effectively addressed in the years ahead. Yet there is a wide gap between declared intentions to conserve land and the biosphere and the actual willingness to adopt or accept the action necessary to realize those declarations. Preparatory negotiations on a treaty to protect the world's biological heritage revealed the dichotomy of nations between the goal of ecological conservation, on which most governments agreed, and the means to that end, on which they did not agree.[31] Can the goal be taken seriously if the means are denied? For the present, we are unable to offer a comparative calculation of advances in environmental protection and coincidental decline in environmental quality and sustainability of land and other natural resources. The political will of nations to reverse that decline is far from certain. Our position is one of hope, but is unavoidably inconclusive.

Part Three

Reconciling Ethics and Politics: Steps Toward Solutions

Is it possible to achieve a policy for land that is both equitable and ecologically, economically, and politically sustainable? Should a national policy for land be codified and adopted as law? On these questions, opinion in America has been sharply divided. Between highly individualistic, traditional libertarian values and considerations of sustainability, societal and transgenerational equity, and environmental integrity, room for compromise may be narrow. We believe that more desirable social and ecological values related to land will be reinforced by trends in science, population dynamics, environmental and technology assessment, and preferences regarding quality of life. Transition to a new ethics and politics of land, however, will not be clearly defined or smooth. Redefining property rights will be difficult and unpleasant. Members of new generations likely will not become wealthy as a result of land transactions, as they did in the past. Regardless of the obstacles it faces, however, a new policy for land should be restored to a position of importance on the national political agenda. For two decades, political representatives have avoided addressing a new land policy, arguing that it was a no-win issue. The losers, however, have been society as a whole and members of future generations.

181

9

The Ecosystem as a Criterion
for Land Policy

Lynton Keith Caldwell

This chapter and the one immediately following examine the relationship between ecology and land policy from two differing perspectives. The first invokes ecology as a guide to policy and planning. It counsels prudence, foresight, and the conservation of those qualities of land and environment needed to sustain biological and economic productivity. It does not look to ecology for direct answers to complex questions of policy, but it sees ecology as a source of information and insight of growing utility in avoiding errors in decisions affecting land and environment. Thus its approach is essentially pragmatic. In contrast, the next chapter is a critique of general ecological theory as a source of land ethics. Its approach is philosophical rather than political; its scope is broader, embracing ecology as a discipline and a guide to ethical and moral conduct. These two essays parallel one another, but they emphasize different aspects of the relationship of ecology to land policy. This chapter considers ecology and ecosystem theory as cautionary guides to policy—as indications of the way the world of nature works. Its thesis does not require the ecosystems concept to be clearly defined. The concept is essentially heuristic, its reliability relative. If the cautionary, explanatory, and predictive capabilities of ecology, however imperfect, equal or exceed those of other inputs to land-use decisions, it is rational to recommend it as a source for guidance. Its utility in defining ethics is an altogether different matter, one whose conclusions depend heavily upon assumptions regarding relationships between human society and the natural world.

Lest the reader be confused by the different evaluations of ecology in relation to policy set out in this and the succeeding chapter, the following observations may help to explain these differences. First, ecology, unlike physics, is not an exact science. Its complexity and the variability of its subject matter make it more like a social science than like the more reductionist fields of biology (e.g., molecular biology). Its lack of predictive power is hardly less than that of economics—in which governments and many people place (unwarranted) confidence. What might be called "practical ecology" draws upon human experience and historical evidence, as well as upon "scientific" methods. Our conventional definition of the scientific disciplines are to some extent arbitrary, and ecology does not fit the narrower molds in which some scientists would pour knowledge.

Second, ecological theory has been changing rapidly and issues that have been controversial have been dissipated by new interpretations of natural processes. These also may change. At present, for example, "balance of nature" (although still in the older literature) has largely given way to the more sophisticated concept of "ecosystem integrity." The integrity concept imputes no teleology or preconceived unity to an ecosystem. It does observe the effects upon species—including humans—and the physical properties of the earth—soil, water, and air—resulting from the disintegration of particular ecosystems. To the extent that ecology is a study of systemic interdependencies it should provide clues to what human interventions in natural (or human-made) systems might prove harmful to human welfare.

Third, ecology might better be described as metascience than science in the narrower sense. Here the holistic outlook on the earth becomes relevant. Like the so-called "balance" concept, holism can be pushed by its adherents and by its critics to a reductio ad absurdum. The holistic way of viewing reality is discounted by some essentially reductionist scientists who value detailed precision over general relevance. The Gaia hypothesis, for example (advanced as a hypothesis, not a theory), takes a viewpoint that is holistic in its inclusiveness. A holistic approach to land policy—considered later in this chapter— does not require that account be taken of every relevant detail, no matter how minor. It does require that the broad context of policy be considered. Even if one concedes the foregoing observations, the relationship of ecology to ethics remains to be considered. Here a different set of issues arises, as Kristin Shrader-Frechette demonstrates in the next chapter.

The Ecosystemic View of the Environment

American land policy has been based upon a set of historically derived assumptions—legal, economic, and political—that provide no means for taking the fundamental ecological properties of land into account. It is, of course, necessary to cope with land problems within the existing context of public attitudes, laws, and economic arrangements. But it is also important to know that there is a larger environmental context for policy with which laws and governments must ultimately reckon: it is the condition of the land as the physical base for human welfare and survival. If human demands upon the natural environment continue to mount, it will become necessary as a matter of welfare and survival to revise present land-policy assumptions for a policy of land management on ecologically valid principles. Public land policy would be public policy for all land, and some traditional rights of ownership would be modified. But prospects for a sustainable future and for enjoyment of privacy and security within socially beneficial uses of the land might be enhanced.

Public policy restricted to lands under government ownership might be politically expedient but it would be ecologically unrealistic. In fact, there are many public policies governing uses of privately owned land so that the issue is seldom public regulation in principle, but rather public policy for what purpose and to what effect. The natural physical and biological systems in the land do not necessarily correspond to the assumptions, boundaries, and uses that law and political economy impose upon them. The stress of human demands upon the land often disrupts ecological processes and impairs the capacity of the natural environment for self-renewal. The obvious tendency of growing numbers and concentrations of human populations is to increase the stress and to make its alleviation more costly and difficult. Impairmᴄnt or impoverishment of the natural life-support system is an ascertainable and measurable phenomena. Recourse to abstract theory such as "balance of nature" is not necessary to establish, for example, interrelationships between overgrazing, soil erosion, stream sedimentation, and desiccation of watersheds. When toxic leaches from landfills poison the adjacent soil, water, and living species, it is clear that the interactive properties of the environment have been invaded and impaired, and that the integrity of the ecosystem has been disrupted.

How would a land policy based upon ecological concepts differ from policies based upon other considerations? Public land policies here and abroad have traditionally been based on juridic, economic, or demographic concepts.[1] Land planning based on sectoral analysis (essentially on economic and social uses) has been predominant in those countries in which the so-called rational allocation of natural resources in land has become accepted policy. Spatial or physical planning, "which considers man and his natural environment in their geographical and historical associations," is an alternative complementary approach to land policy but does not necessarily take ecological considerations fully into account.[2]

Ecological considerations, although not always by that name, have influenced land policies. Yet as early as 1961, G.A. Hills of the Ontario Department of Lands and Forests was advocating an ecological basis for land-use planning.[3] At that time the term "ecosystem" had not come into common usage, but Hills chose an equivalent expression—"a biological productivity system," which he defined as "any area of land together with the organisms which it supports." That "area of land" included its physiographic properties, notably its capability for human uses. But an explicit ecosystemic approach to land policy has seldom been attempted on national or regional scales. The reason does not lie wholly in the complexity and ambiguity of the ecosystems concept, although these are deterring factors.

As a theoretical proposition, the term "ecosystem" has been given several interpretations, ranging from its use as a basic environmental concept to a denial that it has any real scientific validity or any practical utility. An intermediate opinion restricts it to very specific bounded biotic communities. The use of the term in this chapter is as a concept to assist understanding of the interrelating dynamic complexities of the natural world, including its human elements. As previously suggested, it should perhaps be described as a metascience that as of today is largely beyond the reach of reductionist methodologies. However defined, "ecosystem" has been widely accepted as a broad environmental concept and is now well-established in the lexicon of popular usage. Those biologists who wish to restrict the term to a precise scientific definition are, of course, free to do so, but there is little point to their arguing that other and broader interpretations are, for other purposes, less valid.

Ecologists and philosophers may debate the reality of ecosystems and the rationality of using the ecosystem concept as a guide to behavior and policy. As a practical matter, however, the ecosystem concept has already been adopted as a criterion for public policy. For example, the governments of Canada and the United States in the 1978 Agreement on Great Lakes Water Quality declared their intent "to prevent further pollution of the Great Lakes Basin Ecosystem"—and to restore and enhance water quality in the Great Lakes Basin Ecosystem" and to "preserve the aquatic ecosystems."[4] Article I, paragraph (g), of the agreement states that

> Great Lakes Basin Ecosystem means the interacting components of air, land, water and living organisms, including man, within the drainage basin of the St. Lawrence River at, or upstream from the joint at which this river becomes the international boundary between Canada and the United States.[5]

Moreover, in 1985 the governors and premiers of the Great Lakes states and provinces adopted on February 11 at Milwaukee *The Great Lakes Charter*, which declared that "The planning and management of the water resources of the Great Lakes Basin should recognize and be founded upon the integrity of the natural resources and ecosystem of the Great Lakes Basin."[6]

The U.S. Endangered Species Act of 1973 declared as one of its purposes "to provide a means whereby the ecosystems upon which endangered and threatened species depend may be conserved."[7] Executive Order No. 11990 (May 24, 1977) refers to "natural systems," which is essentially the same concept, although perhaps less inclusive than ecosystem if the term "natural" does not include human-made or urban environments.[8] A Scandinavian newsletter on acid rain led off its June 1991 issue with the heading "Sensitive Ecosystems," and the U.S. National Committee for the Man and the Biosphere Program in May 1992 announced the organization of its work into four ecosystem directorates: High Latitude Ecosystems, Human Dominated Ecosystems, Marine and Coastal Ecosystems, and Temperate Ecosystems.[9] Clearly the ecosystem concept is built into the criteria for environmental policy decisions and consequently may be expected to influence policy for land.

The ecosystem, like "health," is not amenable to precise definition but is most commonly applied to "natural" ecosystems. To speak of the "health of ecosystems" compounds the ambiguity, but is nonetheless a useful concept. We can identify the absence of health and can see that ecological conditions may undergo alterations regarded as "unhealthful" (from a human perspective) such as the "plague" of rabbits in Australia, the Chinese water hyacinth in Florida waterways, the Mediterranean fruit fly in California orchards, the increase of schistosomiasis with perennial irrigation, or the spread of mesquite over former grasslands in the American Southwest. We can see that short-term, profit-maximizing, resource-destroying land use is the antithesis of preserving ecosystem health and integrity. We don't dismiss health as a concept for humans because we can't precisely define or measure it. Why dismiss integrity of the ecosystem for similar reasons?

Failure to apply ecological criteria to land-use policies is primarily the consequence of two interactive causes. The first is the inability of society, because of cultural conditioning, inadequacy of knowledge, insufficiency of means, or incapacity of institutions, to build ecologically based land policies into a general system of environmental management. These deficiencies, however, are gradually being remedied by advances in ecology, broadly defined. The second—more obvious and more "political"—is incompatibility of interests among competing land users. An ecosystems approach to land policy encounters resistance to the degree that it is inconsistent with the prevailing values, assumptions, expectations, institutions, and practices. Yet ecological considerations may be compatible with specific aspects of traditional land-use arrangements. For example, specific legal restrictions in Denmark, the Netherlands, Germany, and the United Kingdom are designed to protect and perpetuate certain traditional uses of the land for ecological benefits as well as for sentimental and esthetics purposes. The results are sustainable long-term economic benefits.

To plan for the future is much easier than to undo errors of the past. Corrective action can be taken, as illustrated by the restoration of the Kissimmee River ecosystem in Florida undertaken after ecologically destructive channelization by the Corps of Engineers.[10] Misconceived policies often follow from ecological ignorance or political compromise. For example, many of the National Wildlife Refuges are too small and erroneously bounded to protect the species for which they were established. To bring these areas into conformity with ecological principles would involve numerous real-estate transactions distasteful to politicians, who develop greater enthusiasm for enlarging airports and building new highways. Of course humans, the impacts of their technologies, and their uses of the land are elements in nearly all present-day ecosystems. Yet they are subject to potentialities and limitations inhering in nature, and their sustainability is dependent upon their compatibility with the renewal requirements of their natural life-support base.

Incompatibility among uses derives as often from the institutional interests of agencies responsible for land-use decisions, (e.g., banks, government agencies, corporate landholders, natural resource industries), as it does from contradictions among the use themselves. Thus the factors involved in money-lending speculation, taxation, insurance, and laws of title, inheritance, and trespass, when woven into a nonecological matrix of public land policy, afford resistant barriers to an ecosystems approach. To establish a land policy in which ecological principles are respected would require that the conventional matrix of aggregate interests be ravelled out and rewoven into a new pattern.

In a colony on the moon there would be an overwhelming presumption in favor a predominately ecological approach. The arguments for survival would outweigh all others. Ecology in this context would be the organizing concept through which interactive influences of temperature, gravity, radiation, artificial atmosphere, and physiological-psychological parameters. On earth, ecological criteria may be expected to modify or override other indices of value as the limits of the closed-system aspects of the planet Earth become increasingly apparent. A land ethic may gain acceptance as a justifying by-product of the trend, but to explain the reorientation of attitude on moral grounds alone could be making a virtue of necessity.

The political context of public policy for land changes when ecological theories develop. As we have previously observed, policy for sustainability cannot be confined realistically to lands in governmental ownership, but must take account of whatever lands are included in particular ecological communities, regardless of who holds title to them. This broadened context would be opposed by persons committed to the inviolate right of private land ownership, or who hold specific interests in land use that they believe might be threatened by public action. Ecological principles are in theory more easily applied to government lands than to private holdings, but it does not follow that public agencies honor these principles in practice. Pressure for early economic returns and the financial or technological inability of the private owner to apply ecological concepts, deter the application of ecological principles to private land management. But if the management of whole ecosystems becomes a matter of public policy, then the formulation of land-use policy must proceed upon the assumption that all land is in some degree public. There are implications in this assumption for all parties concerned—public and private.

To institute a broad ecological approach to land policy, the life-support capabilities of the environment must be ascertained. This environmental consideration, emphasized throughout this volume, implies an ecological viewpoint toward relationships between humans and the rest of nature. But this is not the viewpoint from which pioneers, land speculators, farmers, miners, stockmen, lawyers, bankers, newspaper editors, or local government officials have commonly seen the land. One reason is that to institute an ecological approach to public land policy, a great many other things besides land must be considered. People, in general, do not like to think in complex terms— life is simpler when questions and answers are simple. An ecological policy implies considerations of all the interdependencies among beings on the planet. It would include many things omitted in less comprehensive approaches. And it would limit single-purpose approaches to the environment, thus arousing opposition among those persons, individual or corporate, whose single-purpose pursuits would be frustrated.

Implications of an Ecosystems Land Policy

Before examining more closely the ecological basis for modification of rights of land ownership, the implications of the term "land policy" must be identified, as they are basic to the questions: What approach to land policy is most consistent with the public interest? All things considered, what policy in principle, in the aggregate, is best? The term "best" arouses a multitude of subsidiary questions. Is there a public interest apart from the cumulated interests of individuals? The idea of "best" in any sense is certain to be rejected by persons unwilling or unable to consider normative concepts other than their own which they may believe to have universal validity. Persons who believe that the only practical focus of public policy is upon things as they are would find little interest in considering alternative viewpoints. Nevertheless, if goals and values are implicit in the concept "policy," some policies must, by some criteria, be "better." Not all criteria that may be advanced for the formulation and application of a policy afford equally effective means to its specified ends. Moreover, not all goals or objectives serve equally well the general or long-term interests of society. There are, of course, differences over what long-term interests might be and whether the concept has any practical meaning. Nevertheless there are considerations significant for the future of any human society, whatever its goals or values. For example, policies that permitted massive and continuing loss of topsoil or encouraged the "mining of ground water or deforestation for cattle ranching" would not be good *public* land policies under any criteria, however beneficial they might appear to be to the immediate interests of particular land users or owners.

In the United States, and particularly in the West, ambiguity can easily occur in the use of the expression "public land policy." Does the expression apply to land generally—all land? Or does it refer only to policies regarding lands in public (i.e., governmental) ownership? Conventional American assumptions and word usage tend toward the latter definition as the more appropriate. Yet public exercise of eminent domain, of land-use zoning, abatement of nuisances, and of the public sale of land for tax delinquency make it clear that public jurisdiction over land is not confined to public ownership where application of the state's police power is invoked. An ecosystems approach to policy for land assumes a scope that embraces all land regardless of its ownership or custody under law. The metes and bounds of ecological communities are determined by physical, biological, and cultural parameters. People may impose their own arrangements on natural systems; but engineers, surveyors, and lawyers neither amend nor repeal the so-called laws of nature, although they may alter or destroy biotic communities or they may improve their utility—even quality—for human purposes. And although people have never been able to comprehend fully the ultimate unity of the ecosphere, a complex unity embracing the entire earth, they have been learning more and more about its interrelated workings.

Research on global climate change is enlarging this understanding. As more has been learned, the practicality of introducing ecological concepts into land-use policy has been enhanced. But the word "practicality" may be given two different interpretations. There is a conventional short-run practicality of sociopolitical sanctioned arrangements; and there is also a long-run practicality that takes account of ecological trends, assesses the consequences of their continuation into the future, and estimates the effects of modifying forces that might be employed to advance, retard, or prevent them.

Implicit in ecological thinking is recognition that maintenance of biotic communities depends upon the consistency of human standards, laws, and boundaries with those irreplaceable characteristics of land that have evolved through natural processes. For example, structural works or artificial boundaries, when forced into or across a natural system, may alter, impair, or destroy it. Single-purpose land uses, such as flood control, irrigation, or navigation, if pursued without regard to a full range of consequences, may impose new economic and ecological costs on society. A Southern Pacific Railroad causeway altered the ecology of the Great Salt Lake; the Tamiami highway across southern Florida impaired the hydraulic system that nourishes the Everglades; landfills on coastal estuaries have destroyed numerous and valuable marine and salt-marsh ecosystems; and persistent mining of groundwater has changed the ecology of soils and land surfaces in many parts of the United States, notably in the semiarid West. It is likely that the disrupting of biotic communities will induce consequences that will "feed back" to disrupt civilized society. It is not obvious, however, that human changes must always be destructive to natural communities or that, with thoughtful planning, human-made and natural ecosystems could not more often coexist in harmony.

But why this concern with an ecological basis for land policy? By what reasoning is an ecological approach to land use more useful or more valid than any other? Does ecosystemic thinking have a utilitarian value that recommends it to policy makers quite independent of whatever ethical values might be imputed to ecological concepts? Ecological criteria are beyond the perceived advantage of many economic or political interests. From a conventional "conservative" viewpoint, only nature lovers and a few apprehensive scientists would substitute of a naturalistic ideology—an ecological mystique—for the economic common sense of people who know that the practical business of life continues to be the procuring of food, clothing, shelter, and material wealth. Does ecological thinking impute some teleological design to nature? Are people required to seek out nature's "purposes" and adapt their laws and practices to nature's ends regardless of their own needs and purposes?

Some traditional deists, identifying God's purposes with Nature's, might affirm this proposition. Adherents to natural law concepts might still do so. But in the dominant societies of this technoeconomic age mastery or, at the very least, manipulation of nature toward progress and growth sometimes resembles the practice of a secular religion. Nature, if she has purposes, does not reveal them in language that contemporary people understand. Technological society, however, has defined and developed its own purposes in relation to nature. These purposes are primarily economic and, at minimum, require the obtaining of food, clothing, shelter, and the means of communication from nature. To this end humanity has organized its relationships with the environment on the basis of uses made of the properties of the natural world. These are categorized under the familiar expression "natural resources."

As long as human numbers were few, technology was simple, and demands upon the natural world limited, it was feasible to deal with the land and its products as if they were no more than discrete resources. Society was seldom able to make rapid, progressive, and far-reaching changes in biotic communities. Major ecological changes, such as deforestation, or the spread of cultivation by hoe and plow over grasslands required time, measured in the histories of Europe and Asia by centuries.[11] Some of these changes, as in the brittle, subarid ecosystems of the Middle East were cumulatively destructive.[12] Other changes, as in the clearing of forests for agriculture in Western Europe, largely substituted one ecological system for another of comparable stability and productivity.[13] But modern science and technology have permitted society to upset longstanding ecological relationships. Humans have multiplied without restraint, technology has become powerful and complex with unpredictable side effects, and demands upon the environment have become inordinate. Competition for resources has rapidly increased and conflicts among resource users have become a major phenomenon of international politics, of economic and environmental policy.[14]

If categorizing the products of nature into "natural resources" had been based upon a comprehending, conserving, selective utilization of the ecosystem, the implications of this "development process" for the integrity and survival of the ecosystem might have been sustainable. These concepts and practices might have been codified as principles or as considerations by which conflicts over specific resource uses might have been mediated. But ecological integrity as a criterion for policy choices has followed, not preceded, the natural resources concept of people-environment relationships. As a consequence, public policy for land has shared in the contentiousness associated with the politics of natural resources, and ecological concepts have had, as yet, little mediating effect upon land-use conflicts. Neither in politics nor in public administration has there been a generally accepted body of knowledge or doctrine by which conflicts over resource uses could be readily resolved. In the absence of an "ordering" or organizing concept, efforts to coordinate natural resources policies have been largely ineffectual or have been used as covers to impose one use over others or to prevent such imposition.

Prior to intensification of the water-pollution issue, the major impetus toward coordinative efforts in water policy in the United States were efforts to restrain autonomous and arbitrary exercise of power by the Corps of Engineers or to reconcile differences between the corps and competing agencies, most frequently the Bureau of Reclamation. Ostensibly to mediate conflict, Congress adopted a multiple-use mandate to guide government decision making. But Congress did not establish priorities among uses, with a consequence that disputes over uses continue to prevail.[15]

Public policy for land use, as for natural resources generally, has been decided chiefly through trial by political combat. "Conservation" as a concept has been helpful principally as an intermediary proposition, midway between unrestricted competition among resource users and an ecologically based view of public responsibility for the self-renewing capabilities of the biotic community. Aphorisms such as "conservation means wise use" are of little help in the absence of objective criteria for choice. An ecological approach to public land policy implies the possibility of public decisions based upon empirically demonstrable public interest in environmental quality and in the self-renewing capabilities of biotic communities.

Availability of an objectively rational basis for land-policy decisions (if such a basis is actually possible) does not imply that the option to be guided by this knowledge will be accepted or acted upon. Human beings may be expected to act more often on a subjective level of rationality than upon more general and enduring principles. But, until ecological concepts have been made articulate and their amenability to practical application has been demonstrated, they present a difficult challenge for policy makers. Some observers, however, see the emergence of an ecological rationality that, were it to become more widely adopted, could change the politics of land-use decisions.[16]

At present the ecosystems approach to environmental policy, even when written into law, remains largely on the theoretical level. Nevertheless the approach is available as a strategy for research with a view to practical application at such time as it is perceived as a means toward coping with environmental problems. Ecological criteria are now available for environmental planning and whatever their deficiencies, they are generally more reliable than uninformed, nonecological guesswork. One should allow for the possibility that a scientific proposition believed to be valid may in practice prove to be wrong. But science has a tradition of self-correction—a quality generally deficient in politics. Thus an important distinction should be drawn between the uses of ecology in scientific-environmental problem solving and ecology as a basis for policy decisions.[17]

This distinction may explain why some ecologists—confident in their own science—are critical of or opposed to the use of ecological criteria in public policy decisions. Simply stated, they doubt that politicians and most public administrators are competent to evaluate ecological data, and fear that policies allegedly based on ecological criteria may prove ineffectual or even disastrous and scientists will be blamed. When ecologists sometimes emphasize the incomplete and uncertain state of ecological theory and data, their effort may be to guard against overreliance on ecology and not to dismiss its scientific value. But ecology as a perspective on the complex interrelatedness of the world has escaped the custody of professional ecologists and entered the public domain as an approach to the understanding of nature. Greater effort should therefore be made toward raising the level of scientific literacy among public officials.

In the Water Quality Agreements of 1978 the governments of Canada and the United States adopted a basin-wide ecosystem approach to policy, recognizing that whatever happened on the land of the basins' watershed affected the quality of its water. The International Joint Commission (IJC) is responsible for overseeing the implementation of the agreements and its decisions may possibly provide a model for ecological management if (as is very likely) countervailing political considerations do not intrude.

To understand the environmental predicament of the modern world is to begin to understand why an ecological approach is necessary to human well-being and perhaps even to survival. Unfortunately, understanding of the circumstances now often described as the "ecological crisis" carries no automatic insight in how to correct or prevent conditions that are almost universally conceded to be harmful.[18] If the application of ecological concepts to human assumptions about life and behavior implies a new way of organizing human relations with the natural world, an ecological approach to land policy implies fundamental changes in the rights and responsibilities of individuals, corporations, and government agencies in the possession and use of land. That poses some difficult choices for politics, government, and the law, and for the interpretation of ethical and religious principles.

There should be no doubt that ecologically based public policies imply a thoroughgoing transformation of some major sectors of the nation's political economy. A public land policy based on ecological principles necessarily would be comprehensive and coordinative. The individual land owner would lose certain rights and gain certain protections. With appropriate criteria for decision making, controversies over land use could be more often settled by mediative or administrative means than by judicial procedures, and settlements could be based as often on ecological realities as on statutory law.

Substantial changes could be expected to take place in the practical economics of land use. Application of ecological concepts would find a major obstacle in the indiscriminate treatment of land as a commodity. Private possession of land under ecological ground rules could be made consistent with an ecological approach to land policy. But the freedom to buy, sell, or transfer land without regard to the ecological consequences of the intended or resulting action would not be consistent with an ecological approach. Laissez-faire land economics, although deeply rooted in American folkways, is becoming increasingly inconsistent with the interests of the vast majority of citizens who live in great cities, who own no land, and for whom the needs and amenities of life in land are becoming increasingly costly and difficult of access.

The Substance of an Ecological Approach

The ecological approach has been advanced as a way of developing a conserving and sustainable public land policy. It would differ from policies traditionally dominant in the United States and also to a large extent in other countries. But the specific ways in which ecosystemic relationships could be used as criteria for public policy for land must be defined before their operational feasibility can be assessed. The following summary of the salient properties of ecosystems criteria suggests some of the practical advantages to be gained from their application to land policies.

The first and essential characteristic of the ecological approach is its holistic emphasis.[19] A holistic approach means identifying and taking account of all factors of significant relevance to any situation. In a pluralistic political economy unaccustomed to holistic thinking, this comprehensiveness of outlook and analysis would be a salutary corrective to the tendencies of society to attack problems on a linear or single-purpose basis. The novelty of holistic analysis is now diminished by the growth of systems thinking in government and industry. Indeed, ecosystems criteria that are inherently holistic may be taken as an application of systems thinking to relationships among natural and artificial environments. Ecological criteria, for example, are absolutely essential to the construction of life-support systems for the manned exploration of outer space. There are reductionist scientists and philosophers who discount holistic concepts as unattainable, hence imaginary. They call to mind mechanics who study the minute parts of a watch and their interactions, but believe the whole watch to be incomprehensible. Perhaps the cosmic whole can never be fully understood, but if true, neither can the functions and relationships of the parts be fully comprehended. Fortunately for astronauts, these antiholistic skeptics do not design spaceships. A holistic approach to spaceship design is no more utopian or unattainable than is the question, What can we afford to ignore or leave out in space vehicle design?

Second, ecological criteria are based on scientific knowledge, although science does not yet have adequate answers to all ecological problems (as indeed to any problem that science addresses). Public land policies have not hitherto been based on scientific considerations. To enlist science in determining the goals of public policy is a departure from tradition, although science has often been invoked on behalf of policies adopted by other than scientific reasoning. For example, the U.S. Bureau of Land Management applies many scientific concepts to specific problems in its administration of federal public lands, but there is much less science in the laws under which the total public land system operates. Obviously, science does not contain the answers to all policy questions, but in the present state of confusion and contradiction that characterizes land laws, at least in the United States, scientific criteria might afford an objective basis for resolving (more often than mediating) otherwise irreconcilable disputes.[20]

Third, ecological criteria have the advantage of using mediative or administrative procedures in preference to litigation. This becomes possible to the extent that laws, policies, and actions are based on scientifically ascertainable facts rather than on political or technological fiat. Questions of fact become as important as questions of law (at least in an evidentiary sense), and issues formerly litigated in the courts cease to be issues when certain rights, practices, or beliefs associated with land ownership are confirmed, modified, or extinguished by demonstrable evidence, which may be more inclusive than some of the restrictive rules of evidence admissible in the courts.

An ecosystems approach may appear simple only when stated as a general principle—biotic communities themselves may be infinitely complex. The approach begins with an assumption derived from scientific inquiry. The natural world is a composite of interrelating life systems subsisting in a highly improbably terrestrial environment. This environment—the ecosphere or biosphere—is finite. Some of the components are naturally renewable, others are not. Of its renewable components (or resources), some are capable of restoration within a time dimension meaningful to man. But others, fossil fuels, for example, are incapable of renewal in human time dimensions; although for some resources substitutes may be found, they too may be limited.

The ultimate necessity of an ecosystems approach to environmental policy, including land, follows from the finite amount of land, water, air, and other substances upon which the human economy depends and the infinite character of human demands upon the environment. The heavier the stress of human demands upon the environment, the greater the degree to which those demands must be coordinated and rationalized in order that the economy continue to function. In an economy of scarce essentials and pressing demands, either the strong preempt resources and deprive the weak, or, where democratic collectivism prevails, socialization, rationing, licensing, and police action are instituted to insure fair shares.[21] Political laissez-faire in relation to the environment is feasible only when demands made upon it are relatively light and when natural ecological processes are permitted to operate, renewing the ecosystem so that what is used today is replaced for use tomorrow.

The argument for ecological sophistication in public policies for land and the environment depends no longer primarily on the threat of immanent shortages of food, energy, or raw materials for industry that troubled the early conservationists. The long-range prospect for shortages is real, but more immediate danger now perceived is to the quality of life and to human freedom—especially personal freedom—that would follow from a course of action that presses society to ultimate extremities in the maximum utilization of resources and space. Total resource utilization might require total social control and the loss of choice and variety in life as the price of continuing subsistence.

Throughout nearly all human history, most of mankind appears to have enjoyed extended periods of generally favorable environmental conditions. There were, of course, exceptional circumstances in which natural disasters or human errors impaired a particular localized part of an ecosystem. Earthquakes, floods, droughts, epidemics, and famines have disturbed the relative equilibrium of human societies, but the ecosphere as a whole has maintained its stability over thousands of years, even though suffering and death have resulted from localized oscillations.[22] The cumulative effect of human activities today could, however, result in unprecedented change, for example in the global climate and in disintegration of stratospheric ozone. Technology and science have enabled people to cope more effectively with natural disasters, and in some measure to prevent them. But the very success of the human enterprise has created its greatest danger. Technoscience has now given humans free rein to increase their numbers and their demands. The result has been a runaway increase in human populations and unremitting pressure on all resources, including land.

This rapid inflation of human populations and their demands has already impaired the quality of the environment over large areas of the earth and threatens more serious damage in the years ahead. But at the present stage of human affairs, contemplation of the almost certain consequences of ecological folly is less painful than undergoing the changes that would be required to bring generic man-environment relationships into ecological sustainability. There may yet be time to preserve a margin of personal freedom, of environmental variety, and of unforeclosed opportunities that would approach but probably not equal what has been experienced in the past. But the prospect of these conditions surviving into the next century is every day lessened. Science fiction, which often assumes a role of prophecy, presents, in the main, bleak prospects for personal freedom and variety but a great future for adaptive responses and violence. Yet as René Dubos convincingly argued, adaptation can as easily accommodate to degrading or impoverished conditions as to beneficial innovations.[23] The triumphs of science and technology do not seem to include a mastery of ecological mechanics sufficient to offset many of the limiting processes inherent in nature. To avoid collision with ecological inevitabilities people would first have to bring their impulses under control and exercise a collective self-restraint that has not yet become a strongly marked human characteristic.

The idea of instituting lesser controls now to protect basic values and to avoid more drastic measures later has little contemporary appeal. It is the American way, and indeed the human way, to react to present crises rather than to have forestalled them. For who can be sure that a threatened future crisis will actually materialize? There is no end to conventional wisdom on behalf of procrastination. What candidate for elective public office would advocate unsettling social change in the face of dangers that were neither clear nor present in the perception of his constituents? How many politicians would commit themselves to the prevention of dangers that, if real, could only be prevented by an inconvenient rearranging of present institutions and relationships, and would deprive prospective voters of the happy prospect of something-for-nothing material gains? The evasive tactic for politicians has been to declaim their good intentions rhetorically and to call for more research before action (taking care to avoid "wasting" too much money on research that might produce politically unacceptable findings).

Contrary to allegations sometimes made by persons who see it threatening their particular interests or ideologies, ecologically based policy is not antipeople. Human welfare, now and in the future, is its objective. But the welfare of the individual is ultimately dependent upon the viability of the life-supporting biotic community. Impoverishment of natural world means impoverishment of all society dependent upon it, individuals included. For example, to preserve wetlands and estuaries from being drained or filled for dry-land uses is not to prefer ducks and muskrats to people. It is rather to prefer the interests of the whole of society in a viable relationship over those self-centered interests that would jeopardize the biotic community for immediate and personal monetary gain. Yet our policies and laws should recognize, as they currently do not, that many resource users—especially farmers—are driven by economic necessity to practices that are known ultimately to be self-destructive (e.g., mining groundwater for irrigation).

The substance of an ecological approach to land policy is to identify, to protect, and in the interest of human welfare to manage with caution the biotic communities upon whose continuing viability human welfare depends. So far as feasible, an ecological approach allows natural processes to carry on the work of self-renewal unassisted by human effort. To the extent that nature can be relied upon to renew the ecosystem, human effort that might otherwise be required for the sustainable management of nature is freed for other purposes. The pressure of human needs or the drive for material wealth have often forced the substitution of artificial for natural ecosystems. Elaborate systems of irrigation, drainage, and flood control are examples of artificial environments that are stable and productive only at the price of unremitting attention to their maintenance. The great city is, of course, the most artificial and vulnerable environment and exacts a heavy toll for systems maintenance. The giant megalopolis of the late twentieth century is a socioecological experiment whose outcome is not yet reliably foreseeable. Experiments with nonhuman life forms (e.g., rodents) suggest the possibility of eventual catastrophe. But few people appear to take seriously warnings based on this sort of evidence.[24]

To describe urban systems as artificial is not to disparage them or to suggest that they are intrinsically inferior to natural systems. Civilization requires the construction of artificial ecosystems. The ecological approach to their management is not to return them to nature, but rather to benefit to the fullest extent from the operation of natural processes. The ecological approach implies an understanding of and respect for the potentialities of natural systems. To substitute wherever possible the economy of nature for human effort is the essence of economic as well as ecological good sense. Obviously, it is often necessary to channelize and direct natural forces in order to benefit from them. The extent to which human intervention in natural systems is economically or ecologically justifiable cannot be determined in the absence of demonstrable evidence. A particular high-level dam, for example, may or may not be justifiable under an ecological approach and in comparison with alternative ways of achieving its objectives. If the high dam carries ecological liabilities—often cumulative—it also probably entails unwanted economic costs in the long run. It is, however, safe to surmise that a blanket injunction to put *all* rivers under engineering management, or to ignore them altogether, would be very dubious ecological or economic wisdom in the context of human welfare.

Unwise policies often tend to perpetuate unwisdom. When human society puts itself into an unecological straightjacket, the biotic community itself may be destroyed in efforts to break out of self-induced but unintended deprivations and constraints. Ecologically overstressed societies are impelled to further intensification of pressure on their environments in an effort to survive. Examples such as El Salvador and Haiti have been cited elsewhere in this volume. Shortsighted economic development projects have too often made bad situations worse.[25] Political leaders of overpopulated, ecologically impoverished nations have seldom given serious attention to natural resources conservation or to the protection of human rights. Survival for them often means getting from the environment whatever can be gotten today, regardless of the consequences for tomorrow.[26] At the 1992 United Nations Conference on Environment and Development (Earth Summit), representatives from the less-developed countries showed greater willingness to cooperate in environmental protection measures than was evident twenty years earlier at Stockholm. Yet the crucial issue of population growth outrunning the life-support capabilities of the land was generally evaded. An ecological approach to land policy thus also implies a policy of population control. Unless population pressure is manageable, no other aspect of the biotic community can be managed for a sustainable future. Ultimately the pressure of sheer numbers and the attendant demands upon the biotic community would force all environmental policies into serving the one overpowering objective of obtaining a minimal existence for the human masses.

There are alternatives to such a course of folly and futility. Among these, one should perhaps be classed under the heading of unthinkable thoughts. This course would be for a tough-minded and ecologically sophisticated elite to impose ecological order on their less perceptive or self-disciplined brethren. How this might be done is, however, not clear. Some critics of "environmentalism" see this as a danger. Some warn against the rise of environmental "fascism."[27] Unfortunately, or as the critics of environmentalism might prefer, political astuteness and charisma seem to be most often found among the ecologically illiterate members of society. A socioecological catastrophe would probably be necessary for environmentalist dictatorship to occur.

Compulsory population control through biomedical science, or Malthusian control if all other means fail, could very well be the outcome of the current unwillingness of human societies to assess their ecological predicament realistically. Land is a substantially inelastic resource and this means that as human populations multiply, land use is increasingly affected by population policy. The inseparable connections between land use, population, and the public interest have been identified with clarity by Garrett Hardin in his well-known essay "The Tragedy of the Commons" and in other writings, but the literature on this subject is voluminous and the viewpoints vary widely.[28]

As elaborated in the following chapter, some ethicists take strong exception to the idea of an imposed ecological order. For some, the objection would remain even though the health, material well-being, and security of everyone were ultimately improved, perhaps at the cost of having only two children rather than ten. To argue that the "natural right" of humans to procreate should never be infringed upon suggests the dictum of "let social justice prevail even though the world perish." Education and persuasion are less stressful ways of obtaining behavioral change. But these noncoercive methods take time and may not be effective remedies for self-imposed ignorance or greed.

Is it unethical for society to protect itself and future generations from antisocial behavior toward the environment which ultimately will be harmful to all individuals? Social learning can, and has, dramatically altered human attitudes and behaviors, but time and concentrated effort are needed to reorder human conduct through voluntary acceptance of reform. At present, there seems to be too little of either for voluntary reform to avert apocalypse for much of humanity.

Among the contradictions of our future-oriented technoscientific society is its fragmented and contradictory treatment of time. The relativity of time has become commonplace, and for certain purposes as in space flight, atomic technology, and medicine, very refined concepts of time are employed. With respect to the dynamics of the biotic communities, however, the time perceptions of modern persons are both more and less developed than those that characterized their agrarian ancestors. Moderns live by the clock, but are largely unaware of the dynamics of natural systems. People in the aggregate have not learned to perceive the world as a complex of dynamic interrelated systems. Their behavior suggests that they believe the world to be an infinitely open system. Within this open system, time and change have a different meaning than they have when the system is closed, when there is no escape from mistakes, and when the consequences of a chain reaction once started in time cannot be avoided by interplanetary flight. Space exploration has reinforced the illusion that the infinity of the cosmos offers a way out for earthbound man. The reality for human society in the ascertainable future is that the earth must be considered a closed system, even though, in a physical sense it is in continuing interaction with the cosmos.[29]

Within this essentially closed terrestrial system, change goes on continuously. Societies' future is inextricably involved with changes in the air, the water, the land, and the biota (especially the microorganisms) that are the gross elements of the biosphere. People have themselves become a principal change agent. Human numbers and technologies have the effect of accelerating changes in time, of cutting down land forms, of increasing the salinity of the sea, of altering the chemistry of the atmosphere. Only comprehensive surveillance of the side effects of technology, and carefully evaluated application of science and technology to biotic communities can prevent inadvertent damage to the self-regenerating capabilities of the biosphere. And to be effective, ecological management must conform to the appropriate time table of nature, not merely to the convenience of people. To illustrate, a dollar crisis or a Middle Eastern war may offer politically defensible but ecologically invalid arguments for delaying efforts to save the Great Lakes from degradation by pollution, or a self-destructive economic policy may force the Ogallala aquifer below the Great Plains to exhaustion. Today there may be higher political priorities but, ecologically, tomorrow may be too late, and the economic priorities will have been destroyed by failure to respect the conditions for sustainability.

In Defense of an Ecological Land Policy

Our intention is not to describe the content of a particular ecological land policy. To attempt this without reference to specific places, times, and circumstances would be to contradict the very thesis that we have developed. It is the ecosystems *approach* to policy that has been introduced, not a set of ecological policy prescriptions. With perhaps the exception of the Great Lakes Basin, no such comprehensive approach to land policy has been declared in the United States today. If such a policy based on ecological concepts were to be adopted seriously, some major changes in the laws, expectations, and governmental arrangements in American society would also have to occur. These changes are not of the kinds that were of primary concern to the Public Land Law Review Commission, nor have they been the responsibility of the Division of Lands and Natural Resources of the United States Department of Justice nor of the Departments of Agriculture or Interior. The Soil Conservation Service and the Environmental Protection Agency have concerns, but no truly comprehensive agendas. But if they are not the practical concerns of the present, ecological protection may well be compelling policy objectives in the future. If present indicators are correct, American society, and indeed people generally, will eventually be forced into something like an ecological policy for land. But our present land-as-commodity policies, and our disregard for biotic communities in agriculture and building development will make corrective action costly and its effectiveness uncertain.

Our predicament today is that of passengers on a spaceship whose destination is unknown, whose numbers and appetites are increasing, and who have been long accustomed to quarrelsome and improvident conduct. The passengers assume that the builders of the spaceship endowed it with self-renewing mechanisms so that they need take little thought of its maintenance. Moreover, because the ship is very large, they act as though it were infinite, although they are quite capable of calculating its carrying capacity for given levels of safety and convenience, and they know that there could come a day when its resources could be taxed beyond capacity. Meanwhile, being confirmed democratic equalitarians, they insist on electing a captain on grounds of responsiveness to their preferences rather than to the viability of the enterprise. They are possessed by the optimistic thought that before a day of disaster arrives, they will land on some habitable planet. And so there is disbelief among them as to the practical necessity for restraint.

This is the paradigm of Spaceship Earth, whose passengers are only now beginning to realize where they are. Only the ecologically informed among them are aware of the potential precariousness of their condition. Unfortunately, the practical people who are the leaders and managers of the enterprise, although well-informed in many important ways, are generally uninformed or misinformed in this important respect. Their attention is on the lesser mechanics of the enterprise and on the mediation of quarrels among the passengers that might destroy the ship prematurely.

Must we then concede that the outcome of the voyage is hopeless, that the passengers are unteachable, and that the officers and crew are unwilling to learn or are prevented from learning? No incontrovertible evidence compels this conclusion but none refutes its possibility. It is equally plausible to assume, because human civilization is in itself a highly improbable phenomenon, that the limits of its improbability have not yet been reached. Unlikely as it may be, it is possible that American society, if not people generally, may reassess its circumstances with sufficient realism and insight to avoid ecological foreclosure. It is conceivable that people may voluntarily adopt ways of organizing their economy and of behaving in relation to the natural environment so as to bring the economy and the ecosystem into a dynamic, self-sustaining, relative equilibrium. It is conceivable, but at present it seems improbable.

It is hardly to be expected that the ecological policy can be made attractive to persons who would suffer real economic or emotional loss through its implementation. These persons, however, constitute a relatively small, although disproportionately vocal and influential, element of society. The greater number of Americans appear to be wedded to certain fundamental concepts and institutions that in the near term as well as the long run do not serve them well. Incongruity between real needs and postulated values has been especially strong in matters of land-use regulation and environmental management and control. Urban apartment dwellers appear in significant numbers to subscribe to environmental policies appropriate only to the life and times of Daniel Boone. A more adequate understanding of the values, attitudes, and behaviors of urban Americans in relation to natural systems is greatly needed.

If present demographic projections are valid, the America of the twenty-first century, and even before, will be politically dominated by culturally diverse residents of the great urban areas. Their beliefs and wishes could reshape public policies toward land. Few of the millions of urban residents will be owners of land; few will have a personal stake in returns from its rental, sale, or exploitation. But all would be in some measure dependent on it for the realization of other values. The great mass of urban dwellers are therefore not likely to be hostile to ecological concepts per se but may be turned against them if persuaded that they cost jobs. At the lower economic and educational levels people are likely to be totally unfamiliar with ecological concepts and unable to appraise their significance or meaning for their lives. Defense of ecological concepts among landless urbanites is thus largely a matter of inculcating an understanding of ecology and its implications for human welfare and public policy. Under present circumstances this is a difficult task but it is even now being undertaken.

During the decades of the 1980s and 1990s, nongovernmental organizations for conservation and environment have grown dramatically in numbers, membership, and influence. Environmental education has entered the curricula of schools and a large number of professional societies and journals, professional and popular, are widely disseminating ecological concepts and values. Earth Day and World Environmental Day have became civic rituals. More change in social attitude may be occurring than is evident in present-day law and policy. Opinion studies suggest that this is in fact the case. Here, and abroad, there appears to be a generation gap in response to environmental issues. The youth are far more concerned than the old.[30]

There is, of course, a difference between popular acceptance of an ecological paradigm and its application in public affairs. A practical objection to the plausibility of an ecologically oriented public policy is the complexity of the biotic communities themselves. Targeting their criticism on exaggerated interpretations of ecology, certain critics say that if everything relating to an ecosystem must be taken into account, nothing can be taken into account. This, they say, is because ecology provides no method for assessing priorities among the properties of ecosystems in relation to human values. Their conclusion follows that many findings of ecological science are inapplicable (although not necessarily irrelevant) to the economics and politics of land policy. Conservative and libertarian opponents of "environmentalism" and ecological considerations in public policy scornfully reject ecological protection as no more than self-serving maneuvers by well-to-do clients.[31] Boldly assertive of the impracticality and unfairness of environmental protection, they are regarded by environmentally concerned people as representing an invincibly underinformed and prejudiced constituency.

The critics would have greater plausibility if an ecological approach to land policy did in fact imply an extension of ecological concepts to everything having to do with land tenure and management and nothing to do with other concerns, or if it required every aspect of a biotic community to be examined in relation to every land use decision. But this totalitarian interpretation is neither necessary nor feasible. The fact is that ecologists *are* sometimes able to present alternative sets of policies for public consideration, together with their probable consequences. These may be reviewed by the public or by its representatives, who are then better prepared establish priorities in public law and policy.

It is doubtful that a land policy designed to preserve and protect ecosystems would necessarily be more complex than the accumulated mass of laws, policies, and regulations affecting the ownership and use of land today. The effectiveness of an ecological land policy does not depend upon its mirroring the complexities of community ecology. On the contrary, an ecological approach might simplify and clarify public land policy. A policy for protection and ecological management could, by the establishment of standards and guidelines, reduce the confusion, conflict, and uncertainty that currently characterizes land-use policy throughout the United States. It may be unrealistic to believe that the American people will adopt an ecosystems approach to land policy on its merits, but an ecological approach would almost certainly, in a fundamental sense, be more realistic in its treatment of the real problems of land than are some of the policies now prevailing. For the truth is that a great part of public policy for land is only tangentially concerned with the land as a major element in the human life-support system. Land policies are not necessarily framed with primary reference to the land itself, but are often consequent to decisions made in banks, bars, and bedrooms. In any case, land-use policy has been and will doubtless continue to be instrumental to broader social objectives. The nature of these objectives and their relevance to the continuing maintenance of the land as an element in the ecosphere must therefore be taken into account in any serious effort to understand or to modify land-use policy and practices.

Policy for land does not begin with the land, but with our dependencies upon the land. Measured by ultimate human welfare, the most important of these dependencies are the basic functions of land in the complex systems through which life on earth is sustained. Yet these ecological functions are not the ones accorded the higher priorities in our society. Matters of land economics, of law, of land-use technologies, and of public relations push to the forefront of our attention. Our concepts of public law and private property dichotomize our thought and action so that we tend to conceive of public land policy as legitimate primarily for resolving economic differences. The idea of a policy for all lands regardless of formal title of ownership would be consistent with ecological realities. From a conservative legalist viewpoint, however, a public land policy for "private" lands might appear to be a contradiction in terms. The immediate and practical problems of land policy under the prevailing laws and assumptions require attention, and most students of public land policy examine them in this context. And yet the larger view is also needed. Our preoccupation with immediate and practical problems should not prevent our questioning whether in our own best interest we are addressing ourselves to all of the right questions, at the right time, and in the right way.

Public land policy is amenable to treatment at several levels of discourse. We have in this discourse sought a broad and theoretical level of treatment on the premise that unless the context of public land policy is consistent with ecological realities, specific land policies will ultimately prove to be ineffectual or harmful. Our argument has been that the sociopolitical context of public land policy in America is ecologically unrealistic, and the conclusion follows that a fundamental change of public attitude will be required if our society is not to ultimately fall victim to its own self-imposed illusions.

More than public attitudes may have to change, however, if ecologically rational land policies are to prevail. As described in previous chapters, "the iron triangle" of politically powerful economic interests has time and again defeated rational land use proposals in legislatures. The National Land Use Planning Act of 1970 was a casualty of a well-concerted, self-interested effort to block action on the measure in the U.S. House of Representatives. The power of money in politics too often checkmates efforts to advance public interest measures that would disadvantage self-serving private interests upon whose generosity legislators depend for funding their inordinately costly campaigns for election. Electoral reform might go a long way toward facilitating the consideration of public policies for land on their merits.

Changing circumstances in society, if more widely understood, should work against narrow individualism in land-use policy. Garrett Eckbo, landscape architect and planner, observes that "As consciousness of the ecological character of environmental quality expands, the area of public interest expands as well while that of private interest shrinks."[32] Environmental designers like Garrett Eckbo and Ian McHarg, among others, have shown that the artificial and the natural elements of the human environment may be compatible if the requirements of natural systems are respected. At the beginning of the last decade of the twentieth century, the long-established dominance of the "iron triangle" of development—lender, land owner, and developer—is weakening, although it is still powerful in many communities and in the capital of the United States.[33]

It may be that only an end to population growth will create the conditions under which ecosystemic criteria can be regularly applied to land-use policy decisions. Yet by the year 2000 the extent to which attitudes toward land use divide on generational lines should become clearer. There is also a possibility that even with larger populations, their greater concentration and recognition of the many values inherent in natural environments unoccupied by humans may induce positive measures for ecosystem protection. People who are concerned to protect wildlife and prevent the extinction of species must surely become aware of the findings of ecology, ecosystems research, and conservation biology. Ecosystems criteria include identification of the essentials of plant and animal habitat. Application of those criteria to land-use decisions—some of which could require changes in current land uses—may be decisive to the preservation of biological diversity and species survival.[34]

Finally, despite the foregoing arguments for an ecosystemic approach to land-use policy, some readers may still dissent on grounds of impracticality. It may be argued that the ecosystem concept is too large, amorphous, and inclusive to be manageable as a policy criterion. The following chapter by Kristin Shrader-Frechette examines the criticisms of the ecosystem concept from scientific and philosophical perspectives. Her critique addresses the idea of "holism" that is certainly implicit in ecosystems thinking. Evaluations of holism and ecosystems depend in large degree upon the perspective taken. Reductionist methods of science, necessary and appropriate to penetrating the innermost properties of matter, are not applicable to the phenomena of large and complex systems. As George Sarton, founder of the study of the history of science appears to imply, the general need be no less scientific than the particular. Ecology is a synthesizing metascience of the general and ought not be evaluated by criteria appropriate to the particular, which is essentially reductionist. To paraphrase Sarton, we may say that both approaches to understanding reality are equally valid, each in its own way. "Both subjects are equally unexhaustible; they are equal in infinitude. All that we can say is that the two subjects are very different."[35]

Problems with Ecosystemic Criteria for Land Policy

Kristin Shrader-Frechette

Many of us probably believe that ecologists ought to play a central role in helping to formulate environmental ethics and to justify many of our claims regarding land policy.[1] Indeed, we argued in the last chapter that we need to employ ecosystemic criteria, such as the ability of natural systems to sustain themselves, in our decision making about how to use land. We need to employ ecology, as we argued in chapter 9, as a source of information and insight for our practical decision making regarding land use. Many other scholars have come to the same conclusion as we. Ecological science needs to provide part of the framework for environmental and land-related decision making. Philosopher Paul Taylor, for example, explicitly affirms both our duty to preserve environmental integrity and the necessity of our relying on biologists and ecologists in helping us to recognize the scope of our ethical obligations.[2]

Many other philosophers,[3] scientists,[4] and lawmakers[5] have made a similar point: good ecology is a necessary (but not a sufficient) condition for sound environmental ethics and policy regarding land. Moreover, they claim, technological and industrial activities are harming the entire biosphere; ecologists, because of their expertise, have an obligation to help create wise public policy.[6] For example, we need trustworthy ecological data on species decline relative to reserve size,[7] if our ethical and policy conclusions about the optimal size of tropical forest reserves are to be justifiable. Likewise we need to know whether ecologists are correct in believing that phosphorus is a limiting nutrient in causing lake eutrophication, if environmental policy makers are to have a clear scientific basis for not allowing pollution of freshwater lakes with phosphorus effluents.[8]

Introduction: Ecology as a Foundation for Land Policy

According to Arthur Cooper, former president of the Ecological Society of America, the most direct example of ecological influence on environmental ethics and land policy is the role that findings about coastal and estuarine ecosystems played in stimulating government programs for coastal zone management.[9] Cooper also claimed that findings of ecologists were directly responsible for environmental decisions limiting use of DDT, for national forest-management policies favoring the diversity of multispecies forests, and for drawing attention to the problem of acid rain.[10]

Given the fact that environmental ethics and land policy ought to rely at least in part on ecological data,[11] it is reasonable to ask how successful the science has been in informing environmental ethics and land policy generally. Although we wish that it were otherwise, our main argument in this chapter is that ecology, at least at present, cannot perform all the tasks that many moral philosophers and environmental policy makers often assign to it,[12] perhaps because it is such a young science, and because many of its parameters are much more resistant to prediction than are those of physics. Our argument is that, despite the *heuristic* power of ecology—power that we discussed in the last chapter—ecology is often lacking in the *predictive* power that is essential to land-use policy making. Given this lack, it is also important for us to direct land policy by means of ethical, legal, and political arguments.

To support our conclusion, we shall argue for three related claims: (1) Many philosophers who write about environmental ethics and land policy presuppose that their normative conclusions gain support from certain confirmed ecological theories and laws. (2) Ecologists cannot, at least at present, provide a complete and uncontroversial account of two absolutely central ecological notions, biological holism and "equilibrium" or the "balance of nature." These concepts are just as problematic as is the notion of "species," for example. (3) Finally, ecology contributes at the policy, heuristic, and intuitive levels to a correct worldview in terms of which to conceive and direct environmental or land ethics. It, however, has little general theory and few precise predictions, in the strict scientific sense, that provide a universal foundation for resolving particular controversies in environmental/land policy and ethics.

Can Ecologists Help Justify Environmental/Land Policy?

Insofar as moral philosophers and policy makers look to ecology to support their views about environmental or land ethics, they often assume that ecologists can provide them with clear, precise guidelines for a holistic, ecosystemic ethics and for maintaining some sort of balance in nature. In other words, they typically accept what we call, respectively, the "holism presupposition" and the "balance presupposition."[13]

Discussing the role of the balance presupposition, Holmes Rolston focuses on "the paramount law in ecological theory . . . that of homeostasis,"[14] and connects morality with maintaining ecological balance or stability. According to Rolston, humans have an obligation to promote ecological homeostasis or balance, since it is a necessary condition for maximizing human well-being or survival. Paul Sears, Garrett Hardin, Thomas Colwell,[15] Paul Taylor,[16] and Bryan Norton[17] are some of the persons who subscribe to variants of the balance presupposition.

Rolston also claims that environmental ethics in the biocentric sense focuses on what we have called the "holism presupposition." This ethics is based on the discovery of a moral "ought" inherent in recognition of the unified character of the ecosystem. It defines right actions as those that preserve the wholeness or integrity of the ecosystem, actions that "maximize ecosystemic excellences."[18] In addition to Rolston,[19] Callicott, Dubos, Goodpaster, Leopold, Shepard, and perhaps Sagoff[20] also subscribe to variants of the holism presupposition.[21] Goodpaster, for example, invokes Lovelock's notion of Gaia,[22] suggesting that "the biosystem as a whole" exhibits feedback behavior, such as being sustained by metabolic processes for accumulating energy and maintaining an equilibrium with its environment.[23] On the basis of the holism presupposition, Goodpaster follows Leopold[24] and argues for extending moral considerability to ecosystemic wholes. Callicott says much the same thing, that ecology has made it possible to apprehend the biosphere as an "organic whole" of "integrally related parts,"[25] a whole that has rights on the basis of "ecological entitlement."[26]

Problems with Appeals to the Balance of Nature

Whether one appeals (like Bryan Norton) to the balance presupposition or (like Goodpaster and Callicott) to the holism presupposition, one runs into difficulties. Although both the balance and holism theses have significant heuristic power, for both science and policy, neither ecological notion provides an uncontroversial and precise foundation for resolving particular, second-order disputes in environmental ethics and in policy making regarding land. In both cases, but for different reasons, ecology cannot always do the precise, predictive job demanded of it by those who wish to use it as a basis for resolving environmental conflicts. Perhaps the greatest problem with appealing to the balance presupposition is that there is no precise, confirmed sense in which one can claim that natural ecosystems proceed toward homeostasis, stability, or some "balance."[27] Admittedly, the concept of a balanced or stable ecosystem has great heuristic power, and there appears to be some general sense in which nature is balanced or stable. Nevertheless, in the specific case of the ecosystemic view of the balance of nature, to which Norton and Taylor appeal, there is no consensus among ecologists, and they have called for pluralistic theoretical treatments.[28] Nor is there support for the diversity-stability view held by MacArthur, Hutchinson, and Commoner.[29]

The reasons for the disfavor attributed to the view of MacArthur et al. are both empirical and mathematical. Salt marshes and the rocky intertidal provide only two of many classical counterexamples to the diversity-stability view. Salt marshes are simple in species composition, but they are stable, and they are not diverse ecosystems. On the other hand, the rocky intertidal is one of the most species-rich and diverse natural systems, yet it is highly unstable, since it may be perturbed by a single change in its species composition.[30] Empirically based counterexamples of this sort have multiplied over the last fifteen years, and May, Levins, Connell, and others have seriously challenged the diversity-stability hypothesis on both mathematical and field-based grounds.[31] Yet, numerous policy makers continue to cite the hypothesis, the most famous version of the balance of nature, as grounds for supporting many tenets of environmental ethics and law, such as the Endangered Species Act. Most ecologists, however, have either repudiated the thesis or cast serious doubt on it.[32]

Their doubts have arisen in part because we cannot say, in all cases, what it would be to hinder the balance of nature. Ecosystems regularly change, and they regularly eliminate species. How would one use an ethic based on some balance of nature to argue that humans ought not modify ecosystems or even wipe out species, for example, when nature does this herself, through natural disasters such as volcanic eruptions and climate changes like those that destroyed the dinosaurs? Nature doesn't appear merely to extirpate species, or cause them to move elsewhere because their niches are gone. But if not, then one cannot obviously use science, alone, to claim that it is always wrong on *ecological grounds* for humans to do what nature does, wipe out species. However, given a number of ecocentric or biocentric ethics based on notions such as teleology, inherent worth, or intrinsic value—nonscientific notions—it is possible to argue against species extinctions.[33] Likewise, there are obvious *anthropocentric grounds* for alleging wrongness in such cases (for example, because it is wrong for humans to cause unnecessary suffering or to destroy something in a wanton or selfish manner). But if one's only basis for condemning such actions is anthropocentric, because there are no adequate and universal theories of ecological "balance," then it is not clear how ecological theory (as apposed to philosophical notions) can support purely ecocentric environmental or land ethics.[34] Thus, there is no problem with supporting land ethics, but only with supporting land ethics based on predictive, general, ecological theory.

Moreover, the criterion for justifiable species extinction, for those who appeal to the balance presupposition, cannot be that what happens naturally is good, while what happens through human intervention is bad; this would be to solve the problem of scientific and empirical meaning with a purely stipulative and ad hoc definition. Nor can the difference be merely that humans do quickly (e.g., cause lake eutrophication) what nature does slowly. One must have some arguments to show that accelerating ecosystemic changes is bad, even if the changes themselves (e.g., wiping out species) are natural.

In several ways, medical science (if it is a science) also faces problems of defining what is "balanced" or "healthy," problems that are similar to those of ecological science. Both disciplines need to specify criteria for health or for "balance" in order to evaluate the success of their scientific practice. With medical science, however, it is relatively easy to do so because one's goal is always the well-being of the *individual* patient. The analogue in ecology would be the well-being of an individual organism (e.g., the redfish) or an individual species. Environmental and land-use problems, however, almost never focus on the health of one organism or species at the expense of others. Ecological prescriptions for what is healthy or natural must take into account thousands of communities, species, and individuals, all relative to the health of an entire ecosystem—or the entire biosphere, and then specify how to maintain the health or balance of the *entire system*. This is a far more difficult enterprise than specifying the health of one individual within some system.[35] Because it is so difficult, it is not clear how one could specify an ecological "balance" without knowing precisely how to define the system that is allegedly being balanced. (This biological difficulty is analogous to the economic problems associated with defining a theory of social choice; here one of the difficulties is knowing how to specify the whole that aggregates, combines, or represents numerous individual choices.) Thus, despite its obvious heuristic value, there are precise scientific problems with defining ecosystems, for example, and hence with using this concept in precise, predictive cases of decision making.

Problems with Appeals to Holism or Organicism

As a foundation for environmental ethics and land-use policy, appeals to organicism or to the holism presupposition, despite their heuristic power, likewise suffer from both ethical and epistemological problems. Obviously, holistic approaches to land-use policy, in the sense of taking account of all factors relevant to decisions about land, make sense. We argued for such holistic decision making in the last chapter. One runs into difficulties, however, with ethical and scientific versions of holism. For one thing, to presuppose ethically that ecosystems are holistic units that maximize their well-being, as Rolston and Callicott claim, or to presuppose that humans are bound to maximize ecosystemic well-being,[36] is to attribute interests to ecosystems. Yet, within the accepted philosophical tradition, "interests" logically presuppose desires, aims, or wants.[37] And ecosystems do not have desires, aims, or wants.[38] Moreover, the capacity for suffering or enjoyment is presumably a prerequisite for having interests, as we already pointed out in chapter 3.[39] If it were not, then we would be forced to say, for example, that water had an interest in not being drunk.[40] This means that attributing interests to ecosystems (via a first-order ethical principle) is incomplete and problematic (because of the multiplication of entities said to have interests), unless one likewise formulates second-order ethical principles for how to adjudicate conflicts among beings whose interests differ. One might argue, for example, that when there are conflicts of interests among different beings, human interests ought to receive top priority only in cases in which human lives are at stake; otherwise, environmental interests ought to have top priority, even when property rights are at stake.[41] In the absence of such second-order principles—that specify priorities in cases of conflict—it does not seem reasonable to attribute interests to ecosystems, because there would be no way to adjudicate conflicts among different interests or different beings.

A second ethical problem with the ethical version of the holism presupposition—that one ought to maximize ecosystemic well-being—is that, if the biosphere or ecosystems were organic wholes having a good, then it would be very difficult for us, as moral agents, to know what that good is. They cannot tell us what their good is, and there is no general, predictive theory in ecology that can tell us, uncontroversially, what their good is. Moreover, it is not clear (apart from human interests) how we ought to define the good for ecosystems, since they cannot experience pleasure or pain. Obviously, the good for an organism is life, nourishment, and so on. Since the ecosystem is a whole comprised of both living and nonliving components, it is difficult to say what its precise good is. Obviously there are purely anthropocentric grounds for condemning wanton destruction or misuse of the environment, because such behavior manifests selfishness or greed. It would be very difficult in every case, however, to specify purely ecological, or solely nonanthropocentric, criteria for praising or blaming moral actions concerning ecosystems.[42] Third, as we already pointed out in chapter 3, the ethical version of the holism presupposition could lead to what Regan calls "environmental fascism."[43] If one follows ethics of maximizing ecosystemic well-being, then—in the absence of second-order principles like those just mentioned—one thereby presupposes that the welfare of the ecosystem or biosphere ought to come before individual, human welfare. This means, for example, that massive human deaths, or violations of basic civil liberties, could be justified, even required, on the grounds that this would help check the population problem and contribute to the good of the biosphere. Such an argument has already been made by Garrett Hardin in his famous discussion of "lifeboat ethics."[44]

Fourth, as we also noted in chapter 3, within a holistic ethics, there is a dilemma. Either we humans are on a par with other creatures on the planet, or we are not. Either we humans are equal members of the biotic community and therefore have no special responsibilities—contrary to what all our ethical traditions have taught—or we humans are not equal members of the biotic community. If we are not, because of our moral primacy, then in many cases we have no obligations to any nonhuman entity whenever its basic welfare conflicts with our own needs for bodily security. Following the consequences of this dilemma, the presupposition of ethical holism appears to create a dilemma. Either it leads to actions (such as murder) that are heinous (in the case of human equality with other beings). Or it is inconsistent with the prescriptions of most environmentalists (in the case of human superiority over other beings).[45] Hence, the ethical version of the holism presupposition is highly doubtful, despite the desirability of pragmatic holism defended in chapter 9.

Scientific versions of holism are also problematic. Obviously there are communities of different species, as well as interactions and interdependencies among the abiotic and biotic elements of the environment. Nevertheless, there is no precise, empirically confirmed ecological whole, although pragmatic, holistic thinking clearly has heuristic value, as we argued in the previous chapter. For one thing, most well known ecologists have either remained agnostic or rejected the Gaia hypothesis, the basis of many accounts of holism. They regard it as possibly correct, but at present only unproved speculation. Of course, they admit the ecological fact of interconnectedness and convolution on a small scale. Moreover, an ecosystem, as the same collection of individuals, species, and relationships, certainly does not persist through time. Hence any notion of the "dynamic stability" of an ecosystemic whole is somewhat imprecise and unclear.[46] Also, the selection of the "ecosystem" as the unit which is or ought to be maximized is peculiar.[47] Why not choose, as the unit, the community,[48] or the association,[49] or the trophic level? Clements said that the community is an organism;[50] if so, then why is the ecosystem also an organism? Which is it, and what are the criteria for a holistic organism? Or, if one is a holist, why not choose the collection of ecosystems, the biosphere, as that which is maximized in nature and which we are morally enjoined to optimize? Once one abandons an individualistic ethic, then how, from a scientific point of view, does one choose among alternative nonindividual units to be maximized?[51] Such questions suggest that ethical or scientific holism—organicism—despite its apparent heuristic power, is an arbitrary and imprecise notion, akin more to metaphysics than to empirical science or to practical ethics.

Fourth, as an empirical notion, holism is further undercut by the current reductionist dispute in ecology among Gleasonian individualists and Clementsian holists. Their controversy indicates that the "levels problem" has not been solved in ecology. Admittedly, various ecological conclusions are valid within particular spatial and temporal scales. Nevertheless, a given ecological conclusion (regarding balance) typically holds for some (but not other) "wholes" (e.g., populations, species, communities). For example, there may be some sort of stability or balance for a given species within a certain spatial scale, but not for other species, or not within another such scale. Ecologists cannot optimize the well-being of all these different wholes (having different spatial and temporal scales) at the same time. Because they cannot, there is no general level at which ecological problem solving takes place, and no general temporal or spatial scale within which a stable "whole" is exhibited. Likewise, because of the absence of a universal ecological theory that can be appealed to, in defining the "whole" that is balanced, ecologists are forced to work on a case-by-case basis. They recognize that there is no universal level (across species, populations, or communities) at which some balanced or stable whole exists. In part this is because numerous alleged "wholes" (e.g., populations) exhibit density vagueness rather than density dependence, while other "wholes" do not.[52] This suggests, therefore, both that there is no universal level at which a balanced or stable whole is evident, and that there is a "levels problem" in ecology. But if so, then there is no clear, precise, universal sense of biological holism to which environmental ethicists can appeal, despite its apparent heuristic value.

A fifth scientific problem with the scientific and ethical presupposition that ecosystems are holistic units that maximize their well-being is that ecosystems are not agents in any meaningful sense. Moreover, it is scientifically wrong to suggest that ecosystems, rather than populations, adapt. Admittedly species may evolve in a way that benefits a given ecosystem, but there is no selection at the level of the ecosystem.[53] Adaptation is restricted to heritable characteristics; no alleged knowledge of the past operates in natural selection, and the individual that is better adapted to the present environment is the one that leaves more offspring and hence transmits its traits.[54] Given neo-Darwinian theory, Dobzhansky, Goodpaster, Lovelock, Mayr, Rolston, Wright, and other holistic philosophers and ecologists are fundamentally wrong when they suggest either that natural selection operates to produce organs of a given kind because their presence gives rise to certain effects, or that ecosystemic processes operate in certain ways because they maximize ecosystemic excellence.[55] Moreover, although it is possible to claim that adaptation maximizes individual survival, in the sense already discussed, it is not clear what a community or an ecosystem maximizes. Traits advantageous to the individual are not always advantageous to the species or the ecosystem, as in the case of traits such as an individual's "taking all the food."[56] And what are advantageous to the species or to the ecosystem are not always advantageous to the individual, as in the case of dying young to hasten the cycling of nutrients.

Sixth, despite their heuristic power, many ecosystemic or holistic explanations are neither falsifiable nor even testable. This is probably why ecosystems ecology has been called by at least one scientist "theological ecology."[57] There is a clear definition neither of what it is to maximize some pattern of excellence (e.g., based on interspecific competition) nor of the ecosystem that is the subject of this alleged excellence. Theorists simply do not agree on the underlying processes that structure communities and ecosystems.[58] Hence, despite their apparent heuristic value, holistic/ecosystemic notions cannot always contribute practical and precise accounts necessary for resolving environmental conflicts.

Ecology and Its Contribution to Environmental and Land-Use Policy

So far, we have argued that neither the ethical nor the scientific versions of the balance and holism presuppositions can assist us, in every case, in doing environmental ethics and in resolving disputed land-use policy. As we argued in the previous chapter, however, holism (in the pragmatic sense of taking account of all relevant factors) is nevertheless important in policy making regarding land. There is also a sense in which ecology, considered more generally, could contribute to a correct paradigm for environmental ethics. However, the contributions do not seem to lie in the areas mentioned by Cooper in his 1982 Presidential Address to the Ecological Society of America. Recall that Cooper argued that ecological findings about the value of wetlands provided "the most direct example of ecological influence on public policy."[59] Although Cooper cites the wetlands example as an ecological victory for environmental policy, it really appears to be a case in which environmental policy makers accepted untested, highly doubtful *beliefs* of ecologists.[60] Indeed the acclaimed theoretical ecologist John Maynard Smith noted that "ecology is still a branch of science in which it is usually better to rely on the judgment of an experienced practitioner than on the predictions of a theorist."[61] As a consequence of this reliance, the battlefields of environmental policy are littered with the carcasses of untested, now-rejected hypotheses (like the wetlands example and DDT biomagnification)[62] that were once used as ecological "facts" to support arguments for environmental protection.[63]

In the United States's longest legal conflict over environmental policy, for example, general ecological theory was of little help. The controversy began in 1964 and was between the U.S. Environmental Protection Agency (EPA) and five New York utility companies. The basic problem was that the disputants disagreed over the effect of water withdrawals by the utilities on the Hudson River striped-bass population. After spending tens of millions of dollars, scientists could still not estimate the precise ecological effects of the water withdrawals. In other words, they knew, at the level of a first-order ethical principle, that they wished to avoid serious harm to the striped-bass population. Because of the inadequacy of ecological theory, however, they were unable to specify some second-order principle for adjudicating the dispute between those attempting to protect the utility and those attempting to protect the bass.[64] This controversy (between the utility and the EPA) suggests a number of reasons why it is difficult for ecologists to get a hold on fundamental processes allegedly underlying the balance and the holism presuppositions.

1. For one thing, many important ecological problems, such as the causes and consequences of global carbon dioxide or acid rain, involve many parameters and a high degree of complexity and uncertainty. The presence of numerous parameters means both that there is

too much "going on" in natural communities to be captured by any model (e.g., Lotka-Volterra[65]), and that ecologists are not certain which factors are the significant ones.[66]

2. Data bases in ecology are still so limited that they do not provide enough information for making land policy or environmental policy.[67] Because of inadequate data bases, different ecologists often claim evidential support for inconsistent hypotheses.[68]

3. Ecologists are encumbered with masses of untested hypotheses.[69] Just by mere dint of repetition, often these hypotheses achieve the status of facts.[70] Many of them are not testable in the first place,[71] some are mere tautologies,[72] and most are not evaluated against null models.[73]

4. Ecologists often advocate overly simple theories about ecosystem response because empirical data are hard to obtain. Such simple theories (e.g., regarding linear relationships between two parameters) are easily challenged, even though more complex ones are difficult to establish.[74]

5. Ecologists are forced to examine and understand ecosystems that are constantly changing, and changing in ways that are not always predictable or uniform. In other words, the natural-selection foundations of ecology undercut any uncontroversial notion of ecosystemic holism, equilibrium, or balance of nature.[75] Moreover, even if ecologists could arrive at some noncontroversial notion of balance or equilibrium, it would not be very useful, for two reasons. Unlike the mathematical models used to portray them, natural ecosystems are not typically at equilibrium; if they were, they would have far fewer species.[76] Also, it is not clear that adverse environmental effects come from loss of system stability rather than from direct impacts.[77]

6. Virtually every ecological situation can be said to be so unique that there are no obvious "state variables" and few similarities across cases. Hence there may be no general theoretical laws in ecology, since the diversity of the biological community often fails to converge under similar physical conditions.[78]

7. Often scientists cannot make ecological measurements, e.g., for r (the intrinsic rate of natural increase of a population), as closely as the legitimate use of proposed equations might require.[79]

8. Ecologists often must know how to optimize a situation involving many individual entities, species, communities, and populations. As was already mentioned, an analogous problem arises in economics: how to develop a theory of social choice that represents the interests of each person, but makes the good of the entire group paramount. We can't solve the problem in economics or ecology.

Although the eight reasons just listed mean that ecology often cannot give us fundamental, predictive, theoretical laws capable of informing particular environmental decisions, they suggest both some useful methodological rules[80] and some insights regarding what ecology can tell us.[81] It can tell us very general things and can give us first-order ethical principles, such as: "behave as if everything is connected to everything else," or "do not exceed the carrying capacity of the area or the planet." But none of these generalizations is very helpful in practical, environmental decision making, especially when we need either specific answers or a second-order ethical principle that tells us how to adjudicate disputes, for example, over precisely *how* everything is connected to everything else.[82] Ecology can also tell us how to solve very specific problems whose solutions may be subjected to short-term empirical testing. Problems of this kind are exemplified by successful control of vampire-bat populations, California red scale, and lake eutrophication.[83]

Likewise ecologists can often tell us, for example, what interventions in ecosystems are likely to reduce species diversity. Following an anthropocentric account, *if* we define "balance" in terms of species diversity, *then* indeed ecologists can give us some help in environmental ethics and policy making. That is, given the *end* of maximizing species diversity, ecology can tell us about the *means* of attaining it. Ecologists, however, cannot provide us with a general definition of an end or goal of ecosystemic activity, but they can often reveal the best means of attaining some goal, once it is specified. This is in part because, as a recent U.S. National Academy of Sciences report noted, there is typically no general, predictive, ecological "theory" that can be applied to solve environmental and land-use problems, even though particular ecological facts, gained from specific cases, have often been useful in environmental policy making.[84] In other words, ecologists can rarely tell us how to protect entire ecosystems or how to define such protection, although they can often help us manage particular species so as to benefit human interests.[85]

How Can Ecology Help Us?

Where does all this leave us? Ecology can't tell us that more diverse ecosystems are more stable, that tropical rainforests contribute net oxygen to the atmosphere,[86] that there is a testable balance of nature, or that organochloride pesticides magnify along food chains. McIntosh puts the point well: all the schools of ecology have failed to provide it with a general ecological theory having predictive power.[87] As we suggested in the last chapter, however, ecology can provide us with much insight and information regarding the environment. Ecology has great heuristic, if not always predictive, power. Until ecology is able to give us precise and predictive theoretical explanations, as a basis for environmental ethics and land-use policy, we have several interim suggestions: First, we ought to avoid defending our views by means of controversial ecological hypotheses like diversity-stability, or the ethical and scientific versions of the holism and balance presuppositions.[88] Second, following the example of the famous Hudson River controversy over the striped-bass population, we ought to conceive of environmental and land-use policy, not as justified by appeals to questionable ecological hypotheses, but as established on the basis of a negotiated settlement for mitigating impacts.[89] Third, just as we ought to avoid untestable grand theories in ecology as a basis for environmental and land-use policy, so also we ought to avoid assuming, as Sagoff does,[90] that ecology can never become anything more than natural history. Environmental ethics and land-use policy, like good science, must remain open to new discoveries. Fourth, we can nevertheless argue, as does Robert Colwell, that all aspects of nature have "intrinsic value." Or, we can argue that all living beings have inherent worth,[91] and we can thereby establish the presupposition that the burden of proof is on the person who aims to destroy, manipulate, or otherwise tamper with nature. In other words, we can claim that, all things being equal, we have a prima facie duty to recognize the intrinsic value or inherent worth of all beings and therefore a duty not to interfere with anything in nature without good reason. This duty might be said to exist, at least in part, because most nonhuman species existed on the planet before we did, and because all of us on the planet are interdependent. One could also argue that, because we did not create nature, we have a duty not to interfere with it without good reason. We might help others to recognize this duty by encouraging persons to have experiences in nature (e.g., backpacking, camping, birdwatching) and by trying to be aware of the ways in which we are dependent on nature.[92]

Once we make the first-order (or intuitive) ethical claim that all of nature possesses intrinsic value or inherent worth, we make it more difficult for humans to ignore their duties to the land. Nevertheless, such claims do not provide *sufficient* conditions for practical decision making; we still need second-order (or critical) ethical rules to specify criteria for how to adjudicate conflicting claims among natural entities, all of which have inherent worth or intrinsic value.[93] For example, there might be a conflict between the first-order principles that all humans possess a right to life (and therefore can eat plants in order to live) and that all beings (including plants) have intrinsic value. If both principles hold, then we need to specify second-order principles in order to resolve the controversy. Presumably these latter principles would enable us to justify the fact, for instance, that although plants have intrinsic value, nevertheless there are some occasions when humans are justified in eating them. As this example illustrates, merely agreeing with the first-order ethical claim that all of nature has inherent worth or intrinsic value does not resolve the most difficult environmental and land-use conflicts. This is because often those who destroy the environment do *not* deny (at the first or intuitive level) that nature possesses intrinsic value; instead they merely claim (at the second or critical level of analysis) that human concerns are superior to those of nature. In other words, they disagree (at the level of second-order principles) about how to resolve controversies when human concerns (e.g., jobs) are set against environmental well-being (e.g., protecting wilderness). For this reason, an appeal to intrinsic value or inherent worth is a necessary first step in environmental ethics, but it is incomplete or insufficient as a basis for practical environmental decision making. This is because most ethical controversy probably occurs at the second level.

One possible solution to some conflicts among first-order principles (as in the plant example) or among second-order principles (as in the jobs example) might be to specify additional second-order principles. These principles might be, for example, that only humans (or only sentient beings) have "interests" and therefore rights, and that only certain strong rights (as explained by Dworkin) "trump" other obligations arising out of considerations of intrinsic value.[94] For example, only (strong) human rights to life take priority over environmental welfare, in cases of conflict. In all other situations, environmental welfare takes primacy, even over property rights. In order to use these two second-order principles to resolve a conflict, however, we must be able to spell out and defend a notion of "strong rights," a task too extensive to be undertaken here. Nevertheless, this brief mention of rights, interests, and conflicts should suggest some of the possible ethical avenues still open to us. Despite the limitations of ecology as a predictive basis for environmental and land-use policy making, it nevertheless possesses much insight and information important for this task.

Objections to This Account

A number of persons, however, might object to these arguments that the ethical and ecological notions of "balance" and holism or organicism provide little basis for environmental policy making. They might claim, for example, that: (1) The earlier analysis amounts to "ecology bashing." (2) It ignores the fact that we humans *need* balanced, holistic thinking, both for our own welfare and for that of the entire biosphere. (3) Likewise the earlier analysis ignores the fact nature might have a "right" to exist. (4) Moreover, objectors might claim that ecology does give us a number of answers to environmental and land-use questions.[95] Let's consider each of these disagreements in order.

The first objection, regarding "ecology bashing," is warranted only if ecology is currently able to provide more of a foundation for environmental ethics and land-use policy making than has been alleged in the preceding analysis. If so, then this foundation needs to be demonstrated, in spite of the fact that there is no agreement on general ecological theory, and in spite of the fact that there are few, if any, successful predictions issuing from general ecological theory. In other words, a claim of ecology bashing is justified only if the bashing is unfair, if ecology is able to do more than has been alleged. In the absence of arguments to show this unfairness, the charge of ecology bashing amounts to begging the question. Moreover, the account is not so much bashing ecology as such, as it is bashing two unconfirmed, interpretational concepts (balance and holism) that threaten the clarity and testability for which most ecologists strive.

The second objection, that humans need balanced, holistic thinking, also seems to miss the point. Admittedly, at a practical level, as we argued in the previous chapter, the notions of balance and holism have heuristic power. However, to posit the existence of something (e.g., ecological balance) just because we need it would be wishful thinking at its worst, wishful thinking of the sort that Freud condemned in his *The Future of an Illusion*. Moreover, just because we need something does not mean that it exists. We may need intelligence, for example, but that does not mean that we have it. The limits of reality are not determined by our desires, but by what exists and what is defensible. In particular, we may need holistic thinking, but this does not mean that we can provide a rationally defensible account of holism, an account robust enough to undergird environmental policy making and likely objections to it. The earlier analysis indicated some of the fundamental conceptual difficulties besetting holistic/organismic ecology and ethics. If this account is correct, then although a given individual may be able to accept some sort of holism as a pragmatic or heuristic hypothesis at the personal level, it is unlikely that scientific or ethical holism is defensible at the level of predictive ecological theory, because of the conceptual problems already noted. Of course, one *individual* may decide what "whole" to maximize, on the basis of her personal beliefs. For holism to undergird a *societal* approach to policy making, however, requires that it be free of the conceptual difficulties already noted, be precisely defined, be rationally defensible, and therefore be acceptable to many people. Moreover, the set of beliefs that are acceptable to all members of society is much smaller than the set that is acceptable only to one person. This is why society does not legislate morals; it cannot typically do so successfully. For this reason, the content of environmental law and public policy must be narrower than the content of personal, environmental morality, since law must be acceptable to a variety of persons with different beliefs. This suggests that, although we may need a holistic way of thinking, and although it has immense heuristic power, we may not be able to ground societal environmental policy on an ethical or scientific framework based on holism, even though holism is often pragmatically desirable. Nevertheless, we may be able to adopt holism at the level of personal morals, at the level of a working hypothesis, or as we have defined it in the previous chapter.

Like the first objection, the third objection (that this analysis ignores nature's "right" to exist) also begs the question. It can only be wrong to ignore something that is apparent. Yet, it is not apparent that nature has a right to exist, for reasons already explained earlier (viz., the fact that nonsentient beings do not have interests, in the philosophical sense, and therefore they likely do not have rights). If this objection is a proposal to accord rights to nature, then the proposal (if it is to be successful) must include at least two things: (1) a criterion by virtue of which nature is said to have rights, and (2) a criterion or second-order ethical rule that enables us to adjudicate rights conflicts. Without (1), it would be impossible to tell what/who has rights and why they do. Without (2), according rights to all beings would mean that nothing has them. If everything has said to have rights, and if there is no way to adjudicate among conflicting rights claims, then (practically speaking) nothing has rights. This is analogous to the observation that, if everything is said to be true, and if there is no way to adjudicate among conflicting truth claims, then nothing is true. Likewise, according to most contemporary philosophers, natural rights (if accepted at all) are typically accorded only to humans, and only on the basis of the criterion of rationality. Rights claims, on the current view, also are adjudicated on the basis of the types of rights in conflict, so that strong rights take precedence over weak ones.[96] (See note 94.) It may be reasonable, of course, to change the criteria for according rights and adjudicating rights conflicts. Without specific, alternative criteria, however, such a proposal for change is (at best) incomplete or (at worst) unworkable as a basis for environmental ethics and land-use policy.

The fourth objection (that ecology does give us a number of answers to environmental problems, in part because it does have a notion of ecological "balance") is partially correct and partially incorrect. It is correct insofar as ecology can help us along the lines already suggested near the end of section five earlier. For example, ecology can give us natural-history and case-study answers that are often capable of being subjected to short-term empirical testing. The fourth objection is incorrect insofar as it postulates a notion of balance or equilibrium that is universal, long-term, and predictive. There is no universal equilibrium, in the predictive sense, (1) because not all populations (e.g., many insects) exhibit density dependence, (2) because populations are affected by unpredictable environmental factors, and (3) because many populations never show a balance or equilibrium but instead exhibit cycles or chaotic changes. Evidence of radical changes in community composition and structure throughout history also suggests that there are no stable or balanced community "types" existing through time; such types may appear stable only because our time frame of examination is relatively short. Moreover, communities of organisms cannot be classified (into balanced, stable types), on the basis of climate. Both spatial and temporal fluctuations/perturbations undercut, at least at present, any universal notion of balance.[97]

Conclusion

Despite the fact that there appear to be no precise and predictive scientific notions of "balance" and "holism" that we can use as a foundation for ecology, ethics, and environmental policy making, we have seen in the previous chapter that ecosystem and holistic concepts nevertheless have significant heuristic value for ecological science and pragmatic value for environmental policy making. Hence, the purpose of this chapter has not been to leave environmental ethics and land-use policy without a foundation. Rather, the goal has been merely to point out that the foundation is not as simple as many persons currently suppose. As a recent U.S. National Academy of Sciences report on ecology noted:

> the point of discussing the many obstacles to making accurate predictions is not to argue the futility of trying, but to show that the process of prediction must be viewed as complex and probabilistic. An appropriate approach to managing ecological systems recognizes the random component of population dynamics. . . . Environmental manipulations will always be experimental to some extent, and our most promising

course is to structure each one so that we can learn as much as possible from it.[98]

If the Academy report is correct, then ecological notions such as "balance" are not so much foundations on which to build an ethics. Rather, as the previous chapter argued, they are heuristic tools, working hypotheses, and idealizations that provide a useful context for learning more about the environmental perturbations and fluctuations that preclude precise prediction, balance, or stability in ecology. Once we have learned more about these perturbations and fluctuations, we may be able to provide a new paradigm for balance or stability, a paradigm that provides more guidance for environmental ethics and land-use planning. Meanwhile, in the absence of a new ecological paradigm, there remain good political, legal, moral, and economic reasons for developing a sound land-use policy. We shall provide an overview of these reasons in the next chapter and then, in the final chapter, suggest what a national land-use policy should be.

11

Practical Steps and Ethical Justifications

Kristin Shrader-Frechette

History, reduced to its basics, is one real-estate transaction after another.[1] So far in this volume, we have shown why policy and history, the real-estate transactions of the past, have not served the public interest. In this chapter, we suggest some of the ways that we need to write the history of the future so that land-use decisions do serve the public interest. First, we shall outline the political, moral, legal, environmental, and economic reasons why we need new land-use ethics, and in the process of doing so, we shall offer a number of legal and political mechanisms able to achieve these reforms. Next, we shall respond to a number of objections that can be brought to our land-use proposals.

Solutions: Restricting Property Rights in Land

To correct the abuses associated with misuse of land, we have a moral imperative to control land use and property rights so that they serve the public, as well as private, interests. One of the best ways to serve the common good and the public interest is to restrict some of the many "rights" included in the bundle known as "property rights." As we explained in chapter 3, included in the set of rights known as "property rights" are eleven subrights typically known as "incidents of ownership." These are the right to possess; the right to use; the right to manage; the right to income; the right to the capital; the rights to security; the incident of transmissibility (the right to pass on property to one's successors); the incident of absence of term (the right to hold on to property forever, if one lived forever); the prohibition of harmful use; the liability to execution (property may be taken to cover debts); and residuary rights (full rights to property after other limited interests in it cease).[2] When one speaks of limiting property rights in land, therefore, one typically means limiting at least one of these eleven incidents, as they apply to land ownership.

Some of the goals of restricting these "incidents of ownership" are to provide public-interest, rather than private, control of land; to force land users to pay the real costs of their land-related activities; to reward landowners for public-interest uses of their land; and to force private land markets to meet public needs. In other words, land-use controls would aim at curbing: private profits from public contributions to land value; uncosted and uncompensated spillovers; uncosted and uncompensated geographical and intergenerational inequities; and laissez-faire use of land, rather than community planning for optimal use. Many of these goals of land-use ethics typically are implemented by restrictions on the right to use property. Such restrictions are accomplished through mechanisms such as zoning, taxation, building permits, and land-use planning. For example, communities might control development rights, pricing, and taxing of land on the basis of the public interest. Indeed, they might prohibit some land activities altogether (e.g., filling in wetlands). Or, they might heavily tax community-added land value, for instance, the value added to a parcel of land because of sewers and roads being available for it. They could also tax noxious activity (strip mining and failure to reclaim land) so that landowners understood that it was uneconomical to misuse land in certain ways. Likewise, they could tax poor farming and industrial practices, and in that way provide incentives for preserving the soil and promoting less polluting industries. Or, communities might buy up land and then create reserves in certain environmentally sensitive areas, like those threatened by heavy pollution. Alternatively, a community might buy up land, as has been done in European countries, and then lease it for planned development.

On the legal and political side, much land-use control could also be achieved by reinterpreting our notions of "police power," "takings," and "nuisance." (See later discussion and note 23.) In this way, as chapters 9 and 10 explained, ecological and other scientific criteria could be used to define what is harmful to land. Most importantly, as the next chapter will explain, we need a national set of land-use standards. For a number of reasons, we need something like the proposed 1970 National Land Use Policy Act. Those who argue that there is a great need for new land-use ethics, politics, and law point out that land has not been used in ways consistent with the public interest (e.g., valuable forest land has been destroyed, and some of the world's best cropland has been either misused and eroded or paved over for parking lots and suburbs). Proponents of sharp restrictions on property rights in land also point out that there are numerous spillovers, or negative externalities, arising from poor land use and threatening the common good.[3] Each year, for example, three billion tons of topsoil are eroded from U.S. farmland. Not only does this erosion threaten the future of U.S. food-growing capacity, but pollution of U.S. waterways from soil runoff is estimated to cost more than $2 billion per year in material damages alone, apart from loss of wildlife.[4] The joint problems of soil loss and water pollution could be addressed by a number of reforms: heavy taxation of those who cultivate erosive soils or leave mined soils unreclaimed; withholding subsidies from them; or simply prohibiting certain uses of erosive land. Whether such spillovers are addressed through land-use controls, however, is in part a function of whether a solid case can be made for new land-use ethics, ethics that justify further restrictions on property rights.

There are at least five different types of arguments that can be used to defend further restrictions on property rights in land. They are arguments from political philosophy, moral philosophy, legal philosophy, environmental welfare, and economic well-being. Let's look at the arguments from political philosophy first.

Arguments from Political Philosophy

At first glance, there are a number of reasons why American political philosophies seem diametrically opposed to any restriction of property rights in land. America has developed as a bourgeois society based, in large part, on property rights. Even now, as earlier chapters in the volume have pointed out, Americans are very sensitive about relinquishing more of their control over their property in land.

Jefferson was one of the prime movers in early land policy, and he strongly supported abolition of the feudal system of landholding and creation of a society of freeholders. He made clear that Saxon common law supported the notion of freemen holding land. He repeatedly speaks in his writings of allodial rights, rights to an estate held in absolute dominion without obligation to some feudal lord. This is why Jefferson believed that the lands of North America belonged to the people living there and not to the king of England. Being a property owner, for Jefferson, was the key way in which the first Americans exhibited their independence from government and from the British king. Jefferson expressly denied what many British, including the king and philosopher Hobbes, affirmed: that land belongs to the sovereign or the government, or that apportionment of land ought to be controlled by the sovereign or government.[5]

Jefferson also believed that a nation of persons owning property was the surest safeguard of democracy. People would have a vested interest in their land and would work to protect it. He assumed that the owner was an individual person living *on* his land—not the Prudential Life Insurance Co. or a nation-wide development corporation. Because of the close connection between the strength of democracy and property holdings in land, Jefferson strongly supported various homestead laws whose effect was to take land out of the public domain and put it in the hands of citizens, especially small farmers. His draft of the Virginia Constitution included a provision (later removed by others) giving every person of full age the right to fifty acres of land "in full and absolute dominion."[6] Much of Jefferson's emphasis on the importance of property rights, especially property rights in land, derives from John Locke. Locke gave primacy to property rights as the hallmark of freedom and democracy, because private property in land was the chief vehicle enabling persons to be free rather than serfs working on a lord's land. To give up control of private property in land would be to risk a return to the feudal era and to the alleged divine right of kings to control land. For all these reasons, both Locke and Jefferson have long been portrayed as staunch defenders of full rights to private property in land. (See chapter 4, however, where we argue that this interpretation of Locke may be incorrect.) Hence it was no accident that, late in the nineteenth century, Jefferson's views were being cited in opposition to the preservation of Yellowstone.[7]

This strong property-rights tradition has been taken up in recent American philosophy, most notably in libertarian philosophy, especially as exhibited in the views of Harvard philosopher Robert Nozick. Virtually no right is more firmly entrenched, in the minds of Nozick and other libertarians, than the right to property. Nozick, like Madison before him, even goes so far as to say that owning property is essential to the concept of personhood. It is impossible to be a person without owning property. Moreover, nothing, whether dire social need or government decree, for Nozick, justifies taking away even part of one's property. Property is that to which a person is entitled, and (for Nozick) the only thing justifying limitations on property is proof that the property was obtained fraudulently.[8] All the way from Jefferson to contemporary thinkers like Nozick, there appears to be a strong tradition of almost absolute property rights. Hence any talk of additional land-use controls raises the specter of interference with basic American liberties and rights.

As one might suspect, however, the picture is not quite so simple as this. During the years prior to writing the Declaration of Independence, not all Americans held the notion that property rights ought to be as absolute as contemporary libertarians have claimed. In the early days of the Unites States, James Madison was on one side of the property issue and Benjamin Franklin was on the other. Madison sided with those who preferred bicameral legislatures, with an upper chamber elected by property owners, so as to protect landholders against the masses. On the other side, Benjamin Franklin expressed just the opposite sentiment. He wrote: "Private property is a creature of society and is subject to the calls of society, whenever its necessities shall require it." He expressed great regret that some people in Pennsylvania were disposed, as he put it, "to commence an aristocracy, by giving the rich a predominancy in government." Franklin and others, at the time of the American Revolution, challenged the notion that individuals ought to be allowed to accumulate vast amounts of private property, especially private property in land. Their arguments were that the earth was given to humankind in common, that humans have rights only to that which is required for subsistence, and that the inheritance of property should be controlled by society. Hence, even though subsequent traditions have hardly emphasized the fact, the idea that private property was the most absolute of rights was not universally accepted among those who founded this country. They had strong political arguments that land was a commons given to all, and hence something subject to community control.[9]

Moreover, if one reads Jefferson carefully, one discovers that ownership, for Jefferson, represented merely the right to use land during one's lifetime. Jefferson fought for the repeal of the laws of entail, and he argued against inheritance of property. His reasoning was that such laws of inheritance stood in the way of equal opportunity and created vast pockets of power. This is a surprising insight for a man who could not envision the oligopolies controlling the United States today. Jefferson even went so far as to say that wherever there was unused or uncultivated lands and poor persons needing land, the laws of property have been violated.[10] Together with Franklin, and later, Webster, Jefferson represented a strong tradition in American political philosophy, a tradition for restricting property rights only to what we can use ourselves, only to what we are entitled to through labor (not what we inherit), and only to what we can use in ways that serve the common good. In one sense, as we mentioned earlier, this Jeffersonian tradition goes all the way back to Locke. As we argued in chapter 4, the revisionist account of Locke, as a defender of restrictions on property rights, especially in land, represents a strong political-philosophy argument in favor of land-use planning. In brief, this argument is that, because land was given in common to all persons, the community has the right to control how it is used. Moreover, because we have an obligation to use land (given in common) in ways that make no one worse off, as well as in ways that are most productive, the community has the right to regulate property in land so that these conditions are fulfilled.

A second political-philosophy argument in favor of restrictions on land use is that there is no theory that can explain original acquisition of property rights in land; hence, goes the argument, all land use and land transfer is subject to community control. Surprisingly, one person who recognized the absence of any adequate theory of original land acquisition was Sir William Blackstone. Most political and legal authorities, however, cite Blackstone as an upholder of an absolute right to private property, especially private property in land. He wrote:

> So great, moreover, is the regard of the law for private property, that it will not authorize the least violation of it, no not even for the general good of the whole community. In vain, may it be urged that the good of the individual ought to yield to that of the community; for it would be dangerous to allow any private, or even any public tribunal, to be the judge of this common good, and to decide whether it be expedient or no. Besides the public good is in nothing more essentially interested, than in the protection of every individual's private rights, as modelled by the municipal law.[11]

If this quotation is accurate, then Blackstone apparently believed that one ought not violate private property, even for the common good. The main problem with Blackstone's argument, however, is that neither he nor anyone else, Locke included, has an adequate theory as to the origin of, and justification for, private property, especially private property in land. Even Locke (see chapter 4) could not explain how anyone could own land, because no one labored to create it; one can labor to create only the products of land. Both Marxists and capitalists adhere to some version of the labor theory of value, and hence neither group can justify original land *ownership*, as opposed to rights to land *use*.

Blackstone, the alleged proponent of absolute rights to private property, recognized this same point. He wrote:

> Pleased as we are with the possession [of land], we seem afraid to look back on the means by which it was acquired, as if fearful of some defect in our title . . . not caring to reflect that, accurately and strictly speaking, there is no foundation in nature or in natural law, why a set of words on parchment should convey the dominion of land; why the son should have a right to exclude his fellow creatures from a determinate spot of ground, because his father had done so before him.[12]

But if there is no clear foundation for acquisition of full rights to private property, and especially no clear foundation for full acquisition of rights to private property in resources that we did not create, then it is doubtful that anyone could argue that rights to private property are absolute. Regardless of how such rights were allegedly transferred down a long line of owners, it is questionable whether the first, or any other, owner could be said to possess full rights to property in land or natural resources. And if not, then there appears to be some justification for claiming that land, as a commons, ought to be subject to control in the name of the common good or public interest.

Arguments from Moral Philosophy

In addition to these two arguments from political philosophy (no right to full ownership in land because it was given to humans in common; no justification for the original acquisition of property rights), there are a number of considerations based on ethics or moral philosophy that suggest that the public has a right to control private property in ways that contribute to the public interest. The first argument has already been mentioned in chapter 4, in connection with the discussion of Locke. This argument is that, since private owners have not created all the value in land, therefore they ought not have full profits from, or full control over, the land. It is obvious that no owner could create full value in land merely by labor. Nowhere is the inadequacy of the labor theory of value more obvious than when one talks about natural resources such as land. My laboring to dig up silver surely doesn't give me rights to all the silver, since I didn't create it, but merely rights to that portion of the *value* of the silver *added* by my labor. My laboring on farm land does not give me rights to all the land I cultivate, but merely to that portion of the value of the land added by my labor, since I did not create the land.

It is also obvious that, if I buy a beachfront home, and then sell it later for a profit, I do not deserve the full profit and the full control over the land because much of its value was created by nature (e.g., beautiful beaches). The value of coal land is not created by the company who mines it, nor is the value of mountains created by the ski-resort owner. All these forms of labor merely added to what was already there in nature. To say that part of the value of land was created by no human, and therefore no human, alone, ought to control it, is along the lines of Mahatma Gandhi's thought. He wrote: "Land is like the air, rain, and sun, It belongs to all, because it belongs to no one except to God who made it."[13] Tolstoy says something similar:

> If land has become a matter of property, and not water, air, and sunshine, it is by no means for the reasons that it is not equally with those elements, an essential basis of human life, but simply because it was possible to appropriate it, and not the other elements.[14]

Perhaps persons have alleged that they have full property rights in land, but not in air, because they are able to build fences on the earth, but not in the air. Property rights in water have been established by law, especially in the American West. A number of persons have also claimed air rights, but this area of law is still rather "soft." Admittedly, some economists have argued for the creation of property rights in air and water as a solution to problems of pollution and resource depletion (see chapter 6). Despite the pragmatic benefits of this solution, such proposals appear flawed in failing to address the rights of future generations to clean air and water and in presupposing that one can have property rights to something not created by one's own labor. Economists have also criticized the property-rights-in-air/water notion by pointing out that a system of marketable emission permits (via property rights) has several distinct disadvantages, relative to effluent fees (that involve no property rights). Although both are least-cost methods for reducing pollution, the effluent-fees approach (1) tends to correct distortions in the economy, (2) is more equitable in forcing the polluter to pay, and (3) saves certain transaction costs because there is no transfer of permits. Hence, the property-rights-in-air/water is neither the only, nor the best, solution being offered by economists to address air and water pollution.[15]

Besides value added by nature, much of the alleged value of land (air, or water) might be added or created by society. For example, a mountain ski resort may have added value because the taxpayers have added access roads. Property values on one's home may have gone up because neighbors have planned beautiful landscaping nearby or because they have built expensive houses. One of the most obvious senses in which private property owners have not created all the value in their land has to do with irrigation of farmland. Irrigation, probably costing $2,000 per acre, per year, in government-subsidized water in California, is a clear example of public-added value.[16]

In addition to the argument that individual profits from and control of land ought to be proportional to the individual contributions made to its value, there is a second ethical argument for land-use controls. This one is based on geographical and intergenerational equity. Minimal fairness dictates that a situation is inequitable if it allows some persons to use their property in such a way (e.g., poor mining practices) that harms the interests of others (e.g., in clean water). Focusing on the concept of equity, economists such as Mishan have argued for strict land-use controls on the grounds that every citizen has amenity rights, rights not to "be forced against his will to absorb . . . noxious by-products of the activity of others."[17] While the particulars of such a system of amenity rights would not be easy to work out, it is obvious that a clear case can be made for them on both ethical and economic grounds. Some of the desirable ethical consequences of recognizing a class of amenity rights, as a basis for land-use ethics are (1) that the rich and the poor alike would have more equal access to desirable environmental quality; (2) private enterprise would be less likely to ignore the welfare of the public; (3) citizens would not be robbed of choice regarding such things as quiet and attractive surroundings; and (4) citizens would be prohibited from causing any spillovers for which they were unable to compensate others. At present, only the wealthy are able to avoid many environmental spillovers, simply because they have the resources to buy their way out of environmental or natural-resource problems. They can live where they wish, for example; they can buy bottled water, and they can pay for electrostatic air filters.[18]

Amenity rights can also easily be defended on economic grounds. If land-use controls prohibited property owners from using their land in ways that violated the amenity rights of others, then property owners would be forced either to cease their damaging activities or, at least, to compensate others for the effects of such activities. Appropriate compensation, as one form of land-use control, would thus force markets to operate in a more orderly and reasonable fashion. As Mishan points out, because the real costs of certain actions (e.g., mining coal, developing farmland) could not be hidden and said to be "external" to the market process, property owners would be forced to take account of them. And once forced to take account of them, property owners would be far less likely to engage in questionable environmental activities if they were forced to be fully responsible financially for their consequences. One ethical reason for making others fully accountable for the effects of their environmental activities is that failure to do so, and instead forcing someone to absorb the noxious byproducts of another, amounts to unfair discrimination. If one is forced to breathe dirty air simply because she lives in the same geographical area as a polluting factory, or if one is forced to buy bottled water simply because she lives downstream from some industrial effluent, then she might be called a victim of injustice, of unjustifiable discrimination on the basis of geography. Just as there is discrimination on the basis of sex and race, so also it could be argued that people often are discriminated against purely on the basis of geography. Yet geography, like race, creed, and religion, is not a relevant basis for unequal or unfair treatment that is arbitrary and subjective.[19]

Moreover, if one has rights to life, liberty, and the pursuit of happiness, then it appears that one also has rights to whatever is necessary for exercising those rights. And a right to a clean environment, or a right to protection from pollution, equal to the protection enjoyed by others, might be necessary to exercising one's civil liberties. One could also argue that if there is a right to life, then there is a corresponding right to protection from environmental hazards that threaten that right to life. To argue that there is a right to life, but that there is no right to protection from the many involuntarily imposed risks of pollution, for example, appears inconsistent. This is because, if we have a right to life, then as a consequence we must also have a right to the necessary means of protecting that right.[20] But if we do have something like what Mishan called "amenity rights," and like what I called "rights to a clean environment," then any discrimination purely on the grounds of geography is likely not defensible. Geographical equity appears to demand recognition of the same rights to equal protection and the same rights to life, regardless of whether one lives, for example, in a black ghetto or a white suburb. And recognition of the concept of geographical equity, in turn, requires control over land use, at least in the form of restricting certain noxious spillovers, in protecting groundwater and watersheds, and in forcing property owners to use their land in ways consistent with the public interest.[21]

Much the same argument can be made for intergenerational equity. Just as John Locke required that property rights be subject to the proviso that as much and as good be left for others, so also use of land ought to be subject to the proviso that as many and as good opportunities be left for members of future generations as for members of present ones. (Locke might have been astonished to learn that this argument would be strongly endorsed by the Zero Population Growth Society.) Just as minimal fairness dictates that one pay the cost of his own activities and not impose them on others, especially on unwilling others, so also geographical and intergenerational equity appears to require land-use controls so as to guarantee fair treatment of all persons. Fair treatment, in turn, requires land users to pay the costs of their activities; if they wish to turn prime agricultural land into a shopping center, for example, then they must pay the full costs of their depriving future persons of this resource—which they may be unable to do. For this reason "practical" people discount the future to the level of feasibility. Unless land users pay the full costs of future deprivation, they have taken goods (opportunities) out of the commons and unfairly appropriated them for their private use.[22]

Arguments from Legal Philosophy

In addition to the equity arguments for land-use controls, arguments dictated by moral philosophy, there are several reasons, based on legal philosophy, that also justify restriction of property rights in land. The most basic of these arguments is that the tradition of regulation in the public interest in this country also appears to support extensive land-use controls. We use police power and nuisance law, for example, to stop activities of property owners that are harmful to others. Hence, there is legal precedent for regulating private property in the public interest.[23] It is easy to argue for strict land-use controls preventing filling in of wetlands, for example, on the grounds that doing so would flood the land of other persons and hence constitute a nuisance. Or, as one economic analyst of the law put it, wetlands perform functions worth $50,000 t0 $80,000 per acre, although not to their owner. Since their destruction would result in deleterious effects on surrounding watersheds, it is quite easy to show that land-use controls are consistent with much nuisance law.[24]

One reason for expanding our concept of nuisance law and police power, so as to deal with destructive uses of land, is that our current legal system allows us to regulate many activities having less serious effects on the public good than does regulation of property rights and land-use control. We regulate FCC licenses, telephone service, and liquor sales, for example, all on the basis of promoting the public interest and avoiding public harm. If we can justify all these activities in the name of the common good, then it appears reasonable to justify land-use controls by the same means, since property use appears to have at least as great a potential for harm and benefit as does use of FCC licenses.[25]

A second land-use control argument based on legal philosophy is that there are many precedents in the common law of numerous western democracies that support land-use controls, including public control over the use of allegedly private land. In Sweden, for example, there is a long tradition of public ownership of urban land. The tradition dates back to the Middle Ages, and the city planning office in Sweden dates back to 1640. The basic framework is that of public or municipal ownership, with long leases to the users.[26] British practices are close to those in Sweden. The land is assembled by the city and then leased to private developers. In fact, under English law, the crown has been in theory the ultimate owner of all land since William the Conqueror—A.D. 1066. Hence, in England, no disturbance of basic legal tenets is required to engage in land-use planning. Municipally owned land and housing represents more than one-fifth of all housing stock in England.[27] Similar situations exist in Norway, where cities often possess a prior right of preemption over any land offered for sale in the city. In Oslo, for example, the municiality has purchased 25,000 acres of land within the city boundary and it leases this land out to private developers.[28] Planning and land-use controls have also been quite successful in France, in Switzerland, and in the Nether-lands. Municipal ownership of land in the Netherlands is of long stand-ing, and virtually all Dutch cities pursue a vigorous policy of mu-nicipal land acquisition.[29]

What the experience of other countries teaches us is that there is a widespread legal precedent for exactly the sort of regulation of land most needed to serve the public interest. At least in some countries, land-use planning is neither new nor always a violation of established principles of interpreting property rights.

Objections to Land-Use Controls

In response to arguments about the need for greater land-use controls to promote wise use of land, to prevent environmental degradation, and to restrain spillovers, opponents of the new land-use ethics have raised a number of objections. Four of the most important of these objections are that (1) land-use controls are too expensive to devise and to implement; (2) they interfere with normal market processes; (3) they result in an arbitrary, unfair, and elitist dictatorship of planning; and (4) they violate long-standing rights to private property. Before dealing with these objections, let us point out that they have apparently been quite successful. Most Americans are not convinced of the need for a new land-use ethics. As Lynton Caldwell has noted, all direct attempts to enact national land-use legislation have failed. Even with substantial presidential and congressional support, three successive attempts failed to obtain the adoption either of the proposed National Land Use Policy Act of 1970 or of its modifications.[30]

In only nine states is local planning of land use required, and in only six states is local zoning required. While forty states have adopted tax incentives to give relief to owners of agricultural land and open space, and forty-four have adopted tax incentives to give relief to those holding forest land, only thirty-three states have taken power-plant siting out of the hands of private industry. Only thirteen states have drawn up rules favoring the designation of areas of critical en-vironmental or historical concern.[31] In the 1990 elections, land-use protection initiatives were resoundingly defeated by popular vote in several states, including California, New York, and Washington. Given such a grim outlook on land-use planning, let's look at each of the major objections to it. Consider first the objection that most commu-nities can't afford land-use planning, and that they simply do not have the funds to plan and implement land-use controls.

Are Land-use Controls Too Expensive?

To some extent, this is a legitimate objection. Communities faced with strained budgets and more immediate needs often cannot afford to spend much money on land-use planning. Several facts, however, place the economics of land-use planning in perspective. First, the real question is not whether land-use planning is expensive, but for whom it is expensive. If taxpayers bear the cost of planning and zoning, then attempts to avoid noxious environmental spillovers would be borne fairly equitably. On the other hand, if no planning and zoning takes place, then the costs imposed by some property owners on others are likely to be distributed inequitably. Noxious environmental spillovers will probably be borne by those who cannot move away from them or who have little economic and political power. Hence planning probably does not cost more money,[32] but it does redistribute social costs from a subset of victims of spillovers to the entire taxed citizenry.

Concern about the expense associated with land-use controls can be seen in a more appropriate perspective if one considers a similar objection, often made against attempts to avoid racial discrimination in hiring and in housing. True, such attempts to shape behavior are always expensive, but expense is hardly the most important, although it is a necessary, criterion for social policy making. To the degree that certain behavior violates the rights of persons to equal treatment or to other legally guaranteed rights, to that extent is the question of expense less important. We would, after all, not claim that it was too expensive to try to catch criminals, or too expensive to make societal decisions based on merit, rather than expediency, or too expensive to enforce the due-process provisions of the Bill of Rights. Hence, if one is to argue convincingly that land-use planning is too expensive, the objectors must demonstrate that it is more expensive than inequitable distribution of spillovers, failure to safeguard resources for future generations, and so on. In fact, of course, they are almost never required to do so. Even the disadvantaged "victims" of development frequently do not invoke the arguments in their own favor, having been coopted by means of the prevailing "enterprise ideology."

Second, over the long term, it could well be that planning in the public interest ultimately makes a community a more desirable place to live and do business. Hence, it could be that planning actually saves a community more money than failure to plan. For example, Tom McCall, former governor of Oregon, cited a Florida study that showed that planning was actually cheaper for a community than simply leaving itself open to exploitative development. The study showed that

1,000 new residents in a Florida county would include 270 new families, 200 schoolchildren, 19 blind persons, 68 aged persons, 11 juvenile delinquents, 16 alcoholics, and 30 mentally retarded persons. Therefore it is cheaper to hold the land as a reserve, owned by the community, cheaper to retire the bonds used to purchase the acres, than it would be the develop the services needed to support these 1,000 people, since they cannot pay the real cost of all the goods and services that they need.[33] To some persons, this may appear to be a crass argument, but it addresses some crass economic concerns in exactly the terms in which they have been raised by opponents of land-use planning.

A third point to consider in the economics of planning is to recall that development often only appears more economical than planning or buying up land for reserves. The alleged economics of development are often merely an artifact of using a discount rate for valuing future social costs. If one uses a 5 percent discount rate, according to which a billion dollars in pollution costs, 400 years from now, are worth the same as $1 worth of costs next year, then it is easy to see why use of a discount rate might tend to encourage development rather than conservation or land-use planning.[34] Hence, it may not be that land-use planning is extremely costly, but merely that certain economic techniques—such as discounting—make it appear so.

Do Land-Use Controls
Interfere with the Market?

What of the second objection, that land-use planning interferes with normal market operations? This objection errs, because it presupposes that interference with normal market operations is always wrong. Clearly it is not. Interference with "drug traffic," for example, also obstructs market operations. And, in some areas, drug traffic may be the most normal example of market operation, in the sense that "normal" means "typical" or "pervasive." Obviously, land-use planning interferes with normal market operations, but interference is only a problem if one erroneously presupposes that the market never needs any interference. In a variety of ways, the market does need interference, at least in part to insure that it remains as free and as competitive as possible. Conceivably use of property could conflict with free and open competition, as indeed it does every time there is genuine concern about antitrust violations. Moreover, the intent of land-use planning and control is to insure that there is no free lunch, to insure that property owners bear the full costs of the noxious effects of their activities, rather than to impose them on unwilling victims. Seen in this light, land-use controls are one way to make the market function as a better, more open, more competitive market, by forcing externalities to become internalized and by forcing the market to remain competitive and an authentic indicator of actual values.

Using land-use controls to force a more accurate assessment of the costs and benefits of our use of property might thus be seen, not as interfering with the market, but as correcting market imperfections. Indeed, land-use controls might correct imperfections in the real-estate market, just as shadow pricing also corrects market imperfections. In general, there are at least four ways in which market prices deviate from authentic values. They do not price free goods; they do not take account of externalities; they do not correct for speculative instabilities and monopolies that distort the system; and they do not factor opportunity costs (e.g., alternative use of resources). Land-use controls obviously are one vehicle for attempting to alleviate some of the problems created by the first two market distortions, failure to price free goods and failure to take externalities into account.[35] Admittedly, however, whenever a bureaucrat interferes with the market, the potential for harm is very great. That land-use controls can be misused, however, does not argue for letting the market control property, unless it can be shown, in a particular case, that the market abuses are likely to be less serious than the land-use control abuses. Hence the issue of the market vs. control is, at best, one to be decided on a case-by-case basis.

Does Planning Lead to Dictatorship, Unfairness, Elitism, or Arbitrariness?

A third objection to land-use control is that it could lead to a regulatory and bureaucratic nightmare. While this response is reasonable, its difficulty is that this same objection could be used to argue against virtually any regulatory or democratic process. People have raised the same objections to national health insurance, securities and exchange regulation and, above all, the U.S. income tax code. Any regulatory or democratic process is inefficient and prone to numerous mistakes. Certainly trial by jury is open to these same objections. If one is to fault a regulatory and bureaucratic process, then it is incumbent on him to provide a better option for addressing the problems raised by failure to engage in land-use planning. The realistic way to address this objection appears to be to implement planning in ways that have appeared most successful in the past, and to compare the abuses of democratically controlled planning with the abuses created by failure to employ land-use controls. Houston is a case in point. The failure to employ land-use controls has resulted in a notoriously unpleasant place to live.[36] Likewise, although trial by jury is a bureaucratic nightmare, any alternatives to it would likely result in a notoriously more inequitable and more subjective system of justice.

Moreover, to the degree that land-use planning can be accused of being arbitrary or dictatorial, to that extent is it necessary to implement important democratic controls associated with negotiation, funding public-interest groups, and sponsoring open hearings. It may even be necessary to have some sort of adversary assessment of planning options, so that all sides to a controversy are represented. In other words, planning must be democratized. Regulatory decision making must become sensitive to the demands of democracy, equal representation, and public accountability. The solution to problems of regulatory arbitrariness is not to abandon regulation and leave the citizen to the whims of the most powerful economic interests, but rather to build safeguards into the planning system itself. In fact, there is much that we can learn about such safeguards from planning and assessment in other technology- and environment-related areas.[37] Some of these considerations are addressed in Section 10212 of NEPA, the National Environmental Policy. Ultimately, however, if there are objections to land-use planning and land-use controls, then it must be that we the people have allowed them to occur. The solution is not to take regulatory power away from the people, but to teach them to use it wisely. This is similar to what Thomas Jefferson once said. If we believe the people to be unfit for governing themselves, the solution is not to take the power away from them, but to educate them.[38] Educating the people also includes getting their attention. The big land developers spent millions in advertising to defeat land-use controls in California recently. With equal effort and money spent to educate persons about the benefits of land-use controls, the vote might have been different.

Do Land-Use Controls Violate Rights to Private Property?

A fourth objection often brought against land-use controls is that they violate rights to private property. The most basic problem with this objection is that it begs the very question at issue, namely, that property rights are absolute and not subject to control in the public interest. Yet, if many of the arguments in chapter 4 and in the present chapter are correct, then property rights are not absolute, and they were not conceived as absolute, even by those—like Locke and Jefferson—who most strongly supported them.

Conclusion

Where does all this leave us with respect to solutions to problems of land-use control? Land-use ethics requires only that we reexamine our political, legal, and ethical traditions. Once these traditions are understood correctly and completely, it is possible to see that they are wise and rich and good. Hence it is not clear that we need so much a new ethics, in any conceptual sense, but that, as the Buddhist proverb puts it, that we learn to see with new eyes—we learn to see our own philosophical traditions in a new way. The fundamental insight is that land-use control is not the brainchild of some socialist reformer eager to destroy our American heritage. Rather, land-use control is an attempt to make our land law and policy consistent with the technological burdens that we have imposed on nature and on one another. It is also the product of reinterpreting our English and American traditions as more profoundly equitable and more democratic than we were ever taught.

12

A National Policy for Land?

Lynton Keith Caldwell and
Kristin Shrader-Frechette

We have concluded that a national policy for land would be in the
public interest. Beyond this, we believe that national policies for
equitable, sustainable land use would be in the interest of all persons
and all countries. As long as the national state prevails as our dominant form of political organization, national governments will be the
ultimate guardians of responsibility for uses of land. Because custody and stewardship, however, will remain the direct responsibility
of private or corporate persons and of local governing institutions, at
least in the United States, land use will remain a complex and politically sensitive issue. The federal structure and its historical traditions
likewise will add to the normal difficulty of obtaining consensus in a
diverse and democratic society. Arguments can be made for and against
comprehensive land-use legislation at the federal level, but they often are at cross purposes. They have little practical utility unless there
is a priori agreement on what kind of need for what kind of land
policy and for what purpose.

Land-use planning is often attacked by its opponents as being
against property rights, especially private rights. We neither disregard nor undervalue the importance of proprietary status for defining
and protecting the rights of use in land. But we believe that both law
and ethics should firmly link rights of ownership with responsibilities for conserving land as a resource basic to human welfare now
and in the future. Legal ownership of land-use rights establishes (or
should establish) accountability for how the land is treated. Private
ownership provides the stability and the incentive to take care of land
as an indispensable but vulnerable resource. Hence, we are not
unsympathetic to the legitimate interests of the private owner. We see
the major source of conflict over property rights as between conflicting private-property interests rather than between private owners and
public planning.

As matters stand today, the federal government is unavoidably in-

245

volved in nearly every land-use transaction. National policy in some form will enter into those transactions whether or not it is explicit, codified, or consistent. In our view, responsible private-ownership rights in land would best be assured by explicit, rational, ecologically informed policies at all levels of government. But given the variety and complexity of social, economic, and environmental goals this society has asked government to pursue, many of which impinge upon land-use decisions, the concept of property in land may need to be redefined in order to assist the resolution of differences through law.[1]

Our General Thesis

In this chapter we summarize and recapitulate many of the main themes and arguments of this book. Some of the examples of attitudes and actions on land-use issues are reiterated in the more general context of this chapter. We introduce several strategies for obtaining a conserving and sustainable national policy for land. The underlying premise in all cases, however, is that public understanding and receptivity are necessary for a national land policy. It will require a concerted effort of many interests and organizations to bring about this receptivity. The essence of a new national attitude toward land use will inevitably be a new environmental ethics. There are persuasive utilitarian and scientific arguments for a conserving and sustainable land-use policy, but the fundamental reason, and for many people the most persuasive, is ethical. A concern for human welfare, the future of humanity, and the integrity and quality of life on earth requires a new land-use policy.

But people, preoccupied with personal affairs, are not likely to consider basic land-use issues unless they are personally affected. The political hazards of land-use debate, the concerted pressures of land-development lobbyists, and the lack of sufficient popular concern for national action has hitherto had the effect of discouraging serious consideration of the land-use issue. Following the failure of efforts in the early 1970s to enact national legislation, land use as a general issue disappeared from the federal agenda. Anti-government and privatization ideologies became widespread. Among the states, however, legislation for environmental protection and for regulation of certain land uses was enacted, but it was concentrated where pressures of development on scenic assets and quality of life were most strongly felt and resisted. Yet, we believe that land use will before long be back on the national agenda. Limited land and an expanding population and economy almost assure it. This assurance follows, in part, from growing public disillusionment with the national commitment to undifferentiated growth in a finite environment characterized by a society with changing values. Ultimately, the nation must face the reality that Paul B. Sears described as "the inexorable problem of space."[2] Infinite physical expansion is impossible in finite space. Societies must ultimately confront this reality when the option for growth is gone. It is not the total amount of available land or space, however, that most frequently poses problems of competitive uses and ownership. Rather it is the relatively small amount of highly desirable land in limited locations that has been the common object of contention among would-be users. Large land areas—grasslands, deserts, forests, and polar regions—normally present less intense but no less important policy problems. In recent years, however, large ecosystemic areas such as the polar regions, equatorial rainforests, and virgin grasslands have become objects of land-policy debate, particularly where the preservation of diverse species of animals and plants depends upon safeguarding the integrity of biotic communities or ecosystems.

If one accepts the proposition that national legislation is needed to assist rational and coordinated land-use decisions in the public interest, the question follows: what kind of legislation might accomplish this purpose? Fortunately we have models of possible legislation. There are foreign models, such as Patricios (1984) and Steiner and Van Lier (1986),[3] but the particularities of land-use legislation and adjudication in the United States limit the transferability of the legal conventions from other countries. There are land-use provisions in various federal statutes dealing primarily with public lands. Certain private lands are subject to conditional uses overseen by public health or environmental agencies and often hedged by deed restrictions. There is also a large body of judge-made law at both state and federal levels. In addition, as noted in previous chapters, a number of states have experimented with land-use legislation—often indirectly, as with Arizona restrictions on the pumping of groundwater, New York's constitutional prohibition against development in the Adirondack Forest Preserve, or California's coastal-zone initiative.

We also have models for national land-use legislation in proposed statutes that have been introduced into the Congress. A Model Land Development Code, for example, has been prepared by the American Law Institute.[4] We are not wanting in prescriptions for land-use policy reform. In chapter 7, "Limits to Policy," we recounted briefly the ill-fated land-use legislation that was caught in conflict between the U.S. Senate and the Executive branch. It was also blocked in the House of Representatives by the concentrated efforts of developers, speculators, real-estate interests, and the farm lobby. The proposed act was widely misrepresented as a federal land grab, a bureaucratic invasion of home and hearth, a big step toward socialism, and an abrogation of the natural and constitutional rights of Americans. Although the legislation was supported by a diverse number of organizations, including the American Institute of Architects, the American Institute of Planners, the American Society of Landscape Architects, the League of Women Voters, and the Sierra Club, among others, there was insufficient mobilization of public opinion on its behalf. In contrast to its advocacy role in civil rights issues, the news media coverage tended to feature alarms and controversy. Moreover, some ecologists and environmental activists were nervous over the possibility that policy might be preempted by the politically influential natural-resource interests. In 1967 and 1968 the National Forest Products Association urged "an enlightened public land-use policy for the nation." Environmentalists were concerned about how "enlightened" might be defined.[5]

Does defeat of the national land-use policy proposals in the 1970s demonstrate the impracticality of this legislation? Not necessarily, because circumstances, public opinion, and priorities are not static. If action at the state level is indicative, popular receptivity for land-use planning has been growing. The process of public planning and decision making has become more open, inclusive, and responsive to people's preferences and concerns. As citizen participation in the decision-making process has increased, centralized planning by experts has been a declining factor in popular opposition to land-use planning. The tendency today is to bring experts into collaborative relationships with concerned citizens.

Is More Land-Use Policy Really Needed?

An unequivocal "yes" or "no" to this question would have little meaning. For an answer to make sense, one would need to know what kind of land policy was proposed and for what purpose. One would also want to know what means were contemplated to interpret and apply the policy. Although many advocates of land-use policy see it as protective of ecological values, environmental amenities, and economic stability, other goals are possible, some of which are prejudicial to environmental quality or to ecological integrity. As previously noted, some industrial and commercial interests favor land-use policy that would reduce uncertainties and protect their opportunities for site selection and plant construction. Forestry and livestock interests would like to prevent "preservationist" restrictions on their use of natural areas. They would stop the withdrawal of public lands from timbering, mining, and grazing. Supply-side economists may advocate land-use policies that protect jobs and natural-materials industries from environmentalists who would "lock-up" economically valuable resources for "unproductive" purposes. Owners of land vulnerable to periodic flooding (coastal areas and river bottoms) vigorously defend federal subsidies for flood insurance and denounce efforts to reduce or remove subsidies for building on hazardous sites. This deliberate subsidy may be regarded as an uneconomical and special-privilege aspect of land-use planning. Thus land-use policy may be used against, as well as for, ecological amenity and broader public economic objectives.

Government itself, at both federal and state levels, has been divided over what, if any, land-use policy is needed. Federal agencies have differing objectives affecting the land and some of these appear to be in unreconcilable conflict. During a public hearing on the proposed National Land Use Planning Act of 1970 (Senate Bill 3350), on March 24, 1970, a series of transparent overlays were displayed, each indicating the location of present and projected uses of land by federal agencies. The overlays revealed conflicting intentions of federal agencies at numerous locations across the country, many of which were also in direct or indirect conflict with state or local preferences. The Florida Everglades was a case in point. Here were incompatible plans for use of the same land by the Corps of Engineers, the Federal Aviation Agency, the Federal Highway Administration, the National Park Service, the Fish and Wildlife Service, and Florida state and county agencies.[6] No clear set of enforceable principles was in effect to establish priorities among these competing programs and projects. The intergovernmental character of the competition meant that federal action would be required to resolve the differences. In the absence of settled land-use policy and established priorities, vested interests are likely to continue to engage in political maneuvering in the Congress and the Executive branch.

Unreconciled objectives of federal agencies have also arisen over the multiple-use mandate of the Congress.[7] These conflicts have arisen with respect to public lands with multiple capabilities, since some uses would preclude others. For example, wilderness is hardly compatible with timbering and mining. Mass recreation is not conducive to the protection of endangered species or fragile ecosystems. Prodevelopment and environmental-quality interests regularly take opposing positions on local, state, and federal land issues. State governments cannot easily resolve instate controversies in which opinion is sharply divided between rural, prodevelopment interests and protectionist groups that are largely urban. A case in point is the conflict in Minnesota between local business and development interests in the Boundary Waters Wilderness Area, on the one hand, and environmental, wilderness, and wildlife protectionists in the Twin Cities, on the other hand.[8] Similar conflict has arisen in the states of Oregon and Washington, where small local communities dependent on the lumber industry want to cut the ancient forests now to save jobs and prolong the life of dwindling communities. Opposing them are groups in Portland, Seattle, and throughout the nation that criticize the loss of irreplaceable ancient forests, for a short-term economic advantage, as a destruction of our future.[9] In these and similar cases, federal agencies or certain of their employees often take opposite sides of an issue. The Forest Service and the Fish and Wildlife Service, for example, have disagreed over priorities for timber production versus protection of threatened species. Many additional situations could be cited to support the argument that more policy is needed to resolve or prevent conflicts over land use. But does it follow that comprehensive federal legislation is needed? Couldn't incremental adjustments in existing statutes and policies achieve reconciliation of interests and purposes? Couldn't the states collectively provide enough guidance and adjudication in land-use decisions?

Why Can't the States Meet the Need?

The states play an important role in laying down the ground rules for land use, but there are at least three reasons that preclude reliance upon state governments alone to provide the policies needed to attain land-use objectives that are rational, sustainable, generally fair, and ecologically sound. The first is the unequal ability or interest of the states to enact or enforce protective legislation. The second is the preemptive presence of the federal government, especially in those states with large areas of national public domain. A third reason, not yet widely appreciated, is the need for governmental action capable of responding to international environmental issues. As concerns over global climate change, deforestation, desertification, and loss of genetic diversity increase, international cooperation depends on the responsiveness of national governments responsible for foreign policy. Often state governments are reluctant to protect nationwide interests and priorities.

For example, upstream jurisdictions in America's great river systems may be expected to have less concern over watershed protection than downstream communities confronted by stream siltation, water pollution, flooding, and diversion. This expectation may not hold in all states, yet it has been evident in the politics of the Colorado,

Missouri, and Ohio basins. It was also a factor leading to establishment of river basin authorities such as the TVA (Tennessee Valley Authority) and ORSANCO (Ohio River Sanitation Commission). Watershed protection and riverain equity have likewise been issues of contention among national governments in Africa, Asia, and Europe,[10] and between Canada and the United States over transboundary rivers.[11] Similarly, transboundary air pollution has created international antagonisms, notably over acid rain. These air and surface water issues, and many others involved in environmental policy (e.g., groundwater pumping and airborne toxic deposition), arise from activities originating on the land. River systems cross both Canadian and Mexican borders, and the respective governments have established commissions to deal with conflicts over the uses and quality of the transboundary waters. But the International Joint Commission (Canada and the United States) and the International Boundary and Water Commission (Mexico and the United States) have labored under the politically prudent but ecologically erroneous assumption that the problems confronting them were essentially rights to water. To have faced the reality of the water-use problems would have intruded upon the sovereignties of the respective national states. The reality of water-use problems is that they are land-use problems. Land use is an international issue, but adherence to the national sovereignty doctrine has obscured it.

In the United States, state sovereignty has created similar difficulties. Federal and state land policies have been frequently at odds, especially in the western states. The uneconomical, unecological partition of land in the American West into patterns of checkerboard ownership has resulted in difficulties for land management by all parties concerned, federal, state, local, and private. In southern Utah, for example, federal and state agencies have incompatible objectives.[12] Some federal authorities would maintain undeveloped land, where other federal agencies and many state and business interests push to promote tourism and mass recreation. In Alaska, state officials complain that the federal government has throttled development through its preemption of vast tracts of land for national parks, forests, wildlife ranges, and reservations for native Americans. Military installations and federal highways have become contention points, their expansion not always welcomed by state and local governments or by large sectors of the general public. Nevertheless, proposals to close military bases invariably bring cries of protest and opposition from state and local authorities.

Many land-use conflicts are localized at town or county levels but may be addressed most effectively if solutions are consistent with basic principles prevailing at state and federal levels. Although the states hold the residual power to regulate the uses of land, they cannot always unilaterally protect or control the lands subject to their jurisdiction. All jurisdictions are subject to adjudication by the federal courts on the civil rights, due process, and interstate-commerce provisions of the Constitution of the United States. As a result, land-use decisions at state and local levels have been struck down by federal courts as violations of the "taking" clause of the Fifth Amendment or the civil rights provisions of the Fourteenth Amendment.[13] In the federal system of the United States neither the federal government nor the states can attain exclusive jurisdiction over land use.

Opponents of comprehensive national land-use legislation might admit that national policies are needed for certain purposes but argue that, in general, we have as much land law as we need—perhaps too much. They may point out that the Clean Air Acts of 1970 and 1990 and the Water Pollution Control Act Amendments of 1972 contained land-use implications, just as the Federal Land Policy and Management and the Forest Management Act of 1976 had implications for the Forest Service. Statutory provisions affecting land use also influenced decisions by the Army Corps of Engineers, the Water and Power Administration, and Soil Conservation Service, and the Federal Highway Administration among others. But do these disparate statutes and their derivative regulations aggregate to a coherent national policy for land? The continuing course of controversy suggests that they do not.

The Case for a National Policy

A detailed, quantified analysis of cases and controversies is hardly necessary to establish the need for a national land-use policy appropriate to the federal structure of the U.S. government and to U.S. representation in international environmental policy negotiations. Future opportunities and options have already been discounted severely by past land-use decisions that are neither ecologically nor economically sound. The case developed for a national policy in 1970 is still valid.[14] The legislation did not fail on its merits but was a victim of political maneuvers and intense lobbying by a self-serving organized opposition. The argument is that we cannot safeguard the quality of American life or the soundness of the American economy without a comprehensive, coherent, and scientifically valid policy for land. The stability of natural-resource-based industries, and the future distribution of economic activities and of population, require wise land-use decisions now if costly conflicts and errors are to be avoided in the future. We cannot cope effectively with our problems of land use at any level of government unless we deal with them, in their appropriate aspects, at all levels. In our continental economy, land-use decisions in any area may affect the public welfare and land-use decisions in other places. An airport displaced from the Everglades may seek another location; misplaced industrial development may destroy recreational opportunities; preemption of forest land for recreational or ecological purposes may displace forest industries and increase the cost of timber, although commercial forestry may threaten environmental qualities of higher intrinsic value.

Public jurisdiction over land use is divided among the three major levels of government—none have total jurisdiction. Failure of any level to participate in an effort to establish predictable, national, land-use policies would defeat not only a nationwide effort, but very possibly efforts at the other levels of policy including the international. Yet leadership in a nationwide effort must be provided at the national level. A national policy for land is therefore not just a policy of the federal government, but should be a policy of all levels of government with appropriate allocation of responsibilities and administrative action.[15]

What Are the Proper Objectives of a National Policy?

The guiding objective of national land policy would be to obtain a coherent and effective system for wise land-use decision making, consistent with our constitutional system and with responsible democratic self-government. The right of local communities to shape their futures ought to be respected, but how this is to be accomplished, consistent with nationwide and ultimately with international principles, is uncertain. Judicial denial of the right of communities to control their growth is a serious limitation on land-use planning. It reflects the zealous concern of the courts for civil rights and their relative indifference to environmental values. Since the settlement of the continent and the era of the land office and the Homestead Act, the nation has not had a coherent land-use policy. On the contrary, it has had a policy of no general policy. Vestiges of the old "come and get it" ideology remain, but changed conditions and new concerns have led to efforts toward public restraints on irresponsible uses of land. A consequence has been a growing series of conflicts over land use. A declared policy is, in principle, required to provide a basis for public and private decisions throughout the nation. A second objective, indirect to be sure, is to develop public attitudes, indeed a public conscience, toward the use of land that is appropriate to the real needs of our times and protective of our future health, happiness, and prosperity. These attitudes must have an operational capability. They must commit the nation to a conserving and sustainable policy toward land as a common resource.

Our public attitudes have been molded by the long-vanished experience of free land and the frontier.[16] We need new criteria for land use that are ecologically valid, economically sound, and intelligible to ordinary people. We cannot rely on individual self-interest, local determination, or corporate judgment for optimal land-use decisions. These sources of policy may, however, be legitimated if appropriately incorporated in a responsible way in new policies to enable our present institutions, enterprises, and government agencies to perform consistently with continuing public interests.

How should a national policy be implemented at federal, state, and local levels? We must develop a national system—with allocations of responsibility appropriate to all levels of government and to nongovernmental institutions—that will help us meet the land-use problems of the present and future. And in so doing, we should recognize that most problems of land use are not to be found in the physical land itself, but in individual and social attitudes, ambitions, and values.

Suggested Strategies

In a society with multiple values and poorly developed consensus, national land-use decisions need some widely accepted appropriate criteria to establish priorities and work out accommodations and compromises where feasible. The most apparent need for land policy today is to develop principles and procedures that will enable decisions in particular cases to be consistent with a sustainable future. The principles need to be established in the ethos of society, internalized in the beliefs and values of people. The procedures (e.g., land-capability classification and impact analysis) are largely, but need not be exclusively, the functions of public agencies. Land-use criteria for a sustainable future need ethical, ecological, and economic elements. But these elements—which are both factual and evaluative—will become significant only to the extent that they are consistent with a coherent and compatible view of a preferred future. Without such a vision, policy will not be directed beyond short-range, ad hoc, or expedient considerations. Stated differently, there is need, pointed out in our introductory chapter, for a new environmental perspective that will be consistent with ecological renewal, with a holistic approach, and with long-term sustainability. A holistic *approach* does not mean a policy requiring consideration of everything of possible relevance. It does mean that, so far as feasible, unbiased effort should be made to understand our biotic interdependence and to ascertain the full effects of a proposed policy—an objective of impact analysis. To reject a holistic approach, for whatever reason, is to condemn society to the ultimate tyranny of small decisions, to invite error, to facilitate self-serving opportunism, and to multiply unnecessary losses of future opportunities.

The chapters in this book have presented the argument for a national policy for land that, in theory, is ecologically sustainable, legally feasible, equitable, and ethicaliy defensible. Models for policy have been identified at both state and national levels. Obstacles to an environmentally and economically rational set of land-use principles have also been noted. It remains to propose a strategy for guiding the land-use issue on the agenda of national politics. To attain success in this effort, the reasons for past failures should be considered—a point that we emphasized in the introductory chapter. No effort in this field of policy is likely to succeed unless a firm foundation in public support has been laid. This foundation was not evident before the congressional attempt of the 1970s was undertaken. Although a large number of organizations supported the national land-use legislation, there was widespread misrepresentation of its substance and intent, calculated to arouse apprehension among the general public.

We have therefore outlined the elements of a possible strategy for public information and debate; for countering misinformed, unjustified fears; for reconciling differences among the existing policies of states and communities; and for building popular and political support for effective legislation. We are not offering a prescription for obtaining better land-use policy. Our objective is to suggest the procedures that should be considered by anyone undertaking to improve our policies for land. A series of steps in this process of consideration is as follows.

1. Persons or groups that work toward obtaining land policy of more general benefit and sustainability should identify individuals and organizations throughout the nation that are prepared to assume initiative and leadership toward building public understanding and consensus regarding land-use planning. Simultaneously they should ascertain the sources, arguments, and political strength of the opposition.

2. To bring land-policy advocates together, there should be an agenda for regional conference-workshops on the need for and substance of a land-use policy within the broader context of an environmental future. Interstate meetings might be organized in at least eight geographical regions (e.g., New England, Mid-Atlantic, Southeast,

Southwest, Midwest, Rocky Mountain, California, and the Pacific Northwest). The rationale for regional rather than state meetings, at least initially, is to avoid confrontation over policies in particular states and to facilitate interchange of information among manageable numbers of states. Meetings in individual states could follow.

3. Organizations concerned with land-use planning would need to be collaborative rather than competitive among themselves in order to develop an agenda. Regional interests should be represented, but no conferences or workshops should be scheduled until the relevant organizations have sorted out major issues and developed their collaborative agendas.

4. An item on the agendas of the regional meetings should be consideration of the most effective way to arouse and mobilize a broader popular concern with land-use issues. One alternative (not without risk) might be a call for a national commission. This commission could study the issue and report proposals for programmatic policies and institutional arrangements to the appropriate committees of the Congress, to the president, and to the public. The national-commission concept assumes that the regional conferences are predisposed to favor some measure of national policy regarding land-use, and that members of the Congress in the regions would be invited to, informed about, or otherwise involved. National commissions have not been notably successful in obtaining positive results. Careful thought and preparation should precede any call for a conference or commission. It may be argued that if the political climate is right, such efforts are not needed; if the climate is wrong, they will accomplish nothing. Still, the idea should not be dismissed without consideration. Not all concerned people will associate themselves with these meetings, but openness and efforts to inform should forestall allegations of opponents that a secret cabal of radical environmentalists are trying to impose socialistic, undemocratic measures on an unaware, uncomprehending public.

5. On environmental issues generally, the *New York Times*, the *Los Angeles Times* and the Public Broadcasting Service tend toward a broad public perspective. There is need to obtain a better informed and fairer treatment of land-use issues in the news media. It is our impression that whereas the news media are generally strongly positive in civil rights cases, they tend to be negative where public planning and land policy is perceived as intruding upon private property rights. Many newspapers and commercial broadcasters describe wilderness preservation or subdivision controls as inherently "elitist." There are risks of increased political controversies in efforts to link land policy to civil rights, over and beyond the economic-interest conflicts with

which we are familiar. For example, the proposed "Minority Farmers Rights Act" would seem to require quotas and timetables for maintaining or increasing farm land held by "minority" farmers.[17] All allocations of land holdings have societal implications, and all of these implications will need to be considered.

6. Whether a national conference should be called to consider the recommendations of the new land commission should probably be left as an option to be decided near the time of release of the commission report. In any event, the occasion ought to enlarge and strengthen possible public support, but not necessarily to put pressure on the Congress. Organized and articulate voters in the states can influence members of the Congress, but conferences are unlikely to do so unless they are clearly representative of public opinion.

The foregoing suggestions are only some among others, many of which might be more promising. No one arrives somewhere from nowhere. There must always be a point of departure, and our six suggestions are merely suggested first steps.

Given the present bias of the federal judiciary (and especially of the Supreme Court) against environmental legislation, and given its generally solicitous attitude toward private-property rights, accomplishing new land policy may be difficult. Because of opposition whenever government seeks to acquire land for environmental protection, a more fundamental strategy may be necessary. This would be the incorporation of a basic policy for land in an amendment to the U.S. Constitution. There have been, and doubtless will continue to be, proposals to amend the Constitution to legitimize environmental protection as a governmental responsibility.[18] Even if a land-use statute comparable to those proposed in the 1970s were enacted, its fate might be that of the National Environmental Policy Act of 1969. The courts have treated this act as essentially procedural—enforcing its means (the impact statement) but generally declining to consider its ends. Thus, the Executive branch has been left largely free to ignore the substantive provisions that were the intended purpose of the act.

Essential to a strategy for a reconsideration of land law and ethics is the mobilizing of alliances. There are many groups in American society that would welcome a reorientation of land policy toward environmental protection. Predictability and sustainability into the future could become a common conceptual denominator to join diverse groups in a unified effort. The probable consequence of these efforts might be a new environmental ethics. Unfortunately for self-governance, however, many of the organizations for environmental policy and protection appear to be allies of uncertain reliability. Among themselves they sometimes behave as competitors. They are necessarily membership organizations, with inevitable tendencies toward self-preservation. Coalitions are necessary to develop an effective constituency for land-use policy, but their formation requires great care and foresight. An alternative to special-interest organizations and coalitions, as leaders of land-use legislation, was suggested by the Councils of Urgent Studies proposal made more than two decades ago by John R. Platt.[19] These councils would be formed across the country to consider issues of major significance and to mobilize the great resources outside of government to deal with problems that the political system seems unable to handle. Whatever the strategy—arbitration, negotiation, or citizens' courts, for example[20]—it must involve both extensive public participation and access to as reliable and unbiased information as is obtainable. We do not regard these efforts as "social engineering." We do see them as interactive social learning. The strength and survival of the nation requires some common values shared by its diverse elements. Our national motto "E Pluribus Unum" is a goal appropriate to the achievement of a unifying national policy regarding the nation's basic natural resource.

Conclusion

There cannot be a national policy for land consistent with ecologically rational land ethics unless there is simultaneously, tacitly or by law, social consensus on many related aspects of life—notably on those relating to the broader environment. The uses of land touch every aspect of the national economy, and emotional factors have always been present in controversies over land ownership and use. There have been fundamental differences in ethical positions regarding nearly every aspect of land use. Yet Americans seem to believe that no conflict is unresolvable, no value differences irreconcilable, if people will only reason together. American popular ethos seems to have no place for Alasdair MacIntyre's thesis that some opposing values are unreconcilable.[21] When we assert the need for new land ethics, we are in fact declaring for a set of civic values different from those that have been dominant in our political system. Our preference would be for a new consensus rather than a balancing of old differences.

We have spoken of new ethics for land—but their newness would be chiefly in their formulation and pervasiveness. There has always been an American legacy of respect for land and living nature that is wholly consistent with an ecologically rational view of the relationship between humans and their environment. Perhaps what we will see is the decline of one set of essentially economistic, overacquisitive values and a coincident rise of attitudes long present but recessive in

American society—of values expressed in the writings of Henry Thoreau, Walt Whitman, John Muir, and Rachel Carson. All societies evolve through an interplay of change and continuity. We believe that there are forces latent in American society that could shape its future character and could create emergent values consistent with a new awareness of the vulnerability of life on Earth. Changes in the biophysical environment and the popular perception of the significance of those changes will influence public opinion independent of the preferences of policy makers. How different this society of the twenty-first century will be from the one we know today cannot be foreseen, but we believe that sustainability—rather than growth—will become its guiding objective. Sustainability will be less a matter of choice and more an acceptance of necessity.

The question that should be asked is not whether an aggressive environmentalism will change society. Instead we should ask whether the inevitable changes ahead will be, so far as possible, guided toward a benign and sustainable future, or whether a continuing escalation of populations, technologies, and resource consumption will run its course to ultimate disaster. There is, of course, the cornucopian belief that growth will lead to ever greater heights of security and prosperity. We regard this as analogous to a belief in perpetual motion. Whatever the answer to our land and environmental problems, it will necessarily rest on judgment and the will to survive in a satisfying, sustainable world. Science alone cannot provide a completely reliable answer; neither can religion alone nor social theory alone. Our ethics and our politics must provide part of the answer.

We recognize, although with regret, that displacement of essentially economistic assumptions by ecological values gives rise to bitter political conflict. Some interests are certain to lose. On diverging issues, American confidence in conflict resolution through compromise, mediation, and balancing of equities cannot always be realized. Efforts to accommodate all interests regarded as legitimate in choices involving irretrievable losses suggest Solomon's solution, cutting the child in two. However, cutting land in two, figuratively speaking, often serves neither authentic environmental nor economic interests. Rather, it might destroy an environmental value that cannot be compromised. The effective weight of opinion on land-use policy in American society is today too evenly balanced to permit—in many cases—a clear victory for either economic or environmental values. But a compromising solution may mean a total loss. Oil rigs are incompatible with wilderness. Moderate cutting in ancient forests cannot guarantee indefinite employment in the logging industry.

The American news media today is filled with accounts of land-use controversies.[22] These are trials by political combat, there being neither national, agreed-upon principles nor guidelines for public choice.[23] The two major political parties in the United States may obfuscate or finesse the land-policy issue, although in the early 1970s the logic and rationality of a national land-use policy came close to winning congressional acceptance. But this was before the counteractive commercial and development forces awakened to the threat and mobilized their forces in opposition. They remain in a state of alert, often but not always prevailing.[24] Thus, the conclusion of this book is an inconclusive prognosis for the future of land policy in the nation. Our guess, which doubtless reflects our preference, is that the new land ethics now appearing in various sectors of American society will, in time, prevail. We believe in the probability of this outcome as a consequence of the unwillingness of people generally to continue to bear the costs of socially improvident land development. The traditional practice of privatizing profits and communalizing costs becomes harder to justify as more Americans discover the real consequences of laissez-faire land policy. Americans have become aware that they have been taxed to subsidize land-use practices beneficial to a small minority but harmful to larger numbers of people and to future generations.

One indication of a changing attitude toward land and of a significant incremental change in public policy is the emergence of charitable land trusts. These local and regional trusts, of which there are at least 900 in the United States, represent private initiatives in environmental conservation and preservation of natural areas.[25] Also, in contrast to earlier days, tax laws now enable private land owners to preserve the natural features of their property by deeding development rights to a land trust. The property owners lower their tax burdens by relinquishing their rights to develop the land. Although private initiatives like land trusts help to slow the spread of destructive land practices, however, they are unable to address all land-use issues. The push for expansive growth continues, and often it results in irreversible, destructive impacts on the land. Increasing numbers of such land trusts nevertheless illustrate our point that it is not the land itself that we own. Rather, real property is merely certain rights over uses of the land. To form and adopt a land policy that recognizes this point, that is truly sustainable and broadly equitable, challenges our legal and ethical commitments.

Notes

Preface

1. David E. Dowall, "Land Policy in the United States," *Land Use Policy* 6, no. 1 (January 1989): 110.
2. Frank J. Popper, *The Politics of Land Use Reform*, Madison: University of Wisconsin Press, 1981.
3. Ludwig Wittgenstein, *Philosophical Investigations*, London: Blackwell, 1953, p. 127.
4. Although there are political theorists who question the concept of *a* public interest in a society of diverse values, and although there are linguistic deconstructionists who argue that any use of the term is merely a cover for personal or special interests, there is nevertheless a large literature that seriously addresses the concept as real and knowable. For examination of the idea of public interest see Glendon A. Schubert, *The Public Interest: A Critique of the Theory of a Political Concept*, Glencoe, Ill.: Free Press, 1961, reprinted in 1982 by Greenwood Press; and Carl Friedrich, ed., *The Public Interest*, New York: Atherton Press, 1962. See also Walter Lippmann, *The Public Philosophy*, London: Hamish Hamilton, 1955. Since 1991 a journal, *Public Interest Law Review*, has been published by the National Legal Center for the Public Interest, Durham, N.C.

Chapter 1

1. U.S. Congress, Senate, *Land Use Policy and Planning Assistance Act*, Calendar No. 186, Report 93-197. Report together with Minority and Additional Views [to accompany S. 268] June 7, 1973, p. 155.
2. Nicolas Berdyaev, *The Fate of Man in the Modern World*, translated from Russian by Donald A. Lowrie, London: Student Christian Movement Press, 1935. He wrote that "Capitalism gave birth to economism as a world view, but it was itself born of economism. Economism is something more than an ascription of great significance to economic processes and development as conditions of human life: it is a perversion of the hierarchy of values" (p. 78). See also Herman Daly, *Economics, Ecology, Ethics*, San Francisco: Freeman, 1980.
3. Robert S. Platt, "Environmentalism Versus Geography," *American Journal of Sociology* 53 (March 1948): 351–58. "In this discussion the term 'environmentalism' is used to refer exclusively to that approach to the study

of human life which gives primary consideration to the natural environment as a causal factor, advocates its importance, and looks particularly for evidence of its influence. The term is not used here to refer to the recognition that the natural environment has a real significance and is subject to scientific study" (p. 351).

4. Mark Sagoff, *The Economy of the Earth: Philosophy, Law, and the Environment*, Cambridge: Cambridge University Press, 1988; and Donald Worcester, *Nature's Economy: A History of Ecological Ideals*, Cambridge: Cambridge University Press, 1986.

5. David Orr, *Ecological Literacy: Education and the Transition to a Postmodern World*, Albany: SUNY Press, 1992.

6. The interactions among these elements and the particular role of living material, notably plants, are the substance of the Gaia hypothesis regarding the evolution of life and climate on earth. See James Lovelock, *The Gaia and A New Look at Life on Earth*, Oxford: Oxford University Press, 1979; and *Ages of Gaia: A Biography of Our Living Earth*, New York: Norton, 1988. See also Lynn Margulis and Dorion Sagan, *Microcosmos: Four Billion Years of Evolution from our Microbial Ancestors*, New York: Summit Books, 1986; and Lynn Margulis and Lorraine Olendzenski, *Environmental Evolution: Effects of the Origin and Evolution of Life on Planet Earth*, Cambridge, Mass.: MIT Press, 1992.

7. See Tarston Malmberg, *Human Territoriality*, The Hague: Mouton, 1980. Robert Ardrey ascribed human territoriality in part at least to a genetic predisposition, e.g., in *The Territorial Imperative: A Personal Inquiry into the Animal Origins of Property and Nations*, New York: Atheneum, 1966. This is not a proposition on which anthropologists are agreed. But if behavior is an indicator of a predisposition toward territoriality, humans clearly are land-value animals, whatever the causes—cultural or biological. Altruism in sharing space is often a result of misunderstanding the ultimate intentions of newcomers, as the native Americans discovered to *their* ultimate dismay.

8. *Oriental Despotism: A Comparative Study of Total Power*, New Haven: Yale University Press, 1957. The history of the American West amply illustrates the control of land use by whoever controls the allocation of water. E.g., see Marc Reisner, *Cadillac Desert: The American West and Its Disappearing Water*, New York: Viking, 1986; and Donald Worster, *Rivers of Empire: Water, Aridity and the Growth of the American West*, New York: Pantheon, 1985.

9. See *One Third of the Nation's Lands: Report of the Public Land Law Review Commission*, Washington D.C.: U.S. Government Printing Office, 1970.

10. To John Wayles Eppes, 24 June 1813, *The Works of Thomas Jefferson*, vol. XI, edited by Paul Leicester Ford, New York: G.P. Putnam's Sons, 1904, 298.

11. Woody Guthrie, "This Land is Your Land," *The Weaver's Song Book*, New York: Harper & Bros., 1960: 90–92.

12. New York: Modern Library, 1940, p. 530.

13. "The Beaks of Eagles" in Tim Hunt, ed., *Collected Work of Robinson Jeffers*, vol. II, Stanford: Stanford University Press, 1988, p. 537.

14. "Blueprint for Survival," *The Ecologist* 2, no. 1 (January 1972): whole issue.

15. In Bloomington, Indiana, *Herald-Telephone*, July 27, 1975.

16. For a pro-privatization argument see "Privatization of Public Lands: The Ecological and Economic Case for Private Ownership of Public Lands," *Manhattan Report on Economic Policy* II, no. 3, New York: Manhattan Institute for Policy Research, May 1982. More comprehensive and more objective than most studies is an unpublished honors thesis by John Nagle, *The Sagebrush Rebellion: Questioning the Ownership of Western Lands*, Indiana University, Department of Political Science, 1982. There is a large periodical literature on the Sagebrush Rebellion. For concise coverage of the movement see reports by Dick Kirschen, *National Journal* 11 (November 17, 1979): 1928–31; Lawrence Mosher, *National Journal* 13 (March 31, 1981): 476–81; John G. Francis, *Wall Street Journal* 199 (February 5, 1982): 26; and see the journal *Regulation*, published by the American Enterprise Institute and Cato Institute 1977–1988, 1990.

17. Rufus E. Miles, Jr. *Awakening from the American Dream*, New York: Universe Books, 1976. See also William Ophuls and A. Stephen Boyan, Jr., *Ecology and the Politics of Scarcity Revisited: The Unravelling of the American Dream*, New York: Freeman, 1992.

18. Warren G. Bennis, *Why Leaders Can't Lead*, San Francisco: Jossey Bass, 1989.

19. Aldo Leopold, "The Land Ethic," in *A Sand County Almanac*, New York: Oxford University Press, 1949, pp. 201–26.

20. The case for protecting the opportunities of posterity has been effectively developed by Edith Brown Weiss in *In Fairness to Future Generations: International Law, Common Patrimony, and Intergenerational Equity*, Tokyo: United Nations University, and Dobbs Ferry, N.Y.: Transnational Publishers, 1989. Appendix B, constitutional provisions for environmental protection adopted by 53 different countries and twelve American states. See also Ernest Partridge, ed., *Responsibilities to Future Generations*, New York: Prometheus, 1981.

Chapter 2

1. A 1974 study by the Environmental Protection Agency cited land use and growth as the two most serious problems: see S. Carter, M. Frost, C. Rubin, and E.L. Sumek, *Environmental Management and Local Government*, prepared by the International Management Association for the EPA (EPA Report 600/5-73-016, February 1974). Note especially Richard N.L. Andrews, ed., *Land in America: Commodity or Natural Resource*, Lexington, Mass.: Lexington Books/D.C. Heath, 1979.

2. See William Blackstone, *Commentaries on the Laws of England*, vol. II, *Of The Rights of Things* (1766). Facsimile of the First Election of 1775–1769, with an Introduction by A.W. Brian Simpson, Chicago and London: University of Chicago Press, 1979.

3. A.W. Brian Simpson, *An Introduction to the History of the Land Law*, London: Oxford University Press, 1961, rev. 1986; Frank E. Horack, Jr. and Val Nolan, Jr., *Land Use Controls Supplementary Materials on Real Prop-*

erty, St. Paul, Minn.: West, 1955, chapter 1; and Blackstone, op. cit. supra.

4. Cited by Richard Schlatter, *Private Property: The History of an Idea*, London: George Allen & Unwin, 1951.

5. See Jacob H. Beuscher, Robert R. Wright, and Morton Gittleman, *Cases and Materials on Land Use*, 2d ed. St. Paul, Minn.: West Publishing Co., 1976, chap. 2, "The Law of Nuisance."

6. See, for example, on wildlife destruction: Department of State, *U.S. National Report on the Human Environment*, Washington, D.C.: Department of State Publication 8588, June 1971, pp. 10–12.

7. For example, *Morris County Land Improvement Co. vs. Township of Parsippany—Troy Hills* 40 N.J. 539, 193 A.2d 232 (1963); *Just vs. Marinette County* 56 Wis. 2d 7 201 N.W. 2d 761 (1972). For a general discussion see F. Grad, *Treatise on Environmental Law*, vol. 2, New York: M. Bender, 1977, pp. 16–27; Fred P. Bosselman, David Callies, and John Banta, *The Taking Issue: A Study of the Constitutional Limits of Governmental Authority to Regulate the Use of Privately Owned Land Without Paying Compensation to Owners*, prepared for the Council on Environmental Quality and summarized in the Council's 4th Annual Report, Washington, D.C.: U.S. Government Printing Office, 1973, pp. 121–53.

8. See Glen O. Robinson, *The Forest Service: A Study in Public Land Management*, 2d ed., Baltimore: Johns Hopkins University Press, 1977 for a brief discussion of the history of private land holdings and problems with these holdings. Also see Public Land Law Review Commission, "Occupancy Uses," in *One Third of the Nation's Land*, Washington, D.C.: U.S. Government Printing Office, 1970, chapter 13 for recommendations on occupancy use of public land.

9. For example, in the New York Adirondacks, the Adirondack Park Agency has zoned use of private land in the park into districts based on allowable intensity of use rather than type of use, causing reactions on the part of the local owners complaining about the technical restrictions on their land by the administration of the program itself. Sylvia Lewis, "New York's Adirondacks: Tug of War in the Wilderness," *Planning* 42, no. 8 (September 1976): 9–15 (American Society of Planning Officials).

10. Donald Hagman and Dean Miscynski, eds., *Windfalls for Wipeouts: Land Value Capture and Compensation*, Chicago: American Society of Planning Officials, 1978; and Joseph Di Mento, ed., *Wipeouts and their Mitigations: The Changing Context for Land Use and Environmental Law*, Cambridge, Mass.: Lincoln Institute of Land Policy, 1990.

11. For a good discussion see American Society of Planning Officials Planning Advisory Service, "Transferable Development Rights," Report no. 303, Chicago, 1975; also see *Transfer of Development Rights Bibliography*, Trenton, N.J.: Division of Information and Research, Legislative Services Agency, Room 128, State House, Trenton, N.J., 1975; John V. Helb, B. Budd Chavooshian, and George H. Nieswand, *Development Rights Bibliography*, New Brunswick, N.J.: Rutgers University Press, 1976; *Penn Central Transportation Company vs. City of New York* 273 NY Ct. Ap. (June 23, 1977). See also Di Mento, ed., op. cit. supra., note 10.

12. See Raleigh Barlowe, *Land Resource Economics: The Economics of Real Property*, 2d ed., Englewood Cliffs, N.J.: Prentice-Hall, 1972; Peter J. Lane, *Real Estate and the Environment*, New York: Practicing Law Institute, 1973.

13. See Mary Sullivan Mann, *The Right to Housing: Cost Issues and Remedies in Exclusionary Zonings*, New York: Praeger, 1976; Edward A. Williams, *Open Space, The Choice Before California*, Berkeley: Diablo Press, 1969; Mary Anne Guitar, *Property Power: How to Keep the Bulldozer, the Power Line and the Highwayman Away from Your Door*, New York: Doubleday, 1972; and Natural Resources Defense Council, *Land Use Controls in the US: A Handbook on the Legal Rights of Citizens*, New York: Dial Press, 1977.

14. See *Pennsylvania Coal Co. vs. Mahon* 260 U.S. 393 (1922) especially for rezoning density requirements; *Morse vs. City of San Luis Obispo* 247 Cal. Ap. 2d 600, 55 Cal. Reptr. 710 (1967); *Harnett vs. Austin* 93 So. 2d 86 (Fla. 1956) for shopping centers; and *United States vs. Cansby* 328 U.S. 265 (1946) for airports.

15. S. 3354 (Jackson) 91st Cong., 2d sess. (1970); S. 3354 (Jackson) 92nd Cong., 1st sess. (1971). Following introduction, Nixon announced in a February 8, 1971, message to Congress on environment that the administration would support its own National Land Use Proposal, S. 992, 92nd Cong., 1st sess. (1971). After ten days of hearing before the Senate's Interior, Banking, Housing, and Urban Affairs and Commerce Committee, S. 632 was passed on September 19, 1972, with amendments. H.R.7211 (companion bill) was out of the House Interior but not out of Rules. A version almost identical to S. 632 was introduced in January 1973, S. 268 (Jackson) 93rd Cong., 1st sess. 1973, and so was the administration-sponsored bill. After six days of hearings, S. 268 passed the Senate. For the legal history see U.S. Senate Committee on Interior and Insular Affairs Report to accompany S. 268, Land Use Policy and Planning Assistance Act., S. Rep. no. 93-197, 93rd Congress, 1st sess. (1973); also F. Grad, *Treatise on Environmental Law*, vol. 2, 10–38.

16. California Public Resources Code, sec. 27000 et seq. Proposition 20 required builders of homes on private land that is within 3,000 feet of the ocean to secure a permit with the regional agency. Regional decisions can be vetoed by statewide commissions.

17. See Vermont Statutes Anno. Title 10, sec. 6021 et seq. (Also in *Environmental Reporter—State Solid Waste—Land Use*, sec. 1331, pp. 2101–09.) Act 250 requires all developments of ten acres or more to have a state permit.

18. On land-use issues relating to surface mining see Hodel vs. Indiana, 452 U.S. 314 (1981); Hodel vs. Virginia Surface Mining and Reclamation Association, 452 U.S. 264 (1981); and John D. Edgecomb, "Cooperative Federalism and Environmental Protection: The Surface Mining Act of 1977," *Tulane Law Review* 58 (October 1983): 299ff.

19. Frank J. Popper, *The Politics of Land-Use Reform*, Madison: University of Wisconsin Press, 1981. S. 268 was passed by the U.S. Senate on June 21, 1973 (vote: 64–21) and was almost identical to an earlier land-use bill (S. 632) passed in September 1972. The House Interior and Insular Affairs Committee reported H.R. 7211 on August 7, 1972, but the bill was not considered by the House. The House Interior Committee reported H.R. 10294 in January 1974 by a vote of 26–11, but it was killed by a 9–4 vote of the House Rules Committee on February 26, 1974. Source: Elizabeth Haskell, "Land Use and the Environment: Public Policy Issues," *Environment Reporter*, Monograph no. 20, vol. 5, 1974.

20. "Scarsdale, N.Y. once required a builder to put up $80,000 in a cash bond for a minor subdivision." Quoted in Richard F. Babcock and Fred P. Bosselman, *Exclusionary Zoning: Land Use Regulation and Housing in the 1970s,* New York: Praeger, 1973, p. 13. Source: Raymond Urguhardt, *A Survey of Local Government Restrictions Affecting Home Building in NY State,* New York: New York Homebuilders' Association, 1966, p. 20.

21. East Bibb Twiggs Neighborhood Ass'n. vs. Macon Bibb Planning and Zoning Commission 888 F 2d. 1573 (11th Cir. 1989 and 896 F 2d 1264 (11th Cir. 1989). Also Babcock and Bosselman, *Exclusionary Zoning,* op. cit. supra., note 20.

22. One way is for states to provide use-value assessments or other favorable tax treatment for open space land. See Council on Environmental Quality, *Fifth Annual Report,*Washington, D.C.: U.S. Government Printing Office, 1974. Land is taxed on basis of its current, open space use. For listings of states and further analysis see F. Grad, *Treatise on Environmental Law,* vol. 2, chap. 10, sec. 10.03(6)(b), "Techniques to Encourage Open Space Maintenance."

23. Federal Water Pollution Control Act Amendments of 1972, publication 92-500, title I S. 101(a), 86 Stat 816, 33 U.S.C.S. 1251 (2) 1972. The objective of the legislature is "to restore and maintain the chemical, physical and biological integrity of the nation's water." S.1215(a) states that the discharge of pollutants into navigable waters is to be eliminated by 1985. S.208, 33 U.S.C. 1288(a)(1) requires the administrator, after consultation with the appropriate authorities, to publish guidelines on those areas that "as a result of urban industrial concentration or other factors have substantial water quality control problems" S.1288(a)(1). After publication, the governor identifies the areas and twelve days later designates a program [1288(a)(2)]. This amendment, providing for area wide waste treatment management plans and advocating "tough" clean waters approach has significant land-use implications. For a good discussion see F. Grad, *Environmental Law Treatise,* vol. 1, sec. 3.03 (3)(6)(1975).

24. South Florida provides numerous examples of conflicting practices and proposals affecting the same land areas—especially the Everglades. The proposed Dade County International Airport and its associated highway and development would have seriously impaired the ecology of the Everglades National Park. Subsidized cane sugar and vegetable produce farming are incompatible with preservation of the natural environment, but enjoy cost-free management of the water supplies. The environmental anomalies of South Florida agriculture and development have little to do with laissez-faire free enterprize and much to do with largesse from the U.S. Treasury.

25. For a good general discussion see F. Grad, *Treatise on Environmental Law,* vol. 2, chap. 10, "Land Use Planning and Land Use Controls in the Context of Environmental Protection."

26. Bernard H. Siegan, *Land Use Without Zoning,* Lexington, Mass.: Lexington Books/D.C. Heath, 1972, and "Conserving and Developing the Land," *San Diego Law Review* 27 (1990): 279ff.

27. "A National Policy for Land," in National Land Use Policy Hearings

before the Committee on Interior and Insular Affairs, U.S. Senate, S. 3354, 91st Cong. 2d sess. (March 24 and April 28–29, 1970). Washington, D.C.: U.S. Government Printing Office, 1970.

28. See Mancur Olson, *The Logic of Collective Action, Public Goods and the Theory of Groups,* Cambridge, Mass.: Harvard University Press, 1971, pp. 27–31.

29. Garrett Hardin, *The Limits of Altruism: An Ecologist's View of Survival,* Bloomington: Indiana University Press, 1977.

30. For example, *Village of Euclid vs. Ambler Reality Corp.* 272 U.S. 365 (1926); *Baker vs. City of Milwaukee* 533 F.2d, 772 (Oregon 1975). For general information see R.M. Anderson, *American Law of Zoning,* 4 vols., Rochester, N.Y.: Lawyers Co-operative Publishing Co., 1968; Charles M. Haar, *Land Use Planning: A Case Book on the Use, Misuse & Reuse of Urban Land,* 3d ed., Boston: Little, Brown, 1976, pp. 185–223. But see Bernard Siegan, op. cit. supra, note 26.

31. Highway planning is often cited as an example of the abuses caused by an ad hoc or "mission-oriented" approach. Routing through parks without concern for longer-range needs of cities or carving up community neighborhoods indicate the need for a broader policy approach. For summary case studies on neighborhood resistance to highway builders, see Lynton K. Caldwell, Lynton R. Hayes, and Isabel M. MacWhirter, *Citizens and the Environment: Case Studies in Popular Action,* Bloomington: Indiana University Press, 1976––Cases on Overton Park, Memphis, 30; Berkshire Hills, Mass., 166; and Vieux Carré, New Orleans, 349. See also Madison: University of Wisconsin Press, *Building the American City: Report of the U.S. National Commission on Urban Problems,* House Doc. 91-34, Washington, D.C.: U.S. Government Printing Office, 1968, pp. 231. Also see Richard F. Babcock, *The Zoning Game,* Madison: University of Wisconsin Press, 1966, and Babcock and Bosseiman, *Exclusionary Zoning,* op. cit. supra, note 21.

32. See *Construction Industry Association of Sonoma City vs. City of Petaluma* 375 F. Supp. 574 (N.D. Cal. 1914) rev'd 522 F.2d 897 (9th Cir. 1975) Ap. Dis. 96 S. CT 1148 (1976); *Golden vs. Planning Board of Town of Ramapo* 30 NY 2d 359, 285 N.E. 2d 291, 334 NY 2d 138, App. Dis. 408 U.S. 1003 (1972); *City of Eastlake vs. Forest City Ent., Inc.* 41 Ohio St.2d 187, 324 N.E.2d 740. (1975) rev'd 96 S.Ct. 2358 (1976).

33. Public Law no. 91-190, January 1, 1970, 83 Stat. 852, 42 U.S.C. 4321-4347 (1970).

34. General texts for reference: F. Grad, *Treatise on Environmental Law,* vol. 2, chap. 10 (1977); Daniel R. Mandelker, *The Zoning Dilemma,* Indianapolis: Bobbs-Merrill, 1976; Norman Williams Jr., *American Land Planning Law: Land Use and the Police Power,* Willamette, Ill.: Callaghan, 1974. See also Donald G. Hagman, *Public Planning and Control of Urban and Land Development: Cases and Materials,* St. Paul, Minn.: West Publishing Co., 1973, chaps. 10–12; and Bernhard H. Siegan, *Land Use Without Zoning,* Lexington, Mass.: Lexington Books, 1972, p. 247.

35. See California Coastal Zone Conservation Act, Cal. Publication R Section 2700 et seq. (1976 suppl.); and Vermont, Stat. Anno, Title 10, sec.

6001 et seq. (1973, 1975 suppl.). In Vermont, the statute vests permit grant-ing authority in a State Environmental Board assisted by eight District Com-missioners, all citizen members except the chairman. Under the California statute, all meetings of the commission are open to the public. Public hear-ings are required in connection with issuing regulations by the commission. Any person has standing to maintain an action to restrain violations. For analysis see National Resources Defense Council, Inc., *Land Use Controls in the US: A Handbook on the Legal Rights of Citizens*, chaps. 6 and 12 (1977); J. Adams, "Proposition 20: A Citizen Campaign," *Syracuse Law Review* 24 (1973): 1019; for a general discussion see Douglass Petrillo, "California Coast: The Struggle Today; A Plan for Tomorrow," *Florida State University Law Review* 4 (1976): 315.

36. Jamaica Bay Environmental Study Group, *Jamaica Bay and Kennedy Airport: A Multidisciplinary Environmental Study*, Washington, D.C.: Na-tional Academy of Sciences, 1971.

37. Elinor Ostrom, *Governing the Commons: The Evolution of Institu-tions for Collective Action*, Cambridge: Cambridge University Press, 1991.

38. E.g., see E. Adamson Hoebel, *The Law of Primitive Man: A Study in Comparative Legal Dynamics*, Cambridge, Mass.: Harvard University Press, 1954; and Emilio Moran, ed., *Ecosystems Approach in Anthropology: From Concept to Practice*, rev. ed., Ann Arbor: University of Michigan Press, 1990.

39. See Richard N.L. Andrews and M.J. Waits, *Environmental Values in Public Decisions: A Research Agenda*, Ann Arbor: School of Natural Re-sources, University of Michigan, 1978.

40. See *First English Evangelical Lutheran Church of Glendale* vs. *Los Angeles County*, 482 U.S. 304 (1987), and Sylvia Lynn Gillis, "A Blow for Land-Use Planning—The Takings Issue Re-examined," *Ohio State Law Jour-nal* 49 (1989): 1107ff.

Chapter 3

1. Lynton Caldwell, "Law and Land," in R. Andrews (ed.), *Land in America*, Lexington, Mass.: Lexington Books, 1979, p. 167; hereafter cited as: Caldwell 1979, in Andrews.

2. See A. Dawson, *The Land Problem in the Developed Economy*, Totowa, N.J.: Barnes and Noble, 1984, pp. 1–2; E. Mishan, *Cost-Benefit Analysis*, New York: Praeger, 1976, pp. 128–29; and K. Shrader-Frechette, *Nuclear Power and Public Policy*, Boston: Reidel, 1983, pp. 127–29.

3. C. Stone, *Should Trees Have Standing?*, Los Altos, Calif.: Kaufmann, 1974; hereafter cited as: Stone. See also C. Stone, *Earth and Other Ethics*, New York: Harper and Row, 1987.

4. C. Haar and L. Liebman, *Property and Law*, Boston: Little, Brown, 1977, p. 1055.

5. J. Lewis, *Landownership in the United States, Agriculture Informa-tion Bulletin*, no. 435, Washington, D.C.: U.S. Department of Agriculture, Economics, Statistics, and Cooperative Service, 1984. See also C. Geisler,

"A History of Land Reform in the United States, in C. Geisler and F.J. Popper (eds.), *Land Reform, American Style*, Totowa, N.J.: Rowman and Allanheld, 1984; hereafter cited as: Geisler and Geisler and Popper. See the discussion in chapter 6 of this volume.

6. J. Gaventa and B. Horton, "Land Ownership and Land Reform in Appalachia," in Geisler and Popper; Appalachian Regional Commission, *Land Ownership Study*, Appalachian Studies Center, Boone, N.C.: Appalachia State University, 1981; and Geisler and Popper.

7. D. Warriner, *Land Reform in Principle and Practice*, Oxford: Oxford University Press, 1969, p. xiv; hereafter cited as: Warriner. See also P. Dorner, *Land Reform and Economic Development*, Baltimore: Penguin, 1972, pp. 11, 19; hereafter cited as: Dorner. See also D.W. Bromley, *Environment and Economy*, Cambridge: Blackwell, 1991.

8. W. Blackstone, "Ecology and Rights," in *Philosophy and Environmental Crisis*, ed. W.T. Blackstone, Atlanta: University of Georgia Press, 1974; and K. Shrader-Frechette, *Environmental Ethics*, Pacific Grove, Calif.: Boxwood Press, 1991, ch. 6; hereafter cited as: Shrader-Frechette, EE.

9. See E.C. Hargrove, *Foundations of Environmental Ethics*, Englewood Cliffs, N.J.: Prentice Hall, 1989, pp. 57ff.; hereafter cited as: Hargrove, EE.

10. See Warriner, p. 30; Dorner, p. 123; A. Koo, *Land Market Distortion and Tenure Reform*, Ames: Iowa State University Press, 1982, pp. 15, 24–27; hereafter cited as: Koo. See also D. Holland, *Energy and Agriculture*, in Geisler and Popper, pp. 91ff.

11. R. Nozick, *Anarchy, State, and Utopia*, New York: Basic Books, 1974, Ch. 7; and R. Nozick, "The Entitlement Theory," in D. Lyons (ed.), *Rights*, Belmont, Calif.: Wadsworth, 1979, pp. 154–67; hereafter cited as: Nozick 1979. For arguments against redistribution, see Nozick 1979, pp. 154–67.

12. R. Dworkin, *Taking Rights Seriously*, Cambridge, Mass.: Harvard University Press, 1977, pp. 267–79; hereafter cited as: Dworkin. K. Shrader-Frechette, *Risk Analysis and Scientific Method*, Boston: Reidel, 1985, pp. 64–66.

13. Warriner, pp. 376, 15, 37; Dorner, pp. 30–31, 60, 91; Koo, pp. 15, 24–27.

14. Warriner, pp. 392–413.

15. Koo, p. 91.

16. Dorner, pp. 110–11.

17. A. Honore, "Ownership," in L. Becker and K. Kipnis (eds.), *Property*, Englewood Cliffs, N.J.: Prentice-Hall, 1984; A. Honore, "Ownership," in A. Guest (ed.), *Oxford Essays in Jurisprudence*, Oxford: Oxford University Press, 1964.

18. L. Durrell, *State of the Ark: An Atlas of Conservation in Action*, New York: Doubleday, 1986, p. 160. See also Lester Brown et al., *State of the World*, New York: Norton, 1990, 3ff. and 59ff.

19. H. Rolston, "Is There an Ecological Ethic?", *Ethics* 85 (1975): 93–109. See Shrader-Frechette, EE, pp. 16ff.

20. A. Leopold, *A Sand County Almanac*, New York: Oxford University

Press, 1949, pp. 201–2; hereafter cited as: Leopold, SCA. See also J. Baird Callicott, *In Defense of the Land Ethic*, Albany: SUNY Press, 1989.

21. Leopold, SCA, p. 203.

22. Leopold, SCA, pp. 224–25; see also A. Leopold, "The Land Ethic," *Wilderness* 48 (1985): 5–15; hereafter cited as: Leopold 1985. C. Little, "In a Landscape of Hope," *Wilderness* 48, no.168 (1985): 21–30. E. Partridge, "Are We Ready for an Ecological Morality?", *Environmental Ethics* 4, no. 2 (1982): 175–90. J. B. Callicott, "The Conceptual Foundations of the Land Ethic," in Callicott, *A Companion to the Sand County Almanac*, Madison: University of Wisconsin Press, 1987; hereafter cited as: Callicott 1987.

23. A. Leopold, "Some Fundamentals of Conservation in the Southwest," *Environmental Ethics* 1 (1979): 139–40.

24. J.E. Lovelock, *Gaia*, New York: Oxford University Press, 1979, and J. Hughes, "Gaia," *The Ecologist* 13, no. 2/3 (1983): 54–60.

25. J. Passmore, *Man's Responsibility for Nature*, New York: Charles Scribner's Sons, 1974.

26. R. Atfield, "Value in the Wilderness," *Metaphilosophy* 15 (1984): 294ff.

27. L. Sumner, "Review of Robin Attfield," *The Ethics of Environmental Concern*, *Environmental Ethics* 8 (1986): 77.

28. W. Frankena, *Ethics and the Environment*, in K. Goodpaster and K. Sayre (eds.), *Ethics and the Problems of the 21st Century*, Notre Dame, Ind.: University of Notre Dame Press, 1979, p. 11; hereafter cited as: Frankena in Goodpaster and Sayre.

29. J. Rodman, "The Liberation of Nature?", *Inquiry* 20: 91.

30. P. Singer, *Animal Liberation*, New York, Avon, 1977, p. 8. See also P. Singer, "Not for Humans Only: The Place of Nonhumans in Environmental Issues," in Goodpaster and Sayre, pp. 194–95; hereafter cited as: Singer 1979.

31. See, for example, J. Heffernan, "The Land Ethic: A Critical Appraisal," *Environmental Ethics* 4, no. 3 (1982): 235–47 and J. B. Callicott, Animal Liberation, *Environmental Ethics* 2, no. 4 (1980): 311–38; hereafter cited as: Callicott, AL.

32. Singer 1979, pp. 194–95.

33. For one example of a biocentric or ecocentric land ethics that explains when to give priority to human interests and when to give primacy to environmental concerns, see K. Shrader-Frechette, "A Philosophic Basis for Ecocentric Ethics," *Earth Ethics Report* 1, no. 1 (December 1991): 25–31; hereafter cited as: Ecocentric. See also K. Shrader-Frechette, "Ethics and the Environment," *World Health Forum* 12 (1991): 311–21; hereafter cited as: Shrader-Frechette, EAE.

34. R. Carpenter, R., "Ecology in Court, and Other Disappointments of Environmental Science and Environmental Law," *Natural Resources Lawyer* 15, no. 3 (1983): 573–95. S. Levin and M. Harwell, "Environmental Risks Associated with the Release of Genetically Engineered Organisms," *Genewatch* 2, no. 1 (1985): 15. G. Suter, "Ecosystem Theory and NEPA Assessment, *Bulletin of the Ecological Society of America* 62, no. 3 (1981):

186–92. W. Murdoch and J. Connell, "The Ecologist's Role and the Nonsolution of Technology," in Clifton Fadiman and Jean White (eds.), *Ecocide—and Thoughts Towards Survival*, Santa Barbara: California Center for the Study of Democratic Institutions, 1971, p. 57. A. Cooper, "Why Doesn't Anyone Listen to Ecologists—and What Can ESA Do About It?", *Bulletin of the Ecological Society of America* 63, no. 4 (1982): 348–56. M. Sagoff, "What Ecology Can Do," unpublished essay, 1986. See also E. Johnson, "Animal Liberation Versus the Land Ethic," *Environmental Ethics* 3, no. 3 (1981): 269–70; A. Desmond, *The Ape's Reflexion*, New York: Dial Press/James Wade, 1979.

35. See notes 33 and 40, and, for example, Holmes Rolston, *Philosophy Gone Wild*, Buffalo, N.Y.: Prometheus, 1986.

36. T. Regan, *The Case for Animal Rights*, Berkeley: University of California Press, 1983, p. 262. W. Aiken, "Ethical Issues in Agriculture," in Tom Regan, ed., *Earthbound*, New York: Random House, 1984, p. 269.

37. P. Fritzell, "The Conflicts of Ecological Conscience," in Callicott, 1987.

38. G. Hardin, "The Tragedy of the Commons," *Science* 162 (1978): 1243–48. M. Sagoff, "Do We Need a Land Use Ethic?", *Environmental Ethics* 3 (1981): 303–4.

39. See D. Baxter and J. Olszewski, "Congenital Universal Insensitivity to Pain," *Brain* 83 (1960): 381–93.

40. See Paul Taylor, *Respect for Nature*, Princeton: Princeton University Press, 1986.

41. See K. Shrader-Frechette and E. McCoy, *Method in Ecology: Strategies for Conservation*, Cambridge: Cambridge University Press, 1993.

42. H. Rolston, *Duties to Ecosystems*, in Callicott, 1987. See E. Abbey, *Desert Solitaire*, New York: Ballantine, 1971; hereafter cited as: Abbey. See also note 33.

43. Stone (see note 3).

44. Abbey; Leopold, SCA; R. Nash, "The Significance of the Arrangement: Deck Chairs on the Titanic," *Not Man Apart* (October 1975): 9; T. Watkins, "Amplifications," *Wilderness* 48, no. 169 (1985): 55; hereafter cited as: Watkins. See also Callicott, AL; and J. Muir, *The Wilderness World of John Muir*, ed. Edwin Way Teale, Boston: Houghton Mifflin, 1976.

45. Leopold, SCA, p. 240; Watkins, p. 55. Abbey, p. 20. J. Tallmadge, "Saying 'You' to the Land," *Environmental Ethics* 3, no. 4 (1976): 351–63. J. Bennett, "The Land Ethic," *Philosophy Today* 20, no. 2/4 (1981): 124–32.

46. See Dworkin.

47. Stone, p. 11.

48. Stone, pp. 17, 29, 33.

49. Stone; see S. Lehman, "Do Wildernesses Have Rights?", *Environmental Ethics* 3, no. 2 (1981): 133; hereafter cited as: Lehman.

50. See Lehman, pp. 136ff., and the earlier discussion of sentiency in connection with land-community ethics.

51. See Lehman, pp. 143ff.

52.   See Dworkin; K. Shrader-Frechette, *Science Policy, Ethics, and Economic Methodology*, Boston: Reidel, 1984, pp. 219ff. See note 33.
53.   See Nozick 1979. See note 33.

Chapter 4

1.   See later sections of this essay for discussions of traditional capitalist and Marxist accounts of Locke. For a discussion of recent broadsides against the bourgeois thesis, see N. Wood, *John Locke and Agrarian Capitalism*, Berkeley: Umiversity of California Press, 1984, pp. 15ff.; hereafter cited as: Wood. See also R. Lemos, "Locke's Theory of Property," *Interpretation* 5 (Winter 1975): 226ff.; hereafter cited as: Lemos.
2.   L.C. Becker, *Property Rights*, Boston: Routledge and Kegan Paul, 1977, p. 32; hereafter cited as: Becker, PR.
3.   John Locke, *Two Treatises of Government*, ed. Peter Laslett, Cambridge: Cambridge University Press, 1960, II, pars. 27, 30, 31. Hereafter cited as: Locke, followed by treatise (in Roman numerals) and by paragraph (in arabic numerals).
4.   Locke II, 50.
5.   Locke II, 36–37, 50. See H. George, *Progress and Poverty*, New York: Country Life Press, 1955, pp. 334ff. for a discussion of the labor theory of property; hereafter cited as: George.
6.   David Hume, *Treatise of Human Nature*, ed. L.A. Selby-Bigge, rev. P.H. Nidditch, Oxford: Clarendon Press, 1978, II, p. 209. Robert Nozick, *Anarchy, State, and Utopia*, New York: Basic Books, 1974, pp. 174–75; hereafter cited as: Nozick. See also J. Hospers, "Property," *The Personalist* 53 (Summer 1972): 263–273; hereafter cited as: Hospers.
7.   Locke II, 50; see K. Olivecrona, "Locke's Theory of Appropriation," *The Philosophical Quarterly* 24 (July 1974): 230; hereafter cited as: Olivecrona. See also: Becker, PR. C. Beitz, "Tacit Consent and Property Rights," *Political Theory* 8 (November 1980): 487–502; hereafter cited as: Beitz. M. Davis, "Nozick's Argument for the Legitimacy of the Welfare State," *Ethics* 97 (April 1987): 576–94; hereafter cited as: Davis. A. Gibbard, "Natural Property Rights," *Nous* 10 (1976): 77–86; hereafter cited as: Gibbard. K. Vaughn, "John Locke and the Labor Theory of Value," *Journal of Libertarian Studies* 2 (1978): 311–26; hereafter cited as: Vaughn. David Miller, "Justice and Property," *Ratio* 22 (June 1980): 1–14; hereafter cited as: Miller. J. Waldron, "Two Worries About Mixing One's Labour," *The Philosophical Quarterly* 33 (January 1983): 37–44; hereafter cited as: Waldron.
8.   Locke I, 86; II, 28.
9.   Locke II, 37.
10.   Locke II, 41.
11.   Locke II, 32, 34; see S. Schwartzenbach, "Locke's Two Conceptions of Property," *Social Theory and Practice* 14 (Summer 1988): 154ff.; hereafter cited as: Schwartzenbach.
12.   Locke II, 40–42.

13. See, for example, C. Du Rand, "The Reconstitution of Private Property in the People's Republic of China: John Locke Revisited," *Social Theory and Practice* 12 (Fall 1986): 337–50.

14. See, for example, Becker, PR, and L.C. Becker, "The Labor Theory of Property Acquisition," *The Journal of Philosophy* 73 (October 17, 1976): 656; hereafter cited as: Becker, JP. See also Miller, pp. 6–7ff.

15. See Schwartzenbach.

16. Waldron, pp. 37ff.

17. See, for example, H. Rashdall, "The Philosophical Theory of Property," in *Property: Its Duties and Rights*, ed. C. Gore, London: Macmillan, 1913, pp. 37ff.; hereafter cited as: Rashdall. See also P. Cvek, "Locke's Theory of Property," *Auslegung* 11 (Fall 1984): 390–411; hereafter cited as: Cvek.

18. See Rashdall, pp. 37ff.

19. See D. Post, "Jeffersonian Revisions of Locke," *Journal of the History of Ideas* 47 (January–March 1986): 147–57; hereafter cited as: Post. For different opinions of Locke's influence on U.S. law and government, see O. and L. Handlin, "Who Read John Locke?", *The American Scholar* (Autumn 1989): 545–56 and replies to the Handlin article in subsequent issues of *The American Scholar*.

20. For an argument that Locke's theory can be applied to contemporary situations, see Lemos, pp. 226ff.

21. See C.B. Macpherson, *The Political Philosophy of Possessive Individualism*, Oxford: Clarendon Press, 1962; hereafter cited as: Macpherson, PI. See also: Leo Strauss, *Natural Right and History*, Chicago: University of Chicago Press, 1953; hereafter cited as: Strauss. G.C. Lodge, *The New American Ideology*, New York: Knopf, 1975, pp. 103–4; hereafter cited as: Lodge. H.S. Holland, "Property and Personality," in *Property: Its Duties and Rights*, ed. C. Gore, London: Macmillan, 1913, pp. 170–92; hereafter cited as: Holland. R. Schlatter, *Private Property*, New Brunswick, N.J.: Rutgers University Press, 1951, p. 151; hereafter cited as: Schlatter. K. Minogue, "The Concept of Property and Its Contemporary Significance," in J. Pennock and J. Chapman (eds.), *Property*, Nomos 22, New York: New York University Press, 1980, p. 7; hereafter cited as: Minogue. See also: Du Rand; J.P. Day, "Locke on Property," *The Philosophical Quarterly* 16 (July 1966): 207–20; hereafter cited as: Day. Finally see K.M. Squadrito, "Locke's View of Dominion," *Environmental Ethics* 1 (1979): 255–58; hereafter cited as: Squadrito.

22. Locke II, 50.

23. See Du Rand, p. 339.

24. See, for example, T. Mautner, "Locke on Original Appropriation," *American Philosophical Quarterly* 19 (July 1982): 260; hereafter cited as: Mautner.

25. Du Rand, p. 339. See also D. Ellerman, "On the Labor Theory of Property," *Philosophical Forum* 16 (Summer 1985): 320; hereafter cited as: Ellerman. E. Hargrove, "Anglo-American Land Use Attitudes," *Environmental Ethics* 2 (Summer 1980): 141ff.; hereafter cited as: Hargrove.

26. Macpherson; Strauss; see Lodge, pp. 103–4.

27. Engels, "Preface," to Karl Marx, *Poverty of Philosophy*, New York: International Publishers, 1965, pp. 7–24. See also Schlatter, pp. 271ff.

28. See James Tully, *A Discourse on Property*, Cambridge: Cambridge University Press, 1980; hereafter cited as: Tully. Quote is from Tully, p. 138. For a textual analysis of flaws in Tully's account, see Wood, chapters 2 through 5.

29. See Cvek, pp. 391, 400.

30. Locke II, 25–26.

31. Locke II, 25–27.

32. Nozick, p. 174.

33. Schwartzenbach, p. 143. Mautner, p. 267. C. D. Stone, *Earth and Other Ethics*, New York: Harper and Row, 1987, pp. 212–13; hereafter cited as: Stone.

34. N. Griffin, "Aboriginal Rights," *Dialogue* 20 (December 1981): 694.

35. O. O'Neill, "Nozick's Entitlements," *Inquiry* 19 (Winter 1976): 476; hereafter cited as: O'Neill. One person who does not misconstrue Locke as asserting that land is "unowned" in the state of nature is R.P. Wolff. See R.P. Wolff, "Robert Nozick's Derivation of the Minimal State," in J. Paul (ed.), *Reading Nozick*, Totowa, N.J.: Rowman and Littlefield, 1981, p. 101; hereafter cited as: Wolff.

36. Locke II, 4, 27, 28.

37. Locke II, 4; see Cvek.

38. Locke II, 4-5.

39. Locke II, 6.

40. Locke II, 8. For further discussion of Locke's beliefs about the Law of Nature, see Maurice Cranston, *John Locke*, London, 1957, pp. 64–67, 208–9; hereafter cited as: Cranston.

41. Locke II, 8; II, 30.

42. Locke II, 30.

43. Locke I, 90.

44. Locke II, 120.

45. Locke II, 15.

46. Locke II, 124.

47. Locke II, p. 135; See L.J. Macfarlane, *Modern Political Theory*, London: Nelson, 1970, p. 59.

48. Locke II, 6.

49. Locke I, 42.

50. Locke II, 6.

51. V. Held, "John Locke on Robert Nozick," *Social Research* 43 (1976): 171ff.; hereafter cited as: Held. J.H. Reiman, "The Fallacy of Libertarian Capitalism," *Ethics* 92 (October 1981): 85–95; hereafter cited as: Reiman.

52. Locke II, 31.

53. Thomas Scanlon, "Nozick on Rights, Liberty, and Property," in J. Paul (ed.), *Reading Nozick*, Totowa, N.J.: Rowman and Littlefield, 1981, p. 126.

54. See Cranston, pp. 210–11.

55. Locke II, 45. See Cvek, p. 403.

56. See Schlatter, pp. 155, 159.

57. Locke II, 159.

58. Macpherson, PI, p. 3; see Lodge, p. 2; Lemos, pp. 226ff.

59. Locke II, 135; see Squadrito, p. 260.

60. See Macpherson, PI; Nozick; Steiner, "The Natural Right to the Means of Production," *The Philosophical Quarterly* 27 (January 1977): 44.

61. D.C. Snyder, "Locke on Natural Law and Property Rights," *Canadian Journal of Philosophy* 16 (December 1986): 741; hereafter cited as: Snyder.

62. Locke II, 50.

63. Locke I, 42; see II, 6.

64. Locke II, 50.

65. Macpherson, PI, p. 212; see Cvek, p. 402.

66. Locke II, 135; see I, 42.

67. See Held, p. 175; see J. Winfrey, "Charity vs. Justice: Locke on Property," *Journal of the History of Ideas* 42 (July–September 1981): 432.

68. J. Rawls, "Justice as Fairness," *The Philosophical Review* 67 (April 1958): 164–94; see Held, p. 175.

69. Nozick, p. 176; see Held, p. 175; Steiner, p. 45; and H. Sarkar, "The Lockean Proviso," *Canadian Journal of Philosophy* 12 (March 1982): 47–59, who say that Locke subscribes to a patterned conception of justice; Sarkar hereafter cited as: Sarkar.

70. See J.H. Bogart, "Lockean Provisos and State of Nature Theories," *Ethics* 95 (July 1985): 828–36, esp. pp. 830–31.

71. Locke II, 40.

72. Locke II, 40.

73. P.J. Proudhon, *What Is Property?*, trans. B.R. Tucker, London: William Reeves, 1898, pp. 103–4. See also Mill, *Principles of Political Economy*, ed. William J. Ashley, Fairfield, N.J.: Kelley, 1909, II, ch II, 5–6.

74. George, p. 336. See Miller, pp. 6–7; see Becker, PR, ch. 4.

75. See Minogue, p. 20.

76. George, p. 342. See Mautner, p. 267.

77. Mautner, p. 267.

78. Locke II, 25.

79. See O'Neill, 1976, p. 476. Locke added this "productivity argument" in a revision to the third edition of the *Treatises*; see Lodge, pp. 104–5.

80. See Squadrito, p. 260.

81. Locke II, 11; see Locke I, 42; see Snyder, p. 749.

82. See Locke II, 6; I, 92.

83. Locke II, 37.

84. O'Neill, p. 478.

85. For example, Locke II, 6, 7, 11, 16, 23, 60, 79, 135, 159.

86. John Locke, "Essay, Some Thoughts Concerning Education," in *The Works of John Locke*, Salem, N.H.: Ayer Company, 1877, pars. 103–5; hereafter cited as: Locke, Essay.

87. Locke, Essay, pars. 103–5.

88. Locke, Essay, par. 110; see Schlatter, p. 156. See Squadrito, pp. 258–59. See also F. Whelan, "Property as Artifice," in J. Pennock and J. Chapman (eds.), *Property*, Nomos 22, New York: New York University Press, 1980, p. 103.

89. C.B. Macpherson, "The Social Bearing of Locke's Political Theory," in *Locke and Berkeley: A Collection of Critical Essays*, ed. C.B. Martin and D.M. Armstrong, New York: Doubleday, 1968, p. 215.

90. See Cranston, pp. 239–45.

91. Macpherson, PI, p. 241.

92. Snyder, p. 747.

93. Macpherson, pp. 238–47.

Chapter 5

1. For a historical treatment of land in America society, see Marion Clawson, *America's Land and Its Uses*, Baltimore: Johns Hopkins University Press, 1972. For comprehensive treatments of land ownership and use see Curtis S. Berger, *Land Ownership and Use*, Boston: Little, Brown, 1968; and Charles M. Haar and Michael Allen Wolf, *Land-Use Planning: A Casebook on the Use, Misuse and Re-Use of Urban Land*, 4th ed., Boston: Little, Brown, 1989. Many of the issues regarding land policy and property rights arose in the course of debates in 1973 over the proposed National Land Use Policy and Planning Assistance Act. See Robert K. Lane, comp. Senate Action on the National Land Use Policy and Planning Assistance Act: Selected Excerpts from the Congressional Record and Congressional Documents, January–June 1973, 93d Congress, 1st Session. Washington, D.C.: Congressional Research Service, Library of Congress, July 5, 1973. See also more recent discussions of the ownership concept: John Edward Cribbet, "Concepts in Transition: The Search for a New Definition of Property," *University of Illinois Law Review* (1986): 1ff.; John Martinez, "Reconstructing the Takings Doctrine by Redefining Property and Sovereignty," *Fordham Urban Law Journal* 16 (1987–1988): 157ff.; and Linda Bozung and Deborah J. Alessi, "Recent Developments in Environmental Preservation and the Rights of Property Owners," *Urban Law* 20 (Fall, 1988): 969ff. (Excerpts from the subcommittee reports of the Land Use, Planning and Zoning Committee of the American Bar Association). For a jurisprudential analysis of the meaning of rights, see Wesley Newcomb Hofeld, *Fundamental Legal Concepts as Applied in Judicial Reasoning*, Westport, Conn.: Greenwood Press, 1964 (reprinted from 1919 Yale University Press edition).

2. See James E. Krier, "The Environment, the Constitution and the Coupling Fallacy," *Law Quadrangle Notes* [Michigan] 32, no. 3 (Spring 1988): 34–39. Daniel A. Farber, "Disdain for 17-Year-Old Statute Evident in High Court's Ruling" *National Law Journal* (May 4, 1987): 20–22; and Frederic P. Sutherland and Roger Beers, "Supreme Indifference," *Amicus Journal* (Spring 1991): 38–42; and Lynton K. Caldwell, "The Case for an Amendment to the Constitution of the United States for Protection of the Environ-

ment," *Environmental Law and Policy Forum*—[Duke University] 1 (1991): 1-20.

3. Land Use Policy and Planning Assistance Act Calendar No. 186, Report 93-197, June 7, 1973, p. 147. Reprinted in Lane 161.

4. See Lynton K. Caldwell, "Health and Homeostasis as Social Concepts" in *Diversity and Stability in Ecological Systems–Brookhaven Symposia in Biology No. 22*, Upton, N.Y.: Brookhaven National Laboratory, 1969, 209–210. N.J. Ware, "The Physiocrats," *American Economic Review* 21 (1931): 607-19; and Henry Higgs, *The Physiocrates*, New York: Macmillan, 1896.

5. Henry George, *Progress and Poverty*, 50th Anniversary Edition, New York: Modern Library, 1929; and *The Complete Works of Henry George*, vol. III, *The Land Question: Property in Land and the Condition of Labor*, Garden City, N.Y.: Doubleday and Page, 1911.

6. In *Law and Land*, edited by Charles M. Haar, Cambridge, Mass.: Harvard University Press and M.I.T. Press, 1964, p. 23.

7. The influence of the English legalist William Blackstone on legal concepts was considerable. See his *Commentaries on the Laws of England*, vol. II, "Of the Rights of Things, 1766." Reprinted by the University of Chicago Press, 1979.

8. *Improving Land Tenure: A Survey of the Problems of Adapting Customary Land Tenure Systems to Modern Economic Conditions in the Region Served by The South Pacific Commission*, Naumea, New Caledonia: South Pacific Commission, 1968, p. 2.

9. For the history of English land law, see: Kenelm Edward Digby, *An Introduction to the History of the Law of Real Property*, Oxford: Clarendon Press, 1875; W.S. Holdsworth, *An Historical Introduction to the Land Law*, Oxford: Clarendon Press, 1927; and A.W.B. Simpson, *An Introduction to the History of the Land Law*, Oxford: Oxford University Press, 1961.

10. Lynn White Jr., "Historical Roots of Our Ecological Crisis," *Science* 155 (10 March 1967): 1203–7.

11. Locke's views on property were developed notably in Chapter 5 of his *Second Treatise on Government*. The Nature and extent of his influence have been debated. See, for example, "Who Read John Locke? Words and Acts in the American Revolution," by Oscar and Lilian Handlin, *The American Scholar* 58 (Autumn 1989): 545–56 and "The Reader Replies," in the *American Scholar* 58 (Summer 1990): 475–80.

12. See Lynton K. Caldwell, "The Jurisprudence of Thomas Jefferson," *Indiana Law Journal* 18 (April 1973): 193–213.

13. "A Summary View of the Rights of British America," in *The Works of Thomas Jefferson*, ed. Paul Leicester Ford, New York: G.P. Putnam's Sons, 1904, pp. 64–65.

14. To John Wayles Eppes, June 24, 1813, Ford, *Works* XI: 298.

15. Michael B. Metzger, "Private Property and Environmental Sanity," *Ecology Law Quarterly* 5, no. 4 (1976): 797.

16. "The Answer," in Tim Hunt, ed., *Collected Poetry of Robinson Jeffers*, II, Stanford: Stanford University Press, 1988, p. 536.

17. "Property Rights Threatened." Letter to the editor of the *Daily Herald-Telephone*, Bloomington, Indiana, January 17, 1974 from the Chairman of the Lawrence County Committee to Restore the Constitution.

18. See F.P. Bosselman, D. Callies, and J. Banta, *The Taking Issue: A Study of the Constitutional Limits of Governmental Authority to Regulate the Use of Privately Owned Land Without Paying Compensation To Owners*, Washington, D.C.: U.S. Council on Environmental Quality, 1973. And D.W. Large, "The Supreme Court and the Taking Issue: The Search for a Better Rule," *Environmental Law* 18 (Fall 1987): 3–54. The takings issue is discussed in most casebooks on environmental and land law. The treatment in the law journals is voluminous. Two recent references may suffice here: Richard A. Epstein, *Takings: Private Property and the Power of Eminent Domain*, Cambridge, Mass.: Harvard University Press, 1985 (a conservative point of view); and Joseph Di Mento, ed., *Wipeouts and Their Mitigation: The Changing Context for Land Use and Environmental Law*, Cambridge, Mass.: Lincoln Institute of Land Policy, 1990.

19. Marshall Massey, ed., *Environmental Amendment Circular No. 4*, The Comprehensive Environmental Project, 4353 East 119th Way, Denver, Colo. 80233; Lynton K. Caldwell, "The Case for An Environmental Amendment to the Constitution of the United States for Protection of the Environment," *Duke Environmental Law and Policy Forum* 1 (1991): 1–10.

20. See Ernest H. Wohlenberg, "Economics, Aesthetics, and the Saving of the Redwoods," in *Congress and the Environment*, edited by Richard A. Cooley and Geoffrey Wandesfords-Smith, Seattle: University of Washington Press, 1970, pp. 83–95. For a perceptive analysis of the "taking" issue in the Redwoods case, see Thomas R. Vale, "Objectivity, Values, and the Redwoods," *Landscape* 19, no. 1 (Winter, 1970): 30–33.

21. Digby, op. cit., vi.

22. Charles E. Little and Robert L. Burnap, *Stewardship: The Land, the Landowner, the Metropolis*. Prepared for Landowners in the New York Metropolitan Region by the Open Space Action Committee, 1965.

23. See Aldo Leopold, *Sand County Almanac and Sketches Here and There*, New York: Oxford University Press, 1949; and Susan Flader, *Thinking Like a Mountain*, Columbia, Missouri: University of Missouri Press, 1974.

24. Liberty Hyde Bailey, *The Holy Earth*, New York: Scribner's Sons, 1915.

25. Garrett Hardin, "The Tragedy of the Commons," *Science* 162 (December 13, 1968): 1243–48.

26. D.R. Denman, *Land Use and the Constitution of Property: An Inaugural Lecture*, Cambridge, England: Cambridge University Press, 1969: 2.

27. A source of comparative information, not recent but nevertheless relevant and useful, is "Land Problems—Problèmes Fonciers—Bodenprobleme," *Bibliographia: IULA*, The Hague: International Union of Local Authorities, 1983, N. 1/2: 49–68.

28. See Andre Brun, "Droits de Propriete et Droits d'Usage du Sal Agricole: Un Essai de Description," *Economie Rurale*, no. 75 (1968).

29. D.R. Denham, op. cit.

30. See James E. Krier, "The (Unlikely) Death of Property," *Harvard Journal of Law and Public Policy* 13, no. 1 (Winter 1990): 75–83. For a discussion of the history and moral basis of property rights, see L.C. Becker, "The Moral Basis of Property Rights," in J.R. Pennock and J.W. Chapman, eds., *Property,* Nomos 22, New York: New York University Press, 1980, pp. 187–220. For an alternative historical view of private property in land, see Henry George, *Progress and Poverty,* Garden City, N.Y.: Country Life Press, 1955, Ch. 4.

31. See Mark Sagoff, *The Economy of the Earth: Philosophy, Law and the Environment,* Cambridge: Cambridge University Press, 1988, and "Property Rights and Environmental Law" in *Philosophy and Public Policy* 8, no. 2 (Spring 1988): 9–12.

Chapter 6

1. U.S. Department of Commerce, Bureau of the Census, *1987 Census of Agriculture,* vol. 1, part 5, California, Washington, D.C.: U.S. Government Printing Office, 1989, pp. 366, 356, 341–43; hereafter cited as: Commerce, *1987 Agriculture.*

2. R.C. Fellmeth, *The Politics of Land,* New York: Grossman, 1973, p. 9; hereafter cited as POL.

3. L.M. Womack and L.G. Traub, *US—State Agricultural Data,* New York: U.S. Department of Agriculture, AIB 512, 1987, p. 12; hereafter cited as: Womack and Traub, *Agricultural Data 1987.* See also Fellmeth, POL, p. 12, and J. Hightower, "The Industrialization of Food,: in Peter Barnes (ed.), *The People's Land,* Emmaus, Pa., Rodale Press, 1975, pp. 81–85; hereafter cited as: Barnes, PL.

4. Commerce, *1989 Agriculture,* p. 16.

5. Fellmeth, POL, p. 12. See A. Strong, "Land as a Public Good," in I. de Neufville (ed.), *The Land Use Policy Debate in the United States,* New York: Plenum, 1981, pp. 217–33.

6. Fellmeth, POL, pp. 14–16. See R. Andrews (ed.), *Land in America,* Toronto: D.C. Heath, 1979, pp. 127–47.

7. See note 23 for a definition of procedural justice.

8. See M. Friedberger, *Farm Families and Change,* Lexington: University Press of Kentucky, 1988, pp. 73, 223ff., and B. Galeski and E. Wilkening (eds.), *Family Farming in Europe and America,* Boulder, Colo.: Westview, 1987. See also S.W. Hamilton and D.E. Baxter, "Government Ownership and the Price of Land," in *Public Property,* Vancouver: Fraser Institute, 1977, pp. 91–96. See also Paul Davidoff and N. Gold, "The Supply and Availability of Land for Housing for Low- and Moderate-Income Families," in David Listokin (ed.), *Land-Use Controls,* New Brunswick, N.J.: Rutgers University Press, 1979, pp. 279–84.

9. See Fellmeth, POL, p. 74 for an explanation of this situation.

10. Quoted by Fellmeth, POL, pp. 75–76. See J. Dangerfield, "Sowing

the Till," in Barnes, PL. See L. Tweeten, *Causes and Consequences of Structural Change in the Farming Industry*, Washington, D.C.: National Planning Association, 1984.

11. Fellmeth, POL, p. 78. See A.W. Griswold, *Farming and Democracy*, New Haven: Yale, 1952, pp. 5–6; hereafter cited as FD. The Land ownership continues to become more and more concentrated; see, for example, A.J. Fritsch, *Green Space*, Lexington, Ky.: Appalachia Science in the Public Interest, 1982, pp. 15–19; hereafter cited as: GS.

12. Commerce, *1989 Agriculture*, p. 1.

13. Commerce, *1989 Agriculture*, p. 1.

14. Commerce, *1989 Agriculture*, p. 380. See also T.A. Carlin and S.M. Mazie, *The US Farming Sector Entering the 1990's*, Washington, D.C.: U.S. Department of Agriculture, 1990.

15. Fellmeth, POL, p. 81; see notes 8, 10, 11, 19, 21.

16. See, for example, L. Brown, "The Illusion of Progress," pp. 1–16; S. Postel, "Saving Water for Agriculture," pp. 39–58; L. Brown and J. Young, "Feeding the World in the Nineties," pp. 59–78; and A. Durning, "Ending Poverty," pp. 135–53, all in L. Brown et al. (eds.), *State of the World 1990*, New York: Norton, 1990; hereafter cited, respectively, as: Brown, Progress; Postel, Agriculture; Brown and Young, Feeding; and Durning, Poverty, in *World 1990*.

17. See K. Griffin, *The Political Economy of Agrarian Change*, London: Macmillan, 1979, p. 40; hereafter cited as PEAC. See also Griswold, FD, p. 131.

18. See notes 8 and 19.

19. John Egerton, "Appalachia's Absentee Landlords," *The Progressive* 45, no. 6 (June 1981): 43; hereafter cited as: Egerton, Landlords. (The absentee landowners are often called "landlords" because nearly all the corporations owning Appalachian land lease it to other groups to mine. Almost none of these corporations engages in mining as its primary business.) See also John Gaventa and Bill Horton, *Ownership Patterns and Their Impacts on Appalachian Communities: A Survey of 80 Counties*, vol. 1, Washington, D.C.: Appalachian Regional Commission, February 1981, pp. 25–29, 210–11; hereafter cited as: Task Force, ALOS. Interestingly, Harvard University is the largest, private, nonprofit owner of mineral rights in Appalachia and pays no tax at all on them (Task Force, ALOS, p. 63). Finally, see Fritsch, GS. For further information on absentee ownership and the decline of the small farmer, see M. Strange, *Family Farming*, Lincoln: University of Nebraska Press, 1988, pp. 171, 199–200, and W. Whyte (ed.), *Our American Land*, Washington, D.C.: U.S. Government Printing Office 1987, pp. 122ff.

20. Task Force, ALOS, esp. pp. 210–12. Part of this problem has been created, of course, by underassessment of resource-rich land. See R. Nader, "Property Tax Evasion," in Barnes, PL, pp. 144–47.

21. Womack and Traub, *Agricultural Data 1987*, pp. 36, 86.

22. Task Force, ALOS, p. 212. See Mike Clark, Director of the Highlander Center, New Market, Tennessee, quoted by Egerton, Landlords, p. 44. See also Blaine Moss, Natural Resources Defense Center, *Land Use*

Controls in the United States, New York: Dial Press/ James Wade, 1977, pp. 235–36; hereafter cited as: Moss, Land Use. Finally, see Fellmeth, POL, p. 85, and G. Faux, "The Future of Rural Policy," in Barnes, PL, pp. 187–91, and K. Griffin, *Land Concentration and Rural Poverty*, New York: Holmes and Meier, 1976, pp. 1–11; hereafter cited as: LCRP. See also D.E. Albrecht and S.H. Murdoc, *The Sociology of US Agriculture*, Ames: Iowa State University Press, 1990; and L.M. Lobao, *Locality and Inequality*, Albany: State University of New York Pess, 1990.

23.   End-state principles provide reasons for a *particular distribution* of goods, whereas historical, or procedural-justice, principles describe fair or *correct methods* for arriving at any distribution, regardless of what it is. (See Robert Nozick, *Anarchy, State, and Utopia*, New York: Basic Books, 1974; hereafter cited as: Nozick, Anarchy. See also Nozick, "Locke's Theory of Acquisition," in Becker and Kipnis, pp. 146–48; hereafter cited as: Nozick, LT.)

John Rawls (*A Theory of Justice*, Cambridge, Mass.: Harvard University Press, 1971, p. 86; hereafter cited as: Justice) says that "pure procedural justice obtains when there is no independent criterion for the right result. Instead there is a correct or fair procedure such that the outcome is likewise correct or fair, whatever it is, provided that the procedure has been properly followed." Because procedural justice requires use of no independent criterion, e.g., entitlement, or equality of shares, whereas end-state justice does require use of such a criterion, it can be argued that distributions based on procedural principles are often less controversial than those based on end-state principles. See, for example, William Nelson, "The Very Idea of Pure Procedural Justice," *Ethics* 90, no. 4 (July 1980): 502–11.

24.   See notes 19–21 of this essay as well as supporting text.

25.   See notes 15–20, 28–31 of this essay as well as supporting text.

26.   See the discussion in the text (in this section) for an account of "background conditions." See also note 36.

27.   See, for example, Griffin, PEAC, pp. 223–25; and Griffin, LCRP. In the latter book, especially, Griffith shows that the degree of land concentration directly affects both the distribution of income in the agricultural sector and the standard of living of the majority of the rural population. See also W. Samuels, "Welfare Economics, Power, and Property," in G. Wunderlich and W. Gibson (eds.), *Perspectives of Property*, Pennsylvania State University: Institute for Land and Water Resources, 1972, pp. 140–41. See notes 7, 10, 19, 23.

28.   Because concentrations of property limit the economic options of others, they limit their choices (J.R. Pennock, "Thoughts on the Right to Private Property," in J.R. Pennock and J.W. Chapman (eds.), *Property*, Nomos 22, New York: New York University Press, 1980, p. 269. As the authors of the California study of land ownership, POL, put it (quoted in Task Force, ALOS, p. 28): "almost by definition, highly concentrated ownership and control of land means more political and economic power and greater ability to oppose contrary interests than do widely diffused ownership or control. Large landholders direct a greater portion of their earning toward political

ends than do smaller holders. And the large owners' land-use decisions have greater public impact, thus giving him greater bargaining power with officials."

29. See Rawls, Justice, pp. 111–13, 342–47 (sections 18, 52), and Nozick, Anarchy, pp. 90–93. See note 39.

30. See Thomas Aquinas, *The Summa Theologica*, First Part of the Second Part, Vol. 2, New York: Benzinger Brothers, 1947; David Hume, *Concerning Human Understanding*, Sections 51–53, Oxford: Clarendon, 1966; F.H. Bradley, *Collected Essays*, Freeport, N.Y.: Books for Libraries Press, 1968, pp. 272–83; C.A. Campbell, "Self Activity and its Modes," *Contemporary British Philosophy*, Third Series, New York: Macmillan, 1961; A.I. Melden, *Free Action*, London: Routledge and Kegan Paul, 1961, pp. 2, 213ff.; G. Ryle, *The Concept of Mind*, New York: Barnes and Noble, 1949, p. 70; G.E. Moore, *Ethics*, London: Oxford University Press, 1963, p. 126 (hereafter cited as: Ethics); D.F. Gustafson, "Voluntary and Involuntary," *Philosophy and Phenomenological Research* 24, no. 4 (June 1964): 493–501, esp. p. 498. See also J.E. Brady, "Indifference and Voluntariness," *Analysis* 32, no. 3 (June 1972), pp. 98–99; and J.E. Sweeney, "G.E. Moore and Voluntary Actions," *New Scholasticism* 51, no. 2 (Spring 1977): 196–10, esp. pp. 196–97, 201, 204, 209.

31. See K.W. Rankin, "Doer and Doing," *Mind* 69, no. 275 (July 1960): 361–71, esp. p. 371. See also Moore, *Ethics*, pp. 131–32. Melden, "Actions," *Philosophical Review* 65, no. 4 (1956): 523–41. See note 27.

32. P.H. Nowell-Smith, "Comments and Criticism: On Sanctioning Excuses," *Journal of Philosophy* 67, no. 18 (September 1970): 609–19, especially p. 609.

33. G. Ryle, *The Concept of Mind*, New York: Barnes and Noble, 1949, p. 75. P. Foot, "Hart and Honore: Causation in the Law," *Philosophical Review* 72, no. 4 (October 1963): 505–15, especially p. 514. H.L.A. Hart and A.M. Honore, *Causation in the Law*, Oxford: Clarendon Press, 1959, pp. 254–55. See also R.A. Samek, "The Concepts of Act and Intention and Their Treatment in Jurisprudence," *Australasian Journal of Philosophy* 41, no. 2 (August 1963): 198–16, esp. p. 216; R.F. Stalley, "Austin's Account of Action," *Journal of the History of Philosophy* 18, no. 4 (October 1980): 448–53, esp. p. 453.

34. See H.L.A. Hart, "Prolegomenon to the Principles of Punishment," *Proceedings of the Aristotelian Society* LX (1959–60); H.L.A. Hart, "Ascription of Responsibility," in *Freedom and Responsibility*, ed. H. Morris, Stanford: Stanford University Press, 1961, esp. p. 145; hereafter cited as Morris, FR. See also J.L. Austin, "A Plea for Excuses," in Morris, FR, p. 8; and Graham Hughes, "Omissions and *Mens Rea*," in Morris, FR, p. 230. P.H. Nowell-Smith, *Ethics*, Baltimore: Penguin, 1954, esp. p. 296; John Austin, *Philosophical Papers*, Oxford: Clarendon Press, 1961, esp. p. 128. See also P. Bronaugh, "Freedom as the Absence of an Excuse," *Ethics* 74, no. 3 (April 1964). See also V. Haksar, "Responsibility," *The Aristotelian Society* XL (1966): 187–22, and C. Whiteley, "Responsibility," *The Aristotelian Society* XL (1966): 223–26. For Austin's and Hart's claim that their

view about the defeasability thesis was also held by Aristotle, see J.L. Austin, "A Plea for Excuses," in Morris, FR, p. 8, and J.L.A. Hart, "Ascription of Responsibility," in Morris, FR, p. 145. See also J. McGinley, "Aristotle's Notion of the Voluntary," *Apeiron* 14, no. 2 (December 1980): 125–33, esp. pp. 126–27.

35. Haksar, "Responsibility," p. 205, and Whiteley, "Responsibility," p. 231, also make this point.

36. Haksar, "Responsibility," p. 205, also makes this point. See Whiteley, "Responsibility," p. 232.

37. Alan Gewirth, *Reason and Morality*, Chicago: University of Chicago Press, 1978, pp. 27–34, esp. pp. 32–34; hereafter cited as: Gewirth, RM.

38. Gewirth, RM, p. 34.

39. See Gewirth, RM, pp. 33–34; see also pp. 256–58 for additional treatment of voluntariness and forced consent. Finally see Alan Gewirth, *Human Rights*, Chicago: University of Chicago Press, 1982, esp. pp. 28, 114–17, 268–69. See also Stephen Cohen, "Gewirth's Rationalism: Who is a Moral Agent?", *Ethics* 89, no. 2 (June 1979): 179–90; N.K. Bell, "Nozick and Fairness," *Social Theory and Practice* 5, no. 1 (Fall 1978): 65–73; R.D. Heslep, "Gewirth and the Voluntary Agent's Esteem of Purpose," *Philosophy Research Archives* 11 (March 1986): 379–91.

40. Nolette and Fritsch, LT, p. 4. See notes 7, 10, 19, 23

41. A similar point is made by Virginia Held, "John Locke on Robert Nozick," *Social Research* 43, no. 1 (Spring 1976): 171–72. See also James P. Sterba, "Neo Libertarianism," in J.P. Sterba (ed.), *Justice: Alternative Political Perspectives*, Belmont: Wadsworth, 1980. See also V. Ray, "They're Destroying our Small Towns," in Barnes, PL, pp. 176–81.

42. See note 21 of this essay. The term, "property rights" is purposely used in the plural, since what we mean by the words encompasses a number of sub-rights (L.C. Becker "The Moral Basis of Property Rights," in J.R. Pennock and J.W. Chapman (eds.), *Property*, Nomos 22, New York: New York University Press, 1980, pp. 190-91).

43. See Fellmeth, POL, p. 85; P.S. Taylor, "The Battle for Acreage Limitations," in Barnes, PL, pp. 113–17; and O. Staley, "The Family Farm Anti-Trust Act," in Barnes, PL, pp. 222–24.

44. See P. Kaufman, "The Severance Tax," in Barnes, PL, pp. 152–53; John McClaughry, "Taxes for Land Acquisitions," in Barnes, PL, pp. 154–59; and J. de Neufville, "Land Use," in J. de Neufville (ed.), *The Land Policy Debate in the United States*, New York: Plenum, 1981, pp. 31–49; hereafter cited as: LPD.

45. See Peter Dorner, *Land Reform and Economic Development*, Baltimore: Penguin, 1972, and D.W. Bromley, *Environment and Economy*, Cambridge: Blackwell, 1991.

46. Rawls, Justice, p. 87. See note 23. Rawls holds that, without just background conditions, institutions carefully "regulated and corrected," then "the social process *will cease to be just*, however free and fair particular transactions may look when viewed by themselves." ("The Basic Structure as Subject," *American Philosophical Quarterly* 14, no. 2 (April 1977): 160).

47. See John Locke, *Second Treatise of Government*, chapter 5, par. 27 for a discussion of the proviso; hereafter cited as: Locke, ST. See also John Locke, "Of Property," in L. Becker and K. Kipnis (eds.), *Property*, Englewood Cliffs, N.J.: Prentice-Hall, 1984, p. 138; hereafter cited as: Locke, P, and Becker and Kipnis, P. Finally, see L. Becker, *Property Rights*, London: Routledge and Kegan Paul, 1977, pp. 89–94; hereafter cited as: PR. Finally, see chapter 4.

48. I am grateful to E. Partridge and D. Den Uyl for spelling out this objection.

49. Thomas Scanlon, "Nozick on Rights, Liberty, and Property," *Philosophy and Public Affairs* 6, no. 1 (Fall 1976): 8; hereafter cited as: Scanlon, Property.

50. In other words, the argument assigns to pattern a purely instrumental role. The control that concentrated property holdings give one over others is the problem.

51. The argument is neither for nor against a particular level of concentration in land holdings, but that whenever (e.g., in Appalachia) and whatever structures limit the voluntariness of transactions, there are procedural grounds for removing those limits. As Nozick puts it, speaking of his own principles, "patterning (or end-state) considerations" are not introduced when one seeks merely to remove the disadvantages affecting given persons. Nozick, Anarchy, p. 343.

52. Nozick, Anarchy, p. 181.

53. Nozick, Anarchy, p. 238.

54. Anarchy, p. 262. Nozick's exact claim is: "Other people's actions place limits on one's available opportunities. Whether this makes one's resulting action non-voluntary depends upon whether these others have the right to act as they did." Nozick also remarks: "A person's choice among differing degrees of unpalatable alternatives is not rendered non-voluntary by the fact that others voluntarily chose and acted within their rights in a way that did not provide him with more palatable alternatives." (Anarchy, p. 264.) However, whether an act is voluntary or not depends on various psychological-physical considerations. It is not clear that, in a transaction between person A and person B, Nozick ought to "define" person A's act as *voluntary*, in terms of whether person B had a right to act as he did regarding A. Nozick is wrong to argue that, provided that one has a *right* to act as he does, then no undesirable control is exercised by landlords having concentrated holdings. Whether B has a right or not, his actions may still cause A's act to be non-voluntary. The *psychological/physical quality* of B's act (its voluntariness) is not causally affected by the *moral quality* of B's act, but only by whether B exercises overt or covert power over A.

55. See Locke, ST, V; Locke, P; Nozick, Anarchy, pp. 174–78, and Nozick, LT, pp. 146–49. See also Becker, PR, pp. 43–45.

56. See Locke, ST and Locke, P. See also Becker, PR, pp. 43–45.

57. See L.C. Becker, *Property Rights: Philosophic Foundations*, Boston: Routledge and Kegan Paul, 1977, pp. 109–10; hereafter cited as: PR. Mark Nolette and Albert Fritsch, *The Community Land Trust*, Lexington, Ky.: Appalachia-Science in the Public Interest, 1982, p. 3.

58. See Nozick, LT, p. 148.

59. D.H. Meadows, D.L. Meadows, J. Randers, *Beyond the Limits*, Post Mills, VT: Chelsea Green Publishing Company, 1992, chs. 2, 4; hereafter cited as: Meadows et al., Limits 1992.

60. Meadows et al., Limits 1992, chs. 2, 4, 6. See D.H. Meadows et al., *The Limits to Growth*, New York: New American Library, 1974, pp. 40, 60, 69, 81. See also K. Shrader-Frechette, *Environmental Ethics*, Pacific Grove, Calif.: Boxwood, 1991, pp. 171ff.

61. Locke, ST, par. 34.

62. See Becker, PR, p. 44 and Hastings Rashdall, "The Philosophical Theory of Property," in J.V. Bartlett (ed.), *Property: Its Duties and Rights*, 2d ed., London: Macmillan, 1915, pp. 54–56.

63. For similar suggestions, see Becker, PR, p. 117.

Chapter 7

1. Lynda L. Butler, "State Environmental Programs: A Study in Political Influence and Regulatory Failure," *William and Mary Law Review* 31 (Summer 1990): 823–933; Jeffrey L. Amestoy and Mark J. Stefano, "Wildlife Habitat Protection Through State-wide Land Use Regulation," *Harvard Environmental Law Review* 14 (1990): 45–71; and *California Coastal Commission* vs. *Granite Rock Co.*, 480 U.S. 572 (1987)—federal land use regulations do not preempt state environmental regulations applicable to federal lands.

2. J. Ise, "Too Much and Too Poor," in *The American Way*, published by faculty members, Department of Economics, School of Business, Lawrence: University of Kansas, 1955, p. 103.

3. This opinion corresponds to the conclusion reached by N. Wengert, "the general stance of the federal courts, including the Supreme Court continues to be to avoid land use planning and control litigation," in "Constitutional Principles Applied to Land Use," *Natural Resources Journal* 19, nos. 1–2, (1979): 1–20. This observation remained partially valid a decade later, but the federal courts as of 1992 appeared to be moving toward a more rigorous test of public purpose in land use controls and a more vigorous defense of private property rights.

4. See *Vermont's Act 250: Reflections on the First Decade and Recommendations for the Second* South Royalton, Vt.: Environmental Law Center—Vermont Law School, 1980; *Vermont Planning, Development and Land Use Regulation*, Oxford, N.H.: Equity Pub. Co. (Butterworth), 1990.

5. For analysis of court action striking down or imposing conditions on local efforts to restrict or delay growth see D. Brower and J. Pannabecker, "Growth Management Update: An Assessment and Status Report," *Natural Resources Journal* 19 (January 1979): 161–81. See also case note by R. Soloff, *Rutgers Law Review* 15 (1984): 789–99; Godschalk et al., *The Constitutional issues of Growth Management*, Chicago: A.F.P.O. Press, 1977; and W. Reilly, ed., *The Use of Land: A Citizens Policy Guide to Urban Growth*, New York:

T.Y. Crowell, 1973; *Construction Industry Association of Sonoma County* vs. *Petaluma*, 522 F. 2d 987 (1975); *City of Boca Raton* vs. *Boca Villas Corporation* 371 So. 2d 154 (1979).

6. For all aspects of zoning as an instrument of land-use control in addition to citations under n. 15 supra see Patrick J. Rohan, *Zoning and Land Use Controls*, eight volumes plus index and notes (Albany, N.Y.: Matthew Bender, 1984). See also Robert H. Nelson, *Zoning and Property Rights: An analysis of the American System of Land-Use Regulation*, Cambridge, Mass.: MIT Press, 1977.

7. For example, in re Appeal of M.A. Kravitz Co. 501 Pa. 200, 460 A2d 1075 (1983) case note by F. McTiernan, Jr., *Duquesne Law Review* 23 (1983): 249–62; and in re Appeal of Elocin, Inc., 501 Pa. 348, 461 A2d 771 (1983), case note by J. Hanlon, Jr., *Duquesne Law Review* 23 (1983): 263–78.

8. *Golden* vs. *Planning Board of the Town of Ramapo*, 30 NY 2d., p. 359.

9. For accomplishments of TNC see its annual reports and *The Nature Conservancy News*.

10. "Practical Conservation: The Third Force—Environmental Charities as Owners or Managers of Property," summary of a conference, *Journal of the Royal Society of Arts* 134 (March 1986): 226–43.

11. A. Strong and J. Keene, *Environmental Protection Through Public and Private Development Controls*, Washington, D.C.: Government Printing Office 1973; F.P. Bosselman and D. Callies, *The Quiet Revolution in Land Use Control*, Washington, D.C.: Government Printing Office, 1972; Ervin and J. Fitch, "Evaluating Alternative Compensation and Recapture Techniques for Expanded Public Control of Land Use," *Natural Resources Journal* 19 (1979): 21–41 discusses transferable development rights and zoning by eminent domain and zoning auctions. See also J. Brown, "Concomitant Agreement Zoning: An Economic Analysis," *University of Illinois Law Review* (1985): 89–116.

12. *McIlhinney* vs. *Zoning Board* 455 Atl. 2d. 128; *Fairfax Co.* vs. *Snell Construction Co.*, 202 SE 2d 889, 1974.

13. *Lucas* v. *Carolina Coastal Commission* (404 SE 2d. 895) 1991.

14. *Chino Valley* vs. *State Land Department* 580 p 2d 704, Arizona 243 (1978); *Chino Valley* vs. *Prescott* 638 p 2d 1324, 131 Arizona 78 (1982).

15. Resources Rivers Act 9 F/a. Laws 85-347.

16. *Burn's Indiana Statutes Annotated—Code Edition Title 4, State Administration* 1990 Replacement Volume, Charlottesville, Va.: Michie, 1990; Article 21, United States—States Ceding of Jurisdiction and Consent to Acquisition of Indiana Land," Chapter 7, "United States Acquisition of Natural Forest Land," 521–22.

17. *One Third of the Nation's Land Report of the Public Land Law Review Commission*, 1970. See also H. Nathan, ed., *America's Public Lands: Politics, Economics and Administration,* Conference on the Public Land Law Review Commission Report, Berkeley: Institute of Government Studies, University of California, 1972; and H.K. Pyle, *What's Ahead for Our Public Lands? A Summary Review of the Activities and Final Report of the Public*

Land Law Review Commission, Washington, D.C.: Natural Resources Council of America, 1970.

18. G. Wunderlich, "Landownership: A Status of Facts," *Natural Resources Journal* 19 (1979): 105. The status of case law regarding the authority of state and local governments to control the land uses of private owners or of other public agencies is no less ambiguous. N. Wengert, commenting on the large volume of land-use litigation in state courts, concluded that: "First, land use control has not been readily accepted by many parties in interest. Second, state courts have not been able to decide cases in such a manner as to establish principles that might have obviated subsequent challenges." ("Constitutional Principles Applied to Land Use Planning and Regulation: A Tentative Restatement" *Natural Resources Journal* 19 (1979): 1–20.) Judicial difficulties in the absence of generally accepted guiding principles is illustrated in *Commonwealth, Department of General Services v. Organtz Neighbors Association* Pa 483 A2d 448, 1984, case note by T. Rice in 58 Temp. L.Q. 509-22, 1985. See also R. Healy and J. Rosenberg, *Land Use and the States*, Baltimore: published for Resources for the Future by the Johns Hopkins University Press, 1979.

19. See note 8, Chapter 12, on the ancient forest issue.

20. A. Leopold, "The Land Ethic," in *Sand County Almanac*, New York: Oxford University Press, 1949, pp. 201–26.

21. G. Hardin, "The Tragedy of the Commons," *Science* 162 (1974): 1243–48.

22. R. Stroup and J. Baden, *Environment's Best Friend: Property Rights 3 PERC Reports*, Bozeman Mont.: Political Economy Research Center, 1985. See also Hardin and Baden, *Managing the Commons*, San Francisco: W. H. Freeman, 1977.

23. For an analysis of the land use provisions of the Federal Land Policy and Management Act (FLPMA) and the National Forest Management Act (NFMA), see P. Culhane and P. Friesma, "Land Use Planning for the Public Lands," *Natural Resources Journal* 19 (1979): 43–74. The impact of NEPA on land use has been indirect but nonetheless far reaching, primarily through the requirement in Sec. 102(2)c of an environmental impact statement. For an example of the effect upon land use of the environmental impact statement requirement, adopted by about half of the states (i.e., little NEPAs) see E. Gottschalk, Jr., "Guarding the Land: California Court Ruling on Ecological Impact Throws Builders, Lenders, Unions for a Loss," *Wall Street Journal*, 9 October 1972, p. 26. On management of federal lands see *Workshop on Land Protection and Management* (Pub. 97-101), Committee on Energy and Natural Resources, June 1982.

24. See, for example, L. Milbrath, *Environmental Values and Beliefs of the General Public and Leaders in the United States, England and Germany*, Occasional Papers, Buffalo: State University of New York at Buffalo, 1980; also found in D. Mann, ed., *Environmental Policy Formation: The Impact of Values, Ideology, and Standards*, Lexington, Mass.: Lexington Books, 1981. See also P. Ester, "Environmental Concern in the Netherlands," in T. O'Riordan and R. Kerry Turner, eds., *Progress in Resources Management*

and Environmental Planning, vol. 2, New York: John Wiley, 1980. Most recently, see report of a New York Times–CBS opinion poll, *New York Times*, 28 January 1986, pp. 1 and 14; and John M. Gilroy and Robert Y. Shapiro, "The Polls: Environmental Protection," *Public Opinion Quarterly* 50 (Summer 1986): 270–79.

25. Pub. L. 91-190, 42 USC, 4321, January 1, 1970, as amended by Pub. L. 94-52, July 3, 1975 and Pub. L. 94-83, August 9, 1975.

26. The full effect of NEPA on land use is not easily measured, especially because many disputes over environmental matters and impact statement requirements, although basically land-use cases, are litigated over issues of pollution, endangered species, public health, etc., rather than land use per se. For early assessments, see P. Schaenman and T. Muller, *Measuring Impacts of Land Development: An Initial Approach*, Washington, D.C.: Urban Institute, 1974; D. Keyes, *Land Development and the Natural Environment: Estimating Impacts*, Washington, D.C.: Urban Institute, 1976.

27. The published work on land-use policy is much too large for anything more than a selective sample of sources in an essay of this type. R. Andrews, ed., *Land in America: Commodity or Natural Resource*, Lexington, Mass.: Lexington Books, 1979; G. Bjork, *Life, Liberty, and Property: The Economics and Politics of Land-Use Planning and Environmental Controls*, Lexington, Mass.: Lexington Books, 1980; R. Brenneman and S. Bates, *Land Saving Action: A Written Symposium by 29 Experts on Private Land Conservation in the 1980s*, Covelo, Calif.: Island Press, 1984. Also R. Coward, ed., *Land Use Planning Politics and Policy*, Berkeley: University Extension Publications, University of California, 1976; National Task Force on Research Relating to Land Use Planning and Policy, *Land Use: Issues and Research Needs for Planning, Policy, and Allocation*, Pullman: Washington State University, Department of Agriculture, 1976; K. Davis, *Land Use*, Hightstown, N.J.: McGraw-Hill, 1976; R. Ellickson and A. Tarlock, *Land Use Controls*, Boston, Mass.: Little, Brown, 1981; Ervin *et al.*, *Land Use Control: Evaluation and Political Effects*, New York: Ballinger, 1977; C. M. Haar and M.A. Wolf, *Land Use Planning: A Casebook on the Use, Misuse and Re-use of Urban Land*, 4th ed., Boston, Mass.: Little, Brown and Co., 1989. J. Hite, *Room and Situation: The Political Economy of Land Use*, Chicago, Ill.: Nelson-Hall, 1979; O. Koenigsburger et al., *Review of Land Policies*, Elmsford, N.Y.: Pergamon Press, 1981; and G. McClellan, ed., *Land Use in the United States: Exploitation or Conservation*, Bronx, N.Y.: H.W. Wilson, 1971. D. Mandelker, *Land Use Law*, Charlottesville, Va.: Michie, 1982; E. Moss, ed., *Land Use Controls in the United States*, New York: Dial Press, 1976; Richard H. Jackson, *Land Use in America*, New York: John Wiley & Sons, 1981; E. Netter, *Land Use Law: Issues for the Eighties*, Washington, D.C.: Planners Press, 1981. J. De Neufville, *The Land Use Policy Debate in the United States*, New York: Plenum, 1981; C. Little and R. Burnap, *Stewardship, the Land-the Landowner-the Metropolis*, New York: Open Space Committee, 1965; T. Patterson, *Land Use Planning: Techniques of Implementation*, New York: Van Nostrand Reinhold, 1979; F. Popper, *The Politics of Land-Use Reform*, Madison: University of Wisconsin Press, 1981;

C. Perin, *Everything in Its Place: Social Order and Land Use in America*, Princeton: Princeton University Press 1977; P. Raup, *The Federal Dynamic in Land Use*, Washington, D.C.: National Planning Association, 1980; N. Williams, Jr., *American Land Planning Law: Cases and Materials*, New Brunswick, N.J.: Center for Urban Policy, Rutgers University, 1978; and R. Wright and M. Gittleman, *Cases and Materials on Land Use*, St. Paul, Minn.: West Publishing Co., 1982.

28.   National Land Use Policy, Hearings before the Committee on Interior and Insular Affairs, United States Senate, Ninety-first Congress, Second Session on 53354, March 24, April 28, and 29, 1970 and *Readings on Land Use Policy: A Selection of Recent Articles and Studies on Land Use Policy Issues and Activities in the United States Senate* (June 1975). Also Roger C. Adams, "The Land Use Policy and Planning Assistance Act of 1973: Legislating A National Land Use Policy," *George Washington Law Review* 41 (1973): 604–25.

29.   U.S. Department of Commerce, Biennial Report to the Congress on Coastal Zone Management 1982–83, Sept. 1984. For Assessments of the effectiveness of the Coastal Zone Management Act see *Reauthorization of the Coastal Management Act* in Hearings before the Subcommittee on Oceanography by the Committee on Merchant Marine and Fisheries, House of Representatives Ninety-ninth Congress, First Session Serial 99-4, March 28, April 2, 1985. Note pages 140–44.

30.   *Beauty for America: Proceedings of the White House Conference on National Beauty*, Washington, D.C.: Government Printing Office, 1965.

31.   *One Third of the Nation's Land*, 4–10.

32.   For examples of the case for incremental decision making, see Charles E. Lindblom, "The Science of Muddling Through," *Public Administration Review* 19 (Spring 1959): 79–88; and John M. Pfiffner, "Administrative Rationality," *Public Administration Review* 20 (Summer 1960): 125–32. Both articles annotate other sources.

33.   *Environmental Quality—The First Annual Report of the Council on Environmental Quality*, Washington, D.C.: U.S. Government Printing Office, August, 1970, pp. xii–xiii.

34.   *Statement by Russell E. Train, Chairman, Council on Environmental Quality Before the Senate Committee on Interior and Insular Affairs, May 18, 1971*, mimeo, p. 4.

35.   The full story of the peregrinations of the land-use bill remains to be told. Newspapers of the period are the most accessible source of information. On the House Committee vote in 1975 see syndicated column by Jeff Stansbury and Edward Flattau, July 27, 1975. "Odds are Bad for Environmentalists" and "Federal Land-Use Bill is Killed in Committee." Note also Dennis Farney, "The Unsolved Problems of Land-Use," *Wall Street Journal* (2 February 1973).

36.   For accounts of past state initiatives see John V. Conti, "A Quiet Revolution: With Little Fanfare, States are Broadening Control Over Land-Use," *Wall Street Journal* (28 June 1975): 1,23; Elizabeth Haskell, *Managing the Environment: Nine States Look for New Answers*, Washington, D.C.:

Woodrow Wilson International Center for Scholars, Smithsonian Institution, April 1971, 445 pp.; Slavin, Richard H., "Toward a State Land-Use Policy," *State Government* 46 (Winter 1971): 2–10; Robert R. Linowes and Don T. Allenworth, *The States and Land Use Control*, New York: Praeger, 1975; Frank S. So, Irving Hand, and Bruce D. McDowell, eds., *The Practice of State and Regional Planning*, Chicago: American Planning Association, 1986; Thomas G. Pelham, *State Land-Use Planning and Regulation*, Lexington, Mass.: Lexington Books, 1979.

37.   *Hawaii Housing Authority* vs. *Midkiff*, 467 U.S. 229, and Stephen Werneil, "Justices in a Hawaii Land Case Reaffirm States' Powers in Regulation of Resources," *Wall Street Journal* (31 May 1984): 10. See also *Newsweek* (11 June 1984): 69. "Public use" is coterminous with the states police power, i.e., if an act regarding private property is a legitimate use of the state's police power then that act satisfies the public use requirement, even though property taken by eminent domain is transferred to private benefits. However, the Supreme Court appears to be narrowing its tolerance for use of the state police power where property rights are infringed. See Joseph Di Mento, ed., *Wipeouts and Their Mitigation: The Changing Context for Land Use and Environmental Law*, Cambridge, Mass.: Lincoln Institute of Land Policy, 1990.

38.   The legal concept of a business affected with a public enabled government to regulate privately owned business—but by the same logic permitted the granting of special rights on behalf of the public interest. See *Wolff Packing Co.* vs. *Court of Industrial Relations* 262 U.S. 522 (1923) and *Nebbia* vs. *New York*, 291 U.S. 502 (1934).

39.   Myron B. Thompson, "Hawaii's State Land-Use Law," *State Government* 46 (Spring 1966): 97–100. *State of Hawaii Land-Use Districts and Regulations Review*, Summary prepared for the state of Hawaii Land-Use Commission by Eckbo, Dean, Austin & Williams, June 1970, unpaged.

40.   For example, see California, Legislature, Senate, *The Limits of Land Use Regulation—Summary Report from the Hearing of the Senate Committee on Local Government*, August 13, 1987, Sacramento: The Committee, 1987; Paul Sabatier and Daniel A. Mazmanian, "Can Regulation Work? The Implementation of the 1972 California Coastal Initiative," *Policy Sciences* 20, no. 3 (1987): 279–81; Gallup Organization, *New Jersey Land Use Planning: A Survey of Public Opinion*, Trenton, N.J.: Office of State Planning, 1988; and Michael Heiman, *The Quiet Evaluation: Power, Planning and Profits in New York State*, New York: Praeger, 1988.

41.   Harvey M. Jacobs et al., *Wisconsin's Twentieth Century Land Policy Legacy: A Working Bibliography*, Chicago: Council of Planning Librarians, American Planning Association, 1989; Stephan M. Barn et al., *Future Issues Facing Wisconsin's Land Resources*, Madison: Institute for Environmental Studies, University of Wisconsin, 1990 (Report 138); see also W.A. Rowlands, "Which Way Now, Wisconsin?—The Problem of Land Settlement," in *Wisconsin Counties* (July 1944).

42.   Herbert B. Stroud, "Growth Management and Recreational Land Development in Florida," *Land Use Policy* 6 (January 1989): 2. Also Luther J.

Carter, *The Florida Experience: Land and Water Policy in a Growth State*, Baltimore: Johns Hopkins University Press, 1974; and Lance de Haven-Smith, "Regulatory Theory and State Land-Use Regulation: Implications from Florida's Experience With Growth Management," *Public Administration Review* (September–October, 1984): 416–17.

43. James R. Pease, "Planning for Land Conservation and Development in Oregon," in F.R. Steiner and H.N. Van Lier, eds., *Land Conservation and Development—Examples of Land-Use Planning Projects and Programs*, Amsterdam: Elsevier Science, 1984, pp. 253–71; and G. Gustafson, T.L. Daniels, and R.P. Shirack, "The Oregon Land-Use Act: Implications for Farmland and Open Space Protection," *Journal of American Planning Association* 48, no. 3 (1982): 365–73.

44. "Public Unconvinced About Environmental Problems," *Chemecology* 20, no. 8 (November 1992): unpaged.

45. See *Land Letter: The Newsletter for Natural Resource Professionals* 10, no. 19 (1 July 1991). H. Jane Lehman, "Bill to Limit Federal Land Rules Gains: Measure Targets Impacts on Property Values Use," *Washington Post* (13 July 1991): 1, E13; Michael Satchall, "Any Color But Green: A New Political Alliance is Battling the Environmental Movement," *U.S. News and World Report* (21 October 1991): 74–76; and Cornelia Dean, "Beachfront Owners Face Possible Insurance Cuts: Proposal in Senate Pits Landowners Against Environmentalists," *New York Times* (27 May 1992): A1, 9.

46. See American Law Institute, *A Model Land Development Code* (1975), Washington, D.C.: ALI, 1970–1975. See also Linda Bozung and Deborah J. Alessi, "Recent Developments in Environmental Preservation and the Rights of Property Owners," *Urban Lawyer* 20 (Fall 1991): 969–1069. Excerpts from subcommittee reports of the Land Use, Planning and Zoning Committee of the American Bar Association.

47. In *Environment in a Growing Economy*, ed. Henry Jarret, Baltimore: Johns Hopkins University Press, 1967, p. 148.

48. *In the Matter of Joseph E. Seagram and Sons, Inc.* vs. *Tax Commission of the City of New York* 200 N.E. 2nd 447 (1964).

49. Keith Schneider, "Administration Proposes Opening Vast Protected Areas to Builders," *New York Times* (3 August, 1991): 1,8.

50. E.g., Benjamin F. Bobo and B. Bruce-Briggs, *No Land is an Island: Individual Rights and Government Control*, San Francisco: Institute of Contemporary Studies, 1975.

Chapter 8

1. Charles E. Merriam, *History of the Theory of Sovereignty Since Rousseau*, New York: Columbia University Press, 1900.

2. On the details of the Trail Smelter and Test Ban cases, see D.H. Dinwoode, "The Politics of International Pollution Control: The Trail Smelter Case," *International Journal* 27 (Spring 1972): 219–35; and L.F.E. Goldie, "The Nuclear Test Cases: Restraints on Environmental Harm," *Journal of Maritime Law and Commerce* 5 (1973–74): 491. For general treatments of

international obligations and jurisdiction see Lynton K. Caldwell, *International Environmental Policy: Emergence and Dimensions*, 2d. ed., Durham, N.C.: Duke University Press, 1986; and Andrew Hurrell and Benedict Kinsbury, eds., *The International Politics of the Environment*, Oxford: Clarendon Press, 1992.

3. For texts of these declarations, see *International Legal Materials* 28 (1989): 1303 and 13011.

4. For texts of pertinent sections of national constitutions, see Edith Brown Weiss, *In Fairness to Future Generations: International Law, Common Patrimony, and Intergenerational Equity*, Dobbs Ferry, N.Y.: Transnational Publishers, 1989.

5. Charlotte K. Goldberg, "The Garrison Diversion Project: New Solutions for Transboundary Disputes," *Manitoba Law Journal* 11, no. 2 (1981): 177–89.

6. Dino Ross, "International Management of the Flathead River Basin," *Colorado Journal of International Environmental Law and Policy* 1, no. 1 (Summer 1990): 223–39.

7. Troy L. Pewe, ed., *Desert Dust: Origin, Characteristics, and Effect Upon Man*, Boulder, Colo.: Geological Society of America, 1981; and Joseph M. Prospero and Ruby T. Nees, "Dust Concentrations in the Atmosphere of the Sahelian North Atlantic: Possible Relationship to Sahelian Drought," *Science* 196 (10 June 1977): 1196–98.

8. J. Brian Mudd and T.T. Kozlowski, eds., *Response of Plants to Air Pollution*, New York: Academic Press, 1975. Note chapter 14 by Saul Rich, "Interactions of Air Pollution and Agricultural Practices." See also William Ashworth, *The Late, Great Lakes: An Environmental History*, Detroit: Wayne State University Press, 1987. See also International Convention on Long-Range Transboundary Air Pollution (in force 1983). Note comment by Amy A. Fraenkel, "The Convention on Long-Range Air Pollution: Meeting the Challenge of International Cooperation," *Harvard International Law Journal* 30 (Spring 1989): 447ff.

9. Some of the considerations relating to land use and agriculture are discussed by Mark Sagoff in "Ethics, Agriculture, and the Environment" in *Report from the Center for Philosophy and Public Policy* 7, no. 1 (Winter 1987): 9–12. See also Piers M. Blaikie, *The Political Economy of Soil Erosion*, London: Longman, 1985; and Piers M. Blaikie and Harold Brookfield, *Land Degradation and Society*, London: Methuen, 1987.

10. Gary S. Hartshorn, "El Salvador: An Ecological Disaster," letter to Peter Martin, executive director, Institute of Current World Affairs, Hanover, N.H., 7 June 1961, GSH-1.

11. Mary E. Kelly and Dick Kamp, "Mexico–US Free Trade Negotiations and the Environment: Exploring the Issues," *Border Ecology Project*, Austin: Texas Center for Policy Studies, January 1991; and Malissa McKeith, "Environmental Provisions Affecting Businesses on the US/Mexico Border," *International Environmental Reporter* (4/22/1992): 245–48.

12. U.N. Security Council, *Official Records*, Eighth Year, 629th Meeting, S/3108, 27 October, 1953 and idem, supplements for October, Novem-

ber, and December, 1953. See also further reference to this controversy in Editorials/Letters page, *New York Times*, 13 April, 1991, also letters on water and land issues between Hungary and Czechoslovakia and Egypt and Ethiopia.

13. U.S. Treaty Series 628 *United States Statutes at Large* 65th Congress, 1915–1917, 3a Part 2, 1702-D5; *Missouri* vs. *Holland*, 252 U.S. 316 (1920) upheld the Federal Migratory Bird Treaty Act of 1916, 16 U.S.C. Sec. 703, on the basis of the constitutional treaty power.

14. See articles on "colonization" of the West in *Western Wildlands: A Natural Resource Journal* 3, no. 3 (Winter 1977): whole issue.

15. See the United Nations Environment Program, *Desertification Control Bulletin: A Bulletin of World Events in the Control of Deserts. Restoration of Degraded Lands and Reforestation* Nairobi: UNEP. (published at six monthly intervals.)

16. L. Dudley Stamp. *Land for Tomorrow: Our Developing World*, new and revised edition, Bloomington: Indiana University Press, 1969.

17. *Soil Map of the World*, 10 vols., Rome: Food and Agriculture Organization of the United Nations (FAO), 1970–1979; FAO and UNESCO, *Soil Map of the World: Revised Legend*, Rome: FAO, 1988, (World Soil Resources Report, 1988). See also Eward John Russell, *The World of the Soil*, London: Collins, 1957.

18. Stamp, op. cit. 64–66.

19. Soil Conservation Act of 1935, chap. 5, 49 stat. 163, sec. 5, and D. Harper Sims, *The Soil Conservation Service*, New York: Praeger, 1970.

20. For example, see M.G. Wolman and F.G.A. Fournier, *Land Transformation in Agriculture* (SCOPE 32), New York: John Wiley, 1987.

21. Ricardo Umali, "Landsat: Uninvited Eye," *East-West Perspective* 1 (Winter 1980): 12–21.

22. *Remote Sensing: Prospects for Developing Countries*, Report of the Ad Hoc Committee on Remote Sensing for Development. Washington, D.C.: National Academy of Sciences, 1979. But international governance implies multinational agreement on data gathering and this involves the further implication of consensus on the policies toward land that may be implicit in the data. Monitoring of changes in land use could be greatly facilitated. Thus technology may drive policy. But as of 1992 the U.S. General Accounting Office found that international agreements are not well monitored. See RCED-92-43.

23. See bulletins of the North American Cartographic Information Society and special issue of the *American Cartographer*, 13, no. 3. (July 1988). The first GISs to become operative were Canadian and British, see David Rhind, "Why GIS," *ARC News* 11, no. 3 (Summer 1989).

24. E.g., see Blaikie, *op. cit* note 9, supra.

25. Kenneth A. Dahlberg, *Beyond the Green Revolution: The Ecology and Politics of Global Agricultural Development*, New York: Plenum Press, 1979.

26. Caldwell, *International Environmental Policy* op. cit. supra, note 1, and *World Environmental Report* 9 (3 March 1983): 3.

27. *International Legal Materials* 19 (July 1980): 837–38. See also "CIDIE to Address Looming Crisis," *Our Planet* 1, nos. 2/3 (1989): 11.

28. Arnold Toynbee, *Mankind and Mother Earth*, New York: Oxford University Press, 1976.

29. Christian de Saussay, *Land Tenure Systems and Forest Policy*, Rome: Food and Agriculture Organization of the United Nations, 1987.

30. Additional sources of land-use policy of international significance are the following publications of the Council of Europe: *Land Use Policies in Regional Planning—Economic Aspects* Report of the European Seminar— European Conference of Ministers Responsible for Regional Planning (CEMAT), Antalya, Turkey, 21–25 September 1987 (Study Series 49), Strasbourg: The Council, 1989; *Socio-political Instruments of Land Use in Urban Areas* Report of the European Seminar, Falun, Sweden, 29 June–1 July, 1989 (Study Series 50), Strasbourg: The Council, 1989; *Instruments for Rational Land Use: Administrative Instruments* Report of the Second European Seminar, Strasbourg, 14–15 November, 1989 (Study Series 51), Strasbourg: The Council 1990; also Gregory K. Wilkinson, *The Role of Legislation in Land Use Planning in Developing Countries,* Rome: Food and Agriculture Organization of the United Nations, 1985; and Jacques J. Kozub, Norman Meyers, and Emmanuel D'Silva, *Land and Water Management*, Report of seminar held in Washington, D.C., November 20–21, 1986, Washington, D.C.: World Bank Economic Development Institute Report Series, No. 6, 1987.

31. Jane Perlez, "98 Nations Adopt Biological Treaty; US May Not Sign," *New York Times* (23 May 1992): 1, 5; Keith Schneider, "US Will Oppose Species Treaty that Would Promote Preservation," *New York Times* (30 May 1992): 1, 2. For a comprehensive account of the biodiversity issue, see *Global Biodiversity Strategy: Guidelines for Action to Save, Study, and Use Earth's Biotic Wealth Sustainably and Equitably*, New York: World Resources Institute, The World Conservation Union and the United Nations Environment Programme, 1992. Note especially chapters 4 and 5.

Chapter 9

1. Charles M. Haar and Michael Allan Wolf, *Land-Use Planning: A Casebook on the Use, Misuse and Re-use of Urban Land*, 4th ed., Boston: Little, Brown, 1959, and, ed., *Law and Land: Anglo-American Planning Practice*, Cambridge, Mass.: Harvard University Press and the MIT Press, 1964. See also Curtis L. Berger, *Land Ownership and Use*, Boston: Little, Brown, 1968; and Arnold W. Reitz Jr., *Environmental Planning: Law of Land and Resource*, Washington, D.C.: North American International, 1974. Basic legal principles governing land-use have not changed greatly during most recent decades, and in some fundamentals not since Blackstone's *Commentaries* in 1766 on *The Rights of Things*.

2. Edward A. Ackerman, "A View of Terrestrial Space," *Science* 157 (1 September 1967): 1031–32 (a review of *L'Organization de l'espace: Elemente de geographie voluntaire* by Jean Labasse, Paris: Hermann, 1966, p. 605).

Labasse's book is a significant contribution to the literature of land policy and planning.

3. G.A. Hills, *The Ecological Basis for Land-Use Planning*, Research Report No. 46 Toronto: Ontario Department of Lands and Forests, December 1961.

4. Lynton K. Caldwell, ed., *Perspectives on Ecosystem Management for the Great Lakes*, Albany: State University Press of New York, 1985.

5. Caldwell, op. cit., Appendix B, pp. 355–57.

6. Ibid., Appendix C, pp. 359–61.

7. Endangered Species Act of 1973, Public Law 93-205–-Dec. 28, 1973 (87 STAT 885), Sec. 2 (b).

8. Executive Order No. 11990, May 24, 1977, U.S.C. 42-4321.

9. Jens Busch and Christer Agren, "Sensitive Ecosystems," *Acid News: A Newsletter from the Swedish and Norwegian Secretariats on Acid Rain*, no. 2 (June 1991).

10. Keith Schneider, "Returning Part of Everglades to Nature for $700 Million," *New York Times* (11 March 1991): 1, 8; Marjory Stoneman Douglas, *The Everglades: River of Grass*, rev. ed., Sarasota, Fla.: Pineapple Press, 1988; and Marjory Stoneman Douglas, "Still Fighting the Good Fight for the Everglades," *Audubon* 93, no. 4 (July–August 1991): 31–37.

11. William L. Thomas Jr., ed., *Man's Role in Changing the Face of the Earth*, Chicago: University of Chicago Press, 1956. See also Clarence J. Glacken, *Traces on the Rhodian Shore: Nature and Culture in Western Thought from Ancient Times to the End of the Eighteenth Century*, Berkeley: University of California Press, 1967. A "classic" account is George Perkins Marsh, *Man and Nature or, Physical Geography Modified by Human Actions*, Cambridge, Mass.: Harvard University Press, 1965 (a reprint of the 1864 edition).

12. Rhoads Murphy, "The Decline of North Africa since the Roman Occupation: Climatic of Human?", *Annals of the American Association of Geographers* 41 (June 1951): 116–32.

13. Glacken, op. cit., n. 5 sup.

14. Gerald Garvey and Lou Ann Garvey, eds., *International Resource Flows*, Lexington, Mass.: Lexington Books/ D.C. Heath, 1977.

15. Efforts to establish a multiple-use mandate for the public lands have been widely regarded as having failed owing to absence of an authoritative criterion for setting priorities. See the Multiple-Use, Sustained Yield Act of 1960, 16 U.S.C. 528-31 (1970), ELR 41406, and the Classification and Multiple-Use Act of 1964, 43 U.S.C. 1411-18 (1970), ELR 41406. Portions of this latter act appeared to have expired in December 1970 but were restored by the Federal Land Policy and Management Act of 1976, the organic act for the Bureau of Land Management (43 U.S.C. 1712). Commenting on the multiple-use concept, Arnold W. Reitz Jr. writes that "The concept of multiple-use both in theory and practice is so vague as to be often meaningless, or worse yet, to have completely different meanings for dozens of its users" and "too vague to offer much policy guidance," *Environmental Planning: Law of Land and Resources*, Washington, D.C.: North American Inter-

national, 1974: Part Six, 4–5. See George R. Hall, "The Myth and Reality of Multiple-Use Forestry," *National Resources Journal* 3 (October 1963): 276–90; D. Michael Harvey, "Public Land Management Under the Classification and Multiple-Use Act," *National Resources Lawyer* (July 1969): 238–49; and Warren A. Starr, "Multiple Land Use Management," *Natural Resources Journal* (November 1961): 288–301; Gilbert F. White, "The Choice of Use in Resource Management," *Natural Resources Journal* (March 1961): 23–40; and Michael D. Bowls and John V. Krutilla, *Multiple-Use Management: The Economics of Public Forestlands*, Washington, D.C.: Resources for the Future, 1989. In its issue of 21 October 1991, *U.S. News and World Report* (page 76) identified at least eight anti-land-use planning coalitions working for multiple-land-use and environmental deregulation, e.g., the National Inholders/Multiple-Use Land Alliance.

16. Robert V. Bartlett, "Reason and Environmental Policy," *Environmental Ethics* 8 (Fall 1987): 221–39, and J.S. Dryzek, *Rational Ecology: Environmental and Political Economy*, Oxford: Basil Blackwell, 1987.

17. There is a significant difference between the uses of ecology in solving environmental (i.e., "scientific problems") and ecology as an instrument of policymaking. For the use of ecology by scientists, see *Ecological Knowledge and Environmental Problem-Solving: Concepts and Case Studies*, Committee on the Applications of Ecological Theory to Environmental Problems, Commission on Life Sciences, National Research Council, Washington, D.C.: National Academy Press, 1986. For a specific example of ecosystems criteria for policy and management see Masters thesis by B. Riley McClelland, *The Ecosystem—A Unifying Concept for the Management of Natural Areas in the National Park System*, Colorado State University, 1968. For a pioneering study see G.A. Hills, *The Ecological Basis for Land-Use Planning*, Research Report No. 46, Toronto: Ontario Department of Lands and Forests, 1961. Also, *Land Classification in the United States: Report of the Land Committee to the National Resources Planning Board*, Washington, D.C.: U.S. Government Printing Office, 1941, and notes 6, 7, and 8, supra. For urban land use, see Richard Register, "Ecopolis Now," *Amicus Journal* 14, no. 2 (Summer 1992): 28–31.

18. For a different and more comprehensive interpretation of the "crisis" concept, see Eric Ashby, *Reconciling Man With the Environment*, Stanford: Stanford University Press, 1978; and Lynton Keith Caldwell, *Between Two Worlds: Science, The Environmental Movement and Policy Choice*, Cambridge: Cambridge University Press, 1990.

19. O.P. Dwivedi, "Man and Nature: A Historic Approach to a Theory of Ecology," *Environmental Professional* 10 (1988): 8–15. Also, Jan Christian Smuts, *Holism and Evolution*, London: Macmillan, 1926.

20. The need for more adequate criteria for policy to remedy the present confusion and contradiction in the laws governing public (government) land was outlined by Irving Sensel, Assistant Director, Bureau of Land Management, U.S. Department of the Interior in a paper, "Public Land Laws and Effective Management," in *Proceedings of the 10th Annual Western Resources Conference*, Fort Collins: Colorado State University, July 1–3, 1968.

21. For a prospective view, see William Ophuls and Stephen Boyan Jr., *Ecology and the Politics of Scarcity Revisited: The Unraveling of the American Dream*, New York: W.H. Freeman, 1992.

22. Thomas, op. cit., note 11 supra.

23. René Dubos, *Man Adapting*, New Haven: Yale University Press, 1965.

24. John B. Calhoun, *The Ecology and Sociology of the Norway Rat*, Bethesda, Md.: U.S. Dept. of Health, Education and Welfare, U.S. Public Health Service, 1963.

25. An impressive documentation of evidence to this effect was assembled by the Conference on the Ecological Aspects of International Development, Warrenton, Virginia, December 8–11, 1968. A published volume containing the papers and proceedings of this conference was edited by John P. Milton of the Conservation Foundation and M. Faghi Farvar of the Center for the Biology of Natural Systems, Washington University. See *The Careless Technology: Ecology and International Development*, New York: Natural History Press, 1972.

26. For a powerful description of this tragedy, see Alison Jolly, *A World Like Our Own: Man and Nature in Madagascar*, New Haven: Yale University Press, 1980.

27. I regard the expression "environmental fascism" as an inaccurate and misleading expression. It is an inappropriate term for identifying attitudes that its users deplore. But see Tom Regan, *The Case for Animal Rights*, Berkeley: University of California Press, 1983, p. 262; and Paul Taylor, *Respect for Nature*, Princeton, New Jersey: Princeton University Press, 1986, p. 118. See also Mark Schapiro, "Browns and Greens: Europe's Eco-Fascist," *Amicus Journal* 14, no. 1 (Winter 1992): 6–7; But also see responses to Schapiro in *Amicus Journal* 14, no. 2 (Summer 1992): 3.

28. *Science* 162 (13 December 1968): 1243–48. The population versus land issue has also been forcefully stated by Paul B. Sears in "The Inexorable Problem of Space," *Science* 127 (3 January 1958) and by George Macinko in "Saturation: A Problem Evaded in Planning Land Use," *Science* 149 (30 July 1965).

29. The impact of the closed-system reality on politics and economics has been effectively described by Kenneth Boulding in "The Economics of the Coming Spaceship Earth," in Henry Jarrett, ed., *Environmental Quality in a Growing Economy*, Baltimore: John Hopkins Press for Resources for the Future, 1966, pp. 3–14.

30. Ronald Inglehart, *Cultural Shift in Advanced Industrial Society*, Princeton: Princeton University Press, 1989.

31. See published writings by B. Bruce Briggs, Dixie Lee Ray, Julian Simon, and William Tucker. For example, an article by Bruce-Briggs, "Needless Fuss About Land Use," *The Alternative* (June–July 1976).

32. Garrett Eckbo, *Public Landscape: Six Essays on Government and Environmental Design in the San Francisco Bay Area*, Berkeley: University of California, Institute of Governmental Studies, 1978.

33. Lynton K. Caldwell, "Law and Land: The Ecology and Sociology of Land Use Planning" in Richard N.L. Andrews, ed., *Land In America: Com-*

modity Or Natural Resource, Lexington, Mass.: Lexington Books/ D.C. Heath, 1979.

34. See Michael E. Soulé, "Land Use Planning and Wildlife Maintenance: Guidelines for Conserving Wildlife in an Urban Landscape," *Journal of the American Planning Association* 57, no. 3 (Summer 1971): 313–21. See also *Putting Wildlife First: Recommendations for Reforming Our Troubled Refuge System: Report of the Commission on New Directions for the National Wildlife Refuge System*, Washington, D.C.: Defenders of Wildlife, 1992.

35. George Sarton, *A Guide to the History of Science: A First Guide for the Study of the History of Science With Introductory Essays on Science and Tradition*, Waltham, Mass.: Chronica Botanica, 1952, p. 54.

Chapter 10

The author is grateful to philosophers Sara Ketchum and Bryan Norton for criticisms of an early draft and to biologists Robert Colwell and Earl McCoy for detailed, constructive criticisms.

1. See R.P. McIntosh, *The Background of Ecology: Concept and Theory*, Cambridge: Cambridge University Press, 1985, pp. 289–323; hereafter cited as: Background.

2. Paul Taylor, *Respect for Nature*, Princeton: Princeton University Press, 1986, p. 299; hereafter cited as: Taylor, Respect.

3. See K. Shrader-Frechette and E. McCoy, *Method in Ecology*, Cambridge: Cambridge University Press, 1993, esp. chs. 2–3; hereafter cited as: Shrader-Frechette and McCoy, ME, see also Richard Watson, "A Critique of Anti-Anthropocentric Biocentrism," *Environmental Ethics* 5, no. 3 (Fall 1983): 252–56.

4. See Taylor, Respect, p. 49, and E.O. Wilson, *Sociobiology: The New Synthesis*, Cambridge: Harvard University Press, 1975. For a criticism of the attempt to use biological findings as a guide to life, see Michael Ruse, *Sociobiology: Sense or Nonsense*, Dordrecht: Reidel, 1979, esp. chapter 9.

5. In part, U.S. scientists' views of their ethical responsibilities regarding environmental policy have been a result of the passage of the U.S. National Environmental Policy Act of 1969 (NEPA). This act gave ecologists a role somewhat like that of engineering scientists who provide information to policy makers so that they can do what is right. See S.I. Auerbach, "Ecology, Ecologists, and the E.S.A.," *Ecology* 53, no. 2 (Spring 1972): 205–6; W. Van Winkle et al., "Two Roles of Ecologists in Defining and Determining the Acceptability of Environmental Impacts," *International Journal of Environmental Studies* 9 (1976): 247–54; G. Suter, "Ecosystem Theory and NEPA Assessment," *Bulletin of the Ecological Society of America* 62, no. 3 (1981): 186–92; hereafter cited as: NEPA. See also Mark Sagoff, "Fact and Value in Environmental Science," *Environmental Ethics* 7, no. 2 (Summer 1985): 100; hereafter cited as: Sagoff, Fact.; see also Nelkin citation in the next note.

In addition to NEPA, a number of environmental laws also presuppose this ecologist-as-expert view. They speak of the "health" and "balance" of ecosystems and leave it to ecologists to define such concepts in scientific terms. For example, the Marine Protection, Research, and Sanctuaries Act of 1972 enjoins the nation to preserve the "health of the oceans." The Federal Water Pollution Control Act of 1972, likewise, requires polluters to demonstrate that their effluents are such that they "assure the protection and propagation of a balanced, indigenous population of shellfish, fish, and wildlife." (Quoted by Sagoff, Fact, p. 101.)

6. See, for example, D.B. Botkin, "Can There Be a Theory of Global Ecology?", *Journal of Theoretical Biology* 96 (1982): 95; hereafter cited as: Botkin, Theory; L.B. Slobodkin, "Aspects of the Future of Ecology," *Bioscience* 18, no. 1 (January 1968): 16; see also D. Nelkin, "Ecologists and the Public Interest," *Hastings Center Report* 6 (February 1976): 38–44; hereafter cited as: Nelkin, Ecologists.

7. See, for example, R.F. Noss, "Dangerous Simplifications in Conservation Biology," *Bulletin of the Ecological Society of America* 67, no. 4 (December 1986): 278–79. See also J. Diamond, "The Design of a Nature Reserve System for Indonesian New Guinea," in *Conservation Biology*, ed. M.E. Soulé, Sunderland, Mass.: Sinauer, 1986, pp. 485–503; hereafter cited as: Soulé, CB. See also T.E. Lovejoy, R.O. Bierregaard, et al., "Edge and Other Effects of Isolation on Amazon Forest Fragments," in Soulé, CB, pp. 257–85, and M.E. Soulé, "Land Use Planning and Wildlife Maintenance," *Journal of American Institute of Planners* 57, no. 3 (Summer 1991): 313–22.

8. D.W. Schindler, H. Kling, et al., "Eutrophication of Lake 227 by Addition of Phosphate and Nitrate: the Second, Third, and Fourth Years of Enrichment, 1970, 1971, and 1972," *Journal of the Fisheries Research Board of Canada* 30, no. 10 (1973): 1415–40.

9. Cooper claimed that ecologists were responsible for the discovery that coastal wetlands support high levels of both primary and second production of fish. This discovery, he said, formed the basis for the Coastal Zone Management Act of 1972 and for state environmental legislation to protect coastal wetlands. (Arthur Cooper, "Why Doesn't Anyone Listen to Ecologists—and What Can ESA Do About It?", *Bulletin of the Ecological Society of America* 63, no. 4 (December 1982): 348; hereafter cited as: Cooper, Why.)

10. Cooper, Why, pp. 348–49.

11. Sagoff, Fact, p. 99.

12. See preceding note. Philosophers, naturalists, and policy makers such as Rolston, Leopold, Shepard, and McKinley maintain that the science of ecology provides us with a model to follow in the domain of environmental ethics. (See H. Rolston, "Is There an Ecological Ethic?", *Ethics* 85, no. 2 (1975): 93–109 (reprinted in *Ethics and the Environment*, ed. T. Attig and D. Scherer, Englewood Cliffs, N.J.: Prentice-Hall, 1983; hereafter cited as: EE, with page citations to the 1983 reprint); Aldo Leopold, *A Sand County Almanac*, New York: Oxford University Press, 1966; hereafter cited as: SCA;

and Paul Shepard and Daniel McKinley (eds.), *The Subversive Science: Essays Toward an Ecology of Man*, Boston: Houghton Mifflin, 1969. See also C. Little, "In a Landscape of Hope," *Wilderness* 48, no. 168 (1985): 21–30; E. Partridge, "Are We Ready for an Ecological Morality?", *Environmental Ethics* 4, no. 2 (1982): 175–90; and J.B. Callicott (ed.), *A Companion to the Sand County Almanac*, Madison: University of Wisconsin Press, 1987; hereafter cited as: Companion.

13. See Taylor, Respect, pp. 47–58, for criticisms of these two views.

14. Rolston, EE, pp. 42–46.

15. Thomas B. Colwell claims that "The balance of nature provides an objective normative model which can be utilized as the ground of human value." (Rolston, EE, p. 45.) See also Mark Sagoff, "On Preserving the Natural Environment," in D. Scherer and T. Attig, Englewood Cliffs, N.J.: Prentice-Hall, 1983, p. 28; hereafter cited as: OP.

16. Philosopher Paul Taylor presupposes one version of the "balance presupposition" when he argues that we ought to preserve ecological integrity. (Taylor, Respect, p. 299.)

17. Likewise philosopher Bryan Norton adopts another variant of "the balance presupposition" when he argues that we have an ethical obligation to pursue preservationism, which he characterizes in terms of maximizing "dynamic stability." Bryan G. Norton, "Conservation and Preservation: A Conceptual Rehabilitation," unpublished essay, pp. 29–31. See also Bryan Norton, *The Spice of Life: Why Save Natural Variety?*, Princeton: Princeton University Press, 1987, chapters 2, 4; hereafter cited as: Spice. See R. Lewontin, "The Meaning of Stability," in *Diversity and Stability in Ecological Systems*, ed. G. Woodwell and H. Smith, Brookhaven, N.Y.: Brookhaven Laboratory Publication No. 22, 1969. See also D. Futuyma, "Community Structure and Stability in Constant Environments," *American Naturalist* 107 (1973): 443–46; G. Innis, "Stability, Sensitivity, Resilience, Persistence. What is of Interest?", in *Ecosystem Analysis and Prediction*, ed. S. Levin, Philadelphia: Society for Industrial and Applied Mathematics, 1974, pp. 131–39; hereafter cited as: Levin, SS; L. Wu, "On the Stability of Ecosystems," in Levin, SS, pp. 155–65; D.L. De Angelis, "Stability and Connectance in Food Web Models," *Ecology* 56 (1975): 238–43; and K. Shrader-Frechette and E. McCoy, ME, chapter 2.

There are three kinds of diversity in ecology (alpha, beta, gamma), and many types of stability have been postulated. For some of the most famous discussions of trophic and community stability, see R. MacArthur, "Fluctuations of Animal Populations, and a Measure of Community Stability," *Ecology* 36 (1955): 533–36; hereafter cited as: Fluctuations; G.E. Hutchison, "Homage to Santa Rosalia, or Why Are There So Many Kinds of Animals?", *American Naturalist* 93 (1954): 145–59; C. Elton, *The Ecology of Invasions by Animals and Plants*, London: Methuen, 1958, pp. 143–53; Daniel Goodman, "The Theory of Diversity-Stability Relationships in Ecology," *The Quarterly Review of Biology* 50 (1975): 237–66; hereafter cited as: Theory. The MacArthur-Hutchison notion of diversity-stability, however, was challenged by authors such as May and Connell (see note 33). See also

McIntosh, Background, pp. 187, 252–56; and Donald Worster, *Nature's Economy: The Roots of Ecology*, San Francisco: Sierra Club Books, 1977, chapter 15, for a discussion of holism and stability in the development of ecology.

18. For an account of the holism-versus-reductionism controversy in ecology, see R.P. McIntosh, Background, pp. 252–56.

19. Rolston claims that nature "has been enriching the ecosystem," and that we should get in gear with nature, which is maximizing ecosystemic excellences (Rolston, EE, pp. 53–54).

20. Sagoff appeals to the holism presupposition when he enjoins us to preserve nature for its own sake (Sagoff, OP, p. 27), as if the whole of nature were a living organism had interests of its own.

21. Rolston, EE, pp. 46–54, esp. pp. 52–54. See also note 12.

22. J.E. Lovelock, *Gaia*, New York: Oxford University Press, 1979; hereafter cited as: Gaia.

23. K. Goodpaster, "On Being Morally Considerable," in *Ethics and the Environment*, ed. T. Attig and D. Scherer, Englewood Cliffs, N.J.: Prentice-Hall, 1983, p. 39; hereafter cited as: OB. Attig and Scherer hereafter cited as: Attig and Scherer, EAE.

24. Goodpaster's move here is a more sophisticated version of what Leopold did years earlier. Leopold claimed that because the earth is indivisible and its parts are interdependent, it is a living organism. (A. Leopold, "Conservation as a Moral Issue," in Attig and Scherer, EAE, pp. 139–49. See also Lovelock, Gaia.)

25. B. Callicott, "Animal Liberation: A Triangular Affair" in Attig and Scherer, EAE, pp. 61–62; hereafter cited as: AL.

26. "Ecological entitlement" refers to the fact that natural beings are part of living biotic processes in ecosystems. Callicott claims that we are bound by our moral theories to do whatever maximizes ecosystemic excellence (Callicott, AL, p. 68).

27. P. Taylor, for example, urges us to "preserve ecological integrity" (Taylor, Respect, p. 299) but he never tells us what ecological integrity is. For criticisms of the balance presupposition, see Shrader-Frechette and McCoy, ME, ch. 2.

28. Taylor, for example, denies that ecology can inform environmental ethics (Taylor, Respect, p. 8). For an example of calls for "pluralistic theoretical treatments," see G. Cooper, "The Explanatory Tools of Theoretical Population Biology," *PSA 1990*, vol. 1, ed. A. Fine, M. Forbes, and L. Wessels, East Lansing, Mich.: Philosophy of Science Association, 1990, pp. 165–78.

29. See Sagoff, Fact, pp. 107–10, and Taylor, Respect, p. 8.

30. Sagoff, Fact, p. 109; and M. Sagoff, "Environmental Science and Environmental Law," College Park, Md.: Center for Philosophy and Public Policy, March 1985, unpublished essay, p. 8; hereafter cited as: ES.

31. See works by May, Levins, and Connell cited in note 33; see also Sagoff, Fact, p. 109, and McIntoch, Background, pp. 187–88.

32. See, for example, U.S. Congress, Senate, *Congressional Record*, 93rd

Congress, First Session, 119 (24 July 1973): 25668; B. Commoner, *The Closing Circle*, New York: Knopf, 1971, p. 38; and N. Myers, *A Wealth of Wild Species*, Boulder, Colo.: Westview Press, 1983. For evidence of the way ecologists have cast doubt on the thesis, see Sagoff, Fact, p. 107. See also R.T. Paine, "A Note on Trophic Complexity and Community Stability," *American Naturalist* 103 (1969): 91–93; R. Lewin, "Fragile Forests Implied by Pleistocene Data," *Science* 226 (1984): 36–37; R.M. May, *Stability and Complexity in Model Ecosystems*, Princeton: Princeton University Press, 1973; R. Levins, "The Qualitative Analysis of Partially Specified Systems," *Annals of the New York Academy of Sciences* 231 (1974): 123–38; J.H. Connell, "Diversity in Tropical Rain Forests and Coral Reefs," *Science* 199 (1978): 1302–10; Daniel Goodman, "The Theory of Diversity-Stability Relationships in Ecology," *The Quarterly Review of Biology* 50, no. 3 (September 1975): 237–66. See also M.E. Soulé, "Conservation Biology and the 'Real World'," in Soulé, CB, pp. 6–7, and R.P. McIntosh, Background, pp. 142. See B. Norton, *Why Preserve Natural Variety?* Princeton: Princeton University Press, 1988, and B. Norton (ed.), *The Preservation of Species*, Princeton: Princeton University Press, 1986. B. Norton also expressed his views about his variant of the diversity-stability hypothesis in a phone conversation with K. Shrader-Frechette on Friday, December 13, 1985. Norton's variant of the *ecosystemic* diversity-stability hypothesis, however, fares no better than earlier versions because concepts like succession cannot be operationalized. For him to maintain that diverse and mature ecosystems are hence stable is to assume (1) that there is a pattern by means of which ecosystems proceed toward maturity, even though he cannot state what it is, and (2) that there is some neutral way to define a *mature* ecosystem.

33. See note 41 and Taylor, Respect.

34. Paul Taylor clearly recognizes this point, since he argues that natural ecosystems provide the criteria for human actions regarding the environment (Paul Taylor, Respect, pp. 4–6; 81, 85, 174–76). Note, however, that Taylor also claims that ecology provides no help to environmental ethics (Taylor, Respect, p. 8). Following the principle that nature knows best, even when it eliminates species, Taylor also consistently argues that humans have no obligations to rescue or restore species diminished by nature (Taylor, Respect, pp. 50, 52, esp. 177). What follows, if Taylor and I are reasoning correctly, is that it may well be impossible to argue consistently that "nature knows best" and yet to argue (as many environmentalists do) for giving species more protection than nature herself gives them. For philosophical arguments in favor of environmental protection, see note 33 and K. Shrader-Frechette, "Island Biogeography, Species-Area Curves, and Statistical Errors," *PSA 1990*, vol. 1, ed. M. Forbes, A. Fine, and L. Wessels, East Lansing, Mich.: Philosophy of Science Association, 1990, pp. 447–56.

35. Imagine how difficult the practice of medicine would be if medical doctors, instead of taking as their goal the survival of the individual patient, had to take as their goal, the health or well-being of the entire system of which the individual was a member. Once their criteria for medical action became societal or global, rather than based on the Hippocratic Oath and an

individual patient's well-being and rights, then medical doctors would face some of the same problems ecologists face in attempting to use the balance presupposition to dictate particular environmental policies.

36. See notes 24–26.

37. For discussion of the philosophical notion of "interest," see J. Feinberg, "The Rights of Animals and Unborn Generations," in *Philosophy and Environmental Crisis*, ed. W.T. Blackstone, Athens: University of Georgia Press, 1977, pp. 49–51; and W. Frankena, "Ethics and the Environment," in *Ethics and the Problems of the 21st Century*, ed. K. Goodpaster and K. Sayre, Notre Dame: University of Notre Dame Press, 1979, p. 11; hereafter cited as: Goodpaster, Ethics, and Frankena, Ethics.

38. An ecosystem, as a whole, is not a living thing; since it is not, it is unclear how it could either have interests or be a beneficiary. See John Rodman, "The Liberation of Nature," *Inquiry* 20 (1977): 91, for an analysis of the view known as sentientism, that it is only possible to benefit or harm a conscious, sentient human being. See also Taylor, Respect, p. 18.

39. See P. Singer, *Animal Liberation*, New York: Avon, 1977, p. 8; hereafter cited as: Singer, AL. See J. Heffernan, "The Land Ethic: A Critical Appraisal," *Environmental Ethics* 4, no. 3 (1982): 235–47, and B. Callicott, "Animal Liberation," *Environmental Ethics* 2, no. 4 (1980): 311-336, who argues against Singer's view.

40. Even if assigning interests to ecosystems or organic wholes somehow made sense, Singer points out that we would begin using the term "interest" in a very nonphilosophical, loose sense (P. Singer, "Not for Humans Only," in Goodpaster, Ethics, pp. 194–95ff.). Moreover, our obligations to meet such interests would multiply to preposterous and counterintuitive levels. Also, we do not typically accord rights or interests to beings, even human beings, who have no possibility of being sentient. This suggests that it might be difficult for Leopold and others to argue that ecosystems have interests and are members of our moral community, even though we do not consider living, breathing, brain-dead humans as having interests and as being members of our moral community. See H.K. Beecher, Report of the "Ad Hoc" Committee of the Harvard Medical School to Examine the Definition of Brain Death, "A Definition of Irreversible Coma," *Journal of the American Medical Association* 205 (5 August 1968): 85–88.

41. One example, already mentioned in chapter 3, of a biocentric or ecocentric land ethics that prescribes when to give priority to human interests and when to give primacy to environmental concerns is K. Shrader-Frechette, "A Philosophic Basis for Ecocentric Ethics," *Earth Ethics Report* 1, no. 1 (December 1991): 25–31; K. Shrader-Frechette and E. McCoy, ME; and K. Shrader-Frechette, "Ethics and the Environment," *World Health Forum* 12 (1991): 311–21; hereafter cited as: EAE.

42. Frankena, Ethics, makes a similar point.

43. T. Regan, *The Case for Animal Rights*, Berkeley: University of California Press, 1983, p. 262, uses the term "environmental fascism." See Taylor, Respect, p. 118, who makes a similar criticism of Leopold and Rolston, both of whom hold organicist views; he says that they give no place to the

good of the individual. Several thinkers, among them Holmes Rolston, have attempted to respond to the charge of "environmental fascism." (See H. Rolston, "Duties to Ecosystems," in Callicott, Companion.)

44. See Garrett Hardin, "Living on a Lifeboat," *Bioscience* 24 (October 1974): 561–68.

45. See P. Fritzell, "The Conflicts of Ecological Conscience," in Callicott, Companion. On a more general level, environmental philosophers face a similar problem when they argue for "species impartiality" and for a nonhierarchical view of nature, yet maintain that humans have special rights and duties to the environment and to nonhumans. See Taylor, Respect, pp. 45–46, 225–26, 246, 259, 281–82. They can't have it both ways and yet remain consistent.

46. See Shrader-Frechette and McCoy, ME, ch. 2. See Norton, Spice, chapter 4, section 2; see also MacArthur, Fluctuations, and Goodman, Theory, p. 239. See also K. Shrader-Frechette, "Organismic Biology and Ecosystems Ecology," in *Current Issues in Teleology*, ed. N. Rescher, Pittsburgh: Center for Philosophy of Science, 1985, pp. 77–92, for difficulties with the ecosystem concept.

47. The main reason for this peculiarity is that different camps of ecologists would probably claim that different units ought to be maximized.

48. This is the response that many community ecologists would probably make.

49. Ecologists who follow Clements are likely to make this claim. See McIntosh, Background, pp. 44,79, 107.

50. McIntosh, Background, pp. 228, 252–56.

51. B. Norton, "Environmental Ethics and the Rights of Nonhumans," *Environmental Ethics* 4 (1982): 17–36, raises a similar point. See McIntosh, Background, for a discussion of community ecology (pp. 69–146, 263–67), population ecology (pp. 146–93), and ecosystems ecology (193–242).

52. Many ecologists follow the Platonic, holistic paradigm of reifying and studying organic entities like ecosystems, while others follow the nominalistic and reductionistic paradigm of examining the individual or the species, and refrain from creating higher-level holistic entities such as ecosystems. Neither side has won acceptance, but most of the predictive power is on the side of the reductionists, despite the fact that advances are possible through holistic approaches. McIntosh, Background, pp. 126ff., 157ff., 181-182ff. and 252; see K. Shrader-Frechette, "Organismic Biology and Ecosystems Ecology," in *Current Issues in Teleology*, ed. N. Rescher, Pittsburgh: University of Pittsburgh Center for the Philosophy of Science, 1986, pp. 77-92; hereafter cited as: Biology. For information on density dependence, see D. Strong, "Density Vagueness: Abiding the Variance in the Demography of Real Populations," in *Community Ecology*, ed. J. Diamond and T. Case, New York: Harper and Row, 1986.

53. I am grateful to R. Colwell of the Biology Department of the University of California, Berkeley, and to D. Botkin of the Biology Department at the University of California, Santa Barbara, for discussions of natural selection and adaptation.

54. Rather than that each species adapts to the present environment, Lovelock (Gaia, pp. 109, 127–28) claimed that whole ecosystems, as well as individual species, adapt. Despite such assertions, he maintained that he assumed that the "world evolves through Darwinian natural selection" (Lovelock, Gaia, p. 127).

55. According to neo-Darwinian theory, an organism possesses heritable traits because of genes it carries; which genes it transmits to its progeny are determined by random processes taking place during division and fertilization of the sex cells, not by the effects that the genes produce in the organism carrying them or in its offspring and not by the effects that the genes are alleged to produce in the ecosystem. To presuppose otherwise is to confuse environmental poetry with biological science. In sum: flamingoes didn't get their long legs by trying; Darwin didn't welcome the maker of Paley's famous watch; and ecosystems didn't go through successions of species by "desiring" excellence. See Shrader-Frechette, Biology.

56. Thanks to Sara Ketchum for this example. See note 58.

57. McIntosh, Background, p. 193. Ecosystems ecology is allegedly empirical, but the ecosystemic entity about which it centers is not defined clearly.

58. What pattern of excellence is it which an ecosystem maximizes? Ecologists cannot answer the question. Theorists such as Diamond and Gilpin, following MacArthur, claim that interspecific competition is a major factor in patterning natural processes of ecosystems. Other ecologists, such as Simberloff and Strong, argue that the Diamond and Gilpin theories are untestable. (See M. Cody and J. Diamond (eds.), *Ecology and the Evolution of Communities*, Cambridge, Mass.: Harvard University Press, 1975; D. Strong and D. Simberloff (eds.), *Ecological Communities*, Princeton: Princeton University Press, 1984; especially M. Gilpin and J. Diamond, "Are Species Co-occurrences...?", in *Ecological Communities*, ed. D. Strong et al., Princeton: Princeton University Press, 1984, pp. 298–315. See also note 73.) Moreover, the evolutionary foundations of ecology seem to suggest that many, many different happenings in ecosystems might be stable, integral, and balanced. It is not clear that there is a moral reason, short of human welfare, to prefer one temporal arrangement or stability over another. One scientist claims that competition has survived as an hypothesis merely because it fits in with our notions of homeostasis and the balance of nature. (R. Lewin, "Santa Rosalia Was a Goat," *Science* 221 (12 August 1983): 636–39.) See also K. Shrader-Frechette, "Interspecific Competition, Evolutionary Epistemology, and Ecology," *Evolution, Cognition, and Realism*, ed. N. Rescher, New York: University Press of America, 1990, pp. 47–61.

59. See Sagoff, Fact, p. 104.

60. Sagoff, Fact, p. 107. See, for example, S.W. Nixon, "Between Coastal Marshes and Coastal Waters," in *Ecological Processes in Coastal and Marine Systems*, ed. R.J. Livingston, New York: Plenum Press, 1979, pp. 437–525; see also Mark Sagoff, "Environmental Science and Environmental Law," College Park, Md.: Center for Philosophy and Public Policy, March 1985, esp. pp. 5ff.

61. Quoted in McIntosh, Background, p. 321.

62. Not only do ecologists now believe that wetlands do not supply nutrients for estuarine production, as Odum and others presupposed, and that more diverse ecosystems often are unstable, but they have rejected other hypotheses as well. One example is the frequent environmentalist claim that persistent pollutants such as DDT and PCBs concentrate and accumulate along the food chain, leading to biomagnification. (See K. Shrader-Frechette, *Environmental Ethics*, Pacific Grove, Calif.: Boxwood Press, 1991, pp. 294–301.)

63. Although the biomagnification hypothesis has now been largely dismissed, it was used for several decades as an argument against the use of persistent organochloride pesticides. (See Sagoff, Fact, p. 110; see E. Hunt and A. Bischoff, "Inimical Effects on Wildlife of Periodic DDD Application to Clear Lake," *California Fish and Game* 46 (1960): 91–106, for a tentative statement of the hypothesis. See F. Moriarty, *Ecotoxicology*, New York: Academic Press, 1983, pp. 135–54, for a review of the literature leading to the demise of this hypothesis.)

A number of policy makers and scientists have pointed to the failure of ecology to provide clear directives for decisionmaking. They have claimed that ecology "has not been able to deliver the facts, understanding, and predictions" needed for environmental reform. (R. Carpenter, "Ecology in Court," *Natural Resources Lawyer* 15, no. 3 (1983): 573–95; see also 44 *Federal Register* 71456 (December 11, 1979); S. Levin and M. Harwell, M., "Environmental Risks Associated with the Release of Genetically Engineered Organisms," *Genewatch* 2, no. 1: 15; Suter, NEPA; W. Murdoch and J. Connell, "The Ecologist's Role and the Nonsolution of Technology," in *Ecocide—and Thoughts Towards Survival*, ed. Clifton Fadiman and Jean White, Santa Barbara, California: Center for the Study of Democratic Institutions, 1971, p. 57; Cooper, Why; and M. Sagoff, "What Ecology Can Do," unpublished essay, 1986.)

64. The controversy focused on the potential environmental impacts of Consolidated Edison's proposed Cornwell Project, a pumped-storage facility to be built on a mountain overlooking the Hudson valley. At the focus of the debate was the potential impact of the facility's water withdrawals on the Hudson River striped-bass population. (L.W. Barnthouse et al., "Population Biology in the Courtroom: the Hudson River Controversy," *BioScience* 34, no. 1 (January 1984): 17–18. The classic Hudson River case suggests that ecologists may influence public policy, but that their influence derives largely from appeals to their authority, rather than from empirical evidence for their specific claims. Ecology simply cannot come up with specific, practical claims, in many cases, because the science does not yet have a hold on the underlying natural processes that allegedly support some balance of nature or some holistic, ecosystemic maximization of excellence.

65. See Mark Sagoff, "On Explanation in Ecology," unpublished manuscript, 1986, p. 17; hereafter cited as: Explanation.

66. Scientists often are not even sure which factors are relevant to un-

derstanding the problem. (Cooper, Why, p. 350. See also McIntosh, pp. 247, 249, 268, 273–74, 278, 284.)

67. Most environmental impact statements are forced to employ data bases that are inadequate (a) because of the lack of complete resource inventories (e.g., soils, vegetations, fauna), even for federal lands, (b) because of the lack of knowledge about the state of environmental variables such as air and water, and (c) because of the lack of knowledge of process phenomena such as physiology, population, and functioning of ecosystems. (See Cooper, Why, pp. 350–51.)

68. Some ecologists, for example, claim that stressed ecosystems are less resistant to additional stress than unstressed ones, and they substantiate this claim with the observation that bark beetles invade oxidant-weakened pines; meanwhile, however, they often ignore masses of counterexamples. This allows other ecologists to promote the inverse claim, that stressed systems are more resistant to added stress than unstressed ones. (This example is from Suter, NEPA, p. 186.)

69. See D. Simberloff, "The Sick Science of Ecology," *Eidema* 1, no. 1 (1981), and T.W. Poole, "Periodic, Pseudoperiodic, and Chaotic Population Fluctuations," *Ecology* 58 (1977): 210–13. See also McIntosh, Background, pp. 249, 269–70, 273, 284.

70. This is what happened with acceptance of the diversity-stability view, the estuarine production view, and the food-chain biomagnification view, all of which were accepted for decades without any real testing. (See Sagoff, Fact, pp. 110–11.)

71. See D.S. Simberloff, "Competition Theory, Hypothesis Testing, and Other Community Ecological Buzzwords," *American Naturalist* 122 (1983): 626–35.

72. See, for example, R.H. Peters, "Tautology in Evolution and Ecology," *The American Naturalist* 110, no. 971 (January–February 1976): 1–12. See also the previous note. Although there are some deficiencies in Peters' account, nevertheless his basic point, that ecologists need to use null models, remains sound. See also R.H. Peters, *A Critique for Ecology*, Cambridge: Cambridge University Press, 1991; hereafter cited as: Peters, Ecology.

73. See note 71.

74. See Suter, NEPA, p. 186, who makes this point; see also McIntosh, Background, pp. 244, 268. For an analysis of when use of criteria of simplicity might be desirable in ecology and population biology, see Richard Levins, "The Structure of Model Building in Population Biology," *American Scientist* 54, no. 4 (December 1966): 421–31.

75. See E. Johnson, "Animal Liberation Versus the Land Ethic," *Environmental Ethics* 3, no. 3 (1981), and A. Desmond, *The Ape's Reflexion*, New York: James Wade, 1979.

76. One ecologist affirms, "ecosystems are rarely if ever at equilibrium. They are continually being perturbed . . . and are therefore in a permanently unstable state. . . . If they ever did come to equilibrium I don't think we would like them very much. The reason is that, in coming to equilibrium, the rich ecosystems we see today would inevitably lose many of their spe-

cies." (Roger Lewin, "In Ecology, Change Brings Stability," *Science* 234 (28 November 1986): 1072.)

77. Continuing along a similar vein, another scientist claimed that the threat of habitat destruction and pollution derives primarily from direct impacts rather than from loss of system stability. (R.E. Ricklefs, "Community Diversity: Relative Roles of Local and Regional Processes," *Science* 235 (9 January 1987): 171; hereafter cited as: CD.)

78. R.E. Ricklefs, CD, 167. Or as another researcher put it: one can present numerous criticisms of any "test" using natural systems, because each is literally unique. Hence a single field study is not enough to falsify or to support an ecological hypothesis. (See Amyan Macfadyen, "Some Thoughts on the Behaviour of Ecologists," *Journal of Animal Ecology* 44, no. 2 (June 1975): 351.)

79. Ecological equations and models tend to be extremely sensitive to small increments, for example, in the value of r; this means that a slight error, even to the second decimal point, may yield an outcome vastly different from the correct one. For this reason, it is difficult to establish the correctness of the equations in the first place. (See Sagoff, Explanation, p. 18.)

80. The existence of these difficulties suggests that ecologists need to pay careful attention to their techniques and to the methodological presuppositions underlying them. It also suggests that a healthy antidote for what has been called "theological ecology" is an increased emphasis on field experimentation and testability. (See E.C. Pielou, "The Usefulness of Ecological Models: A Stock-Taking," *The Quarterly Review of Biology* 56, no. 1 (March 1981): 17–31; Suter, NEPA, p. 189.)

81. Apart from the scientific reasons for emphasizing the testability of ecological hypotheses, it is also politically important for them to be scientifically sound, especially if decisionmakers and ethicists attempt to use ecological findings as the basis for public and environmental policy. (Cooper, Why, p. 351.)

82. At the level of case-by-case decision making, general ecological statements, like "don't exceed the carrying capacity," are only a little more useful to the person doing environmental ethics than is the dictum "do good and avoid evil" to the person doing normative ethics. In both cases, real problems arise at the level of interpreting exactly what ought to count as good, and exactly what level is the carrying capacity.

83. The vampire bat and red scale examples are taken from Daniel Simberloff, "Can Basic Ecology Guide Environmental Policy?" an address given at the University of Florida, December 11, 1986. This information is also in G.H. Orians, Chair, Committee on the Applications of Ecological Theory to Environmental Problems, Commission on Life Sciences, National Research Council, *Ecological Knowledge and Environmental Problem-Solving*, Washington, D.C.: National Academy Press, 1986, pp. 151–90; hereafter cited as: Orians, EKEP.

See R.H. Peters, "From Natural History to Ecology," *Perspectives in Biology and Medicine* 23, no. 2 (Winter 1980): 197ff., and his account of the transformations of phosphorus in lakes; this is a good example of the precise, empirical sort of work at which ecologists can be quite successful. See also R.H. Peters, Ecology.

84. This example is from Sagoff, Facts, p. 101. For the National Academy of Sciences report, see Orians, EKEP, esp. p. 1.

85. See Sagoff, Fact, p. 103, for the management/protection distinction.

86. See Sagoff, Fact, p. 111.

87. McIntosh writes: "It is unfortunate that the demand for theoretical ecological insights with which to support rhetorical ecology [ecology at the service of environmental ethics and policy] comes at a time when ecology is in a condition sometimes described as...confusion. The press in recent decades to produce a theoretical ecology has coincided with a multiplicity of theoretical ecologies philosophically and methodologically at odds with each other." All schools have failed to provide the hoped-for predictive capacity for ecology. (McIntosh, Background, p. 321.)

88. This is what Bryan Norton argues in one of his arguments in his book, *The Spice of Life*. (Norton, Spice.)

89. Such a mitigation would not require that we be able to predict the effects of certain environmental actions, but merely that we work out details, perhaps on a benefit-cost scheme, of how to mitigate adverse impacts. (See Barnthouse et al., in note 64. See also Sagoff, ES, pp. 14–55.)

90. Just as we ought to avoid begging the question that ecology can provide fundamental laws, so also we ought to avoid begging the question that ecology cannot provide fundamental laws. (See Sagoff, Explanation.)

91. R. Colwell, "Natural and Unnatural History," in W. Shea and B. Sitter (eds.), *Scientists and Their Responsibility*, Canton, Mass.: Watson, 1989, pp. 1–40. See also K. Shrader-Frechette and E. McCoy, ME. See note 41.

92. All these points need more justification than can be given here. See Taylor, Respect, who makes them a central theme of his book.

93. R.M. Hare, in *Moral Thinking*, New York: Oxford, 1981, makes the distinction between first-order, or intuitive ethical principles and second-order, or critical ethical principles.

94. For a discussion of strong versus weak rights, see R. Dworkin, *Taking Rights Seriously*, Cambridge, Mass.: Harvard University Press, 1977. See Shrader-Frechette, EAE (1991). See also note 41.

95. The first objection was formulated by Berkeley ecologist Rob Colwell, the second by Colwell and by University of Bern (Switzerland) geographer Bruno Messerli. Philosopher Beat Sitter and attorney Peter Saladin made the third objection, and Saladin made the fourth objection.

96. See note 93.

97. See the Strong reference in note 52. See also M.B. Davis, "Climatic Instability, Time Lags, and Community Disequilibrium," in *Community Ecology*, ed. J. Diamond and T. Case, New York: Harper and Row, 1986, pp. 269–84; hereafter cited as Diamond and Case, CE. See also R.W. Graham, "Response of Mammalian Communities to Environmental Changes During the Late Quaternary," in Diamond and Case, CE, pp. 300–13.

98. Orians, EKEP, pp. 91–92.

Chapter 11

1. George Condon, quoted by W.H. Gould, "A National Land-Use Policy," in R.N. Andrews, *Land in America*, Lexington, Mass.: Lexington Books, 1979, p. 167; hereafter cited as: Andrews.

2. A.M. Honore, "Ownership," in A.G. Guest (ed.), *Oxford Essays in Jurisprudence*, Oxford: Clarendon Press, 1961, pp. 107–47; see also T.C. Grey, "The Disintegration of Property," ed. J. Pennock and J. Chapman, *Property*, Nomos 22, New York: New York University Press, 1980, pp. 69ff.; hereafter cited as: Grey in Nomos. See also D. Large, "This Land is Whose Land? Changing Concepts of Land as Property," *Wisconsin Law Review*, no. 4 (1973): 1039–83.

3. For an analysis of declining productivity, owing to poor land use, see L. Brown, "The Illusion of Progress," L. Brown et al., *State of the World 1990*, New York: Norton, 1990, pp. 3–16; hereafter cited as: Brown 1990 and *World 1990*. See R.G. Healy, "Land Use and the States," in Andrews, pp. 7–23; hereafter cited as: Healy. For discussion of taxation as a form of land-use control, see H. George, *Progress and Poverty*, Garden City, N.Y.: Country Life Press, 1955, pp. 404ff., 422ff. See also H. Daly and J. Cobb, *For the Common Good*, Boston: Beacon Press, 1989; and L.R. Brown and J.E. Young, "Feeding the World in the Nineties," in *World 1990*, pp. 59–78; hereafter cited as: Feeding 1990.

4. L. Durrell, *State of the Ark*, New York: Doubleday, 1986, p. 160. See Lester Brown, "Viewpoint," in C.E. Little, *Land and Food: The Preservation of US Farmland*, Washington, D.C.: American Land Forum, 1979, p. 27. Finally, see C. Mills, "Should We Save the Family Farm?", *Philosophy and Public Policy* 8, no. 3 (Summer 1988): 1–5. For other data on topsoil losses, see L.R. Brown and J.E. Young, Feeding 1990, pp. 61, 64; and L. Brown, C. Flavin, and S. Postel, "Picturing a Sustainable Society," in *World 1990*, p. 184.

5. Thomas Jefferson to Edmund Pendleton, 13 August 1776, in *Papers of Thomas Jefferson*, ed. J. Boyd et al., vol. 1, Princeton: Princeton University Press, 1950, p. 491; and Thomas Jefferson, "A Summary View of the Rights of British America," in *The Portable Thomas Jefferson*, ed. Merrill D. Peterson, New York: Viking Press, 1975, pp. 4–5; hereafter cited as: Portable Jefferson. See also Eugene Hargrove, "Anglo-American Land-Use Attitudes," *Environmental Ethics* 2 (Summer 1980): 131ff.; hereafter cited as: Hargrove.

6. Jefferson to John Jay, 23 August 1785, in Portable Jefferson, p. 384. Jefferson, *Notes on the State of Virginia*, in Portable Jefferson, p. 217. See also Hargrove, pp. 131–38, and Marion Clawson, *The Land System of the United States*, Lincoln: University of Nebraska Press, 1968, pp. 55–66 for a summary of the ways land was given away in the United States.

7. Hargrove, p. 137. For an analysis of Jefferson's views on property rights, see D. Post, "Jeffersonian Revisions of Locke," *Journal of the History of Ideas* 47 (January–March 1986): 147–57.

8. Robert Nozick, *Anarchy, State and Utopia*, New York: Basic, 1974,

esp. chapter 7. For discussion of Madison's views, see the next note. The elitist case against land-use controls has been articulated by B. Bruce-Briggs, *No Land is an Island*, San Francisco: Institute of Contemporary Studies, 1976, and by William Tucker, *Progress and Privilege*, Garden City, N.Y.: Anchor/Doubleday, 1982. For other libertarian approaches, see Rothbard and Block in note 15.

9. See R.W. Bryant, *Land: Private Property, Public Control*, Montreal: Harvest House, 1972, pp. 4–6; hereafter cited as: Bryant. For discussion of Madison's views, see L. Sager, "Property Rights and the Constitution," in *Nomos*, pp. 376–84.

10. The Jefferson quotation is given in R. Schlatter, *Private Property*, New Brunswick, N.J.: Rutgers University Press, 1951, p. 196; hereafter cited as: Schlatter. For discussion of Jefferson's views on property in land, see Schlatter, pp. 195–201, and Hargrove, pp. 131ff.

11. Quoted in Bryant, p. 137. Grey, pp. 73ff.

12. Quoted in F. Whelan, "Property as Artifice," in *Nomos*, pp. 118–19; for brief analyses of Blackstone's views on property, see Whelan, pp. 114–29, and L. Brown, *Conservation and Practical Morality*, New York: St. Martin's Press, 1987, pp. 51–54.

13. Quoted in Bryant, p. 136.

14. Quoted in Bryant, p. 136.

15. For other solutions to problems of air and water pollution, solutions that avoid assigning property rights to air and water, see H.F. French, "Clearing the Air," in *State of the World 1990*, ed. L.R. Brown et al., New York: W.W. Norton, 1990, pp. 112–18, who discusses economic incentives such as the "deposit-refund" system. See also W.J. Baumol and W.E. Oates, *The Theory of Environmental Policy*, New York: Cambridge University Press, 1988, pp. 159–89, who defend effluent fees, rather than marketable emission permits (property rights), for controlling pollution. For related arguments, see D.W. Bromley, *Environment and Economy: Property Rights and Public Policy*, Cambridge, Mass.: Blackwell, 1991. For arguments in favor of the property-rights scheme see, for example, M.N. Rothbard, "Law, Property Rights, and Air Pollution," in *Economics and the Environment: A Reconciliation*, ed. W. Block, Vancouver, B.C.: The Fraser Institute, 1990, pp. 233–80, and W.E. Block, "Environmental Problems, Private Property Rights Solutions," in Block (ed.), *Economics and the Environment*, pp. 281–332.

16. R.C. Fellmeth, *The Politics of Land*, New York: Grossman, 1973, pp. 9–74. For related problems with water, see, S. Postel, *Conserving Water: The Untapped Alternative*, Worldwatch Paper 67, Washington, D.C.: Worldwatch, 1985.

17. E. Mishan, *Technology and Growth*, New York: Praeger, 1969, p. 39; hereafter cited as: Mishan, TG.

18. For discussion of amenity rights, see Mishan, TG, pp. 37–41; and Mishan, *The Costs of Economic Growth*, New York: Praeger, 1967, pp. 55, 128–29.

19. See E. Mishan, *Cost-Benefit Analysis*, New York: Praeger, 1976, pp. 128–29. For a discussion of geographical equity and geographical discrimina-

tion, see, K. Shrader-Frechette, *Science Policy, Ethics, and Economic Methodology*, Boston: Reidel, 1985, Chapter 7; hereafter cited as: Shrader-Frechette, SP.

20. See Shrader-Frechette, SP, pp. 220ff.

21. See Shrader-Frechette, SP, pp. 222ff.

22. For arguments for duties to members of future generations, see E. Partridge, *Responsibilities to Future Generations*, Buffalo, N.Y.: Prometheus, 1981.

23. See C.M. Haar and L. Liebman, *Property and Law*, Boston: Little, Brown, 1977, pp. 113ff., 963–1055. For an analysis of takings and police power, with respect to reform of these concepts and their application to private property in land, see the classic essay, J.L. Sax, "Takings, Private Property, and Public Rights," *Yale Law Journal* 81 (1971): 149–86. See also D. Macrae, "Scientific Policymaking and Compensation for the Taking of Property," in *Nomos*, pp. 327–40. Finally, for a more philosophical and more contemporary analysis, see Mark Sagoff, "Property Rights and Environmental Law," *Philosophy and Public Policy* 8, no. 2 (Spring 1988): 9–12.

24. For the wetlands statistics, see J.G. Sobetzer, "American Land and Law," in Andrews, pp. 214–16. See also C. Clark, "Clean-Cut Economies," *The Sciences* 29, no. 1 (January/February 1989): 17–19; D. Malakoff, "Restoring the Earth," *Not Man Apart* 18, no. 1 (January/February 1988): 16–17; and B. Norton, *The Spice of Life: Why Save Natural Variety?* Princeton: Princeton University Press, 1987.

25. See R.F. Babcock and D.A. Feurer, "Land as a Commodity," in Andrews, pp. 123–24.

26. Bryant, pp. 198–200.

27. Bryant, p. 147.

28. Bryant, p. 201.

29. Bryant, pp. 206–7.

30. L. Caldwell, "Land and the Law," *University of Illinois Law Review* (Summer 1986): 1–2; see also chapters 5 and 9 in this volume.

31. A. Dawson, *The Land Problem in the Developed Economy*, Totowa, N.J., Barnes and Noble, 1984, pp. 155–56.

32. For arguments about the efficiency of planning and other restrictions on property rights, see Bromley, EE (note 15) and Baumol and Oates, TEP (note 15).

33. Cited in Healy, p. 10. For similar examples, see C.F. Little, "Preservation Policy and Personal Perception," in Andrews, pp. 83–98. For discussion of the view that private property in land is inconsistent with the best use of land, see H. George, *Progress and Poverty*, Garden City, N.Y.: Country Life Press, 1955, pp. 397ff.; hereafter cited as: George. For discussion of the view that land-use control, so as to prevent degradation, is economical, see Brown 90, pp. 7ff.

34. C. Clark, "Clean-Cut Economies," *The Sciences* 29, no. 1 (January/February 1989): 17–19. See also D. Malakoff, "Restoring the Earth," *Not Man Apart* 18, no. 1 (January/February 1988): 16–17; and B. Norton, *The Spice of Life: Why Save Natural Variety?* Princeton: Princeton University Press, 1987.

35. Shrader-Frechette, SP, pp. 129ff., 261ff.

36. See C.M. Haar and L. Liebman, *Property and Law*, Boston: Little, Brown, and Company, 1977, p. 841, for a discussion of the problems in Houston; hereafter cited as: Haar and Liebman. For a discussion of this third objection, based on arbitrariness and dictatorship, see Haar and Liebman, pp. 851ff.

37. For discussion of alternative assessment and negotiation as ways of solving policy problems, see, for example, K.S. Shrader-Frechette, *Risk and Rationality*, Berkeley: University of California Press, 1991, chapters 11 and 12.

38. Cited in Shrader-Frechette, *Risk Analysis and Scientific Method*, Boston: Reidel, 1985, p. 189.

Chapter 12

1. E.g., see John Edward Cribbet, "Concepts in Transition: The Search for a New Definition of Property," *University of Illinois Law Review*, no. 1 (1986): 1–42; and John Martinez, "Reconstructing the Takings Doctrine by Redefining Property and Sovereignty," *Fordham Urban Law Journal* 16 (1987–1988): 157–194. However, strongly held views of the fundamental right of property ownership in land are current in the United States today. See Richard A. Epstein, *Takings: Private Property and the Power of Eminent Domain*, Cambridge, Mass.: Harvard University Press, 1985. But even judicial opinion appears to be divided over what rights should be predominant. See Robert A. Williams Jr., "Legal Discourse, Social Vision, and the Supreme Court's Land Use Planning Law: The Genealogy of the Lochnerian Recurrence in First English Lutheran Church and Nollan," *University of Colorado Law Review* 59 (Summer 1988): 427ff.

2. Paul B. Sears, "The Inexorable Problem of Space," *Science* 127 (3 January 1958): 9–16. See also George Macinko, "Saturation: A Problem Evaded in Planning Land Use," *Science* 149 (30 July 1965): 516–21.

3. Nicholas N. Patricios, ed., *International Handbook on Land Use Planning*, Westport, Conn.: Greenwood Press, 1986, and F.R. Steiner and H.N. Van Lier, eds., *Land Conservation and Development: Examples of Land-Use Planning and Programs*, Amsterdam, Netherlands: Elsevier Science Publishers.

4. American Law Institute, *A Model Land Development Code*, Washington, D.C.: ALI, 1970–1975.

5. E.g., Gene C. Brewer, "Forging an Enlightened Public Land Use Policy for the Nation," Address at the Annual Meeting of the National Forest Products Association, May 9, 1967, and Mortimer B. Doyle, "The Need for a National Land Policy," presentation before the National Resources and Agricultural Committees of the U.S. Chamber of Commerce, February 2, 1968. Both Gene Brewer and Mortimer Doyle were officers of the National Forest Products Association.

6. National Land Use Policy Hearings before the Committee on Interior

and Insular Affairs, United States Senate, Ninety-First Congress, Second Session on S. 3354, March 24, April 28, and April 29, 1970, Part I.

7. Efforts to establish a multiple-use mandate for the public lands have been widely regarded to have failed owing, at least in part, to absence of an authoritative criterion for setting priorities. See the Multiple-Use, Sustained Yield Act of 1960. 16 U.S.C. 528-31 (1970), ELR 41406, and the Classification and Multiple Use Act of 1964, 43 U.S.C. 1411-18 (1970), ELR 41406. Portions of this latter act appeared to have expired in December 1970 but were restored by the Federal Land Policy and Management Act of 1976, the organic act for the Bureau of Land Management (43 U.S.C. 1712). Commenting on the multiple use concept, Arnold W. Reitz Jr. writes that "The concept of multiple-use both in theory and practice is so vague as the be often meaningless, or worse yet, to have completely different meanings for dozens of its users" and "too vague to offer much policy guidance" (*Environmental Planning: Law of Land and Resources*, Washington, D.C.: North American International, 1974: Part Six, 4–5). See George R. Hall, "The Myth and Reality of Multiple-Use Forestry," *National Resources Journal* 3 (October 1963): 276–90; D. Michael Harvey, "Public Land Management Under the Classification and Multiple-Use Act," *National Resources Lawyer* (July 1969): 238–49; and Warren A. Starr, "Multiple Land Use Management," *Natural Resources Journal* (November 1961): 288–301; Gilbert F. White, "The Choice of Use in Resource Management," *Natural Resources Journal* (March 1961): 23–40; and Michael D. Bowls and John V. Krutilla, *Multiple-Use Management: The Economics of Public Forestlands*, Washington, D.C.: Resource for the Future, 1989.

8. James N Gladden, *The Boundary Waters Canoe Area: Wilderness Values and Motorized Recreation*, Ames: Iowa State University Press, 1990.

9. The issue of preserving a irreplaceable natural system versus its sacrifice to extend the life of a declining local industry was brought before the Congress by Representative Jim Jontz of Indiana in H.R. 842, The Ancient Forest Protection Act of 1991, 102d Congress, 1st Session, February 6 1991. See also U.S. Congress, House of Representatives, *Management of Old-Growth Forests of the Pacific Northwest*: Joint Hearings, June 20 and 22, 1989, before the Subcommittee on Forests, Family Farms and Energy of the Committee on Agriculture and the Subcommittee on National Parks and Public Lands of the Committee on Interior and Insular Affairs. 101st Congress, 1st Session, 1989; and Mark Bonnett and Kurt Zimmerman, "Politics and Preservation: The Endangered Species Act and the Northern Spotted Owl," *Ecology Law Quarterly* 18, no. 1 (1991): 105–71. See also *American Forests* 97 (March–April 1991); Philip A. Davis, "From Shade to Spotlight: Protection of Old Growth Forests and Biodiversity," *Congressional Quarterly Weekly Report* 49 (June 1991): 1439; and Alyson Pytte, "Panels Struggle to Balance Timber, Owl Interests," *Congressional Quarterly Weekly Report* 48 (15 September 1990): 2906. As of mid-1992 this issue was still in sharp conflict. See Timothy Egan, "Strangest US Environment Law May Become Endangered Species," *New York Times* (May 26, 1992): 1, 13.

10. Various issues are described in Lynton K. Caldwell, *International Environmental Policy: Emergence and Dimensions*, 2d ed., Durham, N.C.:

Duke University Press, 1991; see references in this volume. Indications of the internationalizing of recognition that riverbasin policy is primarily a land use issue involving allocation of water rights was an NGO information-sharing and strategy workshop, "Lessons from the Great Lakes and Global Rivers" held in Rio de Janeiro on June 8, 1992, at the time of the United Nations Conference on Environment and Development.

11. See John Carroll, *Environmental Diplomacy: An Examination and Prospective of Canadian-United States Transboundary Environmental Relations*, Ann Arbor: University of Michigan Press, 1983. See forthcoming *National Resources Journal* 33, no. 1 (January 1993). Entire issue on the United States, Canada, Mexico, transboundary issues, and institutional implications.

12. See Jim Woolf, "If Feds Don't Buy Parkland, Utah Threatens to Develop It," *Salt Lake Tribune* (13 May 1992), sec. A: 1.

13. G. Richard Hill, ed., *Regulatory Taking: The Limits of Land Use Controls*, Chicago: Section of Urban, State and Local Governmental Law, American Bar Association, 1990 bibliographical references. Selected articles originally appearing in *Urban Lawyer*. See also note 1, supra, especially Epstein, *Takings*. For more recent judicial developments see Stewart E. Sterk, "Government Liability for Unconstitutional Land Use Regulation," *Indiana Law Journal* 60 (Winter 1984/1985): 113ff.; Lawrence Blume and Daniel Rubinfeld, "Compensation for Takings: An Economic Analysis," *California Law Review* 72 (July 1984): 569ff.; Anne R. Pramaggiore, "The Supreme Court's Trilogy of Regulating Takings: Keystone, Glendale, Nollan," *De Paul Law Review* 38 (January 1989): 441ff.; and Sylvia Lynn Gillis, "A Blow for Land Use Planning--The Takings Issue Reexamined," *Ohio State Law Journal* 49 (1989): 1107ff. For what may become a critical case, see *Lucas* vs. *South Carolina Coastal Council*, 404 South Eastern Reporter, 2d Series 895ff. (S.C. 1991).

14. *National Land Use Policy: Hearings Before the Committee on Interior and Insular Affairs*, U.S. Senate, Ninety-First Congress, Second Session on S.3354, March 24, April 28, and April 29, 1970. Part 1, p. 36.

15. Ibid., 30.

16. E.g., see Frederick Jackson Turner, *The Frontier in American History*, New York: Henry Holt, 1920.

17. Senate Bill 2881, introduced July 19, 1990—*Congressional Index* 101st Congress, 1989–1990.

18. Lynton K. Caldwell, "A Constitutional Law for the Environment: 20 years with NEPA Indicates the Need," *Environment* 31, no. 10 (December 1989): 6–11, 25–28; and commentaries 2–5, 31–32. See The Comprehensive Environmental Amendment Project, Marshall Massey, ed., *Environmental Circular* no. 4, Denver, Colo., June 1991. On the negative attitude of the Supreme Court and its inability to find authorization for environmental protection in the Constitution, see Daniel A. Farber, "Environmental Law: Disdain for 17 Year-Old Statute Evident in High Court's Rulings," *National Law Journal* (4 May 1987): 20–23; and Frederic P. Sutherland and Roger Beers, "Supreme Indifference: The National Environmental Policy Act has not had a friend on the Supreme Court since the retirement of William O. Douglas," *The Amicus Journal* 13, no. 2 (Spring 1991): 38–42. On the in-

ability of the courts to find a mandate for environmental protection in the Constitution and the right and responsibility of the president and the Congress in interpreting the Constitution, see James E. Krier, "The Environment, the Constitution and the Coupling Fallacy" (University of Michigan) *Law Quadrangle Notes* 32, no. 3 (Spring 1988): 35–39.

19. John R. Platt, "What We Must Do," *Science* 166 (28 November 1969): 1115–21, and John R. Platt and Richard Cellarius, "Councils of Urgent Studies: Coordinating Councils Could Focus and Legitimize Research on Solutions of Our Major Crises," *Science* 177 (25 August 1972): 670–76. See also Lynton K. Caldwell, *The President As Convener of Interests: Policy Development for the 21st Century*, Bloomington: Indiana University, School of Public and Environmental Affairs, 1984.

20. For discussion of arbitration, negotiation, adversary proceedings, and citizens' panels, see K.S. Shrader-Frechette, *Risk and Rationality*, Berkeley: University of California Press, 1991, chs. 11–12, and *Science Policy, Ethics, and Economic Methodology*, Boston: Reidel, 1985, chs. 8–9.

21. Alasdair MacIntyre, *After Virtue: A Study in Moral Theory*, Notre Dame: University of Notre Dame Press, 1981.

22. E.g., the following examples pertaining to national parks: "The Silent Scandal," *Wall Street Journal* (25 May 1982): 22 (editorial); "As an Alaska Road Opens, So Does Dispute Over Use," *New York Times* (30 July 1990): A6; "US Urged to Take Guru's Land," *New York Times* (27 May 1989): 7; "Discussing Yellowstone, Lujan Creates New Stir," *New York Times* (27 August 1990): 12; "Aisle Seats to a National Park? Well, Maybe," *New York Times* (14 February 1991): 1,6.

23. Richard L. Settle, "Regulating Taking Doctrine in Washington: Now You See It Now You Don't," *University of Puget Sound Law Review* 12 (April 6, 1988). Washington state courts are trying to reconcile ambiguous rulings by the U.S. Supreme Court regarding exercise of the state police power.

24. See Katherine Bishop, "New Tool of Developers and Others Quells Private Opposition to Projects" *New York Times* (26 April 1991) (Law). "Real-estate developers, alleged polluters and even public servants who encounter citizen opposition to their projects have been increasingly using civil lawsuits to discourage such opposition. . . . And while citizens who are targets usually prevail, the time, expense and stress involved keeps many others from speaking out on public issues."

25. Jerry Adler with Daniel Glick, "Put Your Trust in Land: Owners are turning their property into preserves," *Newsweek* (10 December 1990): 78; Russell L. Brenneman, *Private Approaches to the Preservation of Open Land*, New London, Conn.: Conservation and Research Foundation, 1967. Russell L. Brenneman and Sarah M. Bates, eds., *Land-Saving Action: A Written Symposium by 29 Experts on Private Land Conservation in the 1980s*, Covelo, Calif.: Island Press, 1984; Molly Selvin, *The Public Trust Doctrine in 1985*, Santa Monica, Calif.: Rand Corporation, 1985; and Pamela K. Stone, comp., *National Directory of Local and Regional Land Conservation Organizations: 1985-86*, Bar Harbor, Maine: Land Trust Exchange, 1985.

Name Index

317

Subject Index

About the Authors

Lynton Keith Caldwell is the Arthur F. Bentley Professor Emeritus of Political Science and Professor of Public and Environmental Affairs at Indiana University, Bloomington. He holds degrees in English and political science, including a Ph.D. (1943) from the University of Chicago. He has served on faculties of the University of Chicago, the University of Oklahoma, Syracuse University, and the University of California, Berkeley. Dr. Caldwell has served as advisor to numerous national and international groups, including the U.S. Office of Technology Assessment and the United Nations. He is a principal architect of the National Environmental Policy Act of 1969. Author of more than 200 articles and 12 books, Caldwell was named for distinguished environmental services by the UNEP. Among his 12 books are *The Administrative Theories of Hamilton and Jefferson* (1944), *Science and the National Environmental Policy Act* (1982), *Biocracy, Public Policy, and the Life Sciences* (1987), *International Environmental Policy* (1990), and *Between Two Worlds: Science, the Environmental Movement, and Policy Choice* (1990).

Kristin Shrader-Frechette is Distinguished Research Professor of Philosophy at the University of South Florida, Tampa. She holds degrees in mathematics, physics, and philosophy, including a Ph.D. (1972) from the University of Notre Dame. She has held professorships at the University of California and the University of Florida and has held offices or served on committees in the American Philosophical Association, the Philosophy of Science Association, and the U.S. National Academy of Sciences. Editor-in-Chief of the Oxford University Press monograph series on Environmental Ethics and Science Policy, she has also served government, industrial, and environmental groups throughout the world, including the United Nations, the World Health Organization, and the national academies of science in three different countries. She has published more than 130 articles and 12 books, including *Nuclear Power and Public Policy* (1983), *Risk Analysis and Scientific Method* (1985), *Risk and Rationality* (1991), *Environmental Ethics* (1991), and *Method in Ecology* (1993).